Contents

Acknowledgments

Thanks are due to many, but especially to Dirce Waltrick do Amarante in Brazil; Arnd Bohm, Evelyn Cobley, Beth Coward, Michael Kenneally, Hana Stanbury, Margaret Maliszewska, and Colin Wright in Canada; Friedhelm Rathjen and Ulrich Blumenbach in Germany; Anne Fogarty in Ireland; Rosa Maria Bollettieri Bosinelli and Gerald Parks in Italy; Geert Lernout in the Netherlands; Tadeusz Szczerbowski in Poland; Marissa Aixàs and Teresa Caneda Cabrera in Spain; Ruth Frehner, Fritz Senn, and Ursula Zeller in Switzerland; Robert Weninger in the United Kingdom; Tim Martin and Jolanta Wawrzycka in the United States. Thanks also to colleagues during a fellowship at the Camargo Foundation in Cassis, France, especially Rudolf Binion and Stefano Mula; to Richard Ratzlaff and two anonymous readers at the University of Toronto Press; and to Maureen Epp for her eagle-eyed copy editing.

Particular thanks are due to the National Library of Ireland in Dublin, the British Library in London, and the Zurich James Joyce Foundation, as well as to Queen's University at Kingston, Canada, and the Social Sciences and Humanities Research Council of Canada.

Blanket acknowledgments are of course also due to many of the standard and indispensable works of *Wake* scholarship: Campbell and Robinson, Tindall, Glasheen, Mink, McHugh, the numerous contributors to *A Wake Newslitter*, and the many contributions over the years of Fritz Senn, Joycean grandmaster. Finally, and as always, my sincere thanks are due to my wife, Trudi, for her unflagging support and tolerance over the years.

Two works appeared too late to be considered: Krzysztof Bartnicki's *Finneganów Tren* (Krakow: Ha!Art, 2012), a complete Polish version of

FW, and Congrong Dai's *Fennigan de Shouling Ye* (Shangai: Shangai People's Publishing House, 2012), a Chinese version of *FW* I. i–viii, the first of three planned volumes of a complete Chinese rendition.

IMPOSSIBLE JOYCE

Introduction

In the buginning was the woid

(*FW* 378.29)[1]

Finnegans Wake is a literary machine designed to generate as many meanings as possible for as many readers as possible. *Impossible Joyce: Finnegans Wakes*, the present exercise in the long and widening wake of the *Wake*, focuses on the extended capabilities of that machine in the course of a sustained examination of transtextual effects (a concept to which we shall return) generated by comparative readings, across a range of languages, of translated excerpts from a work that has repeatedly been declared entirely untranslatable.

Fritz Senn has commented that 'everything Joyce wrote has to do with translation, is transferential' (1984, 39). The central question with regard to a translation of *Finnegans Wake*, that 'lexicographer's paradise' (Magalaner and Kain 1962, 240), is whether such a possibility can be envisaged in the first place, and scholarly discussions of the issue over the past several decades have been numerous.[2] Competent authorities have categorically stated that the task is theoretically impossible. Theory and practice do not always go hand in hand, however,

---

1 Page references to *Finnegans Wake* are preceded by *FW* and give either the page alone (*FW* 44) or the page and lines cited (*FW* 44.24–8). References to individual chapters of *FW* are in the form I.viii (referring to part I, chapter 8); the sequence of all seventeen chapters is I.i–viii, II.i–iv, III.i–iv, IV.

2 Discussions of the translatability of *Finnegans Wake* include, among many others, Senn (1967b; 1984, 39–56; 1998), Knuth (1972), Eco (1978, 1996), Blumenbach (1990, 1998), Topia (1990), Parks (1992), Milesi (1985, 1996, 2003, 2004), Versteegen (1998), and Bosinelli (2000, 2001).

and the alleged impossibility of the task has not deterred a number of likewise competent translators from undertaking it – usually to the extent of only a page or two, admittedly, but in a small number of heroic cases (Philippe Lavergne in French, Dieter Stündel in German, Erik Bindervoet and Robbert-Jan Henkes in Dutch, Donaldo Schüler in Portuguese, Chong-keon Kim in Korean, Naoki Yanase in Japanese) encompassing the entire 628-page text. Various others have published extensive though less than complete translations (Luigi Schenoni in Italian, Víctor Pozanco in Spanish, Kyôko Miyata in Japanese) of the work, and yet others have translated complete individual chapters, especially the eighth chapter, a first version of which appeared in print as early as 1928 under the title *Anna Livia Plurabelle*.

Joyce himself, according to his biographer Richard Ellmann, had no doubts at all about the translatability of the *Wake*: '"There is nothing that cannot be translated," said Joyce' (Ellmann 1982, 632). Joyce, indeed, as is well known, instigated and participated himself in both French and Italian translations from *Anna Livia Plurabelle*, and kept an interested eye on the progress of a German version.[3] In so doing, he led the way in suggesting that what would become *Finnegans Wake* would also, all appearances to the contrary, be indeed translatable, at least in some sense of that term. Following Joyce's lead, Alberte Pagán has argued that to say the *Wake* is untranslatable is to say that it is illegible – and since an already vast body of exegesis proves that it is legible, it follows that it is also translatable (2000, 147). More provocatively, Umberto Eco has even suggested that *Finnegans Wake* may in fact be 'the easiest of all texts to translate, in that it permits a maximum of creative liberty' on the part of the translator (1996, xi; translation mine). Despite Joyce, however, despite Eco, and even despite a number of highly impressive complete renderings, *Finnegans Wake* is still generally and by no means unreasonably regarded as an essentially untranslatable text in any normal understanding of the concept of translation.

My primary interest here, however, is not in theoretical considerations of translatability or untranslatability but rather in the comparative exploration, across languages, of textual effects generated by actual (would-be) translations. It is now a commonplace that the activity of

---

3 See Beckett and Joyce (1931), Joyce and Settanni (1940), Joyce and Frank (1979), and Goyert (1946, 1970).

literary translation is done considerably less than justice by an exclusive critical focus on the degree to which the results are deemed to be unwaveringly faithful to an original text. Fidelity is of course a crucial factor in the process, but so is the realization that translation itself involves a process of rewriting, of continuing the original text, a process that also presupposes both creativity and originality. A great deal has been written and no doubt still remains be written about the theory of literary translation. The specific reasons why the *Wake* in particular is not susceptible of translation have been discussed in detail and at length by scholars and theorists more competent than myself to adjudicate on such matters. Despite this principled objection, however, it remains the case, as we have already seen, that a surprisingly large number of heroic – or heroically misguided – souls have nonetheless undertaken the Herculean (or Sisyphean) task to at least some degree.

The present work has a deliberately narrow focus, comparing individual choices made by individual translators in a necessarily very limited corpus of examples from *Finnegans Wake*. The object of the exercise is to examine in some detail some of the ways in which attempts across a range of a dozen or so European languages to translate Joyce's astonishing text can be said to result cumulatively in an *extension* of that text into a multilingual macrotext. Michael Groden has observed that Joyce's interim title for many years, *Work in Progress*, signalled the state of his evolving text as one that was 'moving and changing every part of the time' (2007, ix). That text, considered here as also including its multilingual transpositions, is very evidently still in progress, still moving, still continually changing.

There are of course readers who are still waiting for Joyce's book to be translated into English. *Finnegans Wake* is written in a multilevelled, multilingual, polysemous, dreamlike language that explores several dozen world languages for allusive echoes and suggestions that enrich, question, and continually relativize a text less written *in* English than constructed on a linguistic foundation of English. It has been suggested that the language of *Finnegans Wake* might more aptly be called 'Eurish' – 'a base of Irish-English with a superstructure of Aryan loan-words' (Burgess 1966, 22). More productive in the context of its possible translation, however, is the suggestion that the language of the *Wake* is less 'English' than 'Anglo-Wakean,' which its various would-be translators duly attempt to render into 'Franco-Wakean,' 'Germano-Wakean,' and the like (Blumenbach 1990, 1).

Purely as a set of convenient shorthand devices, however, I will continue to refer to the language of Joyce's text as 'English,' though it is only partially so; to renderings into 'French,' 'German,' and the like, though the results frequently deviate extravagantly from the normal usage of these and other target languages; and to 'translations' and 'translators' of *Finnegans Wake*, for all that Joyce's text may indeed, by its very nature, be untranslatable. Alternative terms that have been variously proposed to replace the debatable concept of a 'translation' include *refiguration*, *transfiguration*, *transposition*, *transcreation*, and the like. While I will continue to refer to 'translations,' in short, the term is used purely *as if* a true translation of *Finnegans Wake* were indeed possible in the first place.

Impossible Joyce is primarily a sustained exercise in an activity once described by Fritz Senn, tongue in cheek, as 'pedestrian semantic rummaging' (1995, 226). The conceptual framework in which the present rummagings occur, however, involves considering the literary text not only as a unique and historically specific original work (the *prototext*), but also as always constituting a potential *macrotext* by virtue of its possible extensions backwards and forwards in time.[4] Extensions backwards in time, the *pre-texts*, include the work's genetically earlier forms, as revealed by notebooks, manuscripts, typescripts, prepublication extracts, and the like; extensions forwards in time, the *post-texts*, include film versions, stage adaptations, literary digests, and the like – and, of course, and most importantly for our present purposes, literary translations. The model, however, involves regarding literary translations not as mere secondary texts, whose attempts to replicate an original and always primary text are in principle always inadequate, but rather as what I have called *transtexts*. The term usefully designates a specific variety of the broader category of literary intertexts, namely translations regarded as independent texts characterized primarily by their complex relationship, involving both sameness and difference, with the original text translated and with other competing translations of it.

A *transtextual reading* thus involves a comparative reading of the original and as many as possible of its translations in various languages. Paying only incidental attention to the obvious fact that some translations will inevitably be better or worse than others, a transtextual reading focuses, as already intimated, on the degree to which multiple

---

4 The conceptual framework draws on a model first proposed in my book *Polyglot Joyce: Fictions of Translation* (2005, 5–16).

translations of a literary text, compared across languages, can be said to contribute cumulatively to an *extension* of that text into a multilingual macrotext. While a great deal of work has been done in recent years in Joycean genetic studies (which play no further part in this book), relatively little has been done (with a small number of notable exceptions) in the field of transtextual studies. The two undertakings, however, for all their differences, have a similar aim. As genetic studies extend the potential meaning of the original text by a comparative consideration of its genetically earlier forms, so transtextual studies extend its potential meaning by a comparative consideration, across languages, of its collective translations.

Impossible Joyce, then, is based on the assumption that the entire corpus of translations of the *Wake* can, together with the original text, be productively regarded as constituting a single and coherent object of study, a single polyglot macrotext. To phrase it differently, this book is an exploration of what one might call the literary polysystem constituted by *Finnegans Wake* and its collective international translations.

Our transtextual reading should of course ideally involve a comparative examination, across texts and across languages, of the complete network of linguistic and cultural relationships between and among the original work and *all* its translations. Lacking such ideally polyglot abilities, I am forced to limit the comparative readings almost entirely to a range of western European languages, with occasional forays of a more or less uncertain nature into one or other of the languages of eastern Europe. The uncertainty of these forays, however, emerges as itself constituting a relatively interesting component of the experiment as a whole, for occasionally the attempt to read a translation in a very unfamiliar language can lead to the discovery of serendipitous and suggestive translingual coincidences. Attempting to read versions of *Finnegans Wake* in languages with which one is largely or even almost entirely unfamiliar, after all, merely replicates the experience, at least in large part, of any reader of *Finnegans Wake*. There is also a sense, of course, in which any reading of *Finnegans Wake*, given its incorporation of an extraordinary number of world languages, necessarily always already involves at least some consideration of transtextual effects. The present work chooses to focus exclusively on those effects.

Northrop Frye once suggested that the real hero of *Finnegans Wake* is the reader (1966, 324) – and one could certainly envisage extending that suggestion to include its harried, heroic, and all too often hapless would-be translators. One could suggest even more appropriately, however, that the real hero of the *Wake* is language itself, for, as its author once wrote to Eugène Jolas, 'I have discovered that I can do anything I want with language' (Magalaner and Kain 1962, 240). Would-be translators (and would-be transtextual readers) cannot claim they have not been given fair and open warning.

The fact that *Finnegans Wake* may indeed be untranslatable in any normal sense makes a study of its various would-be translations all the more interesting. In the nature of things, it will emerge fairly quickly that some renderings of the excerpts under consideration are clearly more impressive or less impressive than others. The renderings, however, as already suggested, will in principle be discussed primarily not for the degree to which, individually, they successfully or unsuccessfully reproduce the original text, but rather for the degree to which they can be read as interestingly contributing to the collective macrotextual *Wake* in progress. One is reminded of Clive Hart's comment: 'Ultimately there is, I think, no such thing as an incorrect reading of *Finnegans Wake*' – a statement based on Joyce's own 'delight in the chance meanings of words, the peculiar interaction often caused by their juxtaposition, and the power of verbal circumstance' (1968b, 4, 7). Joyce's own renderings of passages from *Anna Livia Plurabelle*, as is well known, cheerfully ignored on numerous occasions what one would normally think of as semantic meaning in favour of a rhythmical or a musical or a verbal or quite simply a passing humorous effect. Joyce, in short, was obviously much less interested in providing word-for-word equivalents than in continuing and extending the text – a process after all that is also, voluntarily or involuntarily, engaged in by all readers of the *Wake*. The macrotextual model essentially sees those readers as including its translators – and *their* readers.

'Serious critical attention has been focused on the rule that nothing in *Finnegans Wake* is nonsense, yet it is probably equally true that it is all pure nonsense, subsuming and perpetually violating the limitations of prosaic "sense"' (Benstock 1985, 144). Such a combination presents would-be translators with an extraordinary degree of freedom, as Umberto Eco observed, but also with a corresponding need for restraint. Translation is the art of the approximate and the compromise, and translators of the *Wake* are continually faced with the question as to how far it is permissible to go in order to achieve a reasonable negotiated compromise. While this challenge holds to a degree for any translation, it is encountered on every page, even in almost every word, of *Finnegans Wake*.

The comparative readings undertaken in the following chapters are those of one single transtextual reader reading. My reactions will not necessarily be those of a native speaker of any of the various languages involved (including English) or those of any other would-be transtextual reader. A key point about transtextual reading, indeed, even if undertaken by a multilingual team rather than by a single individual, is clearly that it inevitably balances occasional moments of apparent insight against large areas of unadulterated blindness – a balance, however, that once again largely replicates the experience of any reader of *Finnegans Wake*.

Finally, a plea for patience. The readings, attempting to chart sympathetically the sometimes very different interpretive pathways undertaken – or taken to be undertaken – by the 'intermisunderstanding minds of the anticollaborators' (*FW* 118.25), rely in many cases on very close attention to linguistic detail in several languages. The gentle reader, ideally already prepared to be ideally indulgent, is nonetheless reminded of the salutary admonition delivered in the pages of the *Wake* itself: 'Now, patience; and remember patience is the great thing, and above all things else we must avoid anything like being or becoming out of patience' (*FW* 108.8–10).

PART ONE

Work in Progress

1 *Finnegans Wakes*

Latin me that, my trinity scholard, out of eure sanscreed into our eryan.

(*FW* 215.26–7)

To begin with, let us briefly survey the international growth of what we may think of as the multilingual *Finnegans Wake* polysystem, constituting a progressive polyglot extension of an already extravagantly polyglot original text. Our survey will involve, first, a rapid overview of the chronological sequence of would-be translations (fragmentary, partial, or complete) into more than twenty languages to date; second, an even more concise overview of the degree to which particular languages have been involved in translations of and from the *Wake*; and, finally, a brief account of how the iconic title *Finnegans Wake*, so obsessively guarded by Joyce himself, has so far survived its multilingual transpositions. Succeeding chapters will explore how the text itself has survived that process.

I

In the interests of both brevity and clarity, a description of the chronological sequence in which *Finnegans Wake*, despite its notorious untranslatability, has surrounded itself with an accompanying multilingual array of attempted translations may perhaps best be presented in tabular form. Full details of all renderings mentioned here will be found in the concluding Bibliography.

1923   *Finnegans Wake* (*FW*) is in at least one sense an anthology. Joyce writes a first sketch (*FW* 380–2) in March 1923.[1]

1924   The first published fragment of *Work in Progress* (*FW* 383–98), as Joyce insisted on calling *FW* before its actual publication, appears in Paris in the *transatlantic review* (April).

1927   Serial publication of *Work in Progress* begins in Paris in the first issue of the journal *transition* in April and continues for eleven years until April / May 1938, finally including all but the last of the seventeen chapters of *FW*.[2]

1928   *Anna Livia Plurabelle* (*ALP*; *FW* 196–216) separately published in New York (followed by publication in London in 1930).

1929   *Tales Told of Shem and Shaun* (*FW* 152–9, 282–304, 414–19) separately published in Paris.

        Georg Goyert, translator of the German *Ulysses* (1927), begins a German translation of *ALP* (see 1933).

1930   *Haveth Childers Everywhere* (*FW* 532–54) separately published in Paris and New York.

        Alfred Péron and Samuel Beckett working on a French translation of the opening pages of *ALP*, entitled 'Anna Lyvia Pluratself' (*FW* 196–201) – and first published only in 1985 (Péron and Beckett 1985).

1931   French translation (Beckett and Joyce 1931), the first translation published in any language, in the *Nouvelle Revue Française* (May) of the opening and closing pages (*FW* 196–201, 215–16) of *ALP* (see 1928): the initial version by Péron and Beckett (see 1930) reworked and extended by Paul Léon, Eugène Jolas, and Yvan Goll, under Joyce's supervision; further reworked

---

1   For a chart describing the composition of *FW* during the first ten years, see Ellmann (1982, 794–6). For a more detailed discussion of the process of composition, see Crispi and Slote (2007, 485–9). Page references to *FW* throughout the present chronology indicate the corresponding pages of the published text, which in a number of cases involved significant subsequent revisions.

2   For details of the various serial incarnations of *Work in Progress* between 1924 and 1938, see Crispi and Slote (2007, 490–4).

by Joyce, Léon, and Philippe Soupault; and finally revised by Jolas and Adrienne Monnier.

1932   *Two Tales of Shem and Shaun* (*FW* 152–9, 414–19) separately published in London.

C.K. Ogden's translation into Basic English of the closing pages of *ALP* (*FW* 213–16) in the journal *transition*.

Complete Czech *ALP* – the first complete version in any language – by Maria Weatherall, Vladimír Procházka, and Adolf Hoffmeister.

1933   Slightly abbreviated German translation of *ALP* completed by Georg Goyert, but published partially only in 1946 and in full only in 1970.

Japanese version of the opening and closing pages of *ALP* (*FW* 196, 213–16) by Junzaburo Nishiwaki.

1934   *The Mime of Mick, Nick and the Maggies* (*FW* 219–59) separately published in The Hague.

1937   *Storiella as She Is Syung* (*FW* 260–75, 304–8) separately published in London.

1939   *Finnegans Wake* published in London and New York (May).

1940   Italian versions of the opening and closing pages of *ALP* (*FW* 196–201, 215–16) in the Roman journal *Prospettive*, translated by Joyce and Nino Frank (Joyce and Frank 1979), with subsequent modifications by Ettore Settanni (Joyce and Settanni 1940).

1941   Joyce dies of a perforated ulcer in Zurich (13 January). The next five years, unsurprisingly in war-torn Europe, produce little or nothing in the way of efforts to translate *FW*.

1946   Georg Goyert's German translation of the opening and closing pages of *ALP* (*FW* 196–8, 213–16) in the Munich journal *Die Fähre* (see also 1933, 1970).

1948   Brief French excerpts (*FW* 3, 196, 419) translated by Michel Butor in an article on Joyce's work.

1949   Further French excerpts translated by Michel Butor (*FW* 627–8) in Maria Jolas's *James Joyce Yearbook*.

1950   French translations by André du Bouchet of excerpts from the final chapter, including the closing pages, in the journal *L'Âge Nouveau* (*FW* 619, 624, 625–8).

1951   French translation of the closing pages (*FW* 627–8) by Maxime Chastaing, Armand Jacob, and Arthur Watt in the journal *Roman*.

1957   French versions by André du Bouchet in the *Nouvelle Revue Française* of excerpts from the final chapter (from *FW* 604–28), including revised versions of his 1950 translations.

Portuguese translations by Haroldo de Campos and Augusto de Campos of excerpts in the *Jornal do Brasil* (from *FW* 3, 159, 196, 214–16, 556, 561, 627–8).

1959   Polish translations by Jerzy Strzetelski of excerpts from *ALP*, including the opening and closing pages (*FW* 196–8, 206–7, 215–16).

1961   Italian versions of more than forty pages of excerpts by J. Rodolfo Wilcock, the most substantial translated selection in any language to that point (*FW* 3, 33–4, 104–9, 112, 169–70, 179, 182–4, 185, 187–8, 189–91, 196, 206–7, 219–22, 249, 258–9, 306–8, 384, 543–5, 558–9, 572–5, 599–606, 626–8).

Italian translation by Mario Diacono of a brief excerpt (*FW* 107–8).

1962   French translation of first and last chapters by André du Bouchet in his volume *Finnegans Wake* (see 1950, 1957), accompanied by the Beckett and Joyce translations of 1931 from *ALP*.

Portuguese excerpts (from *FW* 3, 143, 159, 189, 196, 214–16, 226, 556, 559, 561, 627–8) by Haroldo de Campos and Augusto de Campos (see 1957) appear in book form as *Panaroma do Finnegans Wake*.

1964   French excerpts (from *FW* 3, 44, 169–71, 384, 627–8), translated by Daniel Castelain.

Hungarian excerpts by Endre Bíró (from *FW* 8–10, 169–95, 196–216, 627–8) in the journal *Híd* (see also 1992).

1965   Slovak translation by Jozef Kot of opening two pages (*FW* 3–5).

1966   Japanese translation by Masayoshi Osawa et al. of the opening two paragraphs of I.vii (*FW* 169–70).

1967   French translation by Philippe Lavergne of I.vii (*FW* 169–95) in the journal *Tel Quel*.

1968   French translation by Philippe Lavergne of I.i (*FW* 3–29) in the journal *Change*.

Japanese translation by Masayoshi Osawa and Junnosuke Sawasaki of excerpts, including closing pages (*FW* 206–7, 418–19, 627–8).

Portuguese translation by Manuel Lourenço of the opening page (*FW* 3).

1969   German translation by Arno Schmidt of selected excerpts (*FW* 30–1, 39, 63–4, 142, 166–7, 175, 182–4, 244–5, 259, 308, 403–6).

German translation by Wolfgang Hildesheimer of the opening pages of *ALP* (*FW* 196–7).

Galician excerpt (*FW* 216) translated by Leopoldo Rodríguez.

1970   Separate complete German translations of *ALP* by Wolfgang Hildesheimer (see 1969), Hans Wollschläger, and (slightly abbreviated) Georg Goyert (see 1933, 1946), in a single volume edited by Klaus Reichert and Fritz Senn.

Japanese translation by Masayoshi Osawa et al. (see 1968) of the first twelve pages of *ALP* (*FW* 196–208), serialized in a Japanese journal between 1970 and 1972.

1971   Japanese translation by Yukio Suzuki et al. of the first three chapters (*FW* 3–74).

Spanish translation by Ricardo Silva-Santisteban of the closing pages (*FW* 626–8).

1972   Italian translation by Gianni Celati of excerpts from I.i (*FW* 8–10).

Polish translation by Maciej Słomczyński of excerpts from I.ii and II.iv (*FW* 44–7, 398–9).

1973   French excerpts from the final chapter, including from the closing pages (*FW* 593–628), translated by Stephen Heath and Philippe Sollers.

Luigi Schenoni begins work on a complete (but ultimately un-finished) Italian translation of *FW* (see 1982, 1996, 2001, 2004, 2011).

1975   Italian version by Anthony Burgess of opening pages (*FW* 3–14).

1978   Japanese excerpts translated by Kyôko Ono et al. (*FW* 169–70, 206–7, 418–19, 593, 627–8).

Japanese excerpt translated by Masayoshi Osawa et al. (*FW* 169–70, 206–7, 418–19, 593, 627–8).

1979   French version by Simonne Verdin of the closing pages (*FW* 627–8).

Italian versions by Joyce and Nino Frank (Joyce and Frank 1979) of the opening and closing pages of *ALP* (*FW* 196–201, 215–16), without Settanni's modifications (see 1940), pub-lished in Joyce's *Scritti italiani* (Risset 1979).

1982   Catalan version by Josep-Miquel Sobré of brief excerpts from *FW* (Masoliver 1982, 80–2).

French version by Philippe Lavergne of *FW*, the first complete rendering in any language.

Italian translation by Luigi Schenoni of the first four chapters (*FW* 3–103).

Italian excerpt translated by Roberto Sanesi (*FW* 593).

Complete Japanese translation of *ALP* (*FW* 196–216) by Masayoshi Osawa et al. (see also 1968, 1970).

Spanish version of the opening and closing pages of *ALP* (*FW* 196–7, 213–16) by Ricardo Silva-Santisteban.

1983   German excerpt from I.i (*FW* 4–5) translated by Wilhelm Füger.

1984   German version by Robert Weninger of 'The Mookse and the Gripes' (*FW* 152–9).

1985   French translation of the opening pages of *ALP* (*FW* 196–201) by Alfred Péron and Samuel Beckett (see 1930) finally published after more than half a century (Aubert and Senn 1985).

German excerpts translated by Christian Enzensberger et al. (*FW* 241), Erich Fried (*FW* 403–4), and Uwe Herms (*FW* 17, 55, 68).

Complete Korean *ALP* translated by Chong-keon Kim.

Complete Polish *ALP* translated by Maciej Słomczyński.

1986 German translation by Harald Beck of the opening pages (*FW* 3–5).

1987 German translation of the opening pages by Harald Beck continued (*FW* 5–7).

German excerpts translated by Klaus Schönmetzler (*FW* 3–5, 152–9, 169–75, 383–4, 414–15, 605–6, 626–8).

1988 Further Spanish excerpts (*FW* 3–5, 196–7, 213–16, 626–8) translated by Ricardo Silva-Santisteban.

1989 *Finnegans Wake Deutsch*, edited by Klaus Reichert and Fritz Senn, containing collected excerpts from *FW* (about a quarter of the original text in all) in German, translated by various hands, including Harald Beck, Ulrich Blumenbach, Ingeborg Horn, Kurt Jauslin, Reinhard Markner, Friedhelm Rathjen, Klaus Reichert, Wolfgang Schrödter, Helmut Stoltefuß, Dieter Stündel, Robert Weninger, and the three separate translations of *ALP* (see 1970) by Georg Goyert, Wolfgang Hildesheimer, and Hans Wollschläger, as well as Arno Schmidt's versions of selected passages (see 1969). The volume provides as many as four different translations in the case of some passages.

1990 Portuguese excerpt from I.vii (*FW* 193–5) translated by Arthur Nestrovski.

1991 First volume (parts I–II) of Naoki Yanase's complete Japanese translation of *FW* (see also 1993).

1992 Spanish translation of opening page (*FW* 3) by Salvador Elizondo.

Complete Spanish translation of *ALP* by Francisco García Tortosa, with Ricardo Navarrete and José María Tejedor Cabrera.

Hungarian translation by Endre Bíró (see also 1964) of sub-stantial excerpts (*FW* 8–10, 35, 152–9, 169–95, 196–216, 226, 261–2, 414–21, 499–501, 627–8).

German translation of excerpts (*FW* 282–7) by Friedhelm Rathjen.

1993   Complete German version of *FW* by Dieter Stündel.

Second volume (parts III–IV) of Naoki Yanase's complete Japanese version of *FW* (see also 1991).

Abridged and much simplified Spanish version of *FW* by Víctor Pozanco.

Galician translation of the first two chapters (*FW* 3–47) by Alberte Pagán.

1995   German excerpt from III.iv (*FW* 555–63) translated by Fried-helm Rathjen.

1996   Complete Italian translation of *ALP* by Luigi Schenoni.

Complete Romanian translation of *ALP* by Felicia Antip.

1997   Danish translation of excerpts from final pages (*FW* 618–28) by Peter Laugesen.

1998   Polish translation by Adam Królikowski of the opening page (*FW* 3).

Romanian translation of final pages of *ALP* (*FW* 213–16) by Laurent Milesi.

1999   Additional Portuguese excerpts (*FW* 292, 449) translated by Haroldo de Campos, more than forty years after *Panaroma do Finnegans Wake* (1957).

Portuguese translation by Donaldo Schüler of *FW* I.i (see also 2003).

2000   Russian translation by Henri Volokhonsky of the first six chapters (*FW* 3–168).

Russian translation by Konstantin Belyaev of selected ex-cerpts (*FW* 196, 209–12).

Slovenian translation by Andrej Skubic of selected excerpts (*FW* 30–4, 380–2, 604–6, 611–12, 615–19).

Portuguese translation by Donaldo Schüler of *FW* I.ii–iv (see also 2003).

2001   Italian translation of *FW* I.i–viii (*FW* 3–216) by Luigi Schenoni.

Polish translation of opening pages (*FW* 3–7) by Jacek Malicki.

Complete Swedish translation of *ALP* by Mario Grut.

Portuguese translation by Donaldo Schüler of *FW* I.v–viii (see also 2003).

2002   Complete Dutch translation of *FW* by Erik Bindervoet and Robbert-Jan Henkes.

Complete Korean translation of *FW* by Chong-keon Kim.

Portuguese translation by Donaldo Schüler of *FW* II.i–iv (see also 2003).

Newspaper obituary (Anon. 2002) of Taha Mahmoud Taha, translator of *Ulysses* into Arabic (1982), indicates that he had also completed an abridged (and as yet unpublished) Arabic translation of *FW*.

Nevzat Erkmen, translator of *Ulysses* into Turkish (1996), reportedly begins work on a complete Turkish translation of *FW*.

2003   Portuguese translation by Donaldo Schüler of *FW* III.i–iv and IV, and publication of his complete five-volume Portuguese translation of *FW*.

2004   Complete Catalan version by Marissa Aixàs of *ALP*, together with other excerpts (*FW* 8–10, 15–18, 182–6).

Italian translation by Luigi Schenoni of *FW* II.i–ii (*FW* 219–308) (see also 1982, 1996, 2001).

Abridged and simplified Japanese translation of *FW*, including approximately half of the original text, by Kyôko Miyata.

2005   Polish version by Krzysztof Bartnicki of 'The Mookse and the Gripes' (*FW* 152–9).

2006   Finnish version by Miikka Mutanen of opening pages (*FW* 3–10).

2007   Spanish version by Leandro Fanzone of selected excerpts (*FW* 159, 215–16, 627–8).

2008   Irish version by Alan Titley of opening lines (*FW* 3).

2009   Finnish version by Miikka Mutanen of opening pages continued (*FW* 10–15).

Japanese version by Tatsuo Hamada of parts I and IV, with completion of parts II and III announced as expected in 2012.

Complete Portuguese version of *ALP* by Dirce Waltrick do Amarante.

Spanish translation by Juan Díaz Victoria of I.i (*FW* 3–29).

2010   Anonymous machine-translated Esperanto version of opening lines (*FW* 3)

2011   Italian translation by Luigi Schenoni of *FW* II.iii–iv (*FW* 309–99) (see also 1982, 1996, 2001, 2004).

2012   German translation by Friedhelm Rathjen (2012b) of multiple excerpts from *FW* (some 200 pages).

German translation by Friedhelm Rathjen (2012a) of *Tales Told of Shem and Shaun* (*FW* 152–9, 282–304, 414–19).

II

By 2012, as we can see from the foregoing account, complete versions of *Finnegans Wake* existed in French (Lavergne 1982), German (Stündel 1993), Japanese (Yanase 1993), Dutch (Bindervoet and Henkes 2002), Korean (Kim 2002), and Portuguese (Schüler 2003); substantial abridged and / or adapted versions existed in German (Reichert and Senn 1989), Spanish (Pozanco 1993), and Japanese (Miyata 2004a); a version of the first twelve chapters was available in Italian (Schenoni 2011), a version of the first six chapters in Russian (Volokhonsky 2000), a version of the first eight chapters and the final chapter in Japanese (Hamada 2009), another version of the first three chapters in Japanese (Suzuki et al. 1971), a version of the first two chapters in Galician (Pagán 1993), and the first and last chapters in French (du Bouchet 1962). Substantial collections of translated excerpts are available in Italian (Wilcock 1961) and German (Rathjen 2012b).

Of the individual chapters of the *Wake*, the most popular with translators has always been the eighth chapter (I.viii), *Anna Livia Plurabelle*, first published in separate form in 1928. In addition to its inclusion in the six complete translations of the *Wake* listed above, at least twelve further complete translations of *Anna Livia Plurabelle* exist, namely in Czech (Weatherall, Procházka, and Hoffmeister 1932), German (Goyert 1970; Hildesheimer 1970; Wollschläger 1970), Japanese (Osawa et al. 1982), Polish (Słomczyński 1985), Spanish (García Tortosa 1992), Italian (Schenoni 1996), Romanian (Antip 1996), Swedish (Grut 2001), Catalan (Aixàs 2004), and Portuguese (Amarante 2009). Significant partial translations of *Anna Livia Plurabelle* also exist in French (Beckett and Joyce 1931), Hungarian (Bíró 1964, 1992), Japanese (Nishiwaki 1933), Italian (Joyce and Settanni 1940; Joyce and Frank 1979), and Polish (Strzetelski 1959).

Turning to the degree of translational activity in individual languages, we find that the earliest translated excerpts from *Finnegans Wake* published in any language were those from *Anna Livia Plurabelle* translated into French in 1931 by Samuel Beckett and others, under the supervision of Joyce himself; the first major (if still very partial) translation from the *Wake* in any language was André du Bouchet's 1962 collection of extracts in French translation entitled *Finnegans Wake*, which included du Bouchet's translation of the first and last chapters as well as the Beckett and Joyce excerpts from *Anna Livia Plurabelle*; and the first complete translation of *Finnegans Wake* in any language, by Philippe Lavergne in 1982, was also in French. There also exist various other translated excerpts into French: by Michel Butor in 1949; by Maxime Chastaing, Jacob, and Watt in 1951; by Daniel Castelain in 1964; by Stephen Heath and Philippe Sollers in 1973; and by Simonne Verdin in 1979. There are two different French versions of the opening pages, du Bouchet's and Lavergne's; and seven different French versions of the final page or so, those of Butor, Chastaing and others, du Bouchet, Castelain, Heath and Sollers, Verdin, and Lavergne, respectively.[3]

German translations of *Anna Livia Plurabelle* were prepared first by Georg Goyert in the early thirties (published partially in 1946 and in full in 1970), then by Wolfgang Hildesheimer, partially in 1969 and in

---

3 On *FW* in French, see Allen (2000), Aubert (1965, 1967, 1982), Butor (1967), Cortanze (1983), Costanzo (1972), Debons (1983), Diament (1996), Ferrer and Aubert (1998), Heath and Sollers (1973), Jauffret (1982), Le Bihan (2010), Lernout (1990), Lernout and Van Mierlo (2004, 368–72, 416–21), O'Neill (2005, 41–7), Quigley (2004), Sollers (1982), Soupault (1931, 1943), Topia (1990), Van Hulle (2004), Van Laere (1968), Verdin (1979), and Vouvé (1985).

full in 1970, and finally by Hans Wollschläger in 1970. A volume of collected excerpts from *Finnegans Wake* in German (representing approximately 25 per cent of the whole), edited by Klaus Reichert and Fritz Senn and translated by various hands, appeared in 1989, and in 1993 German became the second European language (after French) to boast a complete (if vigorously contested) *Finnegans Wake*, translated after seventeen years of work by Dieter Stündel. Friedhelm Rathjen's *Winnegans Fake* (2012b) collects around 200 pages of excerpts translated by him on various occasions over some twenty-five years. Various shorter excerpts have also been rendered into German by, among others, Harald Beck, Ulrich Blumenbach, Christian Enzensberger, Erich Fried, Wilhelm Füger, Uwe Herms, Ingeborg Horn, Kurt Jauslin, Arno Schmidt, Klaus Schönmetzler, Wolfgang Schrödter, and Robert Weninger.[4]

Two excerpts from *Anna Livia Plurabelle* translated by Joyce himself in collaboration with Nino Frank and (subsequently) Ettore Settanni appeared in Italian in 1940. More than forty pages of selected excerpts from *Finnegans Wake* translated by Juan Rodolfo Wilcock appeared in 1961, and Luigi Schenoni, after thirty years of exacting work, produced Italian translations of the first ten chapters by his death in 2004, with two further chapters appearing posthumously in 2011. Various shorter excerpts have also been translated into Italian by, among others, Anthony Burgess, Gianni Celati, Mario Diacono, and Roberto Sanesi.[5]

Shorter excerpts from *Finnegans Wake* were rendered into Spanish by Ricardo Silva-Santisteban in 1971, 1982, and 1988; by Salvador Elizondo in 1992; and by Leandro Fanzone in 2007. A complete Spanish *Anna Livia Plurabelle*, translated by Francisco García Tortosa, with Ricardo Navarrete and José María Tejedor Cabrera, appeared in 1992, and an

---

4 On *FW* in German, see Beck (1986, 1987, 1989), Blumenbach (1990, 1998), Drews (1993, 1998), Enzensberger et al. (1985), Fried (1985), Füger (1983, 2000), Gardt (1989), Herms (1985), Hildesheimer (1969), Laman (2007), Lernout and Van Mierlo (2004, 53–9, 67–9), O'Neill (2005, 56–61), Rademacher (1993), Rathjen (1989, 1992b, 1992c, 1993, 1995b, 1998a, 1998b, 1999), Reichert (1989), Schmidt (1969), Senn (1978, 1983, 1993, 1998), Sonnemann (1995), and Weninger (1984, 1985, 2012).

5 On *FW* in Italian, see Bosinelli (1987, 1990, 1996, 1998a, 2000, 2001), Burgess (1975), Celati (1972), del Pozzo (1982), Diacono (1961), Eco (1978, 1996), Federici (1982), Gramigna (1982), Grisi (1982), Lernout and Van Mierlo (2004, 352–8), Lobner (1986), O'Neill (2005, 67–9), O'Sullivan (2006), Parks (1992), Risset (1973, 1979), Sanesi (1982), Schenoni (1974, 1979, 1986), Settanni (1955), Silver and Torrealta (1982), Wilcock (1961), and Zanotti (2004, 2010).

abridged and very much simplified Spanish version of *Finnegans Wake* by Víctor Pozanco in 1993. A Spanish translation of the opening chapter by J.D. Victoria appeared in 2009. There is to date no complete Spanish rendering of *Finnegans Wake*.[6]

The first Portuguese translations of excerpts from the *Wake*, by Augusto de Campos and Haroldo de Campos, appeared in 1957, expanded into a slim volume in 1962 as *Panaroma do Finnegans Wake*. Manuel Lourenço's Portuguese translation of the opening page appeared in 1968. The first fascicle of a complete Portuguese *Finnegans Wake*, by Donaldo Schüler, appeared in 1999, and the complete translation, in five extensively annotated and handsomely produced volumes, appeared in 2003. A complete Portuguese *Anna Livia Plurabelle* by Dirce Waltrick do Amarante appeared in 2009, and brief excerpts have also been translated into Portuguese by Manuel Lourenço and Arthur Nestrovski.[7]

Among other western European languages, C.K. Ogden's Basic English version of the closing pages of *Anna Livia Plurabelle* appeared in 1932, the final ten pages of the *Wake* were translated into Danish by Peter Laugesen in 1997, and a complete Swedish *Anna Livia Plurabelle* by Mario Grut appeared in 2001. A complete Dutch *Finnegans Wake* by Erik Bindervoet and Robbert-Jan Henkes was published in 2002, and a complete Catalan *Anna Livia Plurabelle* by Marissa Aixàs appeared in 2004. Brief excerpts were translated into Galician by Leopoldo Rodríguez in 1969, and Alberte Pagán translated the first two chapters into Galician in 1993.[8] An Irish version of the opening lines was provided by Alan Titley in 2008.

Turning to eastern European languages, we find that a complete and very early Czech *Anna Livia Plurabelle*, by Maria Weatherall, Vladimír Procházka, and Adolf Hoffmeister, appeared in 1932, only a year after the first partial translation into French was organized by Joyce himself.

---

6 On *FW* in Spanish, see Conde-Parrilla (1997), Elizondo (1992), García Tortosa, Navarrete, and Tejedor Cabrera (1992), García Tortosa (1998), Lobner (1994), O'Neill (2005, 75), and Silva-Santisteban (1971, 1982, 1988).

7 On *FW* in Portuguese, see Amarante (2001, 2003a, 2003b, 2005, 2009), Campos (1978, 1999), Campos and Campos (1957, 1962), Nestrovski (1990), O'Neill (2005, 76–7), and Schüler (2003).

8 On *FW* in Basic English, see Sailer (1999); in Swedish, see Grut (2001); in Dutch, see Bindervoet and Henkes (2002), van der Weide (2003); in Catalan, see Aixàs (2004, 2007); in Galician, see Pagán (2000) and Rodríguez (1969).

A Slovak version by Jozef Kot of the opening pages appeared in 1965. Jerzy Strzetelski's Polish versions of brief excerpts from *Anna Livia Plurabelle* appeared in 1959, while Maciej Słomczyński produced a complete Polish *Anna Livia Plurabelle* in 1985. Further brief excerpts in Polish were published by Adam Królikowski in 1998 and by Jacek Malicki in 2001, while Krzysztof Bartnicki translated 'The Mookse and the Gripes' into Polish in 2005. Endre Bíró translated substantial excerpts (including from *Anna Livia Plurabelle*) into Hungarian in 1964 and increased their number in 1992. A Russian translation by Henri Volokhonsky of the first six chapters of *Finnegans Wake* appeared in 2000, as did a Russian version by Konstantin Belyaev of three pages from *Anna Livia Plurabelle*. A complete Romanian *Anna Livia Plurabelle* translated by Felicia Antip appeared in 1996, a Romanian version of the final pages of *Anna Livia Plurabelle* translated by Laurent Milesi was published in 1998, some ten pages of excerpts in Slovenian translation by Andrej Skubic appeared in 2000, and a Finnish version of the opening pages by Miikka Mutanen followed in 2006.[9]

Among non-European languages, finally, the earliest Japanese excerpts from *Anna Livia Plurabelle* appeared in 1933, translated by Junzaburo Nishiwaki. The first three chapters of *Finnegans Wake*, translated by Yukio Suzuki and others, appeared in 1971, and further excerpts from the *Wake* translated by Kyôko Ono and others appeared in 1978. Masayoshi Osawa and a team of collaborators provided Japanese versions of substantial excerpts from the 1960s to the 1980s, culminating in a complete Japanese *Anna Livia Plurabelle* in 1982. A complete Japanese translation of *Finnegans Wake* by Naoki Yanase appeared in 1993, an abridged Japanese version by Kyôko Miyata appeared in 2004, and a Japanese translation of parts I and IV by Tatsuo Hamada was published in 2009, with parts II and III advertised to appear in 2012 or 2013. In Korean, Chong-keon Kim translated *Anna Livia Plurabelle* in 1985, followed by the complete *Finnegans Wake* in 2002.[10]

---

9 On *FW* in Polish, see Szczerbowski (2000), Wawrzycka (1998, 2004); in Hungarian, see Egri (1967); in Romanian, see Milesi (1998).
10 On *FW* in Japanese, see Ito (2004), Miyata (2004b); on *FW* in Korean, see Kim (2004) and Chun (2004).

III

Joyce, as is well known, was obsessively secretive about the title of the book that he called for more than fifteen years by the interim title *Work in Progress*. We may conclude our survey of the international transpositions of what eventually came to be called *Finnegans Wake* by looking briefly at how that carefully guarded title itself has fared in translation.

The earliest translations, as we have seen, were all of (or from) *Anna Livia Plurabelle*, and in almost all cases involved only very minor variations on that title: the earliest French translation (Beckett and Joyce 1931) used the title 'Anna Livie Plurabelle'; the Czech (Weatherall, Procházka, and Hoffmeister 1932) and Italian (Joyce and Settanni 1940) employed the form 'Anna Livia Plurabella,' as does Grut's Swedish version (2001); while the German (Goyert 1970; Hildesheimer 1970; Wollschläger 1970) and the Spanish (García Tortosa 1992) renderings preferred to stay with the original 'Anna Livia Plurabelle.' The one more adventurous exception was 'Anna Lyvia Pluratself' (Péron and Beckett 1985), which gestures reflexively towards the act of translation itself by transposing 'Livia' into 'Lyvia' as well as augmenting the Liffey by adding not only New Zealand's river Lyvia but also, by the suggestion of a lengthened vowel, the Irish river Lee and the English river Lea. Its flaunted strangeness also suggests a problematically compound personality, sometimes almost 'plural,' sometimes almost 'itself,' no doubt a puzzle (German *Rätsel*) even to itself, resulting perhaps in bouts of secret weeping (Latin *plorat*, 'she weeps'), no doubt about many things (Latin *plura*).

André du Bouchet's first attempt at translating further excerpts from the *Wake* was published as 'Dans le sillage de Finnegan' (1950), literally 'in Finnegan's wake' (in the maritime sense); his second appeared as 'Les veilles des Finnegans' (1957), literally 'the waking of the Finnegans' (in the funereal sense). All subsequent French attempts, whether in journals (Chastaing, Jacob, and Watt 1951; Castelain 1964) or in book form (du Bouchet 1962; Lavergne 1982) leave Joyce's title untranslated. The earliest Italian attempt to translate further passages was that of J. Rodolfo Wilcock (1961), published as 'Frammenti scelti da La veglia di Finnegan,' literally 'selected excerpts from The Wake of Finnegan' (in the funereal sense).

Among later translations from and of *Finnegans Wake*, only four attempt also to translate the title. Endre Bíró's Hungarian title *Finnegan ébredése (részletek)* retranslates as 'excerpts' (*részletek*) from, literally, 'Finnegan wakes'; while Dieter Stündel's *Finnegans Wehg* flamboyantly (if, in the opinion of many readers, misguidedly) combines German *Weh* ('woe, labour pains'), *Weg* ('way'), and a stage-German mispronunciation of the English *wake*. The lack of an apostrophe in Stündel's German (as opposed to its absence in the original) title is reductive, producing an unambiguously singular 'Finnegan's' wake – while the interlingual title of Henri Volokhonsky's Russian *Finneganov Wake* is equally unambiguously a plural 'Finnegans" wake. Reichert and Senn's *Finnegans Wake Deutsch* (1989) parodically employs a bilingual title that mirrors the (apparently) ungrammatical absence of an English apostrophe in the original title by the equally ungrammatical presence of a capitalized German adjective (*Deutsch*). The title of Alberte Pagán's Galician translation of the first two chapters as *Velório de Finnegans* derives from the fact that *Finnegans Wake* is frequently referred to in the languages of the Iberian Peninsula as '*Finnegans*,' much as English-speaking readers refer to 'the *Wake*.' Pagán's title can thus be taken to imply 'The Wake of the *Wake*' – but with the noun *velório* unambiguously suggesting a funereal rather than a maritime context.

Donaldo Schüler's particularly evocative Portuguese title, *Finnicius Revém* (2003) is borrowed, with due acknowledgment, from its original coiners, the Campos brothers (Campos and Campos 1962, 13).[11] It can be read as combining 'Finn' and a Latin quasi-comparative *finnicius* ('a thing even more Finn'), with attendant suggestions of 'finishes,' 'finish us,' even 'Phoenicians' (Portuguese *fenícios*) – Joyce, we may remember, considered the *Odyssey* to have Phoenician origins – not to mention an 'end' (Latin *finis*, Portuguese *fim*), all of which 'comes again' (Portuguese *revém*) as if in a 'dream' (French *rêve*). The invented name *Finnicius*, meanwhile, also suggests the Brazilian personal name *Vinicius*, evoking a Portuguese or Brazilian *vinho* ('wine') in at least partial substitution for the good Irish whiskey that brings an ever-thirsty Tim Finnegan back from the dead. The title of a subsequent children's book by Schüler loosely based on the *Wake*, *Finnício Riovém* (2004), improves further on his earlier title and is certainly one of the most ingenious translations of Joyce's title so far. The first word, *Finnício*, now includes 'Finn' as well

---

11 Augusto de Campos and Haroldo de Campos entitle their eleven translated excerpts '*Finnegans Wake / Finnicius Revém*: 11 excerptos,' but the cover and title page both carry the title *Panaroma do Finnegans Wake*.

as both *fim* ('end') and *início* ('beginning'); while the second word, *riovém*, includes not only *revém* ('comes again') and thus by implication the suggestion of a French *rêve* ('dream'), but also *rio* ('river'), and thus Anna Livia Plurabelle, the eternal river that always returns in a commodius vicus of recirculation.

J.D. Victoria's 2009 Spanish translation of the opening chapter uses the quite different title *Estela de Finnegan*, which might initially tempt one to read it as merely a reductive 'Finnegan's wake,' where the wake (*estela*) is in a maritime rather than a funereal sense. The term *estela*, however, has at least four separate implications in the context. As also meaning a 'stele,' an *estela* may carry any one or more of its historical meanings, whether as commemorative marker, as celebratory monument, or as territorial marker. Here it may be read as carrying all three: it implies, first, a commemorative marker for Tim Finnegan, gone but not forgotten; second, it implies a carefully worked monument to and celebration of the original Joycean text, commonly referred to in Spanish by the short form *Finnegans*; and, third, it suggests a territorial marker that instead of being placed between the original and its translation is placed to include in Joyce's text all its translations, including this one. Nonetheless, and finally, the term *estela* does indeed also translate as a (maritime) 'wake,' employed here, as the context indicates, to highlight the concomitant and inescapable fact that a translation, whatever its intentions, ambitions, and achievements, ultimately never has any choice but to follow, by definition, in the wake of its original (2009, 1).

The punning title of Friedhelm Rathjen's *Winnegans Fake* (2012b), a collection of some two hundred pages of excerpts from the *Wake* in German translation, humorously makes a somewhat similar point: translators of *Finnegans Wake* may very well 'win' some and will undoubtedly lose a great many more (such as not getting even the first word of the title right), and however impressive their wins may be, they will also inevitably produce a *Wake* that is fake.

PART TWO

Words in Progress

2 Riverrun[1]

To begin our transtextual explorations, let us turn to a comparative consideration of a group of would-be translations of the opening three-line sentence (or sentence fragment). In doing so, we shall focus on three complementary and interactive questions. First, and very briefly, what are the primary textual features that we are likely to grasp as readers on a first exposure to the opening sentence in the *Wake*'s highly peculiar brand of English – and what do we in all likelihood *not* yet understand but find out subsequently to have been implied from the beginning? Second, how is this progressive layering of textual information handled in individual translations? Third, and once again briefly, what significant macrotextual effects emerge from this comparative transtextual reading?

As already mentioned, the comparative readings here and in later chapters are limited almost entirely to versions in western European languages. Where versions are provided in eastern European languages (Russian, Polish, Czech, Romanian, Hungarian, Finnish), they are intended largely – though admitting of occasional exploratory forays – for the interest of readers more competent than the present writer to deal with them at an appropriate level of linguistic and cultural detail.

---

1 Chapter 2 includes a much expanded version of an earlier discussion in my book *Polyglot Joyce: Fictions of Translation* (2005). A preliminary version first appeared as '*Finnegans Wakes*: Fictions of Translation' (2000).

I

> riverrun, past Eve and Adam's, from swerve of shore to bend of bay,
> brings us by a commodius vicus of recirculation back to Howth Castle and
> Environs.   (*FW* 3.1–3)

Adaline Glasheen, some decades ago, characterized the first two para-graphs of *Finnegans Wake* as 'a dizzying, incredible tour de force' (1965, 5). Shortly afterwards Jacques Aubert (1969) devoted a ten-page study to a single word, the opening 'riverrun.' Even on a first reading, however, the basic meaning of the celebrated opening sentence, despite its surface difficulties, appears to be more or less clear: the course of some unnamed river, on its way from land to sea, brings us, by a circular process of some kind, back to a particular named location. Even as first-time readers we probably know, or can easily find out, that the river is the Irish river Liffey, on which the city of Dublin stands, and that Howth is a rocky promontory, complete with historical castle, to the north of Dublin Bay. As first-time readers, we will very likely be unclear both as to how or why we are already being brought 'back' to Howth and as to what kind of circular process is involved, though we may well suspect that it pos-sibly has something to do either with the natural cycle of precipitation or, if we have consulted a map, with the geographical fact that the Liffey, rising to the southwest in the Wicklow hills, flows in a wide loop first west, then north, and only then finally east into Dublin Bay.

The main thing the first-time reader does not know at this point, of course, is that what we will continue to call the first sentence will even-tually emerge as only the completion of a final sentence begun more than six hundred pages later. All unbeknownst to us, it thus introduces the circular structure of the narrative itself (if it *is* indeed a narrative), which we have still to read but whose conclusion and reinception we will turn out to have been already witnessing. That never-ending circu-lar narrative, it will more gradually emerge, is among much else the story (or at any rate presents aspects of the relationship) of an archetypal pair, the eternal hero and eternal heroine conveniently anthropomor-phosed in two Dublin landmarks, the Hill of Howth and the river Liffey respectively. The first word thus introduces the heroine, who will turn out to be otherwise known as Anna Livia Plurabelle. As for the hero, to use that term very loosely indeed, one of his many names is that of the titular Finnegan, who will turn out to be not only the tipsy hod-carrier of the music-hall song but also a sleeping giant spread across Dublin whose name punningly hints ('Finn-again') at his identity with the mythological Irish hero Finn (or Fionn) mac Cumhaill, anglicized as Finn MacCool, and whose head (at least in Joyce's text) is also Howth Head.

Another of our hero's appellations is the somewhat unusual *Humphrey Chimpden Earwicker* – the components of which may (among other possibilities, to which we shall return in a later chapter) be read as variously suggesting Norman, English, and Viking aspects of an otherwise Gaelic Finn-again. Both Earwicker's initials (*HCE*) and those of Anna Livia Plurabelle (*ALP*) continually recur in the narrative, and HCE puts in a first appearance in 'Howth Castle and Environs.'[2] Yet another of our hero's (implied) names will turn out to be *Adam*, a discovery that may or may not retrospectively inspire us to notice in the 'Eve and Adam's' of the opening sentence an oblique reference to the Garden of Eden and Original Sin; or that the comfortably traditional relationship of the sexes inscribed in the familiar formula 'Adam and Eve' is disrupted in the very first line of the text; or that the progression from female to male, Eve to Adam, parallels that from ALP to HCE in the opening sentence.

At some later stage in our reading we will eventually realize, most likely on fleeing for help to some professional commentator, that the odd formulation 'a commodius vicus of recirculation' refers to the existence not only of a Vico Road in Dublin but also of the eighteenth-century Italian philosopher Giambattista Vico, who in his treatise *Principi di scienza nuova* (1725) anticipated Nietzsche in conceiving of history as an endless process of recirculation; it may or may not also remind us of Lucius Aelius Aurelius Commodus, the second-century Roman emperor in whose reign historians see the beginnings of the Empire's slow but inevitable collapse, an event both allowing and necessitating the inception of a whole new stage of European history. The opening 'riverrun' thus emerges retrospectively also as a Heraclitean reminder that *panta rhei*, that all is flux and we can never step twice in the same river; by the hint of German *Erinnerung* ('memory') it counter-evokes the role of our shared historical and linguistic heritage, reminding us that we can *only* ever step in the same river; and it reminds us finally that we *are* all inescapably what the French call *riverains*, dwellers on the banks of that same river of memory and language and time.

---

2 The initials *HCE* are not 'explained' until *FW* 30–6; the woman and the river are not clearly identified until *FW* 195 (Glasheen 1965, 5).

'The first word of the text,' as Bernard Benstock observes, 'can be allowed to serve as a paradigm of the linguistic condition of *Finnegans Wake*: *riverrun* has readily been accepted as a poetic neologism somehow compounding river and running (flowing) to suggest the river Liffey in Dublin flowing past Adam and Eve's Church, and metaphorically the river of time running past our primal parents toward the present' (1985, 149). But that is far from being the whole story. Other resonances discovered by various readers in that first word have included a French [*nous*] *rêverons* ('we shall dream'), French [*nous nous*] *reverrons* ('we'll meet again, we'll see each other again'), Italian *riverran* ('they'll come again'), and even an English *reverend*, where 'the relationship of a Reverend Father with Adam and Eve's Church satisfies a kind of associative logic that readers quickly assume as operative in the *Wake*' (Benstock 1985, 149). Fritz Senn has noted (1995, 120) that 'riverrun' also recalls the origins of Joyce's own published work, the opening poem of *Chamber Music* containing the words 'There's music *along the river.*' Senn has also noted (1995, 120) an intriguing echo of Coleridge's line 'where Alph the sacred *river ran,*' a suggestion that happily collocates ALP and Alph, HCE and Kubla Khan, Dublin and imperial Xanadu (whose final syllable even replicates phonetically the *dubh* of Dublin), not to mention *Finnegans Wake* itself and the 'stately pleasure dome' decreed by the mighty khan.

All this, of course, raises the whole question of how a reader of *Finnegans Wake* is to decide on what is a relevant and what an irrelevant response for the particular context – assuming that our reader is competent to decide what that context may be in the first place. Various readers have noted that 'riverrun' contains an embedded *err*, a salutary warning as to what readers of *Finnegans Wake* are inevitably going to do in their readings from this point on.

What can a would-be translator possibly make of all this? And what, in turn, is a reader who reads *Finnegans Wake* in translation rather than the original likely to make of the text he or she reads? We may begin to consider the matter by comparing, perhaps rather extravagantly, the sometimes widely varying implications involved in twenty-eight different translations, in thirteen different languages, of the opening (part-) sentence: three of them French (by Michel Butor, André du Bouchet, and Philippe Lavergne respectively), four Italian (by Rodolfo Wilcock, Anthony Burgess, and Luigi Schenoni, who produced two separate versions), three Spanish (by Salvador Elizondo, Víctor Pozanco, and J.D. Victoria), one Catalan (by Marissa Aixàs), four Portuguese (by Augusto de Campos, Manuel Lourenço, and Donaldo Schüler, who also produced two separate versions), one Galician (by Alberte Pagán), five German (by Harald Beck, Kurt Jauslin, Wolfgang Schrödter, Friedhelm Rathjen, and Dieter Stündel), one Dutch (by Erik Bindervoet and Robbert-Jan Henkes), one Russian (by Henri Volokhonsky), two Polish (by Adam Królikowski and Jacek Malicki), one Czech (anonymous), and one Irish (by Alan Titley). Finally, remembering that Arland Ussher once called the language of *Finnegans Wake* a 'Joysick Esperanto' (1957, 125), it is fitting that we now also have an Esperanto version of the opening sentence, translated in this case not by a human being but by a machine translator (Anon. 2010). For ease of comparison, the translations are grouped by language (and chronologically within individual languages).[3]

II

Dividing the sentence into its six component phrases, we may compare in some detail what each of our translators has made of each phrase in turn – and, in so doing, begin to track the ways in which the Joycean text is cumulatively transformed in the process of its multilingual reading.

[1]   riverrun

Butor (French, 1948): cours de la rivière

du Bouchet (French, 1962): courrive

Lavergne (French, 1982): erre revie

Wilcock (Italian, 1961): corso del fiume

Burgess (Italian, 1975): filafiume

---

3 The chronological order of the twenty-eight versions is as follows: Butor (French, 1948), Wilcock (Italian, 1961), du Bouchet (French, 1962), Campos and Campos (Portuguese, 1962), Lourenço (Portuguese, 1968), Burgess (Italian, 1975), Schenoni (Italian, 1978, 1982), Lavergne (French, 1982), Beck (German, 1989), Jauslin (German, 1989), Rathjen (German, 1989), Schrödter (German, 1989), Elizondo (Spanish, 1992), Pozanco (Spanish, 1993), Stündel (German, 1993), Królikowski (Polish, 1998), Pagán (Galician, 2000), Volokhonsky (Russian, 2000), Malicki (Polish, 2001), Bindervoet and Henkes (Dutch, 2002), Schüler (Portuguese, 2003, 2004), Aixàs (Catalan, 2004), Titley (Irish, 2008), Anon. (Czech, 2009), Victoria (Spanish, 2009), Anon. (Esperanto, 2010).

Schenoni (Italian, 1978): fiume che scorre

Schenoni (Italian, 1982): fluidofiume

Elizondo (Spanish, 1992): riocorrido

Pozanco (Spanish, 1993): río que discurre

Victoria (Spanish, 2009): correrrío

Aixàs (Catalan, 2004): fluirderiu

Campos (Portuguese, 1962): riocorrente

Lourenço (Portuguese, 1968): corrio

Schüler (Portuguese, 2003): rolarriuanna

Schüler (Portuguese, 2004, 10): rolarriuanna

Pagán (Galician, 2000): recorrio

Beck (German, 1989): flußlauf

Jauslin (German, 1989): Flußfloß

Rathjen (German, 1989): Flußgefließe

Schrödter (German, 1989): Flußeslauf

Stündel (German, 1993): Flußflaufs

Bindervoet and Henkes (Dutch, 2002): rivierein

Volokhonsky (Russian, 2000): beg reki

Królikowski (Polish, 1998): rzekobieg

Malicki (Polish, 2001): rzekabiegnie

Anon. (Czech, 2009): protéká

Titley (Irish, 2008): rithruthag na habhann

Anon. (Esperanto, 2010): riverkuro

These twenty-eight translations – or transpositions, or transfigurations, or transcreations – constitute twenty-eight proposed solutions that are, of course, also continuing interrogations of the Joycean text. Given the relatively large number of renderings to be considered, the most effective procedure will be to proceed by individual language.

In French, then, Butor, aiming in 1948 at novice readers of the *Wake* needing an introduction, thus limits himself to what he sees as a basic denotative meaning, expressed in a grammatically correct target-language phrase, his 'cours de la rivière' literally meaning 'course of the river.' Two later French versions attempt quite different solutions. Du Bouchet's one-word 'courrive' transforms 'riverrun' into something closer to 'runriver' while also conflating the river and its restraining banks, English *river* and French *rivière* both deriving from the Latin *ripa* ('riverbank'), whence also French *rive* ('bank'). Lavergne's version, the most daring of the three, portrays the slow drift (*erre*, 'momentum') of a 'rivi-ère' recomposed into 'erre revie,' where 'erre' also invokes *errer* ('to rove, wander, stray'), and 'revie' evokes a life (*vie*) to be relived (*revie*), reseen (*revue*), dreamed (*rêvée*), and redreamed (*rerêvée*).

In Italian, Wilcock, aiming as Butor was at novice readers of the *Wake*, similarly limits himself to an explanatory paraphrase, his 'corso del fiume' also literally meaning 'course of the river.' Schenoni's earlier 'fiume che scorre' ('river that runs') makes a similar semantic choice but chooses to employ a relative clause. Two later Italian versions succeed both in using a single word and in retaining the alliteration of the original: thus Burgess's 'filafiume' and Schenoni's later 'fluidofiume' (both approximately 'flowriver').

In Spanish, Elizondo also succeeds in restricting himself, as does Joyce in English (if we agree to call it English), to a single word, 'riocorrido,' conflating the river (*río*) and its course (*recorrido*), while Pozanco's 'río que discurre' (literally 'river that flows') opts for an explanatory relative clause. Victoria's one-word 'correrrío' successfully conflates *correr* ('to run'), *río* ('river'), and *errar* ('to err, to wander, to go astray'). Aixàs's Catalan 'fluirderiu,' meanwhile, literally 'flowing (*fluir*) of river,' is once again primarily explanatory in tone.

In Portuguese, the Campos brothers' version restricts itself to a single word, 'riocorrente' ('riverrunning') while simultaneously hinting at the river (*rio*) as perennially recurrent (*reocorrente*). Lourenço's 'corrio,' more succinct even than du Bouchet's French 'courrive,' once again conflates *correr* ('to run') and *rio* ('river'). Schüler adopts instead a more expansive 'rolarriuanna,' not only conflating *rolar* ('to roll, flow, run') and *rio* ('river') but also firmly, if perhaps unnecessarily, establishing the identity of the river and Anna Livia Plurabelle. Pagán's Galician 'recorrio' echoes Lourenço's Portuguese 'corrio,' but also establishes the centrality of remembering (*recordar*, 'to remember') and repetition by strategically deploying *re-* as the first syllable of the entire 628-page text.

In German, all five versions variously conflate *Fluß* ('river') and either *fließen* ('to flow') or *Lauf* ('course, run'). Thus Beck's 'flußlauf,' a literal 'riverrun'; Jauslin's 'Flußfloß' ('riverflowed'); Schrödter's 'Flußeslauf' ('river's course'); Rathjen's 'Flußgefließe,' literally 'riverflowings'; and Stündel's more complex 'Flußflaufs,' where *Lauf* ('run, course') is at once swallowed up by and imposed upon a repeated *Fluß*. Alternatively, we might read Stündel's 'Flußflaufs' as playing on a syncopated *Flußverlauf*, an unusual but by no means impossible linguistic combination suggesting 'the course (*Verlauf*) of the river (*Fluß*).' The alliterative effect of 'riverrun' is replicated in Jauslin's 'Flußfloß' and Rathjen's 'Flußgefließe,' while a reverse alliteration is suggested by Beck's 'flußlauf' and Schrödter's 'Flußeslauf.'

Bindervoet and Henkes's Dutch 'rivierein,' for its part, conflates *rivier* ('river') and *rennen* ('to run'), while the element *rein* suggests not only a river that is 'clean, pure, chaste' but also provides an echo of the river Rhine as an appropriately international and intercultural Swiss / German / French / Dutch avatar of Anna Livia. The fact that the various names of the Rhine – German *Rhein*, French *Rhin*, Dutch *Rijn* – share their etymological origins with the Irish noun *rith* ('run'), all of them deriving from an Indo-European root **rei-*, may count as our first instance of a pleasingly appropriate translingual serendipity.

Among eastern European languages, we find Volokhonsky's Russian 'beg reki' offering an explanatory two-word 'running (*beg*) of the river (*reká*),' while in Polish, Królikowski's 'rzekobieg' achieves a one-word conflation of the corresponding vocabulary elements, *rzeka* ('river') and *bieg* ('run'), as does Malicki's 'rzekabiegnie,' the adverbial ending *-nie* of the latter suggesting a location 'by the riverrun.' The anonymous Czech 'protéká' likewise achieves a one-word conflation of *proud* ('river') and *útéck* ('run').

Titley's Irish 'rithruthag na habhann,' meanwhile, rather expansively incorporates two separate terms for the noun 'run,' namely *rith* and *rothag*, while also providing two separate terms for 'river,' a clearly identifiable *abha* visible to all eyes and an only dimly discernible *sruth* almost hidden in the hither-and-thithering currents of *rith* and *rothag*. An Esperanto version, finally, produced by the machine translator GramTrans, offers 'riverkuro,' which not only manages to conflate the nouns *rivero* ('river') and *kuro* ('run') but also self-reflexively hints at both the literary work (*verko*) we are reading and the activity needed to produce it (*verki*, 'to write'), invokes the Japanese river Kuro as a Far Eastern avatar of Anna Livia, and leaves readers to discover for themselves the fact that the Japanese adjective *kuro* ('black') shares its meaning with the Irish adjective *dubh*, an element retained in the name of the city of Dublin, home to Anna Livia's riverrun. Translingual serendipity is clearly not restricted to the products of human translators.

Even the first word of Joyce's text introduces its reader to one of the fundamental principles of *Finnegans Wake*: the infinite malleability, suggestivity, and irrepressibility of language. The possibilities afforded by different languages for translating the two elements of the neologism 'riverrun' are accordingly of immediate interest here. In the case of 'river,' du Bouchet's French makes imaginative use of the etymological link between *rive* and *rivière*, while none of the Italian *fiume*, the Spanish *río*, or the Portuguese *rio* proves particularly productive of new meanings. Jauslin and Rathjen are able to make good use of the link between German *Fluß* ('river') and *fließen* ('to flow'). As regards 'run,' German *Lauf*, from *laufen* ('to run'), shows only moderate potential, but etymology happily enables our French translators to use *cours* and *courir*, the Italians *corso* and *scorrere*, the Portuguese and Spanish *corrente*, *recorrido*, and *discurrir*, all of them derived from the Latin verb *currere* or its noun *cursus*, each denoting both running and flowing. The Spanish verb *discurrir*, employed by Pozanco, has a particularly apposite range of connotations, including not only flowing but also meditating, pondering, reflecting, discoursing, and speaking, all of them perfectly suited to the Anna Livia we will encounter throughout the *Wake*.

All of this, of course, raises the question of just how far it is legitimate to go as a translator. A closely related question is whether some readers (Irish readers, for example) are in principle more privileged than others. To some extent, Irish readers will indeed be more familiar with details of Irish locations, ways of speech, and, possibly, Irish history and culture in general. In our present context of investigation, however, the more productive (and more appropriately Joycean) answer to the question is undoubtedly that different readers, including those who read the text in translation, will have (and may be able to take advantage of) privileges of a quite different kind.

[2]   *past Eve and Adam's*

Butor (French, 1948): dépassé celui d'Ève et d'Adam

du Bouchet (French, 1962): passé notre Adame

Lavergne (French, 1982): pass'Evant notre Adame

Wilcock (Italian, 1961): oltre Adamo ed Eva

Burgess (Italian, 1975): dopo da Eva ed Adamo

Schenoni (Italian, 1978): passato Eva ed Adamo

Schenoni (Italian, 1982): passato Eva ed Adamo

Elizondo (Spanish, 1992): más allá de la de Eva y Adán

Pozanco (Spanish, 1993): más allá de Adam and Eve

Victoria (Spanish, 2009): pasados [la iglesia & la taberna de] Eva
    y Adán

Aixàs (Catalan, 2004): que passant per Eva i Adam,

Campos (Portuguese, 1962): depois de Eva e Adão

Lourenço (Portuguese, 1968): depois de Eva e Adão,

Schüler (Portuguese, 2003): e passa por Nossenhora d'Ohmem's

Schüler (Portuguese, 2004, 10): e passa pelo parque de Eva e Adão,

Pagán (Galician, 2000): pasando Eva e Adán

Beck (German, 1989): vorbei an Ev' und Adams

Jauslin (German, 1989): furbay Eva' und Adams dahein

Rathjen (German, 1989): schleunigst Ev' und Adam passiert

Schrödter (German, 1989): Seit' Eve und Adams

Stündel (German, 1993): vorbei an Adam und Eva

Bindervoet and Henkes (Dutch, 2002): langst de Eva en Adam

Volokhonsky (Russian, 2000): mimo Evy c Adamom,

Królikowski (Polish, 1998): pokąt Adama i Ewy,

Malicki (Polish, 2001): mimo Evy i Adamsa,

Anon. (Czech, 2009): za Evou a Adamem

Titley (Irish, 2008): thairis Aoife agus Ádhamhach,

· Anon. (Esperanto, 2010): pasinta Eva kaj tiu de Adamo,

'As Adam and Eve stand at the beginning of human history, so they
stand at the beginning of our book, suggesting Eden, sexual polarity,

the fall of man, and the promise of redemption' (Campbell and Robinson 1961, 25). 'Past Eve and Adam's' already immerses the reader in the swirl of blurring identities and meanings that will pervade the entire *Wake*. The phrase resonates in at least three major ways: first, as suggested, it recalls the Garden of Eden, Original Sin, and Paradise Lost; second, it is a reversal of a familiarly gendered cultural formula, 'Adam and Eve'; and third, it is more specifically a reversal also of the name 'Adam and Eve's,' a popular nickname of the Franciscan Church of the Immaculate Conception on Merchant's Quay on the river Liffey in Dublin. The nickname already resonates strongly in the context of Joyce's Dublin, combining as it does religious observance and more earthly pleasures. The church in question originated in the seventeenth century as a mass house approached by a lane on the corner of which stood a tavern named Adam and Eve's. During the early eighteenth century it was safer politically to visit a tavern than a mass house, and 'it appears that those on their way to mass often said that they were visiting *Adam and Eve's*' (de Courcy 1996, 198).[4] The fact that Merchant's Quay was once part of Viking Dublin provides a supplementary hint of HCE's presence – though only restrospectively, of course, since a first-time reader will necessarily remain blind to the hint.

Among our almost thirty translators, only Butor emphasizes the biblical implication of the phrase, intimating, if rather obscurely, that the meaning of the river and its course is in some sense more important than that of the biblical myth of origin. The gendered implication is of interest to at least four of the translators. While the textually deviant relationship of our first parents is respected by most of our translators, Wilcock, Pozanco, Stündel, and Królikowski all reverse the textual reversal to a more conservatively familiar Adam and Eve. The geographical implication is primary to all of the translators except Butor, but the implied geography is also not without its ambiguities, for the innocuous-looking preposition 'past' involves a play with presence and absence, a river *going* past or a river *gone* past. Beck, Stündel, Pagán, Aixàs, and Królikowski all stress the river's presence, passing rather than gone past the church on its bank; all other versions except Butor's focus on the river's passage *beyond* the church.

Other implications emerge. Victoria's Spanish, introducing an idiosyncratic system of infixed parenthetical annotation, specifies that the

---

4 The church is also referred to in *Ulysses*: 'masshouse (Adam and Eve's tavern)' (*U* 688.38).

river has flowed past both the church (*iglesia*) and a tavern (*taverna*) likewise associated with 'Eva y Adán.' Rathjen's river reveals itself as very different from Lavergne's: unlike the slow drift of Lavergne's lazy river, Rathjen's proves to be rushing past, as demonstrated by the German superlative 'schleunigst' ('at great speed'). Jauslin's 'furbay' conflates the German verb *fuhr* ('travelled'), the adverb *vorbei* ('past'), and, in translingual anticipation of the river's ultimate destination, the English noun *bay*. The river's progress is further specified by Jauslin as 'dahein,' conflating *dahin* ('onwards') and the suggestion that the river is both going 'home' (*heim*) to the sea and simultaneously, as Dublin's own river, already 'at home' (*daheim*). Schrödter's German rendering, 'Seit' Eve und Adams,' conflates geographical space (*Seite*, the 'side' of the river), historical time (*seit*, 'since'), and the literary 'page' (*Seite*) on which our story of space and time will be written. Bindervoet and Henkes have the river flowing 'langst de Eva en Adam,' conflating Dutch *langs* ('along') and the suggestion that the flow of this river will provide a very long story (*langst*, 'longest') indeed. The machine-produced Esperanto version, finally, after a brilliant start with the opening word, quickly comes to grief with 'pasinta Eva kaj tiu de Adamo,' a version that, by confusing the adjectival and prepositional meanings of the English 'past,' produces a meaningless 'former (*pasinta*) Eve and former Adam's.'

Two of the most interesting readings are once again those of du Bouchet and Lavergne, each of whom pushes the play of identities well beyond that reached by Joyce's original text at this point. Du Bouchet's version thus appears at first to have abandoned Eve altogether, but we eventually find her not only hidden in the opening 'courr*ive*' but also amalgamated with her Adam, who, as 'notre Adame' ('our Adam') is also 'Notre Dame,' male shading into female as the Liffey shades into the Seine and Dublin into Paris. Lavergne achieves a similar blurring of borders and identities. Though his errant river's Irishness is evoked by his opening 'erre' – which is, of course, also *Éire*, Ireland – he also provides it with the necessary textual permit (*passavant*) with which it passes in front of (*passe devant*) the French 'notre Adame' again, once again Eving our Adam ('Evant notre Adame'). In the context of an opening sentence that negotiates as an immediate item of the textual agenda the distance and the difference between the river that is Eve / ALP and the land that is Adam / HCE, du Bouchet's and Lavergne's renderings, in other words, clearly succeed in *extending* the Joycean text – and clearly resonate well beyond the microtextual confines of this initial phrase.

As du Bouchet and Lavergne extend the boundaries of Dublin on the Liffey to include Paris on the Seine, Donaldo Schüler's adventurous Portuguese rendering, 'e passa por Nossenhora d'Ohmem's,' extends those boundaries even further to include the Brazilian metropolis of São Paulo on the Rio Teitê. A well-known church in São Paulo, one discovers, is devoted to the popular cult of Nossa Senhora do Ó ('Our Lady of the Sigh'). Combining Ó and the noun *homem* ('man, mankind'), Schüler's version suggests proleptically that ALP is both alpha and omega and that Anna Livia, Our Lady of the Liffey, will also emerge as Our Lady of Mankind. Since Portuguese *homem* also translates Hebrew *adam* ('man'), we thus have both Adam and Eve subsumed in the Blessed Virgin Mary, while the unnecessary and ungrammatical apostrophe in 'Ohmem's' reminds us both of the presence of the apostrophe in 'Eve and Adam's' and the absence of the apostrophe in *Finnegans Wake*.

A year after *Finnicius Revém*, his five-volume translation of *Finnegans Wake*, appeared, the versatile Schüler also produced a highly abbreviated, very much simplified, and very loosely based children's version, *Finnício Riovém* (2004), the first sentence of which is closely based on his version of the first sentence in *Finnicius Revém*. The phrase under consideration here appears in the later version as 'e passa pelo parque de Eva e Adão,' where the river 'passes' (*passa*) not by the church of 'Eve and Adam's' but by the 'garden (*parque*) of Eve and Adam,' suggesting at once the Garden of Eden, the fall of our first parents, and (at the expense of some geographical displacement) the Phoenix Park (*parque*), the site, as we shall discover, of HCE's temptation and fall – however indeterminate – from grace.

As will already have emerged, Eve and Adam undergo various transformations from one language to another. Eve is thus also variously Ève and Eva; Adam becomes Adamo, Adán, and Adão. The Irish Aoife and Ádhamh (the adjectival form being *Ádhamhach*) will be strange to many readers. The oblique forms in the various Slavic versions contribute 'mimo Evy c Adamom' (Russian), 'pokąt Adama i Ewy' (Polish), 'mimo Evy i Adamsa' (Polish), and 'za Evou a Adamem' (Czech), while a Finnish version (Mutanen 2006), to which we shall return, estranges our first parents even further, with 'ohi Eilvan ja Aatomun.' The point is not a trivial one, for it handily exemplifies the tension between the familiar and the strange, the expected and the unexpected, the simple and the complex, that is at the heart of any reading of *Finnegans Wake*, whether in translation or not.

It has occasionally been suggested by readers of the *Wake*, in conclusion, that 'past Eve' might also be read as suggesting 'past nightfall,' thus obliquely signalling the onset of a book of the night. This particular suggestion, though by no means implausible, is not taken up by any of our translators.

[3]   *from swerve of shore to bend of bay*

Butor (French, 1948): de déviation de rivage en courbe de baie

du Bouchet (French, 1962): des courbes de la côte aux bras de la baie

Lavergne (French, 1982): d'erre rive en rêvière

Wilcock (Italian, 1961): dallo scarto della riva alla piega della baia

Burgess (Italian, 1975): da giro di riva a curva di baia

Schenoni (Italian, 1978): da baia sinuosa a costa frastagliata

Schenoni (Italian, 1982): da spiaggia sinuosa a baia biancheggiante

Elizondo (Spanish, 1992): de desvío de costa a encombadura de bahía

Pozanco (Spanish, 1993): desde el recodo de la orilla a la ensenada de la bahía

Victoria (Spanish, 2009): desde viraje de ribera hasta recodo de bahía

Aixàs (Catalan, 2004): canviant de ribera i vorant la costera

Campos (Portuguese, 1962): do desvio da praia à dobra da baía

Lourenço (Portuguese, 1968): ergue-se do braço da praia até à curva da baía,

Schüler (Portuguese, 2003): roçando a praia, beirando ABahia

Schüler (Portuguese, 2004, 10): roçando a praia, beirando ABahia,

Pagán (Galician, 2000): de cámbio de beira a curva de baía

Beck (German, 1989): vom küstenknick zum bug der bucht

Jauslin (German, 1989): vom Klippenrand zur verschlungenen Bucht

Rathjen (German, 1989): vom Strandgestreun zum Buchtgebeug

Schrödter (German, 1989): von der Krümmung der Küste zur
   Biegung der Bucht

Stündel (German, 1993): von KüstenKurven zur BuchtBiegung

Bindervoet and Henkes (Dutch, 2002): van zwier van strand naar
   bocht van baai

Volokhonsky (Russian, 2000): ot beroj izlučiny do izgiba zaliva

Królikowski (Polish, 1998): od wybrzuszenia brzegu do odtoczenia
   zatoki,

Malicki (Polish, 2001): od odchylenia brzegu do wygięcia zatoki,

Anon. (Czech, 2009): od pobřežního pokroucení k zahnutí zálivu,

Titley (Irish, 2008): ó chuas an chuain go bogha na bá,

Anon. (Esperanto, 2010): de turno de marbordo fleksi da golfo,

'The swerve of shore is the coy gesture of the pretty isle herself which
invites the assault of the bay waters,' Campbell and Robinson wrote
at a time when sexist language was not yet an issue for male critics.
'Again, the waters of Dublin Bay continually pounding the Head of
Howth represent, on an elemental level, the perennial invaders of
Ireland continually pummelling the head of the defender' (Campbell
and Robinson 1961, 25). The course of the Liffey, one might add, also
brings it around to beat against Howth.

The surface meaning of the phrase is relatively unproblematic: the
river flows from the shore into the bay. Taking up the rhythm and the
alliteration of the opening 'riverrun,' the locution 'from swerve of shore
to bend of bay' nonetheless plays intriguingly with the reader's sense
of sameness and difference. On an initial reading, most readers will
probably see the 'swerve of shore' and the 'bend of bay' as two distinct
locations, from which and to which the river flows. The 'swerve' of the
shore, however, both defines and is defined by the 'bend' of the bay.
While the movement from shore to bay is real, in other words, there is
no movement from 'swerve' to 'bend,' for these are merely two names
for the same line of demarcation, variably readable as edge of shore or
edge of bay.

Burgess's Italian translation echoes this relationship: his 'giro' and
'curva' are quite neutral in their context, simply 'turn' and 'curve' respectively, but the phrasing 'da giro di riva a curva di baia,' through the

linking final syllable of 'riva' and 'curva,' adroitly hints at identity in difference. Campos achieves a similar effect in Portuguese by different means, translating 'bend of bay' as *'dobra* da baia,' where 'dobra' not only means 'fold' or 'turn' but is also closely related to *dobre* ('double') and *dobradura* ('doubling'), thus likewise suggesting the identity rather than the opposition of 'swerve' and 'bend.'

We notice that Campos translates 'swerve' as 'desvio,' however, a term much less neutral in its etymological resonances than Burgess's 'giro.' It literally means a going off the road, an unplanned diversion or deviation, and here Campos's formulation can also be read as suggesting the opposition of this uncontrolled waywardness and the more restrained curve of the bay. He is by no means alone in this reading. For most of the translations, indeed, it is the relationship of difference rather than identity between the two terms 'swerve' and 'bend' that rather surprisingly emerges as the most significant issue. The English text arguably offers only minimal inducement to see a productive tension between the two terms: 'swerve' functions primarily as a variant of 'curve,' suggested by the alliteration with 'shore' as 'bend' is by 'bay.' The tension, however, between 'swerve' as potentially indicating lack of control (as in 'swerving wildly') and 'bend' as potentially implying the imposition of control (as in 'bending something to one's purposes'), which is no more than a theoretical possibility in the English text, is interestingly developed in several of the translations.

In Butor's French, the coastal swerve thus becomes a 'déviation,' a diversion or departure from a regulated norm, brought back under control by the 'courbe' or 'curve' of the bay. Wilcock's Italian similarly suggests a 'scarto,' an unplanned swerve restrained by the 'piega' ('turn, fold') of the bay. Elizondo's Spanish has a coastal 'desvío' ('deviation') curved back into shape by an 'encombadura' ('curve, bend'). Pozanco's Spanish 'recodo' is a 'twist,' a 'sudden turn' that is restored to rest in the 'ensenada' ('cove, enclosure') of the bay. Victoria's Spanish, on the other hand, applies the term 'recodo' not to the shore but rather to the bay.

In German, Beck's 'küstenknick' also suggests an abrupt coastal distortion rather than a gradual change, while Rathjen's 'Strandgestreun' suggests an undisciplined 'scattering of beach,' both brought under control by the restraining curvature of the bay (Beck's 'bug der bucht,' Rathjen's 'Buchtgebeug,' all three of these nouns – *Bug, Bucht, Gebeug* – deriving from *biegen,* 'to bend'). Jauslin speaks of a progress from a 'rocky cliffedge' ('Klippenrand'), presumably Howth, to a 'winding bay' ('zur verschlungenen Bucht'). Lavergne, for his part, ignores

shore and bay alike, choosing to focus instead on a parallel relationship: that of the river meandering both physically ('erre rive,' or
'wanderriver') and mentally ('rêvière,' or 'dreamriver') between undisciplined drift and disciplined containment, its wanderings defined
by its restraining banks.

The underlying element of personification in all this is apparent: dis-
cipline versus waywardness, maturity versus youth, perhaps even parent versus child. This note is struck most clearly by du Bouchet, who
echoes the *cour-* of his opening 'courrive' in the pluralized and overtly
sexualized 'courbes' ('curves') of the coast, melting into and becoming
one with the 'bras' ('arms') of the bay. Lourenço's Portuguese river similarly 'rises' (*ergue-se*) from the 'arm' (*braço*) of the strand towards the
'curve' (*curva*) of the bay. A similar tone is struck once again by Stündel's
'KüstenKurven' ('coast-curves'), even if less overtly carried through by
his 'BuchtBiegung' ('bay-bend').

A comparison of Schenoni's two translations, both revealing distinctly sexual overtones, is particularly interesting in this context. In the earlier version he contrasts the smoothness of a 'baia sinuosa' ('curving
bay') and the roughness of a 'costa frastigliata,' the 'swerve of shore'
exaggerated into a geographically quite untenably 'jagged coast.' In the
later version, the roles are entirely reversed, implied gender and all: the
adjective 'sinuosa' ('curving, sinuous') is now transferred from the bay
to a coast that is no longer romantically rugged but rather a peacefully
curvaceous 'spiaggia' ('strand, beach'), while the bay is now portrayed
as 'biancheggiante' (literally 'whitening'), an intriguingly ambiguous
term that not only suggests the white crests of the waves but also connotes both 'shining brightly' and 'going grey,' evocatively refiguring
the bay by implication both as youthful lover and as aging father to the
embraced and embracing coast.

Among other versions, Titley's Irish has the river moving elegantly
from the 'hollow' (*cuas*) of the 'strand' (*cuan*) to the 'bow' (*bogha*) of the
'bay' (*bá*). The machine-produced Esperanto version, 'de turno de marbordo fleksi da golfo,' successfully navigates the 'turn' (*turno*) of the
'coast' (*marbordo*), but comes to grief once again in misreading 'to bend'
as an infinitive (*fleksi*, 'to bend'), thus preventing it from ever reaching
the 'bay' (*golfo*). Schüler's Portuguese rendering, finally, 'roçando a
praia, beirando ABahia,' once again incorporates a transatlantic reference to Brazilian geography: the port city of Bahia is located eight hundred miles north of Rio de Janeiro and is situated, like Dublin, on a
picturesque bay. The religious note introduced by Schüler's reference to

the church of Nossa Senhora do Ó in the previous phrase is continued here: the city of Bahia is officially known as São Salvador da Bahia (literally 'Saint Saviour of the Bay'), and the bay on which it stands is the Bahia de Todos os Santos (literally 'All Saints Bay'). Schüler's version literally has the river 'brushing against (*roçando*) the strand (*a praia*), skirting (*beirando*) the bay (*a baía*).' The phrase *beirando a baía* provides the basis for a triple pun: *beirando* ('skirting') generates, by way of a translingual pun, the noun *aba*, which means both 'skirt' and the 'coast around a port'; the noun *baía*, formerly spelled *bahia*, evokes the port city of the same name; and the irregularly capitalized feminine article *a* in 'ABahia' once again hints proleptically at the presence of ALP, alpha in 'ABahia' as she was omega in 'Nossenhora d'Ohmem's.'

Oddly enough, fewer than half of the versions considered attempt to match Joyce's flaunted use of alliteration. The more successful efforts here include du Bouchet's French 'des courbes de la côte aux bras de la baie'; Beck's German 'vom küstenknick zum bug der bucht'; Stündel's German 'von KüstenKurven zur BuchtBiegung'; and Titley's Irish 'ó chuas an chuain go bogha na bá.' Some other versions substitute rhyme for alliteration: Aixàs's Catalan 'canviant de ribera i vorant la costera'; Campos's Portuguese 'do desvio da praia à dobra da baía'; and Schüler's Portuguese 'roçando a praia, beirando ABahia.'

[4]   *brings us*

Butor (French, 1948): nous reporte

du Bouchet (French, 1962): nous rame

Lavergne (French, 1982): nous recourante

Wilcock (Italian, 1961): ci riporta

Burgess (Italian, 1975): ci riconduci

Schenoni (Italian, 1978): ci porta

Schenoni (Italian, 1982): ci conduce

Elizondo (Spanish, 1992): trayéndonos

Pozanco (Spanish, 1993): nos trae

Victoria (Spanish, 2009): nos trae

Aixàs (Catalan, 2004): ens duu

Campos (Portuguese, 1962): devolve-nos

Lourenço (Portuguese, 1968): traz-nos

Schüler (Portuguese, 2003): reconduz-nos

Schüler (Portuguese, 2004, 10): reconduz-nos

Pagán (Galician, 2000): trai-nos

Beck (German, 1989): bringt uns

Jauslin (German, 1989): und er bringt uns wieder

Rathjen (German, 1989): führt uns

Schrödter (German, 1989): bringt uns

Stündel (German, 1993): führt uns

Bindervoet and Henkes (Dutch, 2002): brengt ons

Volokhonsky (Russian, 2000): prinosit nas

Królikowski (Polish, 1998): przenosi nas

Malicki (Polish, 2001): przynosząc nas

Anon. (Czech, 2009): přináší nám

Titley (Irish, 2008): á dtuairt sinn

Anon. (Esperanto, 2010): alportas nin

The phrase 'brings us' is the least ambiguous one in the English text, but again the translations allow for some interesting semantic developments. All versions use terms that indeed mean 'bring,' but ten of them suggest in addition being 'carried' or 'borne,' as on a river – thus Butor's 'nous reporte,' the earlier Schenoni's 'ci porta,' Wilcock's 'ci riporta,' Pozanco's 'nos trae,' Elizondo's 'trayéndonos,' Victoria's 'nos trae,' Aixàs's 'ens duu' (Catalan *dur*, 'to carry, bear'), Lourenço's 'traz-nos,' Pagán's 'trai-nos,' and the Esperanto 'alportas nin.' Five versions suggest being 'led' or 'conducted' instead of carried – thus Burgess ('ci riconduci'), the later Schenoni ('ci conduce'), Schüler ('reconduz-nos'), and both Rathjen and Stündel ('führt uns'). Campos, with 'devolve-nos,' has us 'returned.'

Three versions choose to embellish Joyce's standard English phrase by introducing wordplays of varying complexity. Titley's Irish 'á dtuairt sinn' plays on the similar pronunciation of *tabhairt* ('to bring') and *tuairt* ('rush'), as in the phrase *de thuairt* ('at a rush'), thus suggesting 'bringing us suddenly.' In Lavergne's French, the river more flamboyantly 'nous recourante,' sweeps us back on its current (*courant*) to the strains of a popular seventeenth-century French dance, the *courante*. Du Bouchet's French, finally, visualizes the situation both more concretely and in different terms: we are now quite specifically passengers in a boat on the river, who are not just 'brought' back but rather rowed (*ramer*, 'to row'), not without difficulty (*ramer*, 'to strain'), and by means of a *rame* which, as a noun, is not only an 'oar' but also a 'ream' of the paper on which *Finnegans Wake* is written.

[5]   *by a commodius vicus of recirculation*

Butor (French, 1948): par un *commodius vicus* de recirculation

du Bouchet (French, 1962): par commode vicus de recirculation

Lavergne (French, 1982): via Vico par chaise percée de recirculation

Wilcock (Italian, 1961): lungo un commodo vico di ricircolazione

Burgess (Italian, 1975): per un vico giambattistamente comodo di ricirculazione

Schenoni (Italian, 1978): per mezzo di un più commodo vico di ricircolo

Schenoni (Italian, 1982): con un più commodus vicus di ricircolo

Elizondo (Spanish, 1992): por un cómodio vícolo de recirculación

Pozanco (Spanish, 1993): por un comodius vicus de circumvalación

Victoria (Spanish, 2009): por un comodio vico [road] de recirculación

Aixàs (Catalan, 2004): per commodius vicus tornant-nos

Campos (Portuguese, 1962): por um cômodo vicus de recirculação

Lourenço (Portuguese, 1968): por um commodius vicus de recirculação

Schüler (Portuguese, 2003): por commódios cominhos recorrentes de vico

Schüler (Portuguese, 2004, 10): por cominhos recorrentes de Vico

Pagán (Galician, 2000): por un cómodus vicus de recirculación

Beck (German, 1989): auf kommodem vicus zirkel

Jauslin (German, 1989): in lässigem Circel zurück über Commodus und Vico

Rathjen (German, 1989): im commundiösen Wickelwirken des Rezirkulierens

Schrödter (German, 1989): in einem commoden Rezirkulus viciosus

Stündel (German, 1993): durch einen kommodien Ouikuß der Rezierkuhlation

Bindervoet and Henkes (Dutch, 2002): via een commodius vicus van recirculatie

Volokhonsky (Russian, 2000): prostornym prostranstvom vozratnych tečenij

Królikowski (Polish, 1998): wikiańskim wszechmodem w kole wiecznego

Malicki (Polish, 2001): przez obszerną wieśrecyrkulacji

Anon. (Czech, 2009): od commodia vica koloběh

Titley (Irish, 2008): go timpeallach timthriallach leithreasúil

Anon. (Esperanto, 2010): de kommodiusvikus de recirkulado

One of the most immediately challenging of the phrases in the English text, this one achieves relatively little connotative expansion at the hands of its various translators, largely because of the easy transferability of its Latinate diction. Latin *vicus* (cognate with Greek *oikos*, 'house') originally meant 'village,' then came to mean 'street' or 'route'; the overt surface meaning of the phrase is thus 'by a commodious, or all-encompassing, process of recirculation.' The most immediately obvious keyword here is 'recirculation,' and it reappears with only very slight variations in a large majority of the renderings. Exceptions include three of the German translators: Beck refigures it as a potentially vicious circle ('vicus zirkel'), as does Schrödter ('Rezirkulus viciosus'), while Jauslin ('Circel') adventurously invokes the specific viciousness of Circe, who turns men into swine. Aixàs's Catalan avoids Latinate diction in favour of a more everyday 'tornant-nos' ('turning us'). Schüler's Portuguese 'cominhos recorrentes' similarly prefers to speak in simpler terms of 'roads (*caminhos*) that return.' Pozanco's Spanish rejects the easy solution of 'recirculación' (as employed by both Elizondo and Victoria) in favour of the initially surprising 'circumvalación,' which nonetheless also includes among its Spanish meanings that of 'encirclement.'

'Vicus,' qualifying this process of recirculation as Viconian, likewise appears largely unchanged in by far the greater number of the translations, whether as a Latin 'vicus' or an Italian 'vico' or 'vícolo,' both of the latter terms still meaning 'lane, alley.' Lavergne's recirculation takes place 'via Vico,' invoking both the philosopher and Dublin's Vico Road. In Dutch, Bindervoet and Henkes achieve the same effect rather more elegantly with the formulation 'via een commodius vicus,' while Victoria's Spanish opts for the decidedly clumsy explanatory formulation 'vico [road].' Embellished variations include two German versions: Rathjen's 'Wickelwirken,' literally a 'process of enfolding,' with Vico heavily disguised in the noun *Wickel* ('reel, spool'); and Stündel's 'Ouikuß,' with Vico even more heavily disguised as, literally, a Franco-German 'yes-kiss,' sexualizing the process of recirculation à la Molly Bloom. Burgess's Italian makes sure that his readers will not miss the reference to Giambattista Vico by making his 'vico' not just 'comodo' but 'giambattistamente comodo.'

'Commodius' likewise transfers relatively easily into both the Romance languages and German. Except for Lavergne, all the translators can be read (if we so choose) as also at least hinting at the presence of the emperor Commodus, while in one case, Jauslin's 'Commodus und Vico,' his presence is impossible to miss. Jauslin translates 'commodius' twice, in fact: first as 'lässig' (literally 'lazy'), and then as the proper name. Stündel hints in addition at an element of comedy (German *Komödie*), Rathjen at the universality of the process (German *kommun*, 'common'; Latin *mundus*, 'world'). Titley's Irish rendering, 'go timpeallach timthriallach leithreasúil,' refers to a process involving movement in a fashion at once 'circular (*timpeallach*), circuitous (*timthriallach*), and privy (*leithreasúil*),' the final adjective playing on the everyday use of the noun *leithreas* to designate an Irish public convenience. Pursuing a similar thought, Lavergne, for his part, irreverently jettisons the emperor and history alike, moving from the anterior to the posterior in likewise concentrating on the commode in 'commodius,' propelling us into an earthy process of watery recirculation courtesy of the 'chaise percée,' the toilet seat as site per se of *éternel retour*.

[6] *back to Howth Castle and Environs*

Butor (French, 1948): jusq'au château d'Howth et ses environs

du Bouchet (French, 1962): vers Howth, Château et Environs

Lavergne (French, 1982): vers Howth Castle et Environs

Wilcock (Italian, 1961): al castello di Howth e dintorni

Burgess (Italian, 1975): al Chestello di Howth e dintorni

Schenoni (Italian, 1978): di nuovo a Howth Castle ed Environs

Schenoni (Italian, 1982): di nuovo a Howth Castle Edintorni

Elizondo (Spanish, 1992): otra vuelta a Howth Castillo y Enderre-dores

Pozanco (Spanish, 1993): de vuelta al castillo de Howth y Environs

Victoria (Spanish, 2009): devuelt'a Howth Castel y Enrededores

Aixàs (Catalan, 2004): al Castell de Howth i Entorns

Campos (Portuguese, 1962): de volta a Howth Castle Ecercanias

Lourenço (Portuguese, 1968): de novo a Howthe Castelo Earredores

Schüler (Portuguese, 2003): ao de Howth Castelo Earredores

Schüler (Portuguese, 2004, 10): ao Homem do Castelocaveira Earredores.

Pagán (Galician, 2000): de volta ao Castelo Howth e Extramuros

Beck (German, 1989): wieder zurück zu Howth Castells Engrer umgebung

Jauslin (German, 1989): nach Hoth Castle samt Einzugskreis

Rathjen (German, 1989): zurück zur Burg von Howth con Entourage

Schrödter (German, 1989): zurück zu Howth Castle und Ergebun-gen

Stündel (German, 1993): zurück nach Haus Castell und Emccebung

Bindervoet and Henkes (Dutch, 2002): terug naar Howth Kasteel en Immelanden

Volokhonsky (Russian, 2000): vspjat' k zamku Haut i ego okrest-nostjam

Królikowski (Polish, 1998): powrotu do Zamku Howth i Okolic

Malicki (Polish, 2001): zpowrotem do Howth-Zamku i Otoczeń

Anon. (Czech, 2009): zpět ke hradu Howth a okolí

Titley (Irish, 2008): ar ais go dtí Halla Cheann Éadair agus a bhfuil máguaird

Anon. (Esperanto, 2010): reen al Howth Castle kaj Ĉirkaŭas

Our opening sentence, or partial sentence, brings us from central Dublin to the promontory of Howth on the northern extremity of Dublin Bay, a significant location in medieval Irish literature, for Howth was a temporary hiding place of the young lovers Diarmuid and Gráinne when pursued by Finn mac Cumhaill, the older man whose promised bride preferred the arms and charms of a young follower to those of an old leader. As the sentence begins with ALP, so it ends with HCE, and a primary challenge for all our translators in this phrase is to achieve the necessary initials of 'Howth Castle and Environs,' even if not necessarily in that order.

All three French translators seize gratefully on the fact that 'environs' is originally a borrowing from French in reaching this end, and both the earlier Schenoni and Pozanco also use the term in Italian and Spanish respectively. In Italian, Wilcock achieves his goal rather minimally with 'al castello di Howth *e* dintorni,' while Burgess improves on the same formula by replacing 'castello' with '*che*stello,' thus economically achieving a double CHE while conflating HCE and the castle. Four translators share one particular strategy: Campos, in Portuguese, combines *e cercanias* to produce 'Howth Castle Ecercanias'; Elizondo, in Spanish, does the same with *en derredores* to produce 'Howth Castillo y Enderredores'; and both Lourenço and Schüler, in Portuguese, combine *e arredores* to produce 'Howth(e) Castelo Earredores.' In all four cases, the phrase compressed and capitalized means 'and environs.' Victoria's Spanish opts for 'Howth Castel y Enrededores' and Aixàs's Catalan for 'Castell de Howth i Entorns,' each employing a standard term for the English *environs*.

Several versions reach for other solutions. Beck and Stündel both play on a destabilization of the German *Umgebung* ('surroundings'): Beck's 'Howth Castells Engrer umgebung' subverting standard orthographical usage by capitalizing the adjective 'engrer' ('nearer') while leaving the noun 'Umgebung' uncapitalized; Stündel's splendid coinage 'Emccebung' humorously implicating the solidity of the *Umgebung* ('surroundings') in the unstable realms of Einsteinian relativity, courtesy of the iconic formula $e = mc^2$. Schrödter's German 'Howth Castle und Ergebungen' ignores the glories of martial victory, concentrating instead on necessary *Ergebungen* ('surrenders'). In Galician, Pagán's 'Castelo Howth e Extramuros' glosses Joyce's 'Environs' as 'what lies beyond its walls.' Jauslin's 'Hoth Castle samt Einzugskreis' changes the gloss to 'with catchment area.' Titley's Irish, 'Halla Cheann Éadair agus a bhfuil máguaird,' represents a special case. In Irish, Howth is known as Beann Édair, literally the 'headland (*beann*) of Édar.' Substituting *ceann* ('head') for *beann*, and conflating Édar and the fatal 'jealousy' (*éad*) of the aging and betrayed Finn mac Cumhaill, Titley's version transforms 'Howth Castle and Environs' into 'the hall (*halla*) of Howth and what surrounds it (*a bhfuil máguaird*)' and *HCE* adroitly into *HCÉ*.

Schüler's two Portuguese versions are both striking. The first (2003) reads 'ao de Howth Castelo Earredores' instead of the more normal word order *ao Castelo de Howth*, the simple but surprisingly disruptive linguistic reversal effectively evoking the reversals of history, all too appropriate especially in the case of Howth. The second (2004), retaining the initials *HCE*, reads 'ao Homem do Castelocaveira Earredores.' Here the 'head' (Danish *hoved*) of Howth is transformed into a Portuguese *caveira* ('skull'), a term derived from the Latin *calvaria* ('skull'), Howth Castle becomes Skull Castle, and HCE is transformed at least momentarily into Jesus Christ, the Man (*homem*) of Calvary, the 'place of the skull,' a hero notoriously also destroyed by the ignorance of the mob – but who rose again from the dead, as Finn mac Cumhaill was expected to do, and as Tim Finnegan appears to do.

Several other versions simply abandon the struggle to retain HCE's initials. None of the four versions in eastern European languages, for example, makes any effort to do so – unless one can assume that the intended result is the very unlikely *ZHO* (Russian), *ZHO* or *HZO* (Polish), or *HHO* (Czech). The Esperanto version, 'Howth Castle kaj Ĉirkaŭas,' producing the initials *HCĈ*, similarly ignores the matter. Bindervoet and Henkes's 'Howth Kasteel en Immelanden' represents a special case in this context: since Dutch contains very few words that begin with the letter *c*, the translators made a conscious decision to use *HKI* as their equivalent of *HCE*, a decision consistently sustained throughout their complete translation of *Finnegans Wake*. The term 'immelanden' suggests 'surrounding territories,' thus 'environs.'

Howth undergoes occasional translingual alterations. Lourenço's Portuguese changes it to 'Howthe,' while Stündel similarly builds a German 'Haus' on the foundations of a mispronounced 'houthe,' perhaps on the assumption in both cases that an Irishman's house is his castle.[5] The vagaries of Russian transliteration systems would have Volokhonsky's Howth appear as either 'Haut' or 'Khaut.' Jauslin's 'Hoth' might variously be readable as just a misprint, or as suggesting for German readers the correct pronunciation of the tricky foreign diphthong, or, as in the other cases just mentioned, reflecting the inevitable abrasions, onomastic and otherwise, of history and time.

A number of versions cannot resist carrying out renovations to HCE's castle. Rathjen's German adjusts the geographical 'environs' to a personal 'Entourage,' thus adding a French tower (*tour*) to his Irish castle; and Pozanco's 'circumvalación,' carrying forward from the previous phrase, does double duty as not only 'encirclement' but also 'circumvallation, surrounding by a wall.' One location famously surrounded by a wall was the biblical Garden of Eden, which brings us to the single term that most significantly extends the Joycean text in this final phrase. The later Schenoni, like Wilcock and Burgess, translates 'and environs' as 'e dintorni' but achieves a disproportionately more successful result in simply combining the two words in his 'Edintorni,' a happy coinage that splendidly evokes the Garden of Eden – and thus Eve and Adam once again, standing in at the very last moment as avatars, respectively, of ALP and HCE. Even more splendidly, since the biblical name *Eden* (Hebrew *'ēden*) has been seen as related to the Akkadian *edinu* ('plain') (McKenzie 1965, 211), the more obsessively industrious transtextual reader is happily allowed to think of Joyce's Dublin as one of the 'cities of the plain' ripe for destruction at the hands of a righteous god because of an unnatural wickedness crying translingually to Heaven for vengeance. The hundred-lettered voice of thunder will shortly (and multilingually) resound.

---

5   In normal German usage, 'Haus Castell' would mean 'the house of the Castell family, the House of Castell.' A comma would solve this particular departure, though implying another: 'house, castle, and surroundings.'

III

Finally, there is the third of our opening questions, namely, what significant macrotextual effects may be said to emerge from a comparative transtextual reading of the available translations and their original, the whole ensemble seen as constituting one single multivoiced text, multiple enunciations of a single sentence at once the same and completely different in each enunciation. It would initially seem reasonable to evaluate our findings into three broad categories: first, false notes, misreadings partially or completely out of tune with our overall (if still highly provisional) understanding of the text as a whole; second, interesting but idiosyncratic readings, drawing our attention to something we might otherwise not have seen, but of whose overall validity as renderings we may remain unconvinced; and third, readings that clearly are valid and fruitful textual extensions rather than misreadings or idiosyncratic readings, revealing aspects of the Joycean text that were occluded (or absent) even in the original. We will restrict ourselves to a few symptomatic examples of each category (referring in square brackets for brevity's sake to the individual phrases already examined).

Among the false notes, one would arguably choose to include Stündel's tendency to pun when possible rather than when necessary: 'Ouikuß' for 'vicus' [5], 'Haus' for 'Howth' [6], or 'Rezierkuhlation' [5], which imports the entirely irrelevant German *Zier* ('ornament') and *Kuh* ('cow') into the German *Rezirkulation*. Clearly, the issue here is textual relevance, and our sense of that relevance is the criterion (however debatable) by which we would classify Stündel's 'Rezierkuhlation,' for all that it could be argued as celebrating the unpredictability and malleability of language, as a false note, while applauding Lavergne's distortion of *rivière* into 'erre revie.' At the same time, of course, a reader who read *Finnegans Wake* only in Stündel's translation would have no way of knowing (yet) whether *Zier* and *Kuh* – and possibly also *kühl* ('cool') – are false notes or not; and obviously, one reader's sense of textual relevance will not necessarily be another's.

Among interesting but idiosyncratic readings, seizing our attention for their ingenuity but perhaps not necessarily convincing us of their entire validity, one might want to include du Bouchet's translation of 'brings us' by 'nous rame' [4], Lavergne's humorously scatological reading of 'commodius' [5], and Stündel's 'Emccebung' [6]. Each of these judgments is again immediately contestable, however, for an idiosyncratic reading is by no means ipso facto a misreading.

Finally, one can point to several examples of readings that clearly extend the implications of the original text and reveal aspects of its functioning that were obscured in that original. These would certainly include du Bouchet's identification of Eve and ALP in translating 'riverrun' by 'courrive' [1]; the blurring of Adam and Eve's and Notre Dame, Liffey and Seine, Dublin and Paris, in both du Bouchet's and Lavergne's 'notre Adame' [2]; Pozanco's 'circumvalación' [5], conflating historical 'encirclement' by Viconian recirculation and the architectural encirclement of Howth Castle by its walls; and Schenoni's 'Edintorni' [6], conflating Howth and Eden.

Perhaps the most impressive example of such textual expansion, however, is the transtextual group treatment of 'from swerve of shore to bend of bay' [3], which, as we have seen, very considerably extends the context of reference of this phrase in a manner that is entirely congruous with our overall (if limited) understanding of Joyce's text. The difference between this example and those cited in the previous paragraph is important. Such examples as du Bouchet's 'notre Adame' [2] or Schenoni's 'Edintorni' [6] acquire their force from a direct comparison of the individual translation with the original text; the group treatment of 'from swerve of shore to bend of bay' acquires its force from comparisons of the translations among themselves.

Applying this procedure to other examples can produce interesting results – including the revelation of our three-category evaluative schema as once again a very blunt instrument for *macrotextual* purposes in the case of a text as irrepressibly polysemous as *Finnegans Wake*. Thus Rathjen's having the Liffey rush past in spate, 'schleunigst' [2], might initially seem to be just a misreading, contrary to extratextual geographical fact (if we choose to consider that relevant); taken in conjunction with the dreamy laziness of Lavergne's 'rêvière' [3], however, it appropriately reminds us that we are dealing in Joyce's text not just with one geographically identifiable river but with a single textual representative of all rivers.[6] Schenoni's change from 'da baia sinuosa a costa frastagliata' in his earlier translation to 'da spiaggia sinuosa a baia

---

6   In explanation of the surprising speed of his river, Friedhelm Rathjen writes: 'The puzzlingly swift Liffey in my version of the first sentence of *FW* has a very special reason. Somewhere I had read that the name Stephen is half-hidden in "paST EVE aNd Adam's," and so I tried to do the same in my version by including a word ending -*st* just ahead of "Eve": "schleunigST EV' uNd Adam passiert"' (personal communication, 15 December 2005).

biancheggiante' in the later version [3] is on one level no more than a translator's emendation of his own work, the latter decision necessarily superseding and replacing the former; reading the two versions as transtextual variants of the *same* text serves to emphasize the pervasive textual vacillation throughout the *Wake* between male and female, young and old, here and there, then and now. The several reversals, finally, of 'Eve and Adam's' [2] to the more accustomed formulation might once again, taken in isolation, seem to be either careless misreadings or misguided would-be corrections; taken instead as dissenting voices in a larger transtextual group discourse, they forcefully underscore the gendered implications of the phrase. The same logic, indeed, might lead us to conclude that in the special case of *Finnegans Wake* even blatant individual mistranslations have at least some claim, perhaps even an entirely defensible claim, to macrotextual toleration, as part of the highly inviting noise in which Joyce's final text, before any attempt at translation, is already so rich.

Noise is of course a relative concept. For a Finnish reader, for example, the following version of the opening sentence by Miikka Mutanen (2006) may well be an excellent translation, significantly better than any of the twenty-eight we have examined so far:

> virtavie, ohi Eilvan ja Aatomun, heitseistä rannan kaareen seppellahden, takaisin kiertää avarjen kulco modeus meidät Kuinks Linnaan ja Ympäröivaan.

For someone like the present writer who is completely ignorant of Finnish, of course, it is almost entirely noise. That 'almost' is crucial, however, for we can reasonably assume that 'virtavie' must correspond to at least some degree to 'riverrun,' and 'ohi Eilvan ja Aatomun' likewise to 'past Eve and Adam's.' That is perhaps as far as we can go, beyond noting that the order of appearance of Eve and Adam is retained, while in some other translations, as we have seen, it is conservatively reversed. Resort to a Finnish dictionary reveals that *virta* means 'current' or 'stream,' which is encouraging, but I find myself unable either to account for *-vie* or to understand my inability to do so. Tracking down the extraordinary 'Kuinks Linnaan ja Ympäröivaan,' on the other hand, proves a good deal more satisfactory. The phrase must clearly correspond to 'Howth Castle and Environs' but makes no attempt to reproduce HCE's initials – which is, of course, in itself potentially not at all uninteresting: the translator, for example, might be planning to use the formula *KLY* for HCE throughout (as the Dutch translators use *HKI*), and the Finnish language might (or might not) provide good reasons for doing so.

Returning to my Finnish dictionary, I find that *linna* means 'castle' and that *ympäri* means 'about,' so 'Kuinks,' we might deduce, must refer, however oddly, to 'Howth.' And indeed it does, for further resort to the dictionary reveals that the Finnish adverb *kuinka* translates the English adverb *how*, thus also revealing that Mutanen reads the name *Howth* as consisting of a combination of *how* and *-th*, and, whether humorously or perhaps already in translatorial desperation, constructs his *Kuink-s* on a similar principle. The difference for the English-speaking reader between reading *Finnegans Wake* in Finnish and reading it in English, that is to say, is in principle and in at least one crucial respect a difference of degree rather than of kind, for what is central to both endeavours is the gradual, painstaking, and highly tentative generation of very small areas of meaning in the midst of what very frequently may seem like extraordinarily large areas of textual noise.

3 Tristrams

Sir Tristram, violer d'amores, fr'over the short sea, had passencore rearrived from North Armorica on this side the scraggy isthmus of Europe Minor to wielderfight his penisolate war:

(FW 3.4–6)

du Bouchet (French, 1962): Sire Tristram, violeur d'amores, d'oultre la manche mer, n'avait à corps ravivé du Nord de l'Armorique ès bords d'icel huisthme hérissé d'Europe mineure pour reluivreferre sa guerre péniseulte:

Lavergne (French, 1982): Sire Tristram, violeur d'amoeurs, manchissant la courte oisie, n'avait pâque buissé sa derrive d'Armorique du Nord sur ce flanc de notre isthme décharné d'Europe Mineure pour y resoutenir le combat d'un presqu'Yseul penny:

Wilcock (Italian, 1961): Sir Tristano da oltre il mare piccolo, violista d'amori, non era ancora riarrivato da Nord Armorica, in questa parte dello scabroso rouistmo d'Europa Minore, a brandibattere la sua guerra penisolata:

Burgess (Italian, 1975): Signore Tristano, violatore d'amori, d'attraverso il mare corto, non aveva ancora gettato dell'Armorica del Nord sul cisistmo scosceso dell'Europa Minore per rimuovere la sua guerra penisulata:

Schenoni (Italian, 1978): Sir Tristram, violatore d'amores, d'oltre il mar piccolo, era passencore riarrivato dall'Armorica del Nord su questo lato dell'istmo scabroso dell'Europa Minore per wielderbattere la sua guerra peneisolata:

Schenoni (Italian, 1982): Sir Tristram, violista d'amores, da sopra il mar d'Irlanda, aveva passencore riraggiunto dall'Armorica del Nord su questa sponda l'istmo scosceso d'Europa Minore per wielderbattere la sua guerra penisolata:

Elizondo (Spanish, 1992): Sir Tristram, violer d'amores, habiendo cruzado el corto mar, había pasancor revuelto de Nortearmórica, de este lado del estrecho istmo de Europa Menor para martibatallar en su guerra peneisolar:

Pozanco (Spanish, 1993): Sir Tristán, viola d'amores, del otro lado del pequeño mar, no ha passencore vuelto a llegar de Norte Armórica a este lado del flaco istmo de Europa Menor para librar su penuriósolo combate:

Victoria (Spanish, 2009): Sir Tristram, violamores, de sobre'l mar angosto, había no todavía [pasadotravez] vueltoarrivar desde Norte Armórica a este lado del raquítico istmo de Europa Menor par'empuñapelear su [aislada] guerra peneinsular:

Campos (Portuguese, 1962): Sir Tristão, violador d'amôres, através o mar breve, tinha pazencore revoltado de Norte Armórica a êste lado do áspero istmo da Europa Menor para relutar sua guerra penisolada:

Lourenço (Portuguese, 1968): Dom Tristram, ladcim'pre do estreito mar, violer d'amores, não tinha passancore rechegado da Armórica do Norte a este lado do ossudo istmo da Europa Menor para relutar o seu penisolado combate:

Schüler (Portuguese, 2003): Sir Tristrão, violeiro d'amores, d'além do mar encapelado, não tinha passancorado reveniente de Norte Armórica a estas bandas do istmo escarpado da Europa Menor para o virolento conflito de penisoldada guerra:

Pagán (Galician, 2000): O señor Tristrán, violer d'amores, do outro lado da pequena mareira, non regresara passencore de Norte Armórica a este lado o escuálido istmo de Europa Menor para librar a cabo a sua penisolada guerra:

Beck (German, 1989): Herr Tristram, harpfunier d'amores, räubher über rauhe see, war passencore zurückgekommen aus Nord-Armorica auf diese seite des klüftigen isthmus von Klein-Europa, um seinen penisolaten krieg wieder auszufechten:

Rathjen (German, 1989): Sir Tristram, Wiederholer d'amoore, von jenseits der Kurzsee, war passimkorps aus Nordarmorika rückgelangt an diese Seite des rauhen Isthmus von Kleineuropa um seinen penisolieren Krieg zu fehderführen:

Stündel (German, 1993): Sör Tristram, der LeibesGeiger, von jenseits der kurzen Seh, war noch nicht wieder aus Nord Armorika zu der dunnen Landenge von Klein Europa zurückgekehrt um wieder den Krampf in seinem Peinisolatten Kriech aufzunehmen:

Bindervoet and Henkes (Dutch, 2002): Heer Tristram, violaat d'amores, vannover de korte zee, was passencore weeromgekeerd uit Noord-Armorica deeszijds 't schierlijk eilandje van Klein-Europa voor het widervuren van zijn gepenisoleerde oorlog:

Volokhonsky (Russian, 2000): Sėr Tristram s violoj d'amore iz-za bližnego morja pribyl nazad passažirom transporta Severnoj Armoriki na ėtu storonu izrezannogo perešejka v Evropu Maluju daby samolično vesti penisolirovannuju vojnu na poluostrove:

Królikowski (Polish, 1998): Pan Tristrum, rzępolent z miłości, poprze'z fal niedal, przelewił się na pośród z Północnej Armoryki w tę flankę wężyzn przesmyku Europy Mniejniżmniejszej, prostowzłujbój jej wpółzwyspizolowanej wojny:

Malicki (Polish, 2001): Pan Tristram, woler d'amorów, fru' poprzez krótkie morze, miał przejściowy rdzeń powtórnie przybywając z Północnej Armoryki na tę stronę nieregularnego istmusu Europy niniejszej by wydzierżyć swą penisulową wojnę:

Mutanen (Finnish, 2006): Herra Tristankki, rakkauksien vahinguttaja, yli irlamminmeren, oli ydimääräisen joentakaisin Pohjois-Panssarimerikasta tällä puolen Vähä-Euroopan kannaslaihelia voimistellakseen musterottelunsa niemisodan:

Titley (Irish, 2008): Saír Throstam, feichidveibhlín na mionsearc ar an bhfarraige, a raibh brot a chroí fillte go hanraiththráthuil chun caoil chreagaigh na mionEorpa d'fhonn tréanthroid an chogaigh a eisfhearadh go leaidiniseach.

'The first paragraph states place, the second time,' Adaline Glasheen pithily observed (1977, xxiv). The place, as we have already seen, is Dublin, and the time, though apparently after the Flood – 'rory end to the regginbrow was to be seen ringsome on the aquaface' (*FW* 3.13–14) – is also before the Fall (Finnegan's, at any rate), which will not occur until the third paragraph. The second, with its seven clauses, speaks in a parodic echo of the Book of Genesis of events that had 'not yet' come to pass before that Fall. In the present chapter, we shall concentrate on just the first of these clauses.

The introduction of 'Sir Tristram' immediately introduces a number of interweaving themes. The tragic love story of the Cornish knight Tristan and the Irish princess Iseult – who soon will also put in an early appearance: 'But was iz? Iseut?' (*FW* 4.14) – is one of the great transnational medieval narratives of Europe, its origins clearly Celtic but only becoming widely known first in French and then in German versions in the twelfth and thirteenth centuries respectively. In these early continental versions the hero's name is always *Tristan* (as it is again in Richard Wagner's canonic operatic version of 1854, *Tristan und Isolde*) rather than *Tristram*, a form popularized in the English-speaking world in Sir Thomas Malory's mid-fifteenth-century version of the tale in his collection of Arthurian romances, *Le morte d'Arthur*. The tale received a new lease of life in 1900 with the appearance of the French scholar Joseph Bédier's attempt to reconstruct from the dozens of multiply divergent versions in existence across a wide range of European languages a unitary *Roman de Tristan et Iseult*.

Born in Cornwall, the Tristan or Tristram of the medieval tale is forced by political hostilities to spend his youth in Brittany; returning as a young man to the court of his uncle, King Mark of Cornwall, he is soon sent to Ireland to fetch Mark's promised bride, Iseult (Iseut, Yseut, Isotta, Isolde); the two young people predictably fall in love and the resulting complications occupy the rest of the story, ending equally predictably in tragedy. The archetypal triangle of Tristan, Iseult, and Mark mirrors that of Lancelot, Guinevere, and Arthur in Arthurian romance as well as (and more immediately relevant for *Finnegans Wake*) that of Diarmaid, Gráinne, and Finn or Fionn mac Cumhaill in Irish Fenian lore. The name *Tristan* appears (though there is considerable debate) to derive from an original Celtic *Drust* or *Drystan*, 'associated with "tumult, din,"' later modified by French *triste* ('sad') (Cottle 1978, 389; see also Hanks et al. 2002, 877). Appropriately, Cornish *tristys* (*FW* 449.7) also means 'sadness, sorrow.' The variant *Tristram* is thus punningly suggestive in *Finnegans Wake* (if not in Malory) not only of lovers' trysts and the sad (*triste*) fate of the lovers, but also of an unrestrained sexual energy (*ram*). We may note in passing that the cuckolded Mark and

HCE (associated with Finn and father of a daughter called Issy) are ety-mologically related in Old Irish, in which the two nouns *marc* and *ech* (as in ECH) both mean 'horse.' Finally, there is a glancing reference to yet another Tristram, namely the hero of Laurence Sterne's *Tristram Shandy*, whose multiply postponed entry into his own narrative is evoked by Joyce's multiply repeated 'not yet.'

Joyce, as is well known, provided his own set of notes on what would become the first page of the *Wake* in a letter of 15 November 1926 to Harriet Shaw Weaver (*L* 1:247–8; also quoted in Ellmann 1982, 583–4). 'Sir Tristram,' as Joyce himself observed in that letter, also re-fers to another Tristram, namely Sir Almeric Tristram, a leader of the invading force of Normans that reached Ireland from Britain begin-ning in 1169 – and thus one who, like the legendary Tristan / Tristram, 'also came by sea to Ireland under the direction of his monarch to es-tablish a claim' (Benstock 1985, 166). Sir Almeric, moreover, was born in Brittany, known to the Romans as Armorica, a name based on a pre-vious Celtic designation of the region as *ar mor* ('on the sea'), and his name also appears variously as *Amory*, *Armory*, and *Armoricus*, thus allowing us, as readers of the *Wake*, to associate him not only with Brittany (*Armoricus*) and the martial exploits of knights in armour (*Armory*) but also with the gentler jousts of courtly and not-so-courtly love (*Amor-y*). Etymologically, as it happens, Sir Almeric's name has nothing at all to do with love or war or Brittany: Cottle derives it, via Old French, from the Germanic *Amalric*, which combines two ele-ments, *amal* and *rīc*, meaning 'work' and 'rule' respectively (1978, 36). The serendipitous coincidence, however (it need hardly be said), is more than welcome grist to the Joycean mill.

[1]   *Sir Tristram,*

du Bouchet (French, 1962): Sire Tristram,

Lavergne (French, 1982): Sire Tristram,

Wilcock (Italian, 1961): Sir Tristano

Burgess (Italian, 1975): Signore Tristano,

Schenoni (Italian, 1978): Sir Tristram,

Schenoni (Italian, 1982): Sir Tristram,

Elizondo (Spanish, 1992): Sir Tristram,

Pozanco (Spanish, 1993): Sir Tristán,

Victoria (Spanish, 2009): Sir Tristram,

Campos (Portuguese, 1962): Sir Tristão,

Lourenço (Portuguese, 1968): Dom Tristram,

Schüler (Portuguese, 2003): Sir Tristrão,

Pagán (Galician, 2000): O señor Tristrán,

Beck (German, 1989): Herr Tristram,

Rathjen (German, 1989): Sir Tristram,

Stündel (German, 1993): Sör Tristram,

Bindervoet and Henkes (Dutch, 2002): Heer Tristram,

Volokhonsky (Russian, 2000): Sėr Tristram

Królikowski (Polish, 1998): Pan Tristrum,

Malicki (Polish, 2001): Pan Tristram,

Mutanen (Finnish, 2006): Herra Tristankki,

Titley (Irish, 2008): Saír Throstam,

To begin with, we may notice that the name *Tristram* retains its angli-cized form in thirteen of the twenty-two translations, while being domesticated to a greater or lesser extent in the respective target lan-guage as *Tristano* in two of the four Italian versions (Wilcock, Burgess), *Tristão* in one Portuguese version (Campos) and *Tristrão* in another (Schüler), *Tristán* in one of the three Spanish versions (Pozanco), *Tristrán* in Galician (Pagán), *Tristrum* in Polish (Królikowski), and *Tristankki* in Finnish (Mutanen). The distinction is far from being a trivial one, for the eight versions that favour some variant of the name *Tristan* rather than *Tristram*, and in thus focusing exclusively on the hero of medieval legend, lover of Iseult and reluctant rival of King Mark, necessarily ignore the collateral but crucial presence of Sir Almeric Tristram. Those versions referring, like Joyce's, to *Tristram* refer both to the legendary lover and to the historical Sir Almeric, first ·earl of Howth and builder of Howth Castle, who, indeed, is intro-duced to the reader immediately after the reference to 'Howth Castle and Environs' in the previous line.

Tristram's English title of 'Sir' is likewise retained in nine of the twenty-two versions, while being domesticated in the remaining thirteen transpositions in a rainbow of linguistic variants, including the French 'Sire' (du Bouchet, Lavergne), Italian 'Signore' (Burgess), Portuguese 'Dom' (Lourenço), Galician 'O señor' (Pagán), German 'Herr' (Beck), Dutch 'Heer' (Bindervoet and Henkes), Polish 'Pan' (Królikowski, Malicki), and Finnish 'Herra' (Mutanen).

Among more adventurous versions, Volokhonsky's 'Sėr' suggests a mischievous amalgamation of an English *Sir* and a Russian 'cheese' (*syr*). Stündel opts yet more adventurously for a perhaps appropriately outlandish 'Sör,' which might be read on one level as retaining for German readers (if somewhat unnecessarily) the approximate English pronunciation of *sir*, and on another as gesturing proleptically towards a French *soeur* ('sister'), namely Issy, sister to Shem and Shaun, both of whom (as 'Shem-Shaun,' alias 'Tree-Stone') will eventually emerge as dual aspects of the Tristan of legend, challenging an older man for the love of a younger woman, in this case his daughter, their sister. Alternatively, or in addition, we may see Stündel's 'Sör' as introducing a note of sexual ambivalence – 'sister Tristram' – not yet sounded in Joyce's English but which will recur at fairly frequent intervals throughout the text. Widening the translinguistic range, we might even suspect an element of moral disapproval of 'Sör' Tristram's amorous dallyings, given that Irish *sor* means 'louse.' Titley's Irish 'Saír Throstam,' finally, imaginatively combines English *sir* and the Irish prefixes *saor-* ('noble') and *sár-* ('excellent, outstanding') to characterize a 'Trostam' (the initial *th-* is a grammatical necessity after the prefix, but also plays on the English *thrust*) whose name is based on an Irish *trost* that means both 'thrust' and 'fall': an aristocratic superthruster urging his conquests à la Don Juan to 'trust him' – and whose heroic risings (*trost*) are nonetheless inevitably followed, à la HCE, by a correspondingly unheroic fall (*trost*).

[2]   *violer d'amores,*

du Bouchet (French, 1962): violeur d'amores,

Lavergne (French, 1982): violeur d'amoeurs,

Wilcock (Italian, 1961): violista d'amori,

Burgess (Italian, 1975): violatore d'amori,

Schenoni (Italian, 1978): violatore d'amores,

Schenoni (Italian, 1982): violista d'amores,

Elizondo (Spanish, 1992): violer d'amores,

Pozanco (Spanish, 1993): viola d'amores,

Victoria (Spanish, 2009): violamores,

Campos (Portuguese, 1962): violador d'amôres,

Lourenço (Portuguese, 1968): violer d'amores,

Schüler (Portuguese, 2003): violeiro d'amores,

Pagán (Galician, 2000): violer d'amores,

Beck (German, 1989): harpfunier d'amores,

Rathjen (German, 1989): Wiederholer d'amoore,

Stündel (German, 1993): der LeibesGeiger,

Bindervoet and Henkes (Dutch, 2002): violaat d'amores,

Volokhonsky (Russian, 2000): s violoj d'amore

Królikowski (Polish, 1998): rzępolent z miłości,

Malicki (Polish, 2001): woler d'amorów,

Mutanen (Finnish, 2006): rakkauksien vahinguttaja,

Titley (Irish, 2008): feichidveibhlín na mionsearc

Tristram is a 'violer d'amores' – 'viola in all moods and senses,' as Joyce cryptically commented in his letter to Harriet Weaver. The legendary Tristram was a musician (though his instrument was the medieval harp rather than the seventeenth-century viola d'amore), a lover, and because of that fatal love also a violator of social proprieties and knightly honour. Nor was violence foreign to his nature when called for. The historical Tristram of Howth Castle and environs boasted the given name (among other variants) of Amory, likewise suggesting love, and whatever his musical abilities may have been, he was necessarily also no stranger to violence. Violet, meanwhile, a term deriving from the Latin *viola*, is the liturgical colour of mourning, appropriate for at least the legendary Tristram, who will later appear as a Latin 'Tristis Tristior Tristissimus' (*FW* 158.1), a lover literally 'sad sadder saddest.'

Tristram as 'violer d'amores' is both a 'musician of love' (Campbell and Robinson 1961, 26), playing 'love-songs on the viola d'amore' (Burgess 1966, 22), and also a violator of love and of honour, his own and – for *amores* is plural – others'. Three of our translators (Elizondo in Spanish, Lourenço in Portuguese, Pagán in Galician) simply retain Joyce's own ambiguous quasi-Romance formulation, allowing for a similar range of meanings. Two others prefer to think of Tristram as most importantly a musician: thus Wilcock's Italian 'violista d'amori' and Schüler's Portuguese 'violeiro d'amores,' both meaning a 'violist of love, a musician of love.' Pozanco's Spanish even sees Tristram as himself the very instrument of love, a 'viola d'amores.' One translator revises his opinion significantly to allow for the benefit of the doubt: Schenoni's Italian version of 1978 has 'violatore d'amores,' while his version of four years later adopts 'violista d'amores,' transforming Tristram in the process from a 'violator of love' to a 'violist of love.'

Several versions opt unambiguously for a more negative judgment: for du Bouchet and Lavergne he is a French 'violeur,' for Burgess an Italian 'violatore,' for Campos a Portuguese 'violador,' thus in all cases a 'violator.' For Bindervoet and Henkes Tristram is a 'violaat,' combining a clear suggestion of the English verb *to violate* in the description of a Dutch *violist*, a musician whose fiddling may go on too late (*laat*). In Lavergne's 'violeur d'amoeurs' he is a violator not just of love (*amour*) but of social morals (*moeurs*) in general. Victoria's Spanish 'violamores' succeeds in retaining reference to both the musician and the violator Tristram.

The three German translators choose quite different linguistic solutions. In Beck's formulation, 'harpfunier d'amores,' Tristram employs not only the musician's harp (*Harfe*) but also the hunter's appropriately phallic harpoon (*Harpune*) in his pursuit of love. For Rathjen's 'Wiederholer d'amoore,' playing on two different German verbs sharing the same spelling, *wiederholen*, he is primarily a 'Wiederholer,' one who was sent 'to fetch again' (*er holt wieder*) Mark's promised bride from the bogs (*Moor*, 'bog') of Ireland, and one who continues to 'repeat' (*er wiederholt*) his amorous transgressions. For Stündel, playing on *Liebe* ('love'), *Leib* ('body'), and such idiomatic expressions as *Leibarzt* ('personal physician'), Tristram is 'der LeibesGeiger,' a personal musician (*Geiger*, 'fiddler') of love who plays on the body of his beloved as if it were an instrument.

Titley's 'feichidveibhlín na mionsearc,' finally, succeeds in performing a complex triple wordplay. It conflates first an Irish *feitheid* ('beast of prey') and a Hiberno-English *feck*, which not only means 'to steal' (thus invoking the French *voler*, 'to steal') but also functions as a socially acceptable alternative for the more drastic *fuck*. It then goes on to conflate *veidhlín* ('violin') and the suggestion of *-bhailbhe*, evoking a metathesized 'stammering' (*bailbhe*) à la HCE. It concludes with a combination of *mion* ('small') and *searc* ('love'), suggesting the shallowness of our Trostam's avowed love while playing on the complementary linguistic fact that the Irish *searc* shares its pronunciation with the Hiberno-English *shark*, thus casting our maritime hero firmly as a sexually predatory Brechtian Mac the Knife.

[3]   *fr'over the short sea,*

du Bouchet (French, 1962): d'oultre la manche mer,

Lavergne (French, 1982): manchissant la courte oisie,

Wilcock (Italian, 1961): da oltre il mare piccolo,

Burgess (Italian, 1975): d'attraverso il mare corto,

Schenoni (Italian, 1978): d'oltre il mar piccolo,

Schenoni (Italian, 1982): da sopra il mar d'Irlanda,

Elizondo (Spanish, 1992): habiendo cruzado el corto mar,

Pozanco (Spanish, 1993): del otro lado del pequeño mar,

Victoria (Spanish, 2009): de sobre'l mar angosto,

Campos (Portuguese, 1962): através o mar breve,

Lourenço (Portuguese, 1968): ladcim'pre do estreito mar,

Schüler (Portuguese, 2003): d'além do mar encapelado,

Pagán (Galician, 2000): do outro lado da pequena mareira,

Beck (German, 1989): räubher über rauhe see,

Rathjen (German, 1989): von jenseits der Kurzsee,

Stündel (German, 1993): von jenseits der kurzen Seh,

Bindervoet and Henkes (Dutch, 2002): vannover de korte zee,

Volokhonsky (Russian, 2000): iz-za bližnego morja

Królikowski (Polish, 1998): poprze'z fal niedal,

Malicki (Polish, 2001): fru' poprzez krótkie morze,

Mutanen (Finnish, 2006): yli irlamminmeren,

Titley (Irish, 2008): ar an bhfarraige,

Joyce's Tristram, finally, is a foreigner, 'fr'over the short sea,' the contracted phrase economically suggesting a rover, from over, far over, the sea. Humphrey Chimpden Earwicker will later emerge as also a foreigner by origin, being of Scandinavian blood. Following a later discredited theory concerning the origins of Finn mac Cumhaill, Joyce will likewise suggest HCE's avatar Finn as having both Irish and Norse blood (MacKillop 1986, 23–4).

The phrase 'short sea' may be taken as referring either to the size or the state of the body of water in question. As an adjectival phrase, it is commonly applied to short-distance shipping that does not cross an ocean, as opposed to deep-sea shipping; as a noun phrase, a short sea is one that is rough and choppy, while a long sea is characterized by a calm and unbroken surface. If we read it in the former sense, the primary reference would appear to be to the Irish Sea, across which both the legendary Tristram and the historical Tristram sailed on their way to Ireland. As always, however, nothing in *Finnegans Wake* is ever limited to a single meaning, and some readers, in the light of Joyce's Tristram arriving from 'North Armorica' (to which we shall return), see the phrase as simultaneously referring to the Atlantic Ocean (Wilcock 1961, 1130).

Most of our translators – two of whom (Wilcock, Lourenço) reverse the order of the two phrases 'violer d'amores' and 'fr'over the short sea' – render the latter phrase with relatively slight variations as meaning 'from over the short sea' (Burgess, Campos, Bindervoet and Henkes), 'from the other side of the short sea' (Rathjen, Stündel), 'having crossed the short sea' (Elizondo), 'from across the small sea' (Wilcock), or 'from the other side of the small sea' (Pozanco, Pagán). Victoria's Spanish 'mar angosto' specifically implies a 'narrow sea,' while also gesturing (Spanish *angustia*, 'anguish') towards the legendary Tristram's anguished love for (in Malory's account) La Beale Isoud, daughter of Anguish, King of Ireland. Lourenço's Portuguese is the only version, oddly enough, to devote specific attention to the contracted phrase 'fr'over': his compressed 'ladcim'pre do estreito mar' suggests an arrival on this side (*lado*) from 'over the surface of' (*lá de cima de*) and from 'across' (*sobre*) the expanse of the likewise 'narrow' (*estreito*) sea.

Schenoni translates the phrase in 1978 as meaning 'from beyond the small sea' ('d'oltre il mar piccolo'), revising it in 1982 to 'from over the Irish Sea' ('da sopra il mar d'Irlanda'), somewhat surprisingly offering a more narrowly specific geographical solution. The Finnish 'yli irlam-minmeren' also refers specifically to travel 'over' (*yli*) the 'sea' (*meri*) of Ireland (*Irlanti*), a sea whose smallness is suggested by *lammin*, an oblique case of *lampi* ('pool'). Stündel's German 'von jenseits der kurzen Seh' puns on *See* ('sea') and *sehen* ('to see'), obliquely suggesting (*kurzsichtig*, 'shortsighted') at least the legendary Tristram's disastrous lack of foresight. Volokhonsky's Russian 'iz-za bližnego morja' and Królikowski's Polish 'poprze'z fal niedal' both take the adjective *short* to mean 'nearby' (Russian *bližnij*, Polish *niedaleki*), while Malicki's Polish 'fru' poprzez krótkie morze' replicates the Joycean 'short' (*krótki*). Titley's Irish 'ar an bhfarraige' ignores the adjective altogether with a lapidary 'on the sea.'

The two French versions provide an interesting expansion of the implied geographical reference. Du Bouchet's Sire Tristram arrives 'd'oultre la manche mer,' where Old French *oultre* on the one hand means simply 'beyond' (Latin *ultra*) but in the context of du Bouchet's phrase also generates echoes of modern French *outre-Manche* ('cross-Channel'), *outremer* ('overseas'), not to mention *adultère* ('adultery, adulterous, adulterer'). The 'manche mer' in question is not only *mince* ('small, slender') like the Irish Sea but extends the reference to the English Channel (*la Manche*), across which both Tristrams will also have originally sailed, on their way from Brittany to Cornwall. Lavergne's Tristram arrives 'manchissant la courte oisie,' which, as in du Bouchet's version, suggests *franchissant la Manche* ('crossing the English Channel'), though now also wearing his heart on his sleeve (*manche*) in the name of knightly courtesy (*courtoisie*), the term *courtoisie* punning on the French adjective *court* ('short') and the English noun *sea*.

Only two versions, finally, see the 'short sea' as primarily suggesting stormy weather. Schüler's Portuguese 'd'além do mar encapelado' ('from beyond the swelling sea') portrays a sea that has 'grown rough' (*encapelado*) and thus might also perhaps anticipate stormy times ahead for Sir Tristrão. Beck's German 'räubher über rauhe see' likewise sees a stormy sea, but expands significantly the characterization of his Herr Tristram, now bluntly stated to be a robber (*Räuber*) rather than merely a rover, come from over (*herüber*) a rough (*rauh*) sea, leaving the reader to decide whether the primary reference is to the Tristram of legend or the Sir Amory of history.

[4]   *had passencore rearrived*

du Bouchet (French, 1962): n'avait à corps ravivé

Lavergne (French, 1982): n'avait pâque buissé sa derrive

Wilcock (Italian, 1961): non era ancora riarrivato

Burgess (Italian, 1975): non aveva ancora gettato

Schenoni (Italian, 1978): era passencore riarrivato

Schenoni (Italian, 1982): aveva passencore riraggiunto

Elizondo (Spanish, 1992): había pasancor revuelto

Pozanco (Spanish, 1993): no ha passencore vuelto a llegar

Victoria (Spanish, 2009): había no todavía [pasadotravez] vuelto-arrivar

Campos (Portuguese, 1962): tinha pazencore revoltado

Lourenço (Portuguese, 1968): não tinha passancore rechegado

Schüler (Portuguese, 2003): não tinha passancorado reveniente

Pagán (Galician, 2000): non regresara passencore

Beck (German, 1989): war passencore zurückgekommen

Rathjen (German, 1989): war passimkorps ... rückgelangt

Stündel (German, 1993): war noch nicht wieder ... zurückgekehrt

Bindervoet and Henkes (Dutch, 2002): was passencore weeromge-keerd

Volokhonsky (Russian, 2000): pribyl nazad passažirom transporta

Królikowski (Polish, 1998): przelewił się na pośród

Malicki (Polish, 2001): miał przejściowy rdzeń powtórnie przybywając

Mutanen (Finnish, 2006): oli ydimääräisen joentakaisin

Titley (Irish, 2008): a raibh brot a chroí fillte go hanraiththráthuil

Readers are invited to see the primary surface meaning of this phrase as being that Sir Tristram had 'not yet' (French *pas encore*) arrived from the north coast of Brittany (otherwise, as we have seen, *Armorica*) – which would, of course, situate the scene of his arrival as being King Mark's Cornwall rather than Ireland, and the 'short sea' he has just crossed as indeed the English Channel rather than the Irish Sea. That surface meaning is immediately challenged, and the indeterminacy heightened, by the friction between *pas encore* ('not yet') and *passe encore* ('passes again') as well as by that between an assumed 'arrived' and the actual textual wording 'rearrived' – a friction Joyce identified for Harriet Weaver's benefit as an example of the 'ricorsi storici of Vico': Tristram has both 'not yet arrived' and 'passing again (*en passant encore*), will arrive again.'

Several of our translators, in several languages, opt for discretion as the better part of valour in simply retaining Joyce's 'passencore,' a resolutely minimal form of translation – thus Schenoni's Italian, Pozanco's Spanish, Pagán's Galician, Beck's German, and Bindervoet and Henkes's Dutch. Other solutions include minimal but significant alterations, such as Elizondo's 'pasancor,' suggesting the Spanish *ancora* ('anchor') of sea-faring vessels; Campos's 'pazencore,' unexpectedly contributing a Portuguese *paz* ('peace') instead; and Lourenço's 'passancore,' once again suggesting the anchor (Portuguese *âncora*) of sailing ships, whether sailing for love or war. Rathjen's 'passimkorps' substitutes a punning approximation that suggests army units (German *Korps*) everywhere (Latin *passim*), primarily evoking the Norman invasion represented by Sir Amory Tristram rather than the amorous voyage of Tristram the lover. Some versions opt for a simple but reductive 'not yet' – thus Wilcock's 'non era ancora,' Burgess's 'non aveva ancora,' Stündel's 'war noch nicht.' Schüler's Portuguese successfully plays on the verbs *passar* ('to pass') and *ancorar* ('to anchor') in his 'não tinha passancorado,' while Burgess adopts a related strategy in his Italian 'non aveva ancora gettato,' playing on *ancora* ('again') and the phrase *gettare ancora* ('to drop anchor').

The verb 'rearrived' poses no particular challenge for any of the translators, but inspires a few to displays of verbal fireworks. Schenoni's second Italian version introduces a more complex variant of his earlier 'riarrivato' (*arrivare*, 'to arrive') with 'riraggiunto,' combining a singulative *giungere* ('to arrive') and a duplicative *raggiungere* ('to rejoin'), the latter itself in turn duplicated (*ri-*). Victoria's Spanish version, with its unusual use of a bracketed alternative, 'había no todavía [pasadotravez] vueltoarrivar,' successfully implies at once that Tristram had not yet (*no todavía*) 'passed across' (*pasado a través*), not yet 'passed again' (*pasado otra vez*), and not yet 'repeated his arrival' (*vuelto a arrivar*). Du Bouchet's French 'n'avait à corps ravivé' suggests that, though 'revived' (*ravivé*) 'in body' (*à corps*) 'once again' (*encore*), he had neither 'yet arrived' (*n'avait encore arrivé*), nor arrived 'once again' (*encore*). Finally, no doubt celebrating the maritime origins of the verb *to arrive* as meaning to reach a 'shore' (Latin *ripa*, French *rive*), Lavergne's 'n'avait pâque buissé sa derrive' provides the showiest fireworks display and stretches the limits of French in a complexly tortured series of water-related puns. Taken together, they suggest (reductively) that Tristram had not yet 'passed over' (*pâque*, 'Passover'), whether by 'steamship' (*paquebot*) or otherwise, but had 'only' (*n'avait pas que*) managed to work out (*puiser*, 'to draw water, to derive an idea') the general 'drift' (*dérive*) of his eventual course towards an arrival (*arrivée*), though one as yet only approximately 'derived' (*dérivée*) from his calculations.

Titley's Irish goes entirely its own way with another complex formulaton, 'a raibh brot a chroí fillte go hanraiththráthuil,' whose meaning might be read variously as 'the mantle (*brot*) of whose heart (*croí*) was folded (*fillte*)' or 'the fire (*bruth*) of whose heart had returned (*fillte*)' or 'the fire of whose heart was deceitful (*fillte*) and treacherous (*fillte*),' situations any one of which might be deemed either 'felicitous' (*tráthúil*) or 'disastrous' (*anrathúil*), or both. Added to this rich conflation of indeterminacies is the fact that *brot* ('mantle, cloak, veil') is a variant form of *brat*, which shares all of these meanings but also means 'broth.' Challenging the reader to decide on its degree or lack of relevance is the parallel fact that while *anrath* means 'misfortune, ill-luck,' *anraith* likewise means 'broth, soup.' Of equally uncertain relevance is the fact that since Scottish Gaelic *raith* means 'idle talk,' *anraith*, if we choose to read the first syllable as the intensifying particle *an-* ('very'), may be taken as meaning 'inordinately idle talk.' Readers may consider themselves duly warned.

[5]   from North Armorica

du Bouchet (French, 1962): du Nord de l'Armorique

Lavergne (French, 1982): d'Armorique du Nord

Wilcock (Italian, 1961): da Nord Armorica,

Burgess (Italian, 1975): dell'Armorica del Nord

Schenoni (Italian, 1978): dall'Armorica del Nord

Schenoni (Italian, 1982): dall'Armorica del Nord

Elizondo (Spanish, 1992): de Nortearmórica

Pozanco (Spanish, 1993): de Norte Armórica

Victoria (Spanish, 2009): desde Norte Armórica

Campos (Portuguese, 1962): de Norte Armórica

Lourenço (Portuguese, 1968): da Armórica do Norte

Schüler (Portuguese, 2003): de Norte Armórica

Pagán (Galician, 2000): de Norte Armórica

Beck (German, 1989): aus Nord-Armorica

Rathjen (German, 1989): aus Nordarmorika

Stündel (German, 1993): aus Nord Armorika

Bindervoet and Henkes (Dutch, 2002): uit Noord-Armorica

Volokhonsky (Russian, 2000): Severnoj Armoriki

Królikowski (Polish, 1998): z Północnej Armoryki

Malicki (Polish, 2001): z Północnej Armoryki

Mutanen (Finnish, 2006): Pohjois-Panssarimerikasta

Titley (Irish, 2008): [*text missing*]

The conflation of time suggested by 'passencore' is matched by a conflation of space: the reference to 'North Armorica' clearly (if for as-yet-unexplained reasons) evokes for Joyce's reader not only northern Brittany but also faraway (though for many more familiar) North America. The phrase 'North Armorica' is thus rendered in almost all versions by the particular construction also normally used for 'North America' in the relevant language, including in the two Polish versions, both of which combine the standard terms for 'North America' (*Ameryka Północna*) and 'Armorica' (*Armoryka*). Serendipitously, the Polish *połnoc* ('north') contributes in passing to the conflation of time and space, deriving from *pol* ('half') and *noc* ('night'), north understood in this context as the direction of midnight (Buck 1988, 873). Uncharacteristically, du Bouchet's French 'du Nord de l'Armorique' (unlike Lavergne's 'd'Armorique du Nord') is reductive, unambiguously referring only to northern Brittany, thus excluding the transatlantic echo – which will of course very soon become much stronger with the reference to Laurens County, Georgia, and its county seat, Dublin. Titley's Irish is silent on the matter.

The most elaborate rendering of the phrase occurs in Mutanen's Finnish 'Pohjois-Panssarimerikasta,' which combines the standard term *Pohjois-Amerikka* ('North America') with the Finnish nouns *panssari* ('armour,' translingually punning on 'Armorica') and *meri* ('sea') to achieve the relevant medieval and maritime overtones. Etymology once again contributes serendipitously to the conflation of time and space: Finnish *pohjoinen* ('north') has a similar origin to Polish *północ*, deriving likewise from *puoli* ('half') and *yö* ('night'), north being once again the direction of midnight (Bergman 1968, 455, 630, 638), while *panssari* (a Finnish loanword from German) unexpectedly manages to leap a millennium in linking the ancient shores of Gaulish Armorica with twentieth-century wartime memories of German *Panzer* ('armour').

[6]   *on this side*

du Bouchet (French, 1962): ès bords

Lavergne (French, 1982): sur ce flanc

Wilcock (Italian, 1961): in questa parte

Burgess (Italian, 1975): sul cisistmo

Schenoni (Italian, 1978): su questo lato

Schenoni (Italian, 1982): su questa sponda

Elizondo (Spanish, 1992): de este lado

Pozanco (Spanish, 1993): a este lado

Victoria (Spanish, 2009): a este lado

Campos (Portuguese, 1962): a êste lado

Lourenço (Portuguese, 1968): a este lado

Schüler (Portuguese, 2003): a estas bandas

Pagán (Galician, 2000): a este lado

Beck (German, 1989): auf diese seite

Rathjen (German, 1989): an diese Seite

Stündel (German, 1993): zu

Bindervoet and Henkes (Dutch, 2002): deeszijds

Volokhonsky (Russian, 2000): na ètu storonu

Królikowski (Polish, 1998): w tę flankę

Malicki (Polish, 2001): na tę stronę

Mutanen (Finnish, 2006): tällä puolen

Titley (Irish, 2008): [*text missing*]

The modern English-speaking reader is faced with the slightly destabilizing question as to whether the old-fashioned usage 'on this side' does indeed mean 'on this side *of*.' Almost all our translators, at any rate, by following the phrase with a preposition meaning 'of,' agree, restabilized, that the action does indeed occur 'on this side of' the isthmus in question. Four versions employ other strategies: Pagán's Galician 'a este lado o' (rather than 'a este lado do') replicates Joyce's phrasing exactly and to similar effect; Stündel's German 'zu' ('to') resolves the problem by ignoring it; Titley's Irish continues to remain silent; and Elizondo's Spanish 'de este lado,' literally 'from this side,' is alone in envisaging the action as proceeding *from* rather than towards the isthmus under discussion. We may notice too that while 'side' is translated simply as 'lado' in three Spanish and two Portuguese versions, French and Italian translators differ significantly among themselves as to the best term to employ. Du Bouchet opts in French for a stylized 'ès bords,' Lavergne for 'sur ce flanc,' while four Italian versions choose as many possibilities: Wilcock's 'in questa parte,' Schenoni's earlier 'su questo lato' and later 'su questa sponda,' and Burgess's punning 'sul cisistmo,' to which we shall return below.

[7]   *the scraggy isthmus*

du Bouchet (French, 1962): d'icel huisthme hérissé

Lavergne (French, 1982): de notre isthme décharné

Wilcock (Italian, 1961): dello scabroso rouistmo

Burgess (Italian, 1975): sul cisistmo scosceso

Schenoni (Italian, 1978): dell'istmo scabroso

Schenoni (Italian, 1982): l'istmo scosceso

Elizondo (Spanish, 1992): del estrecho istmo

Pozanco (Spanish, 1993): del flaco istmo

Victoria (Spanish, 2009): del raquítico istmo

Campos (Portuguese, 1962): do áspero istmo

Lourenço (Portuguese, 1968): do ossudo istmo

Schüler (Portuguese, 2003): do istmo escarpado

Pagán (Galician, 2000): o escuálido istmo

Beck (German, 1989): des klüftigen isthmus

Rathjen (German, 1989): des rauhen Isthmus

Stündel (German, 1993): zu der dunnen Landenge

Bindervoet and Henkes (Dutch, 2002): 't schierlijk eilandje

Volokhonsky (Russian, 2000): izrezannogo perešejka

Królikowski (Polish, 1998): wężyzn przesmyku

Malicki (Polish, 2001): nieregularnego istmusu

Mutanen (Finnish, 2006): kannaslaihelia voimistellakseen

Titley (Irish, 2008): chun caoil chreagaigh

Joyce's 'scraggy isthmus of Europe Minor' likewise allows, entirely un-surprisingly, for a variety of readings. An isthmus is by etymological definition (Greek *isthmos*, 'neck') a neck of land joining two larger bod-ies of land. In geological terms, the English Channel and the Irish Sea once formed part of an isthmus joining Ireland via Britain to western Europe. Depending on one's estimation of the importance of Ireland in the global scheme of things, western Europe itself might still be seen as a 'scraggy isthmus' linking Ireland and the greater body of central and eastern Europe. The isthmus of Sutton, meanwhile, scraggy like the neck of a chicken, continues to join Howth, the site at least of Sir Amory Tristram's arrival, to the Irish mainland. Campbell and Robinson note that North Brittany is 'on Ireland's side of rugged Europe' (1961, 26); Wilcock (1961, 1130) sees the isthmus in question as being that of Sutton and also that of western Europe; Europe Minor might also be taken in a Wakean scheme of things as just another name for Ireland, that remarkable island whose saints and scholars once re-civilized Europe.

The Greek origins of the word *isthmus* allow almost all our translators to render it by a conveniently cognate term in the target language: French *isthme* (Lavergne), Italian *istmo* (Schenoni), Spanish *istmo* (Elizondo, Pozanco, Victoria), Portuguese *istmo* (Campos, Lourenço, Schüler), Galician *istmo* (Pagán), German *Isthmus* (Beck, Rathjen). Other versions ring changes on the relevant term. Thus du Bouchet's highly stylized French 'ès bords d'icel huisthme' plays on an archaic *icelui* ('this') and *isthme*; Wilcock's Italian 'rouistmo' plays similarly on *rovo* ('bush, bramble') and *istmo*; Burgess's Italian 'cisistmo' on Latin *cis-* ('on this side') and *istmo*. Stündel's German reductively substitutes the alternative dictionary term 'Landenge' (literally a 'narrowing of the land'); Titley's 'caol' is similarly a standard Irish term for an isthmus; while Bindervoet and Henkes avoid direct reference to an isthmus, preferring to speak instead of a 'schierlijk eilandje,' literally an 'almost islet,' playing on the Dutch term *schiereiland* ('peninsula'). Lavergne's 'notre isthme' ('our isthmus') adopts a somewhat proprietorial stance.

According to David Hayman's *First-Draft Version*, Joyce first wrote 'merry isthmus' rather than 'scraggy isthmus.' While the earlier version has its seasonal charm, English *scrag* anticipates Greek *isthmos* as another term for 'neck,' and a 'scraggy isthmus' is thus literally a 'necky neck.' The adjective *scraggy* means 'lean' and also 'rough, rugged, ragged,' while also evocative of 'craggy,' as in Titley's Irish *creagach* ('rocky, craggy, barren'). Our other translators describe their particular 'scraggy isthmus' in an interesting variety of ways: du Bouchet's is 'hérissé' ('bristly, spiky'), Lavergne's 'décharné' ('emaciated, stripped of flesh'), Wilcock's and the earlier Schenoni's 'scabroso' ('rugged'), Burgess's and the later Schenoni's 'scosceso' ('rugged, precipitous'), Elizondo's 'estrecho' ('narrow'), Pozanco's 'flaco' ('thin, lean'), Victoria's 'raquítico' ('stunted, blighted'), Campos's 'áspero' ('rough, harsh'), Lourenço's 'ossudo' ('bony'), Schüler's 'escarpado' ('steep'), Beck's 'klüftig' ('craggy'), Rathjen's 'rauh' ('rough'), Stündel's 'dunn' (*dünn*, 'thin, narrow'), and Malicki's 'nieregularny' ('irregular'). Pagán's 'escuálido' interestingly combines weakness and disreputability (Spanish *escuálido*, 'weak, squalid, filthy'), while Bindervoet and Henkes choose to focus on the difficulty, precisely, of precise definition, restructuring, as we have seen, the standard Dutch term *schiereiland* ('peninsula') to describe something that is 'almost' (*schierlijk*) a peninsula, almost an island (*eiland*), or perhaps not even that but only just almost an 'islet' (*eilandje*).

[8]   *of Europe Minor*

du Bouchet (French, 1962): d'Europe mineure

Lavergne (French, 1982): d'Europe Mineure

Wilcock (Italian, 1961): d'Europa Minore,

Burgess (Italian, 1975): dell'Europa Minore

Schenoni (Italian, 1978): dell'Europa Minore

Schenoni (Italian, 1982): d'Europa Minore

Elizondo (Spanish, 1992): de Europa Menor

Pozanco (Spanish, 1993): de Europa Menor

Victoria (Spanish, 2009): de Europa Menor

Campos (Portuguese, 1962): da Europa Menor

Lourenço (Portuguese, 1968): da Europa Menor

Schüler (Portuguese, 2003): da Europa Menor

Pagán (Galician, 2000): de Europa Menor

Beck (German, 1989): von Klein-Europa,

Rathjen (German, 1989): von Kleineuropa

Stündel (German, 1993): von Klein Europa

Bindervoet and Henkes (Dutch, 2002): van Klein-Europa

Volokhonsky (Russian, 2000): v Evropu Maluju

Królikowski (Polish, 1998): Europy Mniejniżmniejszej,

Malicki (Polish, 2001): Europy mniejszej

Mutanen (Finnish, 2006): Vähä-Euroopan

Titley (Irish, 2008): na mionEorpa

As 'North Armorica' also evoked the more familiar 'North America,' widening the geographical scope of the reference, so 'Europe Minor' also, and to similar effect, evokes the more familiar phrase 'Asia Minor.' Not all translators may agree on the primary geographical referent of the phrase, but it is clear that 'Europe Minor' provokes a much narrower range of translatorial responses than did the 'scraggy isthmus.'

[9]   to wielderfight

du Bouchet (French, 1962): pour reluivreferre

Lavergne (French, 1982): pour y resoutenir le combat

Wilcock (Italian, 1961): a brandibattere

Burgess (Italian, 1975): per rimuovere

Schenoni (Italian, 1978): per wielderbattere

Schenoni (Italian, 1982): per wielderbattere

Elizondo (Spanish, 1992): para martibatallar

Pozanco (Spanish, 1993): para librar ... combate:

Victoria (Spanish, 2009): par'empuñapelear

Campos (Portuguese, 1962): para relutar

Lourenço (Portuguese, 1968): para relutar

Schüler (Portuguese, 2003): para o virolento conflito

Pagán (Galician, 2000): para librar a cabo

Beck (German, 1989): um ... wielder auszufechten:

Rathjen (German, 1989): um ... zu fehderführen:

Stündel (German, 1993): um wieder ... aufzunehmen:

Bindervoet and Henkes (Dutch, 2002): voor het widervuren

Volokhonsky (Russian, 2000): daby samolično vesti

Królikowski (Polish, 1998): prostowzłujbój

Malicki (Polish, 2001): by wydzierżyć

Mutanen (Finnish, 2006): musterottelunsa

Titley (Irish, 2008): d'fhonn tréanthroid an chogaigh a eisfhearadh

The phrase 'to wielderfight' contains the challenge 'yield or fight' while punningly incorporating the German *wieder* ('again') to imply both 'to refight, to fight all over again' (having perhaps yielded rather than fought on a previous occasion?) and also, in Anthony Burgess's apt formulation, to 'wield weapons in wild fight' (1966, 22). The complementary suggestion of the German *Widder*, meaning 'ram,' taken in conjunction with the second syllable of Tristram's name, already suggests a sexual dimension to the 'penisolate war' he is about to wage.

The phrase 'to wielderfight' is rendered in Italian by Schenoni in both of his versions as 'per wielderbattere,' economically replacing Joyce's 'fight' by its equivalent, *battere*. Burgess prefers 'per rimuovere,' playing on the linguistic friction between *rimuovere*, which would normally (but inappropriately in the context) mean 'to remove' and *ri-muovere* ('to set in motion once again'). Wilcock, finally, has 'a brandibattere,' effectively combining *brando* ('sword, brand'), *brandire* ('to brandish'), *battere* ('to beat), and *combattere* ('to fight'). Of the three Spanish versions, Pozanco has a simple 'para librar combate,' literally 'to engage in battle,' while Elizondo prefers a rather more Baroque 'para martibatallar,' suggesting to battle (*batallar*) like Mars (*Marte*) – or like a martyr (*mártir*). Victoria adopts 'par'empuñapelear,' combining *puño* ('fist'), *empuñar* ('to seize'), and *pelear* ('to fight'). In Portuguese, both Campos and Lourenço opt somewhat reductively for 'relutar,' literally 'to fight again,' while Pagán's Galician prefers 'librar a cabo' ('to bring to a head') – where one may also detect the geographical presence of the headland (*cabo*) of Howth. Schüler's Portuguese, more energetically, refers to a 'virolento conflito,' suggesting a struggle both violent (*violento*) and virulent (*virulento*).

Bindervoet and Henkes opt in Dutch for 'widervuren,' which succeeds, impressively, in combining German *wieder* ('again') and *wider* ('against'), Dutch *weer* ('again'), German *Widder* ('ram,' the animal), Dutch *vuren* ('to fire,' as of a gun), and German *weiterführen* ('to continue'). Stündel's German 'aufzunehmen' ('to take up'), by contrast, is surprisingly colourless. Beck's German prefers 'wielder auszufechten,' adroitly recycling Joyce's 'wielder' in the German context as meaning 'to fight out' (*auszufechten*) his war both 'again' (*wieder*) and 'more wildly' (*wilder*) than before. Rathjen's German prefers the phrase 'zu fehderführen,' combining *Fehde* ('feud') and *federführend* ('in overall control of' and 'with pen in hand'), *einen Krieg führen* ('to conduct a war'), and *erfahren* ('to experience'). In Lavergne's French, 'pour y resoutenir le combat,' we find the need both to continue (*soutenir*) and to resolve (*résoudre*) the struggle. In du Bouchet's French, finally, 'pour reluivreferre sa guerre,' we find in what is certainly the richest version of all those examined so far the necessity 'to polish up' (*faire reluire*) one's weapons (*fer*, 'iron, sword'), 'to give battle' (*livrer bataille*), 'to make war' (*faire la guerre*), and to fight wildly (*ivre*, 'intoxicated') again (*relivrer bataille*) and again (*refaire la guerre*). Titley's Irish, on the other hand, 'd'fhonn tréanthroid an chogaigh a eisfhearadh,' translates without wordplay as 'in order (*d'fhonn*) to engage (*fearadh*) once again (*eis-*) in the fierce (*tréan-*) combat (*troid*) of war (*cogadh*).'

[10]   *his penisolate war:*

du Bouchet (French, 1962): guerre péniseulte:

Lavergne (French, 1982): le combat d'un presqu'Yseul penny:

Wilcock (Italian, 1961): la sua guerra penisolata:

Burgess (Italian, 1975): la sua guerra penisulata:

Schenoni (Italian, 1978): la sua guerra peneisolata:

Schenoni (Italian, 1982): la sua guerra penisolata:

Elizondo (Spanish, 1992): en su guerra peneisolar:

Pozanco (Spanish, 1993): su penuriósolo combate:

Victoria (Spanish, 2009): su [aislada] guerra peneinsular:

Campos (Portuguese, 1962): sua guerra penisolada:

Lourenço (Portuguese, 1968): o seu penisolado combate:

Schüler (Portuguese, 2003): de penisoldada guerra:

Pagán (Galician, 2000): a sua penisolada guerra:

Beck (German, 1989): seinen penisolaten krieg

Rathjen (German, 1989): seinen penisolieren Krieg

Stündel (German, 1993): in seinem Peinisolatten Kriech

Bindervoet and Henkes (Dutch, 2002): van zijn gepenisoleerde oorlog:

Volokhonsky (Russian, 2000): penisolirovannuju vojnu na po-luostrove:

Królikowski (Polish, 1998): jej wpółzwyspizolowanej wojny:

Malicki (Polish, 2001): swą penisulową wojnę:

Mutanen (Finnish, 2006): niemisodan:

Titley (Irish, 2008): go leaidiniseach.

As many readers have already observed, the phrase 'his penisolate war' allows Tristram to be read as encompassing an entire phalanx of adventurers here: as bold but lonely sexual adventurer, he is once more to wage a war of the penis, a Tristan obsessively pursuing his Iseult, whatever his or her particular name may be; as lonely writer (whose name might also be James Joyce), he is to wage a war of the pen; as Sir Almeric Tristram, he is to wage a late twelfth-century peninsular war against the native Irish from his Norman bastion on the peninsula of Howth; as Sir Arthur Wellesley, reluctant Dubliner and eventually first duke of Wellington, he is to wage the early nineteenth-century Peninsular War in Spain and Portugal against Napoleon.

The battle between Wellington and Napoleon evokes the Tweedledum-and-Tweedledee rivalry between the warring brothers Shem and Shaun, two of the three children of HCE and ALP, with whom we shall become familiar in the course of the *Wake*. The third child of HCE and ALP, their daughter Issy, is likewise proleptically evoked by the adjective 'penisolate,' which suggests ('-isol-') both the name *Iseult* and the degree to which Iseult-Issy is an object of sexual desire for both of the brothers, who together will function in this role as 'Tree-Stone,' a dual avatar of Tristan. Such desire is also not without its dangers, etymology suggests: the name *Iseult* appears, by some accounts at least, to derive from the Welsh adjective *ysol* ('consuming, devouring'), and in the medieval story both she and Tristan are indeed eventually consumed entirely by their love for each other. In an early Welsh version of the tale her name is *Esyllt* instead, a name suggested as deriving from the Welsh verb *syllu* ('to gaze'), as in 'she who is gazed upon,' or 'of fair aspect' (Hanks et al. 2002, 786). Issy's favourite occupation in the *Wake* will turn out to be gazing lovingly at herself in any convenient mirror.

The phrase 'penisolate war' is in general rendered less interestingly in translation than is the phrase 'to wielderfight.' All four Italian versions are able to stay close to Joyce's 'penisolate,' but the earlier Schenoni manages to include both 'penis' (*pene*) and the 'pains' (*pene*) of love in his 'peneisolata,' while reverting to a more rigorous 'peniso-lata' in his later rendering. In Spanish, Elizondo and Victoria render 'penisolate' as 'peneisolar' and 'peneinsular' respectively, the former emphasizing isolation (*aislar*), the latter geography. Pozanco, however, apparently thinks of the effects of the campaign ahead in primarily economic terms, characterizing Tristram as 'penuriósolo,' combining *solo* ('alone') and, oddly, *penurioso* ('penurious, poverty-stricken'). While Campos, Lourenço, and Pagán remain closer to Joyce's terminology in referring to a 'guerra penisolada' or a 'penisolado combate,' Schüler's reference to a 'penisoldada guerra' emphasizes the presence of an embedded Portuguese Isolda, alias Iseult.

Beck's German 'penisolaten krieg,' quite close to Joyce's original, strikes a very similar note, while Rathjen's 'penisolieren Krieg' suggests also that the war is specifically an *Irenkrieg*, a war (*Krieg*) against (or among) Irishmen (*Iren*). The Dutch 'gepenisoleerde oorlog' of Bindervoet and Henkes dutifully mentions the war (*oorlog*), the penis (*penis*), and isolation (*geïsoleerd*, 'isolated') but also reveals the shadow of a hidden 'isol … de' whose heart, parted from her lover, is, in German if not in Dutch, *leer* ('empty'). Stündel, for his part, has his Tristram opt for taking up 'den Krampf in seinem Peinisolatten Kriech,' where martial *Kampf* ('combat') and *Krieg* ('war') are jocularly transposed into a Beckettean combination of *Krampf* ('cramp') and *Kriechen* ('crawling'), appropriately abetted by the *Pein* ('pain') if not the *Penis* in his 'Peinisolatten Kriech.' In Lavergne's distinctly idiosyncratic rendering, 'le combat d'un presqu'Yseul penny,' we find the struggle, whether by penis (*pénis*) or pen (*penne*, 'feather, quill') or both, and alone (*seul*) if necessary, for both peninsula (*presqu'île*) and Iseult – even if each, rather surprisingly (not to mention ungallantly), is worth 'little more than a single penny' (*presqu'un seul penny*). In du Bouchet's version, 'sa guerre péniseulte,' we find in 'péniseulte' the French *pénis* ('penis') and *seul* ('alone') as well as the undisguised *Iseult* herself.

In quite a different key, Titley's adverbial phrase 'go leaidiniseach' dispenses altogether with any reference to Iseult, conflating Irish *leathinis* ('peninsula'), the ancient place name *Leatha* ('Armorica'), and the noun *leaid* ('lad'), the latter allowing access to the English slang term for penis, 'old lad,' and rather indulgently implying that our Armorican Trostam, ensconced on his peninsula and vigorously wielding his old lad, is indeed a bit of a lad.

The analysis of translations so far has, for the sake of simplicity and clarity, largely ignored linguistic echoes in languages other than the particular language under specific consideration at any given point. Thus, for example, it was mentioned that the earlier Schenoni manages to include both 'penis' (*pene*) and the 'pains' (*pene*) of love in his Italian reference to a 'guerra peneisolata'; it was also mentioned that Elizondo and Victoria refer in Spanish to a 'guerra peneisolar' and a 'guerra peneinsular' respectively; what was not mentioned, however, is that we can of course also discern the Italian *pene* (meaning both 'penis' and 'pains') in each of the Spanish renderings, not to mention the English *pen* in all three versions, Italian and Spanish alike. With occasional exceptions, we will continue along the same lines, since to attempt to identify *every* multilingual resonance in *every* version considered could very quickly lead to an unreadably cluttered text.

4 Rocks and Fires

nor had topsawyer's rocks by the stream Oconee exaggerated themselse to Laurens County's gorgios while they went doublin their mumper all the time: nor avoice from afire bellowsed mishe mishe to tauftauf thuartpeatrick:

(*FW* 3.6–10)

du Bouchet (French, 1962): marmerocs de sommescieur le long du calme Oconee ne s'étaient pour lors exagerés en gorgios de Laurens County doublin l'arrombe de mot en mot: [*text missing*]

Lavergne (French, 1982): ni près du fleuve Oconee les roches premières ne s'étaient exaltruées en splendide Georgi Dublin de Laurens Comptez en doublant ses membres tout le temps: nulle voix humaine n'avait dessouflé son micmac pour bêptiser Patrick:

Wilcock (Italian, 1961): né si erano le alte rocce accanto al fiume Oconee esagerate fino ai gorghi della contea di Laurens mentre il loro numero si raddublinava continuamente; né la voce dal fuoco aveva risoffiato mishe mishe al tauf tauf tuseipetrizio;

Burgess (Italian, 1975): neppure i sassoni tomsawyereschi huckfinn-eschi sul ruscello Oconee ci erano esagerati ai gorghi gorgolianti di Laurens County (Gorgia) quando sempre sempre dubilavano il loro proprio Dublino; neppure una voce di fuocofuori aveva soffiettato mishe mishe a tauf tauf tu es Pietrorbiera.

Schenoni (Italian, 1978): né i roccoglioni del tommiglior sawyergan-tino presso l'Oconee si altrerano ingigantiti fino ai giorgi della contea di Laurens, continuando a raddublinare il loro mammero; né voce da fuoco aveva mugghiato mishe mishe al tauftauf tuseitorbizio.

Schenoni (Italian, 1982): né le topsawyer's rocks presso il fiume Oconee s'altrerano ingrandite fino ai gorgi della Laurens County mentre continuavano a raddublinare per tutto il tempo il loro mùmpero: né 'navoce da 'nfoco aveva soffiorato mishe mishe al tauftauf tuseipeatrizio:

Elizondo (Spanish, 1992): ni habían las rocas del alto psawrrador, esparcidas a lo largo del arroyo Oconee, exagerádose a sí otras mismas a los gorgios del Condado de Laurens mientras iban dubliando todo el tiempo su mendiganancia; ni una voz salida del fuego surgía diciendo mishe mishe a tauftauf tuespetrarricio,

Pozanco (Spanish, 1993): ni los dentados riscos de junto al Oconee se habían recrecido aún en la exuberancia de Laurens County a fuerza de redublinar sus pobres miembros: ni bramó una voz ardiente la pifia para cortarle el revesino al bautismo de Patricio:

Victoria (Spanish, 2009): ni [había] habido piedras de [jonathan] altosawyer por el riachuelo Oconee exageradas ellasmismás hasta [ser] jorgios [no gitanos] fabulosos del condado de Laurens mientras fueron dubliando su número [de mendigos (má's y padres) ininteligibles huraños & tramposos] todo el tiempo: ni unavoz de unfuego [había] bramadicho mishe mishe [yo(soy)yo] para babautizar túerespetricio:

Campos (Portuguese, 1962): nem tinham os calhaus do altom sawyerrador pelo rio Oconee sexagerado aos górgios de Laurens County enquanto êles iam dublando os bebêbados todo o tempo: [text missing]

Lourenço (Portuguese, 1968): nem as rochas de Pedro Sawyer se tinham dublixagerado, pela corrente do Ocone, até os gorgios do Condado de Laurens enquanto que elas continuavam a dublinar o seu nâmero: nem uma voz vinda do fogo tinha rugido mishe mishe para tauftauf tuespetrício:

Schüler (Portuguese, 2003): nem as pétreas bolotas de Sawyer ao longo do Oconee caudaloso se tinham seggsagerado ao território laurenciano da Geórgia enquanto se dublinavam em

mamypapypares o tempo todo: nem avoz do fogo rebellava
mim-She, mim-She ao tauftauf do pautripedrícioquetués:

Pagán (Galician, 2000): nen os altoms penedos do sawyerrador no
arroio Oconee se converteran outramente na magnífica garganta
de Laurens County redublinando a sua probeza todo o tempo:
nen avoz desde a chamas lle resoprara mixe mixe a tauftauf
tiespedrício:

Beck (German, 1989): noch hatten sich topsawyers felsen am
Oconeeflüßchen nicht hochgestapelt zu Laurens-Lands georgiosem dubling seine schmarotzahl all die weil: noch fauchte kein
stimm fern aus dem feuer mischmisch zu tauftauf dubistpeatrick:

Jauslin (German, 1989): noch hatten sich die Felsen des sawyerlichen Oberschwätzers am Fluß Oconee nicht andersgetürmt zur
GiorgioSchlucht von Laurens County, allweil nur ihren VerdRuß
zu verdublin; noch schrie keine Stimme, vergebens, vom Herdfeuer, vermessin, vermißihn, tauftauf, du gleichst ihm wie ein Ei
dem andern, reingelegt, Stuart Patrick:

Rathjen (German, 1989): noch hatten Topsawyers Felsen am
Oconeelauf einanders aufgeworfen zu Laurensbezirksgeäugiern
während sie die ganze Zeit ihre Unzoll verdopplinten: noch
neStimmede aus deFeuerne michsiemaschsie blaßgebalgt um
Dubistpaetrick taufzutaufen:

Schrödter (German, 1989): noch hatten sich die Topsäygers Felsen
beim Strome Oconee höchstselbst über Laurens Countys gorgos
getrieben während sie doch all die Weil ihre KNümmerlichkeit
verdoubblin gingen: noch anfeuerte eintstimmen von eintflammen mishe mishe zu tauftauf thuartpeatrick:

Stündel (German, 1993): noch hatten sich die Top-Saweiherischen
Felsen nicht am Strom des Oconee aufgehäuft zu Laurens Land,
obgleich sie ihre Anzoll die ganze Zeit über verdublint hatten:
keine Stümme bröllete aus dem Foier Moische Moische zu
tauftauf DubistPehtricks:

Bindervoet and Henkes (Dutch, 2002): noch hadden topzooiers
rotshopen aan de Oconee-stroom zichcelverlei gecumulleerd naar
Laurenslands gorgio's wijl ze gehelenal de tijd hun worpelingen
verdubbelinden: noch bluisbalgde een stem vanuit de vuurte
miesje miesje tot tauftauf giezijtpitriek:

Volokhonsky (Russian, 2000): ne to čtoby vozmyšennye gory u
potoka Okoni razduvalis' do prošorlivych gordšiev grafstva
Lorens, a te vse vremja v tisme dublinirovali vdvoe: ne to čtoby
glas ognja vzduval miš miš dlja poperečnogo viski:

Królikowski (Polish, 1998): i nie miałż skał czeletracznych w potoku
O'Ceanilnym nad miernych ku Hrabstwa Laurennego gardłażom,
gdyże ci dwublinili swój dąspój won wszytek czas: i nie strunił
przed ogniście miechawicznym miszmaszem mordewkubeł
wciupatryka:

Malicki (Polish, 2001): animmiał topka tracza skał przez strumień
Oconee wzmocnionych sami sobą do Laurena Hrabstwa
wielkości gdy oni opuszczali doublin ich mamuśwink cały czas:
ani głos z ognia poniżejwse dzony mishe mishe do tauftauf
takoższtukipawiatryczka:

Mutanen (Finnish, 2006): eipä olleet pohjoisen Okeanoon virran
latvonsawyerin kareikkuet suurennelleet toissijaan Laurenaasian
Kreivicounnan magorgiaisille, kun he menivät äitäi tuplin koko
ajan: eipä palavasta äänen möyrakasta eihän eihän sua suowalea
pietrikkiveä:

'Dublin, Laurens Co, Georgia, founded by a Dubliner, Peter Sawyer, on
r. Oconee. Its motto: Doubling all the time,' Joyce wrote to Harriet
Weaver in November 1926 (*L* 1:247–8). The reference to 'topsawyer's
rocks by the stream Oconee,' a sizeable river in the American state of
Georgia, builds on the potential reference to North America in the phrase
'North Armorica.' The combination of rocks (already suggesting HCE),
a river (suggesting ALP), and a North American Dublin (confirming the
reference to HCE) abruptly, if only temporarily, alters both the place and
the time of the action, from the Old World to the New and from the
European Middle Ages to the American nineteenth century. More importantly, it establishes a link between them, since the new-world Dublin
was founded by a scion of the old-world Dublin. As Anthony Burgess
puts it, 'Joyce is concerned with hinting that the events of history repeat
themselves, not only in time but in space as well: what happens in the
Old World happens also in the New' (1966, 22).

The American context is doubly reinforced by the phrase 'topsawyer's rocks.' Few readers are likely to know without consulting a professional commentary that Topsawyer's Rock is the name of a natural for-
mation on the Oconee River (McHugh 1980, 3), but most English-speaking

readers at least will very likely be struck by the evocation of Tom Sawyer, whose boyhood escapades on the Mississippi River in the American South are recounted in the hugely popular *Adventures of Tom Sawyer* (1876) by the likewise American writer Mark Twain (Samuel Langhorne Clemens). The term *top sawyer* itself was a technical term in American logging circles: a top sawyer worked the upper handle of a two-handled crosscut pit-saw, while the lower handle was worked by a pit sawyer.

Once again, however, the links are bidirectional. 'Topsawyer' evokes Tom Sawyer, which evokes Mark Twain, whose name in turn evokes the Mark of the Tristan legend, suggesting a second Mark, or 'Mark Twain.' One of Tom Sawyer's escapades is to put in an unexpected appearance, alive and well, at his own funeral, thus evoking Tim Finnegan's funeral resurrection. Tom's escapades are shared by his friend Huck Finn – later the protagonist of the *Adventures of Huckleberry Finn* (1884) – whose name echoes that of the Irish giant buried by Joyce under Dublin, Ireland. 'Interestingly enough, Samuel Clemens called his wife "Livy"' (Campbell and Robinson 1961, 28n5). Meanwhile, just as the reference to Sir Tristram's 'penisolate war' evoked the warring pair Wellington and Napoleon, so the mention of a top sawyer implies the existence of a bottom sawyer occupying an inferior position, once again anticipating the rivalry of the warring brothers Shem and Shaun.

The reference to 'the stream Oconee' likewise strongly evokes American culture, the exotic name of the river and the trochaic rhythm of the phrase combining to recall the American poet Henry Wadsworth Longfellow's once immensely popular *Song of Hiawatha* (1855). But again the link is bidirectional, for while the name *Oconee* does indeed have what to European ears is no doubt both an exotic name and an exotic meaning – a totemic 'people (*o*) of the skunk (*conee*)' – in the Muscogee or Creek Indian language of the American Southeast (Anon. 2008), many Irish readers will see it instead as suggesting (parodically or otherwise) the Hiberno-English *ochone* (from the Irish *ochón*, 'alas'), a cry of lamentation very likely uttered by many poverty-stricken nineteenth-century Irish emigrants to the United States.

Fritz Senn sees a link in quite a different key: following on the overtly male sexual possibilities of 'topsawyer's rocks,' he now detects in the stream Oconee 'a strong female (and riverine) element,' reinforcing 'birth (as in *née*) and perhaps the place of birth (if *con* is taken to be French): the first letter, *O* – round and open and gaping – will acquire iconic significance later in the book' (1995, 51).

[1]   *nor had topsawyer's rocks by the stream Oconee*

du Bouchet (French, 1962): marmerocs de sommescieur le long du calme Oconee

Lavergne (French, 1982): près du fleuve Oconee les roches premières

Wilcock (Italian, 1961): le alte rocce accanto al fiume Oconee

Burgess (Italian, 1975): i sassoni tomsawyereschi huckfinneschi sul ruscello Oconee

Schenoni (Italian, 1978): i roccoglioni del tommiglior sawyergantino presso l'Oconee

Schenoni (Italian, 1982): le topsawyer's rocks presso il fiume Oconee

Elizondo (Spanish, 1992): las rocas del alto psawrrador, esparcidas a lo largo del arroyo Oconee,

Pozanco (Spanish, 1993): los dentados riscos de junto al Oconee

Victoria (Spanish, 2009): piedras de [jonathan] altosawyer por el riachuelo Oconee

Campos (Portuguese, 1962): os calhaus do altom sawyerrador pelo rio Oconee

Lourenço (Portuguese, 1968): as rochas de Pedro Sawyer [*text missing*]

Schüler (Portuguese, 2003): as pétreas bolotas de Sawyer ao longo do Oconee caudaloso

Pagán (Galician, 2000): os altoms penedos do sawyerrador no arroio Oconee

Beck (German, 1989): topsawyers felsen am Oconeeflüßchen

Jauslin (German, 1989): die Felsen des sawyerlichen Oberschwätzers am Fluß Oconee

Rathjen (German, 1989): Topsawyers Felsen am Oconeelauf

Schrödter (German, 1989): die Topsäygers Felsen beim Strome Oconee

Stündel (German, 1993): die Top-Saweiherischen Felsen … am Strom des Oconee

Bindervoet and Henkes (Dutch, 2002): topzooiers rotshopen aan de
Oconee-stroom

In French, du Bouchet's decidedly cryptic French version, 'marmerocs
de sommescieur,' renders 'topsawyer' as 'sommescieur,' which combines Latin *summa* ('topmost'), French *scieur* ('sawyer'), and French
somme ('nap, forty winks') to provide an approximate rhyming equivalent (in French phonetics) of 'Tom Sawyer' as well as suggesting a not
particularly energetic Tom who might well emulate Tim Finnegan in
tumbling from his perch. Joyce's simple 'rocks' is exaggerated into
complicated 'marmerocs,' the term conflating two others – ancient and
modern, foreign and domestic – namely Greek *mármaros* and French
roc, both meaning 'rock.' Some readers may detect in this ostentatiously
learned construct a linguistic echo of *mamelouk*s ('mamelukes'), a warlike body of rebellious thirteenth-century Caucasian slaves who 'exaggerated' themselves sufficiently to seize the throne of Egypt. Others
may detect a fluvial hint of the French river Marne, anticipating the
French Somme, both of them exaggeratedly anticipating the American
river Oconee. Lavergne's French version (the only one, incidentally, to
reverse the order of the opening two phrases) chooses a very different
strategy, simplifying things initially with 'les roches premières,' literally 'the first rocks,' but allowing readers to take this as meaning 'the
primeval rocks' and thus invoking the Greek foundation myth of
Deucalion, who sowed rocks that turned into men.

In Italian, Wilcock simplifies the phrase even further to 'le alte rocce,'
literally 'the high rocks,' which he explains in a note as an allusion to the
Flood (1961, 1130). Burgess prefers a more Baroque 'i sassoni tomsawyereschi huckfinneschi,' where *sassoni* means 'large stones' but also puns
on *Sassoni* as meaning 'Saxons,' which in Irish (and Scottish) usage, as
'Sassanachs,' means 'English.' 'I sassoni' may thus perhaps be taken as
indicating the irremediable foreignness of the rocks in question, albeit
adjectivally qualified as both 'tomsawyereschi' and, for good measure,
'huckfinneschi' as well, which is to say, 'à la Tom Sawyer and Huck Finn,'
the latter, of course, permitting a passing reference also to Joyce's Irish
Finn. Burgess's expansive phrasing here is reminiscent of his similarly
expansive 'giambattistamente comodo' in rendering the phrase 'a commodious vicus of recirculation' (*FW* 3.2). This method of what one might
call infixed annotation is somewhat similar to (and considerably more
elegant than) that much later used in various instances in Victoria's
Spanish transposition of the *Wake*'s opening chapter.

In similarly expansive vein, the earlier Schenoni adopts 'i roccoglioni tel tommiglior sawyergantino,' where the rocks have metamorphosed into 'roccoglioni,' a combination of *rocche* ('rocks') and *coglioni* ('testicles'), while Tom Sawyer reveals himself as a sawyer both already 'superior' (*migliore*) and, no doubt in the course of his procreative endeavours, in the process of 'rising' (*ergente*) even further. It is noticeable that Schenoni's 1978 version frequently deviates further from Joyce's text than his 1982 revision of it. In this instance the later and less adventurous version shows him deciding that Joyce's original formulation is preferable and reverting to an interlingual 'le topsawyer's rocks.'

Three quite different strategies also emerge in Spanish, strikingly involving three different renditions of the simple term 'rocks.' Elizondo decides for 'las rocas' ('the rocks') 'del alto psawrrador,' where 'topsawyer' is distributed across the final two words, 'alto' ('high') and a very un-Spanish 'psawrrador,' based on Spanish *aserrador* ('sawyer'). Pozanco opts for 'los dentados riscos,' literally 'the jagged crags,' significantly enhancing the Romantic wildness of the scene but only at the cost of omitting all other resonances. Victoria, for his part, refers to the 'piedras de [jonathan] altosawyer,' where 'piedras de altosawyer' translates as an interlingual 'rocks of high-sawyer.' Victoria's system of infixed annotation, together with a play on the Spanish *piedra* ('rock'), also allows him to correct in passing Joyce's identification of the founder of Dublin, Georgia, whose given name was actually *Jonathan* rather than *Peter* (Spanish *Pedro*).

In Portuguese, we again find three different versions of 'rocks' in as many translations, Campos preferring 'calhaus,' Lourenço 'rochas,' and Schüler 'bolotas.' Campos (anticipating Elizondo's strategy above) distributes Tom Sawyer across his 'do altom sawyerrador,' playing on Portuguese *alto* ('high') and *serrador* ('sawyer'), while Lourenço's 'as rochas de Pedro Sawyer' abandons Tom in favour of his translated namesake, the misnamed Peter. As is frequently the case, Schüler's is the most adventurous of the Portuguese versions: 'as pétreas bolotas de Sawyer' retranslates literally as 'the rocky acorns of Sawyer,' making use of the Greek *pétra* and Latin *petra* ('rock') and their relationship to the name *Peter* – like Lourenço, Schüler sees Peter Sawyer rather than Tom as the more important referent. His use of *bolotas* ('acorns') for 'rocks' overtly emphasizes the sexual connotation of Joyce's term, while also hinting (in colloquial Brazilian usage) that these acorns from which great oaks may grow are likely to lead not only to a 'bunch' (*bolo*) of descendants but also a bunch of 'trouble' (*bolo*). One striking point about all three versions is that none takes advantage of the fact that Portuguese *serra* means both 'saw' and 'mountain, mountain ridge, mountain range,' providing an inviting potential bridge between 'rocks' and 'sawyer.' Pagán's Galician version, 'os altoms penedos do sawyer-rador,' employs a very similar strategy to Campos's Portuguese version discussed above, while translating 'rocks' as *penedos*, a term whose possible sexual implications are considerably enhanced by an embedded Italian *pene* ('penis').

Moving to German, we find that all five translators render 'rocks' as 'Felsen,' with both Beck ('topsawyers felsen') and Rathjen ('Topsawyers Felsen') content to employ a translingual replication of Joyce's original wordplay on 'topsawyer.' The other German translators propose different responses to the latter challenge: Schrödter's 'Topsäygers Felsen' embeds the German *Säger* ('sawyer'), while Stündel's 'Top-Saweiherischen Felsen' embeds the water reference *Weiher* ('pond'), but both of these choices largely occlude the reference to Tom Sawyer. Jauslin's 'Felsen des sawyerlichen Oberschwätzers,' on the other hand, retains the reference in 'sawyerlich,' pronounced almost exactly like the German adjective *säuerlich* ('sour-faced') but only by introducing the noun *Oberschwätzer*, implying a top dog who is also the 'chief wind-bag.'

In Dutch, Bindervoet and Henkes opt for 'topzooiers rotshopen,' where 'topzooier,' substituting *zooi* ('mob') for *zaag* ('saw'), achieves an almost exact translingual echo of our 'topsawyer,' who, however, is momentarily transformed into a top mobster rather than a lumberjack. The individual 'rocks' of Joyce's English, meanwhile, are appropriately exaggerated (Latin *agger*, 'heap of rocks') into nothing less than whole 'heaps (*hopen*) of rock (*rots*).'

The phrase 'by the stream Oconee' generates rather less translatorial excitement, but still allows for some quite interesting divergences of opinion. In French, du Bouchet renders it as 'le long du calme Oconee.' The fact that the stream is now said to be 'calm' (*calme*) may be the result of the possible presence of the river Somme in 'sommescieur,' since toponymists see the name *Somme* as derived from a Celtic *Samara*, meaning 'tranquil, calm' (possibly cognate with Irish *sámh*, 'gentle'). Lavergne limits himself to 'près du fleuve Oconee.' While Lavergne's chosen preposition 'près' merely implies 'near,' perhaps only at one single point, du Bouchet's 'le long de' implies 'along,' suggesting that the rocks in question extend along the river's banks for some distance.

Lavergne translates 'stream' as 'fleuve,' we notice, while du Bouchet leaves the word untranslated. We find a similar situation in Italian, where the earlier Schenoni likewise leaves it untranslated ('presso l'Oconee'), only to reintroduce the noun in his later version ('presso il fiume Oconee'). Wilcock has 'accanto al fiume Oconee,' while Burgess prefers 'sul ruscello Oconee.' The difference in meaning between the various prepositions employed – *presso, accanto a, sul* – does not appear to be significant, but we may notice that Burgess's 'ruscello' suggests a rather less impressive stream, a mere brook, while Wilcock's and Schenoni's 'fiume' implies a more significant river in both cases.

In Spanish, we once again find a similar situation, with Pozanco's 'junto al Oconee' making no reference to the size of the stream, Victoria's 'por el riachuelo Oconee' definitely referring to an insignificant streamlet (*riachuelo*), and Elizondo's 'a lo largo del arroyo Oconee' referring to an only slightly more imposing brook (*arroyo*). Pozanco's 'junto al' suggests the rocks in question are 'near' the river, and Victoria's 'por' suggests they are 'on' the river, while Elizondo's 'a lo largo' seems to 'exaggerate' them once again in implying the existence of numerous rocks 'along' its course, as in the case of du Bouchet's French rendering.

Campos's Portuguese 'pelo rio Oconee' and Pagán's Galician 'no arroio Oconee' call for no further comment, but Schüler's Portuguese version, 'ao longo do Oconee caudaloso,' suggests not only (and like Elizondo's Spanish rendering) various rocks along (*ao longo de*) the course of the river but also a river that, far from being a mere streamlet or brook, is now nothing less than 'mighty, torrential' (*caudaloso*) – perhaps reminding occasional Irish readers that the Liffey too was formerly called *An Ruirthech* ('the tempestuous one'). Among German versions, and near-synonyms describing rivers, Schrödter and Stündel both refer to the Oconee as a 'Strom,' suggesting a broad river, while Jauslin prefers a 'Fluß,' non-committal as to size, and Beck takes the opposite view to Schüler's Portuguese version in calling it merely a 'Flüßchen' ('brook, rivulet'). Rathjen's 'am Oconeelauf' once again implies rocks along the 'course' (*Lauf*) of the river. In Dutch, Bindervoet and Henkes opt for an unadorned and non-commital 'aan de Oconee-stroom.'

While all of the above leave the name of the Oconee untranslated – despite the inviting similarity of the Hiberno-English *ochone* – two other versions undertake to do so. In Mutanen's Finnish rendering ('olleet pohjoisen Okeanoon') the Oconee mutates majestically into the 'Okeanoon,' evoking the world-girdling river personified in Greek mythology by the Titan Okeanos. In Królikowski's Polish version ('w potoku O'Ceanilnym') the same stream (*potok*) of Ocean, on which the entire habitable world floated, is once again evoked, this time in its Latin rather than Greek form – but, given the context of *Finnegans Wake*, decoratively enhanced for good measure by an Irish patronymic apostrophe. *Honi soit qui mal y pense.*

[2] . *exaggerated themselse to Laurens County's gorgios*

du Bouchet (French, 1962): s'étaient pour lors exagerés en gorgios de Laurens County

Lavergne (French, 1982): s'étaient exaltruées en splendide Georgi Dublin de Laurens Comptez

Wilcock (Italian, 1961): si erano ... esagerate fino ai gorghi della contea di Laurens

Burgess (Italian, 1975): ci erano esagerati ai gorghi gorgolianti di Laurens County (Gorgia)

Schenoni (Italian, 1978): si altrerano ingigantiti fino ai giorgi della contea di Laurens,

Schenoni (Italian, 1982): s'altrerano ingrandite fino ai gorgi della Laurens County

Elizondo (Spanish, 1992): exagerádose a sí otras mismas a los gorgios del Condado de Laurens

Pozanco (Spanish, 1993): se habían recrecido aún en la exuberancia de Laurens County

Victoria (Spanish, 2009): exageradas ellasmismás hasta [ser] jorgios [no gitanos] fabulosos del condado de Laurens

Campos (Portuguese, 1962): sexagerado aos górgios de Laurens County

Lourenço (Portuguese, 1968): se tinham dublixagerado ... até os gorgios do Condado de Laurens

Schüler (Portuguese, 2003): se tinham seggsagerado ao território laurenciano da Geórgia

Pagán (Galician, 2000): se converteran outramente na magnífica garganta de Laurens County

Beck (German, 1989): hochgestapelt zu Laurens-Lands georgiosem
dubling

Jauslin (German, 1989): andersgetürmt zur GiorgioSchlucht von
Laurens County,

Rathjen (German, 1989): einanders aufgeworfen zu Laurensbezirksgeäugiern

Schrödter (German, 1989): höchstselbst über Laurens Countys
gorgos getrieben

Stündel (German, 1993): aufgehäuft zu Laurens Land,

Bindervoet and Henkes (Dutch, 2002): zichcelverlei gecumulleerd
naar Laurenslands gorgio's

'Nor had topsawyer's rocks by the stream Oconee exaggerated themselse.' Translators have a number of options in deciding how best to
render 'exaggerated' in the context of Joyce's phrase. First, they can
render the literal dictionary meaning of the verb, namely 'to overstate,
to claim too much.' Second, they can attempt to take advantage of etymology, remembering that the Latin noun *agger* denotes 'heap, mound,
pile,' as of rocks, and that the verb *exaggerare* means literally 'to heap
up, accumulate,' as well as figuratively 'to claim too much.' Third, they
can seize on the fact that 'piling up the rocks' has been slang since the
mid-nineteenth century for 'making money' (Partridge 1972, 771).
Fourth, they may choose to remember that 'rocks' is also slang for 'testicles,' as Molly Bloom – 'O, rocks!' (*U* 4.343) – was well aware. Fifth,
they may attempt to combine any or all of the above. All renderings, it
should be mentioned, incorporate at some point a negative phrase
meaning 'nor' or 'not,' which thus calls for no further discussion.

The first group is well populated, with du Bouchet, Wilcock, Burgess,
and Elizondo all availing themselves of the corresponding dictionary
term for *exaggerated* in the respective target language. Pozanco's Spanish
'se habían recrecido' incorporates a suggestion of 'regrown' (*recrecido*)
as well as 'increased,' while Pagán's Galician 'se converteran' suggests
'had turned themselves into.'

The second group, drawing on etymology, is represented by Stündel's
German 'aufgehäuft,' literally 'heaped up,' and by Bindervoet and
Henkes's Dutch 'gecumulleerd,' roughly 'piled themselves up.' The lat-
ter version might be read by some as a passing nod to our resident giant

Finn, whose father, Cumhall, was once regarded by Celtic scholars as an avatar of the Gaulish war god Camulos, a position since abandoned (Green 1992, 141). The third possibility remains purely theoretical: none of our translators chooses to see any reference to money, despite Campbell and Robinson's observation that in the image of the opposed sawyers 'the sawyer on top is the successful one; his "rocks" (slang for "money") "exaggerate themselves," that is to say, increase' (1961, 28). The fourth group, invoking sex, is only slightly more populated. Campos's 'sexagerado' conflates English *sex* and Portuguese *exagerado* ('exaggerated'), while Schüler's 'seggsagerado' conflates both of these as well as English *eggs*, the latter (whether English or not) a potent symbol of rebirth and regeneration.

The fifth group, involving combinations of various kinds, is the largest. Lavergne's French 'exaltruées' combines *exalter* ('to exalt') and *s'éxalter* ('to grow excited'), with a suggestion of Latin *alter*, French *autre* ('other'). Schenoni's earlier 'ingigantiti' suggests having become 'gigantic' (*ingigantiti*), modified less flamboyantly in his later version to merely 'magnified' (*ingrandite*). Lourenço's 'dublixagerado' combines Portuguese *duplicar* ('to duplicate, repeat') and *exagerar* ('to exaggerate') with a strong hint of *Dublin*. In German, Beck's 'hochgestapelt' combines *stapeln* ('to pile up') and *hochstapeln* ('to swindle someone'), while Rathjen's 'aufgeworfen,' in similar vein, combines *aufwerfen* ('to pile up') and *sich zu etwas aufwerfen* ('to set oneself up as something'). Jauslin's 'andersgetürmt,' suggesting 'otherwise towered up,' economically evokes the Tower of Babel. Schrödter goes his own way with the formulation 'sich ... höchstselbst ... getrieben,' suggesting 'had forced (*getrieben*) their very selves (*höchstselbst*) to great heights (*höchst*).'

As for 'themselse,' which Joyce explained to Harriet Weaver as referring to 'another dublin 5000 inhabitants,' a number of versions domesticate its conflation of self and other by rendering it as meaning simply 'themselves': thus du Bouchet in French, Wilcock and Burgess in Italian, Pozanco in Spanish, all three Portuguese translators, and Schrödter and Stündel in German. Other versions use a variety of compensatory strategies. In French, Lavergne's 'exaltruées' suggests Latin *alter* ('other'). In Italian, Schenoni's 'si altrerano' translates roughly as 'they othered themselves.' In Spanish, Elizondo's 'sí otras mismas' combines 'themselves' (*sí mismas*) and 'others' (*otras*), while Victoria's 'ellas-mismás' conflates 'themselves' (*ellas mismas*) and 'more' (*más*). In Galician, Pagán's 'outramente' means 'otherwise.' In German, Rathjen's 'einanders' conflates 'one another' (*einander*) and 'otherwise' (*anders*), while Jauslin's 'andersgetürmt,' as we noted, also includes 'otherwise.' Beck's 'sich hochgestapelt,' as we have seen, suggests 'swindled themselves in piling themselves up.' In Dutch, finally, Bindervoet and Henkes's 'zichcelverlei' effectively conflates *zichzelf* ('themselves'), an orthographic disruption ('-celv-') of *zelf* ('self, selves'), and a dislocational play on the verb *verleggen* ('to shift, put elsewhere').

Laurens County, one of 159 counties in the state of Georgia, is named for Colonel John Laurens (1754–82), an aide-de-camp to General George Washington during the American Revolutionary War. More immediately important in the context of *Finnegans Wake*, its county seat is the city of Dublin, Georgia. Serendipitously, the name *Laurens* provides an onomastic link to Sir Amory Tristram, under whose leadership a Norman force defeated the Danes and Irish of Howth at the Battle of Evora, just north of the present site of the village of Howth, on 10 August 1177, the feast of the third-century Roman martyr St Lawrence, whose name Sir Amory thereupon adopted in gratitude. A second transatlantic link is provided by the fact that the patron saint of Dublin, Ireland, is St Laurence O'Toole (1123–80), who was archbishop of Dublin at the time of Sir Amory's arrival on Howth. A third link points the reader to Laurence Sterne, author of another highly eccentric narrative, *The Life and Opinions of Tristram Shandy, Gentleman* (1759–67), and whose Irish connections (he was born in Clonmel, County Tipperary), though not yet looming large, will certainly also not remain long forgotten in *Finnegans Wake*. Among the many topics on which Sterne's garrulous narrator expatiates at length is the influence of one's name, in his own case thus none other than *Tristram* (which, he recalls, his father had thought, all things considered, the worst possible name for an infant).

The phrase 'Laurens County' is retained untranslated by several of our translators: thus du Bouchet in French, Burgess and the later Schenoni in Italian, Pozanco in Spanish, Campos in Portuguese, Pagán in Galician, Jauslin and Schrödter in German. Others retain the name *Laurens* but translate or otherwise readjust the term *County*: thus Lavergne's 'Comptez,' playing on French *comté* ('county') and, suggesting successful capitalist endeavour, *compter* ('to count'); Wilcock's and the earlier Schenoni's Italian 'contea'; Elizondo's and Victoria's Spanish 'condado'; Lourenço's Portuguese 'Condado'; Beck's and Stündel's German 'Land'; Rathjen's German 'Bezirk'; Bindervoet and Henkes's Dutch 'land.' Schüler's Portuguese opts for 'o território laurenciano,' literally 'the Laurentian territory.' One may note in passing that Królikowski's Polish 'Hrabstwa Laurennego,' Malicki's Polish 'Laurena Hrabstwa,' and Mutanen's Finnish 'Laurenaasian Kreivicounnan' all appear to be based on a county allegedly named *Lauren* rather than *Laurens*. Readers of these versions would consequently have considerably greater difficulty in recognizing the Irish links provided by the rhyming *Laurens*, *Lawrence*, and *Laurence*.

Considerably greater excitement and variety are generated by Joyce's 'gorgios.' That term, according to the *Oxford Dictionary of English Etymology* (Onions 1966), has its origins in the Romany *gorgio* and entered English during the nineteenth century, initially as a 'gipsies' name for one who is not a gipsy.' Equivalents in other languages include German *gadscho* and Spanish *gacho*. In English, the term came eventually to mean also a 'youngster,' that is to say, one not yet a full gipsy; a 'well-dressed gentleman,' and thus presumably not a gipsy; or even just a 'man' (Partridge 1972, 392). Joyce's use of the term may thus be read on one level as an evocation of the invader motif, the struggle between insiders and outsiders, natives and foreigners. Alternatively, or additionally, we may see the *gorgios* as the 'youngsters' who are the fruit of Topsawyer's testicular rocks (Campbell and Robinson 1961, 28n6). In comparison with the citizens of Dublin, Ireland, those of Dublin, Georgia, are indeed 'youngsters,' who like the gipsies (literally, if mistakenly, 'Egyptians') came from the east, as invaders of Dublin, Ireland, have also typically come. As 'well-dressed gentlemen' of gorgeous aspect or even just as 'men' in general who are born from rocks, a link is established to the Greek myth of Deucalion, a variant of which we shall shortly be encountering in the biblical myth of Noah. In the context of fathers and sons, many readers have also detected the presence of Joyce's own son Giorgio (1905–76) – whose name, we may note, derives from the Greek *geōrgós* ('earth-worker, farmer').

Some of our translators simply leave the term untranslated: thus du Bouchet in French, Elizondo in Spanish, Campos and Lourenço in Portuguese, Bindervoet and Henkes in Dutch. Some are tempted by the surface similarity of the Italian *gorgo* ('whirlpool, abyss'): thus Wilcock's 'gorghi' ('whirlpools'), rendered more picturesquely romantic in Burgess's alliterating 'gorghi gorgolianti' ('gurgling whirlpools') in a Laurens County now situated not in Georgia but in 'Gorgia,' a land presumably of gorges as well as whirlpools – and whose inhabitants speak with a noticeable accent (Italian *gorgia*, 'burr, brogue'). At least one gorge also appears in Pagán's Galician, which opts for 'garganta' (literally 'gorge'), while Schrödter's 'gorgos' adds a German plural ending to an Italian *gorgo* in order to play on the Greek *gorgós* ('grim, fierce, terrible').

Giorgio Joyce appears in several guises and combinations. The early Schenoni chooses 'giorgi,' conflating *gorghi* ('whirlpools') and *Giorgio*; the later Schenoni achieves the same effect more economically with 'gorgi.' Jauslin's German 'GiorgioSchlucht' (literally 'Giorgio gorge') works somewhat less euphoniously, and rather too obviously, with a similar combination. Schüler's Portuguese reference to 'Geórgia' economically includes a reference to Giorgio as well as to the relevant state. Victoria's Spanish 'jorgios' combines Joyce's 'gorgios' and *Jorge*, the Spanish form of the Italian *Giorgio*. Others also detect a reference to the Georgian architecture of Dublin, Ireland: thus Lavergne's rendering, 'en splendide Georgi Dublin,' very roughly 'in splendid Georgian Dublin,' with a complementary hint of *Giorgio*. Beck's German also speaks of a 'georgiosem dubling,' playing interlingually on a 'gorgeous,' 'Georgian,' and doubled Dublin, likewise with an echo of *Giorgio*.

The most complex version is Rathjen's '-geäugiern,' which humorously conflates a colloquial *r*-dropping North German pronunciation of *Georg* (the German form of *Giorgio*), *Georgien* (the German form of *Georgia*), and *Georgier* ('Georgians') with the verb *äugen* ('to ogle'), the latter presumably as a result of the gorgios' gorgeousness. Pozanco's Spanish goes its own way in less complex fashion with 'la exuberancia de Laurens County,' roughly 'the gorgeousness of Laurens County,' while Stündel, possibly inadvertently, omits the term altogether.

[3]   *while they went doublin their mumper all the time:*

du Bouchet (French, 1962): doublin l'arrombe de mot en mot:

Lavergne (French, 1982): en doublant ses membres tout le temps:

Wilcock (Italian, 1961): mentre il loro numero si raddublinava continuamente;

Burgess (Italian, 1975): quando sempre sempre dubilavano il loro proprio Dublino;

Schenoni (Italian, 1978): continuando a raddublinare il loro mammero;

Schenoni (Italian, 1982): mentre continuavano a raddublinare per tutto il tempo il loro mùmpero:

Elizondo (Spanish, 1992): mientras iban dubliando todo el tiempo su mendiganancia;

Pozanco (Spanish, 1993): a fuerza de redublinar sus pobres miembros:

Victoria (Spanish, 2009): mientras fueron dubliando su número [de mendigos (má's y padres) ininteligibles huraños & tramposos] todo el tiempo:

Campos (Portuguese, 1962): enquanto êles iam dublando os bebêbados todo o tempo:[1]

Lourenço (Portuguese, 1968): enquanto que elas continuavam a dublinar o seu nâmero:

Schüler (Portuguese, 2003): enquanto se dublinavam em mamypa-pypares o tempo todo:

Pagán (Galician, 2000): redublinando a sua probeza todo o tempo:

Beck (German, 1989): dubling seine schmarotzahl all die weil:

Jauslin (German, 1989): allweil nur ihren VerdRuß zu verdublin;

Rathjen (German, 1989): während sie die ganze Zeit ihre Unzoll verdopplinten:

Schrödter (German, 1989): während sie doch all die Weil ihre KNümmerlichkeit verdoubblin gingen:

Stündel (German, 1993): obgleich sie ihre Anzoll die ganze Zeit über verdublint hatten:

Bindervoet and Henkes (Dutch, 2002): wijl ze gehelenal de tijd hun worpelingen verdubbelinden:

According to the *New Georgia Encyclopedia* (Anon. 2003), the city of Dublin, Georgia, was incorporated in 1812, and was given its name by the prosperous Irish-born merchant and postmaster Jonathan Sawyer, who also donated the land for the town, in honour of his Irish wife's native city (and, according to local legend, so that having been born in Dublin she could also be buried in Dublin). During a period of rapid

---

1   The Campos translation breaks off here.

growth in the early twentieth century, Dublin, by some accounts at least, proudly laid claim to being 'the only city in Georgia that's doublin' all the time.' Situated halfway between Savannah and Atlanta, Dublin has since quadrupled in size and now boasts a city population of approximately 20,000. Locally known as the Emerald City, it hosts a two-week-long St Patrick's Festival, featuring (by popular demand) both the World's Biggest Irish Stew and a Leprechaun Contest.

Few of our translators have any trouble with 'doublin' and its double reference to two Dublins – but though all render it with a pun on a target-language term for 'doubling,' it is striking that very few render it in the same fashion in the same language. In French, we thus find 'doublin' (du Bouchet) and 'doublant' (Lavergne); in Italian, 'raddublinava' (Wilcock), 'dubilavano' (Burgess), and 'raddublinare' (Schenoni); in Spanish, 'dubliando' (Elizondo, Victoria) and 'redublinar' (Pozanco); in Portuguese, 'dublando' (Campos) and 'dublinar' (Lourenço, Schüler); in Galician, 'redublinando' (Pagán); in German, 'dubling' (Beck), 'verdublin' (Jauslin, Stündel), 'verdopplinten' (Rathjen), and 'verdoubblin' (Schrödter); and in Dutch, 'verdubbelinden' (Bindervoet and Henkes). We may even add Russian 'dublinirovali,' Polish 'dwublinili' (Królikowski) and 'doublin' (Malicki), and Finnish 'tuplin' (Mutanen). Burgess's Italian adds a supplementary doubling flourish: 'sempre sempre dubilavano,' suggesting this doubled Dublin doubling 'always, always.'

The object of all this doubling, the Joycean 'mumper,' extends our translators' efforts to a considerably greater extent. The invaluable Partridge (1972, 602) informs us that the verb *to mump* (from Dutch *mompen*, 'to cheat') entered seventeenth-century English in the sense of 'to deceive, to cheat' and is also found in the sense 'to beg,' resulting in a 'mumper' being thus variously a beggar, a sponger, or, as of the nineteenth century, with blissful disregard for racial equity, a 'half-bred Gypsy.' However, *to mump* can also mean just a relatively inoffensive 'to mumble' (*OED*), and we may also decide to take into account the clearly related Norwegian *mumpa* ('to stuff one's mouth'), Icelandic *mumpa* ('to eat greedily'), and German *mampfen* ('to munch, to chomp'), all suggesting that Joyce's 'mumper' primarily implies the 'number of mouths to feed.' Finally, there is of course the punning implication that the (male) inhabitants of Dublin, Georgia, are doubling their number only by dint of conscientiously doubling the size of their (virile) member 'all the time' in the course of active procreational service.

In French, du Bouchet's 'doublin l'arrombe de mot en mot' conflates *leur nombre* ('their number') and *larron* ('thief'), while 'de mot en mot' (literally 'from word to word') translingually doubles as the English 'more and more.' Lavergne has them doubling 'ses membres,' literally 'their members,' where French allows the same play as English on *membre viril* ('penis'). In Italian, Wilcock has them doubling their 'numero' ('number'), while for Burgess they were doubling 'il loro proprio Dublino' ('their own Dublin'). In Schenoni's earlier version the object of the exercise is their 'mammero,' apparently doubling not only their *numero* ('number') but also the number of ladies who become a *mamma*; his later version prefers a closer approximation to the original, his 'mùmpero' preserving all of Joyce's linguistic indeterminacy.

In Spanish, Pozanco speaks of 'sus pobres miembros,' literally 'their poor members,' where *miembro* can once again also mean 'penis.' Elizondo takes a bleak view of the results of such activity: for him they are merely cynically doubling the amount of financial 'gain' (*ganancia*) they can make from 'begging' (*mendigante*). Victoria has them doubling their 'número' ('number'), but adds parenthetically (and somewhat judgmentally) that that increasing number (*más*, 'more') is composed of 'mendigos' ('beggars'), some of them mothers ('má's') and some of them fathers ('padres'), but all of them unintelligible ('ininteligibles'), unsociable ('huraños'), and swindlers ('tramposos').

In Portuguese, Lourenço sees them doubling their 'nâmero,' conflating *número* ('number') and *namoro* ('love-making'), while Campos, attributing their excessive activity in this area to the effects of alcohol, soberly anticipates a doubling of the number of drunks as well as that of babies, his 'bebêbados' conflating *bebê* ('baby') and *bêbado* ('drunk'). Schüler, deconstructing 'mumper' as composed of English *mum* ('mother') and French *père* ('father'), likewise sees no particularly positive results of the projected growth, likely merely to produce a new generation of 'mamypapypares,' offspring who are carbon copies (Latin *pares*, 'equals') of their mammies and daddies. Pagán's Galician version sees the whole exercise as merely perpetuating their state of poverty, albeit honest poverty: his 'probeza' conflates *pobreza* ('poverty') and *probo* ('honest, upright').

In Dutch, Bindervoet and Henkes characterize their doubled progeny without any marked degree of enthusiasm as 'hun worpelingen,' the numerous products of their *worp* ('litter'), no more individualized than puppies or piglets. In German, Jauslin thinks their excesses are merely doubling their Malthusian 'VerdRuß,' a term conflating *Verdruss* ('frustration') and *Russ*, presumably the 'soot' and smoke of the rampant industrial development necessitated. Other German translators are even more censorious. Beck sees the number being doubled as already a 'schmarotzahl,' which is to say, the number (*Zahl*) of *Schmarotzer* ('parasites, freeloaders'). There is general agreement that the growth of all kinds involved is excessive: Rathjen speaks of an 'Unzoll,' Stündel of an 'Anzoll,' in both cases playing on not just the *Anzahl* ('number') but rather the *Unzahl* ('enormous number') of progeny involved, not to mention a complementary play on *Zoll* ('inch'), suggesting both the measure of procreational endeavour involved and the inevitable 'toll' (*Zoll*) that it will all eventually take. Schrödter similarly sees their efforts as merely doubling their 'KNümmerlichkeit,' which is to say, not just their *Nummer* ('number') but to a corresponding degree their *Kümmerlichkeit* ('wretchedness').

'The drift of this dense passage,' Campbell and Robinson suggest, referring to the whole clause, 'is as follows: A successful son of HCE emigrates from East to West, as his father before him. Settling in America he begets a large progeny and bequeaths them a decent, even gorgeous prosperity' (1961, 28). To which, half a century later, one can only respond: well, maybe, but clearly the drift is not the same for all readers, as we have just seen. The number of possibilities explored by our multilingual translators in rendering the single clause considered here provides striking support for Fritz Senn's wry observation on the cumulative activities of the Joycean critical industry, its participants continually 'exaggerating' themselves and determinedly doubling their numbers all the time, as they unrelentingly 'pile meanings upon meanings in extrapolative excess' (1995, 51).

[4]   *nor avoice from afire bellowsed mishe mishe*

du Bouchet (French, 1962): [*text missing*]

Lavergne (French, 1982): nulle voix humaine n'avait dessouflé son micmac

Wilcock (Italian, 1961): né la voce dal fuoco aveva risoffiato mishe mishe

Burgess (Italian, 1975): neppure una voce di fuocofuori aveva soffiettato mishe mishe

Schenoni (Italian, 1978): né voce da fuoco aveva mugghiato mishe mishe

Schenoni (Italian, 1982): né 'navoce da 'nfoco aveva soffiorato mishe mishe

Elizondo (Spanish, 1992): ni una voz salida del fuego surgía diciendo mishe mishe

Pozanco (Spanish, 1993): ni bramó una voz ardiente la pifia

Victoria (Spanish, 2009): ni unavoz de unfuego [había] bramadicho
mishe mishe [yo(soy)yo]

Lourenço (Portuguese, 1968): nem uma voz vinda do fogo tinha
rugido mishe mishe

Schüler (Portuguese, 2003): nem avoz do fogo rebellava mim-She,
mim-She

Pagán (Galician, 2000): nen avoz desde a chamas lle resoprara mixe
mixe

Beck (German, 1989): noch fauchte kein stimm fern aus dem feuer
mischmisch

Jauslin (German, 1989): noch schrie keine Stimme, vergebens, vom
Herdfeuer, vermessin, vermißihn,

Rathjen (German, 1989): noch neStimmede aus deFeuerne michsiemaschsie blaßgebalgt

Schrödter (German, 1989): noch anfeuerte eintstimmen von eintflammen mishe mishe

Stündel (German, 1993): keine Stümme bröllete aus dem Foier
Moische Moische

Bindervoet and Henkes (Dutch, 2002): noch bluisbalgde een stem
vanuit de vuurte miesje miesje

From the high Middle Ages of Arthurian legend and the Norman invasion of Ireland we found ourselves translated to nineteenth-century
Dublin, Georgia. We now cross the Atlantic and the centuries again, to
fifth-century Ireland in the time of another invader from the east attempting to impose foreign values and culture on the natives, this time
in the form of the Christianizing mission of the man (or men) later ven-
erated as St Patrick. Commenting on the phrase 'avoice from afire,'
Joyce identified it to Harriet Weaver in November 1926 as 'the flame of
Christianity kindled by St Patrick on Holy Saturday in defiance of royal
orders.' Traditionally, the royalty in question was the initially hostile

Lóegaire or Laoghaire (anglicized as Leary), king of Tara and high king of Ireland, to whom the modern town of Dún Laoghaire ('Laoghaire's fort'), just south of Dublin city, owes its name. Joyce's ostensibly helpful explanation tells only part of the story, of course, for most readers are perhaps rather more likely to associate a voice from a fire with the voice of the Lord speaking to Moses from the biblical burning bush, a bush afire, blazing.

Joyce's claim that the fire is the flame of faith kindled by Patrick is also immediately destabilized by the syncopated phrasing 'avoice from afire,' nominalizing the adjective *afire* and in so doing suggesting a privative use of the prefix *a-* (as in *atheism, atypical*) and thus questioning the nature of fire and voice alike. The voice (if it is more than imaginary) from the fire (if it is more than imaginary) also 'bellowsed' to Patrick, combining the verb *bellow* and the noun *bellows*, the action of which latter at least we would normally expect to be exercised on rather than emerge from the fire. Joyce's readers and translators, as one would expect, have reacted variously in their identification and characterization of the voice in question.

Turning first to what our translators have made of 'avoice from afire,' we find that in French, Lavergne, noting the privative prefix, considers it 'nulle voix humaine' ('no human voice'), the formulation evoking an appropriately ecclesiastical atmosphere by playing on the similarly named organ stop (*voix humaine, vox humana*) that can evoke the sound of a singing choir. (Presumably inadvertently, our other French translator, André du Bouchet, omits this entire clause from his version of the opening page.)

In Italian, Wilcock has 'la voce dal fuoco,' literally a much less indeterminate '*the* voice from *the* fire' (emphasis mine). Burgess's 'una voce di fuocofuori,' literally 'a voice of fire (*fuoco*) from without (*fuori*),' plays on the similarity of a voice 'from afire' and 'from afar.' The earlier Schenoni opts for 'voce da fuoco' ('voice of fire'), the later for "navoce da 'nfoco' ('a voice from a fire [*foco*],' with reduced indefinite articles). In Spanish, Elizondo has 'una voz salida del fuego,' literally 'a voice come from the fire'; Pozanco 'una voz ardiente,' a rationalized 'ardent voice'; and Victoria 'unavoz de unfuego' ('a voice from a fire,' with attention drawn, as in the case of the later Schenoni, to the unusual use of the indefinite articles, but no longer with any privative force).

In Portuguese, Lourenço adopts 'uma voz vinda do fogo' ('a voice come from the fire'), while Schüler has 'avoz do fogo,' literally 'the voice from the fire.' The difference is a substantial one, however, for

Schüler ingeniously forces the feminine definite article *a* to function as if it were in fact the privative prefix *a-*, which functions in Portuguese (*ateísmo, atípico*) as it does in English. His 'avoz' thus means both 'the voice' and 'non-voice.' Pagán's Galician achieves almost exactly the same effect with 'avoz desde a chamas,' literally 'the voice from the fire' (*chamas*, 'flames, fire') but also suggesting a 'non-voice.'

German offers several more complex (and some rather adventurous) versions. Beck has 'kein stimm fern aus dem feuer,' suggesting 'no voice afar (*fern*) from the fire,' where the phrase 'kein stimm' is a grammatically altered form of the standard German *keine Stimme* ('no voice'), drawing attention to itself by its challenge to the reader to account for the alteration. Here the meaning of the alteration is less important than the fact of alteration in the first place. Rathjen's 'neStimmede aus de-Feuerne' conflates *eine Stimme* ('a voice'), *stimmte* ('gave voice'), and *entstammte* ('originated') as well as *aus dem Feuer* ('from the fire') and *aus der Ferne* ('from afar'). Stündel's 'keine Stümme ... aus dem Foier' conflates *keine Stimme* ('no voice') and *stumm* ('mute') as well as *aus dem Feuer* ('from the fire'), identified as the fire of 'faith' (French *foi*). Schrödter's 'eintstimmen von eintflammen' conflates *eine Stimme* ('a voice') and *entstammte* ('originated') as well as *eine Flamme* ('a flame') and *entflammen* ('to inflame'). Jauslin opts for 'keine Stimme ... vom Herdfeuer,' literally 'no voice from the fire on the hearth (*Herd*).' In Dutch, finally, Bindervoet and Henkes have 'een stem vanuit de vuurte,' literally 'a voice from out of the fire' (*vuur*, 'fire'; *vuurtje*, 'little fire').

Joyce's voice or non-voice 'bellowsed mishe mishe.' Joyce's own comment to Harriet Weaver on this formulation (before an original 'bellowed' was later changed to 'bellowsed') was: 'bellowed: the response of the peatfire of faith to the windy words of the apostle,' thus encouraging a reading that the fire of faith blazed into roaring life in response to the inspirational message of St Patrick. Translators are thus faced with the challenge to render simultaneously the 'bellowing' of the fire and the action of the saint as 'bellows.'

Some versions translate the verb as if it meant simply 'bellowed' or 'roared': thus in Pozanco's Spanish the voice 'bramó' ('bellowed'); Victoria's 'bramadicho' conflates the same verb *bramar* and *dicho* ('said'); Lourenço's Portuguese 'rugido' means 'bellowed, roared' (*rugir*); and Stündel's German 'bröllete' likewise suggests 'roared' (*brüllte*). Other versions employ a different register, while still assuming a single meaning: thus Elizondo's Spanish 'surgía diciendo' reports that a voice 'came forth (*surgir*) and said'; Jauslin's German 'schrie' suggests merely 'cried' (*schreien*); Pagán's Galician 'resoprara' suggests rather 'had whispered (*soprar*)'; Wilcock's 'risoffiato' incorporates Italian *soffiare* ('to blow, to whisper') and *ri-* , suggesting repeated action; Beck's 'fauchte' suggests a more colourful 'hissed, spat'; and Schrödter's German 'anfeuerte' suggests something like 'urged (*anfeuern*) fierily.'

More complex versions include Lavergne's 'dessouflé,' conflating French *souffler* ('to blow') and *soufflet* ('bellows'); Burgess's 'soffiettato' similarly combines the Italian verb *soffiare* ('to blow, to whisper') and the noun *soffietto* ('bellows'); Rathjen's 'blaßgebalgt' conflates German *blass* ('pale') and the noun *Blasebalg* ('bellows'), employed as a verb; Bindervoet and Henkes similarly opt for 'bluisbalgde,' employing the Dutch noun *blaasbalg* ('bellows') as a verb, but provocatively conflating it with the verbs *blazen* ('to blow') and *blussen* ('to extinguish'). Schenoni's earlier 'mugghiato' literally means 'had bellowed, roared,' but his later 'soffiorato' both reduces the volume and changes the tone significantly in a combination of Italian *soffiare* ('to blow, to whisper') and *fiorato* ('covered in flowers'). Schüler's 'rebellava,' finally, conflates Portuguese *rebelar* ('to rise up, to rebel') and *berrar* ('to bellow'), thus suggesting, roughly, 'bellowed brooking no opposition.'

Joyce's 'bellowsed' also contains the noun 'bells' and the verb 'blows.' Several of our translators, as we have seen, manage to include reference to the latter – Wilcock, Burgess, and the later Schenoni all incorporate Italian *soffiare* and Lavergne the French *souffler*, both meaning 'to blow.' Rathjen's 'blaßgebalgt' incorporates the German *blasen* ('to blow'); Bindervoet and Henkes's 'bluisbalgde' likewise implies the corresponding Dutch *blazen* (as well as *blussen*). The 'low' sounds of church 'bells' ringing remain without echo outside of Joyce's original text, with the one exception of Lavergne's reference to an organ stop. The distant bellowing of bulls and lowing of cattle may of course exist even in Joyce's text only as a pastoral figment of one reader's perhaps over-heated imagination.

As for 'mishe mishe,' seven versions simply retain Joyce's original formulation, and an eighth, Pagán's 'mixe mixe,' merely rewrites it in accordance with the phonetic system of the target language, Galician. Joyce's own explanation of the phrase was 'Mishe = I am (Irish) i.e. Christian' – as if the voice from the fire were answering the question 'Who is already baptized?' Equally feasibly, however, one can think of the 'fire of faith' blazing into life, its new adherents shouting 'Me, me, baptize me, me.' Campbell and Robinson, in the early days of *Finnegans Wake* scholarship, remembering the pagan Irish fire goddess Brigit who later translated seamlessly into the historic sixth-century St Brigid of Kildare, suggested even more specifically that 'from a fire below comes the voice of the virgin lady of the isle – the goddess Brigit,' who, in her 'mishe mishe,' reveals herself as ALP, 'the mother-substance of all being' (1961, 29). This assumption is evidently based on an understanding of 'mishe mishe' as suggesting 'me she, I am she,' and we find Schüler's Portuguese translation adopting exactly this reading in his 'mim-She, mim-She,' literally 'me (*mim*) She.'

Anthony Burgess and Salvador Elizondo both resort to explanatory translators' notes. Burgess, though converting the goddess into a saint, accepts the identification proposed by Campbell and Robinson but attempts to incorporate Joyce's explanation that 'mishe' means 'I am': '"Mishe mishe" is the Erse for "I am, I am" – St. Bridget, as mother of Ireland, affirming her immortality' (Burgess 1966, 22). Elizondo, for his part, improving even further on Campbell and Robinson by means of a conflation of Irish hagiographical legends, sees the voice of Brigit as coming specifically from the subterranean fire of St Patrick's Purgatory (1992, 159). Both Burgess and Elizondo, however, despite these editorial notes, actually retain Joyce's original formulation and make no overt reference to either the divine Brigit or the sainted Brigid in their translations. The Dutch version of Bindervoet and Henkes, 'miesje miesje,' rewrites Joyce's formulation in accordance with Dutch phonetics, but can also be read as mischievously gesturing, courtesy of the Dutch personal name *Miesje* ('Molly'), towards neither goddess nor saint but towards that rather less than saintly Joycean diva Molly Bloom.

For other readers, the burning bush of the Old Testament is the more obvious referent: in Exodus 3:4 the Lord, in the form of a voice from a fire, calls out 'Moses, Moses' (Hebrew *mošeh mošeh*) from the burning bush. Only one of our versions, Stündel's German 'Moische Moische,' reflects this more specifically, conflating the German *Mose*, the Hebrew *Mošeh*, the French *moi* ('me'), and Joyce's *mishe*. Later, in Exodus 3:14, the Lord announces his own name, still from the burning bush, and that name is 'I Am That I Am' – which can in turn not unreasonably be translated into Irish as 'mise mise.' Joyce's suggestion that 'mishe' is the equivalent of 'I am' is only partially correct. The Irish personal pronoun *mise* (anglicized as *mishe*) means 'I am' only in association with a complement: *mise Seán* thus means 'I am Sean.' Unaccompanied, *mise* means 'I, me, myself' (*dúirt mise* 'I said'). *Mise mise* therefore means either 'me, me' or 'I am myself' – evocative of course of the biblical 'I am that I am.'

Victoria's Spanish 'mishe mishe [yo(soy)yo]' opts for this particular reading, his parenthetical 'yo(soy)yo' literally meaning 'I(am)I.'

For yet other readers, the words from the fire appear to be far from divine in origin: thus in Pozanco's Spanish, they are nothing more than a 'pifia' (*pifia*, 'joke, mockery'), and the voice merely 'bellowed out mockingly.' For others again, the words appear to be seen as a mere conjuring trick to impress the gullible: thus in Lavergne's French, the words are just 'micmac' (*micmac*, 'trickery'). Others remain undecided as to their comprehensibility or relevance: Beck's 'mischmisch' thus conflates German *mich mich* ('me me') and an interrogative *Mischmasch* ('mishmash, hodgepodge'); Rathjen's 'michsiemaschsie' similarly includes German *mich* ('me') and *sie* ('she') – perhaps based on Campbell and Robinson's reading, as Schüler's Portuguese version is – but more clearly emphasizes, like Beck, the element of incomprehensible *Mischmasch*. Easily the most idiosyncratic version is Jauslin's German, which chooses to substitute three separate terms, 'vergebens' ('in vain'), 'vermessin' (*vermessen*, 'presumptuous, impudent'), and 'vermißihn' (*vermiss ihn*, 'miss him'), in anticipation, one must assume, of the motif of thwarting in the following phrase.

[5]   to *tauftauf thuartpeatrick*

du Bouchet (French, 1962): [*text missing*]

Lavergne (French, 1982): pour bêptiser Patrick:

Wilcock (Italian, 1961): al tauf tauf tuseipetrizio;

Burgess (Italian, 1975): a tauf tauf tu es Pietrorbiera

Schenoni (Italian, 1978): al tauftauf tuseitorbizio.

Schenoni (Italian, 1982): al tauftauf tuseipeatrizio:

Elizondo (Spanish, 1992): a tauftauf tuespetrarricio,

Pozanco (Spanish, 1993): para cortarle el revesino al bautismo de Patricio:

Victoria (Spanish, 2009): para babautizar túerespetricio:

Lourenço (Portuguese, 1968): para tauftauf tuespetrício:

Schüler (Portuguese, 2003): ao tauftauf do pautripedrícioquetués:

Pagán (Galician, 2000): a tauftauf tiespedrício:

Beck (German, 1989): zu tauftauf dubistpeatrick:

Jauslin (German, 1989): tauftauf, du gleichst ihm wie ein Ei dem andern, reingelegt, Stuart Patrick:

Rathjen (German, 1989): um Dubistpaetrick taufzutaufen:

Schrödter (German, 1989): zu tauftauf thuartpeatrick:

Stündel (German, 1993): zu tauftauf DubistPehtricks:

Bindervoet and Henkes (Dutch, 2002): tot tauftauf giezijtpitriek:

The progression from 'mishe mishe to tauftauf thuart-' suggests a number of things. Most obviously, at least for some readers, it suggests a linguistic opposition of *me* (Irish *mé*, *mise*) and *you* (Irish *tú*, *tusa*). The doubling of both 'mishe' and 'tauf' also suggests a possible opposition: Tindall, indeed, sees the two phrases as 'motifs for Shem (being) and Shaun (pious doing)' (1959, 255n13). The two phrases also introduce the motif of stuttering, which will be constantly associated with HCE, and thus suggests reading 'thuart-' as *thwart*, since stuttering thwarts speech and communication.

Other implications also become apparent at this point, as we pass from the fiery voice to baptism by water: German *taufen*, like Greek *baptízein*, originally meant 'to immerse' in water. For some readers, the combination of fire and water may well evoke the figure of Moses, whose name, from the Hebrew *Mošeh*, is explained by popular etymology in the Bible as deriving from *mashah* ('to draw out'), since he was 'drawn out' from the water (Exodus 2:10). As Moses led the Chosen People out of slavery to the Promised Land, so Patrick led the Irish out of spiritual darkness into the light of Christian belief. As Moses was personally 'thwarted' by the Lord's eventual refusal to let him enter the Promised Land himself, Patrick was a victim of rumours of an unspecified nature, against which he attempts to defend himself in his autobiographical writings – a fact that associates him in turn with HCE.

Why the text should suddenly summon up a German *taufen* ('to baptize') at this point has exercised a number of readers. Campbell and Robinson, for example, see 'tauftauf' as reminding us 'that St. Patrick's spiritual tutor was St. Germanicus' (1961, 29). Seizing on this identification, Burgess observes that 'it is dreamily appropriate that the patron saint of Ireland should use the German to point to the continuity, as well as the supra-national essence, of Christian evangelism' (1966, 21). Patrick's mentor at Auxerre, one might note, was actually St Germanus rather than Germanicus, and the name *Germanus* has nothing to do with 'German,' deriving instead from the Late Latin *germanus* ('brother') – which would not of course have prevented Joyce from seizing gleefully on the homonymy, if indeed he did. Whatever its linguistic *raison d'être*, however, 'tauftauf,' if pronounced in accordance with English rather than German spelling conventions, approximates both English *turf* and German *Torf* ('turf'), an association confirmed in the next word by the appearance of a 'peatrick,' suggesting a rick or stack of peat, more commonly called turf in Ireland, and suggesting Patrick as baptizing the oversized peat rick that is Ireland.

As Fritz Senn has observed, the rocks by the stream Oconee that occupied our attention in a previous clause transform themselves in the present phrase into the very rock on which the Christian church was founded (1995, 51). The expression 'peatrick' clearly also combines *Patrick* and *Peter*. Joyce confirms this in his commentary to Harriet Weaver: 'Thou art Peter and upon this rock etc. (a pun in the original aramaic) / Lat: Tu es Petrus et super hanc petram.' As he once commented to Frank Budgen, 'The Holy Roman Catholic Apostolic Church was built upon a pun. It ought to be good enough for me' (Ellmann 1982, 546).

The name *Peter* thus not only introduces another divinely appointed leader, as the first pope, but also turns our attention both to rocks (once again) and to wordplay – and, incidentally, also to sexual identity, a theme that will recur at various points throughout the text. Greek *Petros* and Latin *Petrus* are both (masculine) given names formed in each case from a (feminine) noun, *petra* ('rock') – the Greek text being a variation on the Aramaic wordplay in John 1:42 referred to by Joyce, where Simon Peter is called *Kēphas*, from the Aramaic *kêpā*, 'rock' (McKenzie 1965, 663).[2] We find a companion rock well hidden in 'thuart-,' for, as Brendan O Hehir points out (1967, 98), Irish *art* also means 'rock' – a point confirmed by Dinneen, whose iconic dictionary, incidentally, is dedicated to his namesake, St Patrick, 'apostle and patron of Ireland.' In addition to Peter – and of course to HCE, whose head is Howth – both Moses

---

2 Matthew 16:18: 'Thou art Peter, and upon this rock I will build my church'; 'Tu es Petrus, et super hanc petram aedificabo ecclesiam meam'; 'Su ei Petros, kai epi tautē tē petra oikodomēsō mou tēn ekklēsian.'

and Patrick are associated with rocks: Moses climbs Mount Sinai to re-
ceive the Tables of the Law from the Lord, Patrick climbs the mountain
called Croagh Patrick in County Mayo, where he is said to have fasted
for forty days. Since 'croagh' is an anglicization of the Irish *cruach*,
meaning 'heap, pile, stack, rick' (Dinneen 1927), 'Croagh Patrick' or
Cruach Phádraig thus literally means 'St Patrick's rick' (O Hehir 1967, 1;
Mink 1978, 275) – or, indeed, 'Patrick's peatrick.' Since Patrick is the
patron saint of Ireland, the Apostle of the Irish, and the highest-ranking
personage in the entire catalogue of Irish saints, we may certainly also
detect a link to Topsawyer's Rock.[3]

Meanwhile, 'peatrick,' in combining *Patrick* and *Peter*, can be read as
also evoking Patrick Pearse (1879–1916), whose family name is a variant of *Peters* (Cottle 1978, 286) and who is also numbered among those
who attempted to lead the Irish out of a perceived servitude, resulting
in his own execution in 1916 for his part in the Easter Rising. While
a student at University College, Joyce studied Irish extramurally for
two years with Pearse, whose collected poetry in Irish was published
in 1914 as *Suantraidhe agus goltraidhe* (literally 'songs of sleeping and
weeping'). One of the poems was 'Mise Éire' (17; literally 'I am Ireland'),
which may also be read as included among the resonances of 'mishe
mishe.'

Turning to our translators, we find that, with only four exceptions,
all retain Joyce's original 'tauftauf.' Of the more adventurous four,
Lavergne opts for 'pour bêptiser Patrick,' where the invented 'bêptiser' conflates the French *baptiser* ('to baptize') and *bêtise* ('nonsense,
stupidity'); Victoria's 'para babautizar' introduces a corresponding
stammer on the first syllable of Spanish *bautizar* ('to baptize'); Rathjen's
'um Dubistpaetrick taufzutaufen' plays on the German *zu taufen* ('to
baptize'), with a hint of a complementary *aufzutauen* ('to thaw out');
and Pozanco's Spanish 'para cortarle el revesino al bautismo de
Patricio' translates roughly as 'to thwart (*cortar el revesino*) the baptism
of (or by) Patrick.'

As for 'thuartpeatrick,' there is considerably less agreement. Lavergne,
as we have just seen, opts for an unambiguous 'Patrick,' while Pozanco
translates the English *Patrick* into a Spanish *Patricio*. Pozanco uses a
Spanish idiom meaning 'thwart' to translate 'thuart-,' while Lavergne

---

3 Adaline Glasheen points out (1977, 232) that there is even a sixth-century Cornish
   St Petrock, who will later put in an appearance (*FW* 203.21).

sees a baptism that is simultaneously a *bêtise* ('nonsense, stupidity') –
and thus also 'thwarted.' Wilcock's 'tuseipetrizio' conflates an Italian *tu
sei Pietro* ('thou art Peter') and an Italian version of *Patrick*, namely
Patrizio. The same result is achieved in Victoria's 'túerespetricio,' conflating a Spanish *tu éres* ('thou art'), a Latin *Petrus*, and a Spanish *Patricio*;
and again in Lourenço's 'tuespetrício,' conflating *Petrus* and *Patrício*; as
also in Pagán's 'tiespedrício,' conflating *Pedro* and *Patrício*. Schüler's
Portuguese 'pautripedrícioquetués' goes one better by promising a 'list'
(*pauta*) and then delivering it, conflating *Pádraig*, *Patrício*, *Pedro*, and *que
tu és* ('that thou art').

Other versions attempt to capture, by a variety of means, Joyce's
triple conflation of the biblical 'Thou art Peter,' the name *Patrick*, and,
if possible, some reference to peat or turf. Schrödter's German version achieves this economically by simply retaining Joyce's original
'thuartpeatrick,' while Beck's 'dubistpeatrick' is an only slightly
modified German 'thou art peatrick.' Rathjen's 'Dubistpaetrick' gives
Patrick precedence over Peter and discreetly disguises the peat, while
Stündel's 'DubistPehtricks' includes a German *Peter* as well as *Patrick*,
pays less attention to the specificity of peat than to the appearance of
'ricks' in general, and is apparently suspicious that 'tricks' of some
sort may be involved.

Peat looms large in more than one version. Bindervoet and Henkes's
'giezijtpitriek' conflates a Dutch 'thou art' (*gie zijt*), a likewise Dutch
Pieter, and a *Patrick*, but is also able to 'smell' (Dutch *rieken*) peat in a
nearby 'burner' (Dutch *pit*) of some kind. The presence of peat is more
flamboyantly celebrated in Burgess's 'tu es Pietrorbiera,' conflating a
Latin *tu es* ('thou art'), an Italian *Pietro*, a likewise Italian *torbiera*
('peatbog'), and a definite hint of a papal greeting to the city and the
world, *urbi et orbe*, adding up to an Italian Pope Peter Peatbog – lacking only, alas, any hint of an Irish (or even British) Patrick. The early
Schenoni's 'tuseitorbizio' conflates an Italian *torba* ('peat, turf') and
Patrizio, perhaps unduly emphasizing Patrick's connections with Irish
bogs – and now excluding any reference to Peter. The later Schenoni's
more sober 'tuseipeatrizio' restores peat, Peter, and Patrizio to their
Joyce-allotted roles.

Two versions are notable for their flaunted eccentricities. Elizondo's
'tuespetrarricio' duly includes a Latin *tu es* ('thou art') and *Petrus* and a
Spanish *Patricio* – but also abandons peat in favour of rice (Spanish *ar-
roz*), presumably imported at this point because of the opportunity for
an interlingual pun, even if left unrealized, on 'paddy' fields. Peat bogs

and paddy fields – the latter so called, incidentally, from the Malay *pādī* ('rice plant') rather than from any putative Irish connection – are of course also linked by their shared dependence on water, entirely appropriate to the immediate context of baptism.

Jauslin, meanwhile, following on his idiosyncratic rendering of 'mishe mishe,' devises an even more idiosyncratic German commentary on 'tauftauf,' based perhaps on a fancied resemblance of that phrase to a repeated French *œuf* ('egg'): 'tauftauf, du gleichst ihm wie ein Ei dem andern,' literally 'tauftauf, you and he are as alike as one egg is to another' – the German idiom corresponding to the English 'like two peas in a pod.' Jauslin then moves on to 'thuartpeatrick,' where we find, first of all, 'thuart-,' evidently interpreted as suggesting 'thwart,' rendered by 'reingelegt,' literally 'tricked, caught you!' (*hereinlegen*). The point of Jauslin's exercise seems to emerge from his immediately following and once again highly idiosyncratic rendering of the now complete 'thuartpeatrick' as 'Stuart Patrick,' which should undoubtedly be understood as a gesture, however tentative and incomplete ('Stuart Pa-'), towards Charles Stewart Parnell (1846–91) as a potential future Moses of the Irish people, and likewise eventually 'thwarted' – as was his eighteenth-century predecessor and partial namesake Charles Edward Stuart, alias Bonnie Prince Charlie, whose presence here is also signalled by the spelling. Parnell is thus seen as another Patrick, another Apostle of the Irish, the two like two peas in a pod – or, as the German idiom would more appropriately have it, as alike as one egg is to another (*wie ein Ei dem andern*), for eggs are of course a traditional symbol of rebirth, new growth, and new beginnings. And while the name *Peter* has been eliminated from Jauslin's rendering of 'peatrick,' its implied return is suggested by association with 'Stuart,' for the surname *Parnell* (like the surname *Pearse*) is derived, as experts tell us, from the given name *Peter* (MacLysaght 1980, 241). The same is true, to add one final link, of *Persse*, which as a surname likewise derives from *Peter* – and as a given name is that of HCE's alter ego Persse O'Reilly. That the Estonian noun *persse* means 'arse' (Tindall 1996, 62) is naturally more than welcome icing on the Joycean cake.

I have already suggested that in the special case of *Finnegans Wake* even blatant individual mistranslations have a claim to macrotextual toleration, as part of the pervasive and proliferating noise in which Joyce's final text, even before any attempt at translation, is already so exorbitantly rich. Jauslin's rendition of the phrase just considered is a good example of this: we may reject it out of hand as being in any sense an accurate rendering of the original text; but as a *commentary* on that text, which of course all translation also always is, it can certainly lay some claim to our interest.

Bernard Benstock has suggested that Joyce playfully hid versions of his own name ('Jhem') and Nora's as well as those of Giorgio and Lucia in the opening page of *Finnegans Wake* (1966, 61). Giorgio, as we have already seen, was triumphantly discovered by several of our translators in Laurens County's 'gorgios.' The suggestion, however, that Nora is hidden in '*nor a*voice' and Lucia disguised in 'bel*low*sed' has found no response in any of the versions considered here.

5 Passencores

not yet, though venissoon after, had a kidscad buttended a bland old isaac: not yet, though all's fair in vanessy, were sosie sesthers wroth with twone nathandjoe. Rot a peck of pa's malt had Jhem or Shen brewed by arclight and rory end to the regginbrow was to be seen ringsome on the aquaface.

(FW 3.10–14)

du Bouchet (French, 1962): pas plus qu'encore, quoique pentecôte près, n'eut son roux cadet filoué un ameugle isaac chevrauné: et bien que rien hait neuf en vanessie, point n'avaient les sus-isthœurs déruthé leur doublempair Nathanjoe. Et mie Jhem ou Shaun, sous volts arctiques, lampé le malt palternel et de l'arc-en-cil l'irroré se pouvait à la ronde boire sur l'aquaface.

Lavergne (French, 1982): pas encore, mais nous y venaisons bientôt, n'avait un jeune blancbec flibutté le blanc bouc d'Isaac: pas encore, bien que tout soit affoire en Vanité, les doubles sœurs ne s'étaient colère avec Joe Nathan. Onc mais n'avaient Jhem ni Shem brassé de becquée le malte paternel sous l'arcastre solaire et l'on voyait la queue rugissante d'un arc-en-cil encerner le quai de Ringsend.

Wilcock (Italian, 1961): né ancora, benché poco dopo, si era un giovincapro scagliato contro un blando vecchio isacco; neppure, benché tutto sia permesso alle vanessie, si erano imbronciate le sosisorelle con un duaun natangiò. Né a luce d'arco avevano Giem o Shem distillato un gallone del malto paterno, né il roriadoso estremo dell'altobaleno regisplendeva girigiocoso sull'acquispecchio.

Schenoni (Italian, 1982): non ancora, benché venisson dopo, una cadaglia aveva buttestato un blando vecchio isacco: non ancora, benché tutto sia lecito in vanessità, le sosie sesterelle s'erano adirate con un duun natangiò. Rutta un poco del malto di pa' Jhem o Shen avevano fatto fermentare con luce d'arco e una rorida fine al regginbaleno si doveva ancora vedere ringsull'acquafaccia.

Elizondo (Spanish, 1992): ni entonces, aunque poco después, el muchacho pseudocabronizado, engañó al viejo blandiciego isaac: no; todavía no, aunque todo se valenvenerecía a lo largo de la rutha en que susuenan las lianas de nathanajo con que tejen las estheras; pudre un pito con malta la cerveza del viejo que Sem y Cam habían caldeado a la luz de lampararea, hacia el último extremo del sarkoliris visto anulosamente sobre la caragua.

Pozanco (Spanish, 1993): aún no, aunque very soon-Venyson-prontísimo, se había un novatillo entrometido con el templado isaac: aún no, aunque todo se lo justificase la vanidad, se habían las me(s)mas hermanas encolorizado con un tal (o dos) Joe Nathan. Ni un cuartillo de la cerveza paterna habían fermentado Jhem ni Shem bajo la achispada bóveda y ya se veían los anillos de la juguetonacola del arco iris sobre el aquaface.

Victoria (Spanish, 2009): no aún, sin embargo [venadeándolo] muy pronto después, habiun chicabrete [engañoso] culacabado [a] un soso viejo isaac [butt]: toda vía no, aunque todo se vale'n vanili-dad, fueron envueltas [& escritas] hermanas sosias iracundas con dosún nathanyjoe [jonathan (swift)]. [Al] Pudrir una pizca de la malta de 'pá había Jhem o Shen hecho cerveza por luzarco y al final del [puente] rory el arco iris [cejarreina] estaba para ser vistos algunosanillos sobre la caragua.

Lourenço (Portuguese, 1968): ainda não, no entanto imeviadamente alguém, numa pele de cabra, iludibuttou um amenocego velho isaque: ainda não, no entanto tudo é justo no jogo de vanessia e ambasirmans estavam iradas com doblum nathanjo. Jhem ou Shem apodreceram um pinto da bebida do pai preparada à luz de

um candelabro oval e paroriente o arquiris podia ser visto sob a
forma de um anel sobre a aquaface.

Schüler (Portuguese, 2003): ainda não, embora desvanessido depois,
um braço novilho tinha iludido um cego revelho Isaque: ainda
não, embora em invernesses fantasvale tudo, as tristes esthernes
tinham dilaceradoo duuno nathandeãojo. Barrica nenhuma de
maltescocês tinham Jhem ou Shen fermentado à luz iriada darco e
a chuvosa-pestana brilhava em anel à tona d'aquaface.

Pagán (Galician, 2000): ainda non, mas porco despois, un canallin
rematara cun isaac vello e débil: ainda non, mas todo se permite
nesa van idade, aborrutheran esters irmás isosi dun dous nathandjoes. Ven un cuartillo da cervexa de papá elaboraran Jhem
ou Shen à luz de arco e xa ser via o roridante cabo do arco da cella
formando aneis na aquaface.

Beck (German, 1989): noch nicht, aber nur ein böckchen später, hatte
ein kitztropf einem blindmütigen isaak den rest gegeben: noch
nicht, aber alles heiligt vanestas, war das doppelte schwestherchen zornig auf zweinen nathandjoe. Kein peck von papas malz
hatten Jhem oder Shen bei archuslicht verbraut unds taurote end
vom regenbrowgen konnt man ringsam sehn auf dem aquaface.

Jauslin (German, 1989): und immer noch nicht, doch baldersohnend, hatte ein Rüpelkind einen altermilden Isaak verspuntet: immer noch nicht, doch 's ist im Venerischwinden alles klar,
waren schickseste Geschwester ergrimmt über Zweieinen:
Nathandjoe. Ein verbeultes Viertelscheffel von Papas Malz
hatten Jhem oder Shen im Regenbogenlicht gebraut und
das Spektakelende der Regginbrühe war ringelklingelnd im
Wassergesicht zu besichtigen.

Rathjen (German, 1989): noch nicht obwohl hirschnell danach, hatte
ein Knirpskniff einen dünkelnobelalten Isaak butterseicht bedickerendet: noch nicht, obwohl man's ja mag vannerstdie Eiteln
kleiden, zürnten sosie Schwesthern zweinem Nathaundjoe. Nücht
einen Viertelscheffel von Pas Malz hatte Jhem oder Shen bis zum
Boginnlicht gebraut und rötaurig Ende zum Gegenbrauen war
allherund zu sehen auf der Aquafratz.

Schrödter (German, 1989): noch nicht, obschon kitz darauf, hatte
ein Kintzluder einen blönden alten isaac ausgeräumt: noch nicht,

obwohl alles jahr ma' gVanns eitel is', waren Susillings-
schwEstthern wRüthend auf zweien Nathandjoe. Vernicht einen
Packen von Paps Malz hatten Jhem oder Shen unter einem arch
de luminiere gebraut und das vertaummte Ende zum Regginbraugen war rgsomm auf dem Euangesicht zu sehen.

Stündel (German, 1993): noch nicht, obgleich nach dem WildBret
hatte ein ZickleinTrick den blünden ollen Isaak gelaimt: noch
nicht, obwohl alles fähr mit Vanässi ist, wahren soßische
Schwustern mit zweins Nathanjöl geschrüben. Einen verrotteten
Haufen von Pas Malz hatten Jhem oder Shem bei BogenLicht
gebraut und das rohrie Ende des ReckenBockens zeigte sich
ringsum auf dem SchnappsGesicht.

Bindervoet and Henkes (Dutch, 2002): nog niet, hoewel zeer wildra
doorna, had een pestploert een zachtzienige isaac kontgebuttst:
nog niet, hoewel alles is geoorloogd in ijdelnijd, waren sosie
zwesthers pruttelig jegens tween nathandjoe. Nocht had Jhem of
Shen bij arklicht een pikkig vaatje pa's tanig malt gebrouwen en
was aan de roriënt ringsom op het watergezicht de reigenbrauw
te zien.

Volokhonsky (Russian, 2000): poka eščë net, no vspore potom malyj
promel starogo slipkogo isaaka: poka net, hot' vce putem sredi
suet vaness, kogda u sester pust' sosi sok vo gneve na dvojnogo
natandšo. Hrena eževičnogo iz papašina soloda varil by Čhem ili
Šem pri svete radugi, i pylajuščij konec eja otražalsja kol'com na
poverhnosti vod.

Królikowski (Polish, 1998): jeszcze nie, chociaż diczwnet potem
zabeczkował swój kałdun w słodziszczach starego izaaka: jeszcze
nie, choć cała ta rusałszczana próżność złojpoliła groszomiłe
siostercje z dwurazuchem natentamjoe. Bo zgorzel ojczulkowego
garnca słodu zwarzył Drzim czy Szim, per jasnygwint i do
zachłodu, niczym królewską zwarzynę Ginę, aż do zważenia
widoku kolizn na nawierzchni wody.

Malicki (Polish, 2001): ani jeszcze, pomimo przybycia później, miał
kupę numerów zaduppionych a blandynowy stary issak: nie jesa
cze, pomimo wszystkich obawy w vanessie, były sosiste sieostry
gniewne z dwujednym natanjóziem. Gnicie dziury taty słodu
miało Jhemczy też Shen c uwarzyćpoprzez świetlny łuk i

rozkuśny koniec do panującej brwi był widabny podobny ringowi na powierzchni aquy.

Mutanen (Finnish, 2006): ei vielä, joskin hirveenpian jälkeen, ollut kilivili puskiinni vanhaa kalkkista iisackia: ei vielä, joskin haihtuu kaikki pätevyys, olleet siskotukset yhteen kirjoen toinensi nathanjajoe. Papan maltaasta hiekiertäen oli melkoisen pilaantuneen ulkoluen Jhem tai Shen pannut valokaarella ja järinsateenkarvan jyrnä otsapäätös nähtiin rinkinä vesikasvoilla.

The list of events that had not yet happened continues, three so far, four more to come. The opening clause in the text considered in this chapter focuses on the enmity of brothers – which will emerge as a central theme, involving the warring brothers Shem and Shaun – and the relationship of fathers and sons, ultimately also warlike in that fathers, in the nature of things, are always vulnerable to being supplanted by sons. Joyce made two explanatory comments to Harriet Weaver in his letter of 15 November 1926: 'The venison purveyor Jacob got the blessing meant for Esau,' and 'Parnell ousted Isaac Butt from leadership' (*L* 1:247–8). The two events are linked by the name *Isaac*. The biblical story of the twin brothers Jacob and Esau (Genesis 27:1–40), sons of Isaac, tells how the two siblings fought even in their mother's womb. Esau, as the firstborn of the two, was in principle the rightful successor to his father's estate, but this right had to be confirmed by a formal blessing by Isaac, who was by now old and blind. The wily Jacob fooled both Esau and Isaac by a trick involving the skin of a newly killed kid goat: knowing that the blind old man was likely to recognize Esau primarily by the latter's unusually hairy skin, kid brother Jacob covered his own smooth face and arms in the goatskin and duly received the blessing and the inheritance intended for his brother.

The biblical Jacob's thus making Isaac the butt of his deceit serves in the world of *Finnegans Wake* as a more than adequate bridge to the ousting in 1877 of the aging, ailing, and beleaguered politician Isaac Butt (1813–79) as leader of the Irish nationalist party at Westminster by the rising young political star Charles Stewart Parnell (1846–91). We may note in passing that the Hebrew name *Yaakov* not only becomes *Jacob* in English; the Latin form of the name, *Jacobus*, eventually gave rise also to a Late Latin byform, *Jacomus*, which in turn became the English *James*, as in the case of one James Joyce, whose alter ego in *Finnegans Wake* is called *Shem*, a Joycean byform of *Séamus*, the normal Irish version of *James*.

[1]   *not yet, though venissoon after,*

du Bouchet (French, 1962): pas plus qu'encore, quoique pentecôte près,

Lavergne (French, 1982): pas encore, mais nous y venaisons bientôt,

Wilcock (Italian, 1961): né ancora, benché poco dopo,

Schenoni (Italian, 1982): non ancora, benché venisson dopo,

Elizondo (Spanish, 1992): ni entonces, aunque poco después,

Pozanco (Spanish, 1993): aún no, aunque very soon-Venyson-prontísimo,

Victoria (Spanish, 2009): no aún, sin embargo [venadeándolo] muy pronto después,

Lourenço (Portuguese, 1968): ainda não, no entanto imeviadamente

Schüler (Portuguese, 2003): ainda não, embora desvanessido depois,

Pagán (Galician, 2000): ainda non, mas porco despois,

Beck (German, 1989): noch nicht, aber nur ein böckchen später,

Jauslin (German, 1989): und immer noch nicht, doch baldersohnend,

Rathjen (German, 1989): noch nicht obwohl hirschnell danach,

Schrödter (German, 1989): noch nicht, obschon kitz darauf,

Stündel (German, 1993): noch nicht, obgleich nach dem WildBret

Bindervoet and Henkes (Dutch, 2002): nog niet, hoewel zeer wildra doorna,

The term 'venissoon,' as well as overtly implying 'very soon,' conflates the *venison* whose hairy skin Jacob used to fool his father and the *benison* or blessing originally intended for Esau. By its similarity to the name *Vanessa* (to which we shall return), it hints at the (as yet unmotivated) presence of Jonathan Swift, and by its inclusion of the sequence -*iss*- it faintly anticipates the figure of Issy, much as the terms 'peni*so*late' and '*isth*mus' have already done. Our translators rise to the combined challenge in a variety of ways. Wilcock's Italian 'poco dopo' and Elizondo's Spanish 'poco después' both literally mean 'shortly afterwards' but abandon all other resonances. Schenoni's 'non ancora, benché venisson dopo' essentially retains Joyce's term, though bringing it somewhat closer to the English *benison*. Stündel's 'nach dem WildBret' misunderstands the phrase as meaning, literally, 'after the venison (*Wildbret*),' as if discussing the progress of a multicourse meal. Bindervoet and Henkes's 'zeer wildra doorna,' on the other hand, successfully employs Dutch *dra* ('erelong') and *doorna* ('thereafter') while hinting at *wildbraad* ('venison').

Various animals are made to play the role of venison: Beck's 'ein böckchen später' conflates German *ein bisschen später* ('a little later') and *ein Böckchen* ('a little goat'); Schrödter's 'kitz darauf' adroitly conflates German *kurz darauf* ('shortly afterwards') and *Kitz* ('kid'); Rathjen's 'hirschnell danach' conflates German *sehr schnell* ('very quickly') and *Hirsch* ('stag'). Victoria's 'venadeándolo' plays on Spanish *venado* ('deer'), *venadear* ('to go deer-hunting'), and English *venery*. Pagán's 'porco despois' changes the species a little, conflating Galician *pouco despois* ('shortly after') and a decidedly non-kosher *porco* ('hog'), while Lourenço's 'imeviadamente' conflates Portuguese *imediatamente* ('immediately') and a rather less specific *vianda* ('meat, fowl').

Other versions rely on more general wordplay. In French, du Bouchet's 'pentecôte près' plays on *bientôt après* ('soon afterwards') and *pentecôte près* ('Pentecost near'), sounding a portentously biblical tone but abandoning all other more specific resonances, while Lavergne's 'nous y venaisons bientôt' plays more successfully on *venaison* ('venison') and *nous y venons bientôt* ('we'll come to it soon'). Pozanco's idiosyncratic 'very soon-Venyson-prontísimo' includes the resonances by annotational accretion rather than by translation, while Schüler's 'desvanessido depois' plays on Portuguese *desvanecido* ('vain'), which evokes 'vanessy' (and thus Swift) in the following clause more strongly than does Joyce's 'venissoon.'

Jauslin, finally, goes entirely his own way with 'baldersohnend,' which duly contains the German *bald* ('soon') but in addition, surprisingly, conflates *ersehnend* ('longing for') and *Sohn* ('son'). The resulting construction ignores any reference to the 'venison' used to trick the old man, suggesting instead that Isaac is 'longing for a son' (*einen Sohn ersehnend*), longing for a rightful heir – and that this longing, as will emerge in the next phrase, makes him an all too easy dupe for a trickster who is admittedly also his son, but not the son Isaac believes him to be. Jauslin's once-again distinctly idiosyncratic choice may be the result of an arcane perceived parallel: apparently detecting in 'venissoon' the presence not of Vanessa but of Venus, the Roman goddess of love and beauty, he 'translates' the Mediterranean goddess into the Scandinavian god Balder, the shining youth associated with light and beauty in Norse mythology. Balder, son of Odin, is best remembered for the story of his tragic death, inadvertently caused by his own brother, and his loss (perhaps seen here as paralleling father Isaac's loss of a rightful heir) makes not only All-Father Odin but all the gods and all of nature weep.

[2]   *had a kidscad buttended a bland old isaac:*

du Bouchet (French, 1962): n'eut son roux cadet filoué un ameugle isaac chevrauné:

Lavergne (French, 1982): n'avait un jeune blancbec flibutté le blanc bouc d'Isaac:

Wilcock (Italian, 1961): si era un giovincapro scagliato contro un blando vecchio isacco;

Schenoni (Italian, 1982): una cadaglia aveva buttestato un blando vecchio isacco:

Elizondo (Spanish, 1992): el muchacho pseudocabronizado, engañó al viejo blandiciego isaac:

Pozanco (Spanish, 1993): se había un novatillo entrometido con el templado isaac:

Victoria (Spanish, 2009): habiun chicabrete [engañoso] culacabado [a] un soso viejo isaac [butt]:

Lourenço (Portuguese, 1968): alguém, numa pele de cabra, iludibuttou um amenocego velho isaque:

Schüler (Portuguese, 2003): um braço novilho tinha iludido um cego revelho Isaque:

Pagán (Galician, 2000): un canallin rematara cun isaac vello e débil:

Beck (German, 1989): hatte ein kitztropf einem blindmütigen isaak den rest gegeben:

Jauslin (German, 1989): hatte ein Rüpelkind einen altermilden Isaak verspuntet:

Rathjen (German, 1989): hatte ein Knirpskniff einen dünkelnobelalten Isaak butterseicht bedickerendet:

Schrödter (German, 1989): hatte ein Kintzluder einen blönden alten
isaac ausgeräumt:

Stündel (German, 1993): hatte ein ZickleinTrick den blünden ollen
Isaak gelaimt:

Bindervoet and Henkes (Dutch, 2002): had een pestploert een
zachtzienige isaac kontgebuttst:

The complexly structured 'kidscad' who (or which) 'buttended a bland
old isaac' generates, as one might expect, quite a number of divergent
translatorial responses. The English term *kid* originally referred to the
young of a goat, then sequentially to a child, a young man, and a thief;
the verb *to kid* initially meant to cheat, then merely to tease or to chaff;
and *scad* was once a cant term for a trick played by a *scadger*, or rascal
(Partridge 1972, 507, 799). A *cad*, meanwhile, once denoted not only
an ill-bred fellow, especially one devoid of any finer instincts, but also
a messenger or errand-boy, or even, eventually, a particular friend
(Partridge 1972, 143–4). A Joycean 'kidscad' might thus variously be
construed as suggesting a cad, with the varying connotations of the
term, among youngsters (perhaps recalling 'gorgios'); merely a childish
trick; a trick specifically involving the young of a goat; or all of the above.

Du Bouchet's French kidscad is a 'roux cadet,' a younger son (*cadet*)
whose apparently red (*roux*) hair is not his own but that of the slain
kid; Lavergne's is, less judgmentally, merely 'un jeune blancbec,' a
young whipper-snapper (*blanc-bec*); neither includes any reference to
goats. Wilcock's Italian, however, makes no bones: he is a 'giovincapro,' a 'young goat,' a kid. For Schenoni, he is 'una cadaglia,' a conflation of a younger son (*cadetto*) and a scoundrel (*canaglia*). In Spanish,
Elizondo has him as a 'muchacho pseudocabronizado,' a boy pretend-
ing to be turned into a goat (*cabrón*); Pozanco thinks him just a 'novatillo,' a mere novice (*novato*); while Victoria less charitably considers
him a deceitful (*engañoso*) 'chicabrete,' a goat-boy (*chico*, 'boy'; *cabra*,
'goat'). In Lourenço's Portuguese he is rather vaguely just 'alguém,
numa pele de cabra' ('somebody in a goatskin'), while in Schüler's he
is 'um braço novilho,' a new (*novo*) young kid (*braço*) whose youthful
vigour and aggressiveness are suggested by the bullfighting term for
a young bull, a *novilho*. Pagán's Galician, less impressed, thinks of him
as just 'un canallin,' a young cad (*canalla*).

Five German versions adopt as many solutions. For Beck, he is 'ein kitztropf,' a rascal (*Tropf*) with something of the baby goat (*Kitz*) about him; for Jauslin, he is 'ein Rüpelkind,' a young lout (*Rüpel*); for Schrödter, he is 'ein Kintzluder,' conflating *Kitz* and *Kindsluder*, a 'brat of a child.' Two of the five, however, concentrate on the trick rather than the trickster: Rathjen thus speaks of 'ein Knirpskniff,' a trick (*Kniff*) played by a whippersnapper (*Knirps*); while Stündel has it as 'ein ZickleinTrick,' using another term for a kid goat, *Zicklein*. In Dutch, Bindervoet and Henkes revert from the trick to the trickster, whom they consider 'een pestploert,' a pestilential (*pest*, 'pestilence') cad (*ploert*). These last three versions, we may note, are the only ones to replicate Joyce's alliteration, Rathjen's perhaps most successfully, in doing so on the same initial /k/.

As for Joyce's 'buttended,' goats notoriously butt; a butt or butt-end is a backside; a butt is also a target and a barrel (anticipating pa's malt); Isaac Butt was fairly unceremoniously replaced by Parnell in the 1870s; and Parnell's nickname as a boy was 'Butthead,' 'from his habit of charging into others who incurred his displeasure' (Glasheen 1976, 16). In French, du Bouchet's assailant has merely swindled ('filoué') his father, displaying the behaviour of a cheating rogue (*filou*) rather than that of a son (*fils*); while Lavergne more ambitiously prefers the expression 'flibutté,' ingeniously conflating Isaac Butt, *butter* ('to bump someone off'), Parnell's use of filibustering as a form of parliamentary obstructionism in bringing Butt down, and *flibuster* ('to act like a pirate'). In Italian, Wilcock's trickster has 'hurled himself' blindly against his blind target (*scagliarsi*, 'to hurl oneself'), while Schenoni's has 'buttestato' his Butt with a head-butt (*testata*). In Spanish, while Elizondo's goat-boy merely 'deceived' (*engañó*) his father, and Pozanco's novice had merely 'meddled with' (*entrometido*) his, Victoria's rather more aggressive young vandal had 'culacabado' his aged parent, finished him off (*acabar*, 'to finish') with a butt to the butt (*culo*, 'buttocks'). In Portuguese, Lourenço's less aggressive 'someone in a goat-skin' merely 'iludibuttou' his victim in a combination of *iludir* ('to deceive') and Isaac Butt, while Schüler's cad had similarly 'iludido' – deceived and deluded – his target.

In Galician, Pagán's young scoundrel had more robustly finished off the old man, giving him the coup de grâce in a combination of *rematar* ('to finish') and *matar* ('to kill'). In German, Beck's old man was similarly 'finished off' (*den Rest geben*, 'to finish someone off'), while Schrödter's was 'ausgeräumt' ('cleaned out'), Stündel's 'taken for a ride' (*leimen*, 'to hoodwink'), and Jauslin's 'made fun of by a young pup,' the locution 'verspuntet' combining *verspotten* ('to make fun of'), a colloquial *ein junger Spund* ('a young pup'), and the verb *spunden* ('to bung,' as of a cask or butt). We shall return to a final German version, by Friedhelm Rathjen. In Dutch, meanwhile, Bindervoet and Henkes prefer the expression 'kontgebuttst,' thus succeeding with admirable succinctness in having their Butt butted in the butt (*kont*, 'arse').

As for the 'bland old isaac' in question, the particular butt of all this aggression and deception, the aging biblical Isaac was blind, literally and (at least in this encounter) figuratively, while the aging politician Isaac Butt's policy on Irish Home Rule was, at least for some younger colleagues, including Parnell, all too unaggressively bland. Joyce's own increasing blindness is ironically included in the biblical reference.

In French, du Bouchet's 'bland old isaac' is 'un ameugle isaac chevrauné,' the invented adjective 'ameugle' playing on *aveugle* ('blind') and an all too bovinely placid *meugler* ('to moo'), while 'chevrauné' invents a verb based on *chevreau* ('a young goat'), thus 'kidded,' with just a hint of *aîné* ('firstborn') – namely Esau, likewise to his cost, 'kidded.' Lavergne, playing on his own translation of 'kidscad' as 'blancbec,' chooses to see the confidence trick played on 'le blanc bouc d'Isaac,' literally 'Isaac's white goat' and, by implication, 'the white-haired old goat, Isaac.' In Italian, both Wilcock and Schenoni opt for the quite literal translation 'un blando vecchio isacco' ('a bland old isaac'). In Spanish, Elizondo's Isaac is a 'viejo blandiciego,' an old man (*viejo*) who is simultaneously blind (*ciego*), bland (*blando*), and, by implication, vacillating (*blandiente*); Pozanco's Isaac is all too blandly 'moderate' (*templado*); and Victoria's 'soso viejo isaac [butt]' is 'vapid, dull' (*soso*). In Portuguese, Lourenço's Isaac ('isaque') is at once mild (*ameno*), blind (*cego*), and old (*velho*), while Schüler's patriarch is not just old (*velho*) but very old (*revelho*) and easily fooled, with things happening 'without the knowledge of' (*à revelia de*) the blind man (*cego*). Pagán's Galician Isaac is just 'vello e débil' ('old and weak').

Among German versions, Beck speaks of a 'blindmütigen isaak,' playing on *blind* ('blind') and *blindwütig* ('in a blind rage') – but actually implying the opposite of the latter, the invented 'blindmütig' suggesting something closer to *kleinmütig* ('timid'). Jauslin speaks of an 'altermilden Isaak,' an Isaac made mild by age (*Alter*); Schrödter of a 'blönden alten isaac,' an Isaac simultaneously blind (*blind*), stupid (*blöd*), and, interlingually, bland; while Stündel employs a similar vowel-shifting strategy with his 'blünden ollen Isaak,' a conflation of German *blind* and English *bland* with a supplementary teasing hint that old Isaac was also either *blöd* ('stupid') or even *blond* ('blonde') or both. In Bindervoet and Henkes's Dutch, old Isaac was 'zachtzienig,' conflating the adjective *zachtzinnig* ('good-natured') and the verb *zien* ('to see'), specifically to see things perhaps too good-naturedly in a light soft (*zacht*), mild (*zacht*), and mellow (*zacht*).

Friedhelm Rathjen's German, finally, goes its own way, elaborately invoking a confidence trick that had 'einen dünkelnobelalten Isaak butterseicht bedickerendet.' Here Isaac is pleasant (*nobel*) and generous (*nobel*) and noble (*nobel*) and old (*alt*), but also, in his blindness, suffering from both *Dunkel* ('darkness') and *Dünkel* ('arrogance'), the arrogance of one who assumes in his blindness that his way of seeing things is the only way. His 'buttending' is flamboyantly described by Rathjen as 'Isaak butterseicht bedickerendet,' suggesting an old man bland (*seicht*, 'shallow') and 'soft as butter' (*butterweich*) who, for his sins, has to endure *das dicke Ende* ('the worst thing of all').

Rathjen's baroque combination succeeds in evoking, almost subliminally, yet a third Isaac, the hoodwinked biblical patriarch and the unseated Irish politician shading into the fictional Isaac Bickerstaff, thus anticipating the appearance in the next clause of his creator, Dubliner Jonathan Swift (1667–1745). 'Isaac Bickerstaff' was a pseudonym used by Swift in a 1708 April Fool's hoax attack on the well-known astrologer and almanac-maker John Partridge (not venison, but certainly fair game), one of whose publications had aroused Swift's ire by sarcastic references to the Church of England. Swift, a kidscad member of the Kit-Cat Club in London, retaliated as 'Isaac Bickerstaff' by first 'predicting' in print the date of Partridge's allegedly imminent demise and then, despite the latter's agitated protests, publishing 'independent' corroboration that this sad event had indeed happened.

[3]   *not yet, though all's fair in vanessy,*

du Bouchet (French, 1962): et bien que rien hait neuf en vanessie,

Lavergne (French, 1982): pas encore, bien que tout soit affoire en Vanité,

Wilcock (Italian, 1961): neppure, benché tutto sia permesso alle vanessie,

Schenoni (Italian, 1982): non ancora, benché tutto sia lecito in vanessità,

Elizondo (Spanish, 1992): no; todavía no, aunque todo se valenvenerecía

Pozanco (Spanish, 1993): aún no, aunque todo se lo justificase la
vanidad,

Victoria (Spanish, 2009): toda vía no, aunque todo se vale'n vanili-
dad,

Lourenço (Portuguese, 1968): ainda não, no entanto tudo é justo no
jogo de vanessia

Schüler (Portuguese, 2003): ainda não, embora em invernesses
fantasvale tudo,

Pagán (Galician, 2000): ainda non, mas todo se permite nesa van
idade,

Beck (German, 1989): noch nicht, aber alles heiligt vanestas,

Jauslin (German, 1989): immer noch nicht, doch 's ist im Venerischwinden alles klar,

Rathjen (German, 1989): noch nicht, obwohl man's ja mag vannerst-
die Eiteln kleiden,

Schrödter (German, 1989): noch nicht, obwohl alles jahr ma' gVanns
eitel is',

Stündel (German, 1993): noch nicht, obwohl alles fähr mit Vanässi ist,

Bindervoet and Henkes (Dutch, 2002): nog niet, hoewel alles is
geoorloogd in ijdelnijd,

While the previous clause, relating to the hoodwinking of the aged patriarch, concerns the relationship of old men and young men, fathers
and sons, we now turn to the relationship of old men and young wom-
en, fathers (even if only spiritual) and daughters; the name *Isaac*, as we
have seen, once again constitutes the link, 'Isaac Bickerstaff' conjuring
up Jonathan Swift. The locution 'all's fair in vanessy' evokes the adage
that all's fair in love and war, as well as Thackeray's *Vanity Fair* (1847–
8). Thackeray's novel, satirizing English social mores of the day,
borrows its title from John Bunyan's *Pilgrim's Progress* (1678): one stop
on Bunyan's pilgrim's allegorical route is a never-ending fair held in a
town called Vanity, representing vain attachment to earthly things.
'Vanessy' also evokes the two much younger women who played a

major if still mysterious role in Swift's life, one of whom he playfully named *Vanessa*, both of whom were actually called *Esther* ('-essy'), and to both of whom we shall return. Joyce's text will also return to Swift and his pair of young ladies, the trio much later referred to as 'Biggerstiff' and his 'two venusstas' (*FW* 413.29).

In French, du Bouchet's 'et bien que rien hait neuf en vanessie' suggests something like 'though there is nothing new in vanity,' while maintaining the polysemy of Joyce's 'vanessy' and introducing a new ambiguity by replacing the expected *est* ('is') with the similarly pronounced *hait* ('hates'). Lavergne opts instead for 'bien que tout soit affoire en Vanité,' suggesting rather 'though everything is at the fair (*foire*) in Vanity,' playing both on an interlingual English *affair* and on the fact that the standard title of Thackeray's novel in French is *La foire aux vanités*.

In Italian, Wilcock's 'benché tutto sia permesso alle vanessie' suggests something like 'though all is permitted for the vanessies,' and Schenoni's 'benché tutto sia lecito in vanessità' something like 'though all is permissible (*lecito*) in vanessity.' Neither chooses to take advantage of the standard Italian title of Thackeray's novel, *La fiera delle vanità*.

Three Spanish versions choose three separate options. Pozanco opts for an unambiguous 'aunque todo se lo justificase la vanidad,' literally 'even though vanity would justify everything to itself.' Victoria's 'aunque todo se vale'n vanilidad' suggests less straightforwardly 'though everything is fine (*todo se vale*) in vanity (*vanidad*) or in silly, empty talk (*vaniloquio*).' More complex still is Elizondo's 'aunque todo se valenvenerecía,' where the final portmanteau word includes *valerse* ('to be fine'), *venéreo* ('sensual, venereal'), and an hispanicized echo of 'vanessy.' Lourenço's Portuguese version, by contrast, is quite straightforward: 'no entanto tudo é justo no jogo de vanessia' ('though all is fair in the game of vanessy'). Schüler's Portuguese, on the other hand, is considerably less so: his 'embora em invernesses fantasvale tudo,' following Campbell and Robinson in seeing the presence of Macbeth, 'seduced by the wiles of the Three Weird Sisters' (1961, 30), understands 'in vanessy' as including a reference to Inverness rather than Vanity Fair or 'vanessy' and asserts that in the combined result everything (*tudo*) is fine (*vale*), at least in fantasy (*fantasia*). In Galician, Pagán reflects philosophically, in one of the more successful renderings, that 'todo se permite nesa van idade,' roughly 'everything is permissible in this silly age of vanity,' where 'van idade' conflates Galician *vano* ('vain, silly'), *idade* ('age'), and *vaidade* ('vanity'), while 'nesa van' reverses *Vanessa*.

German offers an array of solutions. Stündel's 'obwohl alles fähr mit Vanässi ist' approximates the original by the simple expedient of recasting Joyce's 'fair' and 'vanessy' in German phonetics. Beck's 'aber alles heiligt vanestas' suggests that 'vanestas' (conflating *vanitas* and *van-esthers*) justifies (*heiligt*) all. Jauslin takes 'vanessy' as primarily conflating *venery* and *vanishing*, abandons the Swiftian echo, and assures his readers that all is well (*alles klar*) 'im Venerischwinden,' which in turn conflates *im Venerischen* ('in matters venereal') and *im Verschwinden* ('vanishing'). Rathjen's 'obwohl man's ja mag vannerst-die Eiteln kleiden' initially appears to suggest something like 'although one likes it when vain people dress,' but its primary purpose is in fact to conceal / reveal the usual German title of Thackeray's novel, *Jahrmarkt der Eitelkeit*, as well as a disguised 'vanessy.' Schrödter adopts a similar strategy with his 'obwohl alles jahr ma' gVanns eitel is'.'

In Dutch, finally – where Thackeray's novel is usually called *De markt van de ijdelheid* – Bindervoet and Henkes, abandoning the echo of Swift, opt for a complex 'hoewel alles is geoorloogd in ijdelnijd,' implying, roughly, 'though all is permissible (*geoorloofd*) when everybody is at war (*oorlog*) with everybody else as a result of vanity (*ijdelheid*) and envy (*nijd*).' A supplementary translingual resonance reminds the attentive reader that all's fair (*geoorloofd*) in love ('-loof-') and war (*oorlog*).

[4]   *were sosie sesthers wroth with twone nathandjoe.*

du Bouchet (French, 1962): point n'avaient les susisthœurs déruthé leur doublempair Nathanjoe.

Lavergne (French, 1982): les doubles sœurs ne s'étaient en colère avec Joe Nathan.

Wilcock (Italian, 1961): si erano imbronciate le sosisorelle con un duaun natangiò.

Schenoni (Italian, 1982): le sosie sesterelle s'erano adirate con un duun natangiò.

Elizondo (Spanish, 1992): a lo largo de la rutha en que susuenan las lianas de nanathajo con que tejen las estheras;

Pozanco (Spanish, 1993): se habían las me(s)mas hermanas encolorizado con un tal (o dos) Joe Nathan.

Victoria (Spanish, 2009): fueron envueltas [& escritas] hermanas
sosias iracundas con dosún nathanyjoe [jonathan (swift)].

Lourenço (Portuguese, 1968): e ambasirmans estavam iradas com
doblum nathanjo.

Schüler (Portuguese, 2003): as tristes esthernes tinham dilaceradoo
duuno nathandeãojo.

Pagán (Galician, 2000): aborrutheran esters irmás isosi dun dous
nathandjoes.

Beck (German, 1989): war das doppelte schwestherchen zornig auf
zweinen nathandjoe.

Jauslin (German, 1989): waren schickseste Geschwester ergrimmt
über Zweieinen: Nathandjoe.

Rathjen (German, 1989): zürnten sosie Schwesthern zweinem
Nathaundjoe.

Schrödter (German, 1989): waren Susillings-schwEstthern wRüthend auf zweien Nathandjoe.

Stündel (German, 1993): wahren soßische Schwustern mit zweins
Nathanjöl geschrüben.

Bindervoet and Henkes (Dutch, 2002): waren sosie zwesthers
pruttelig jegens tween nathandjoe.

'Swift's Stella & Vanessa both had name Esther,' Joyce explained in his
letter to Harriet Weaver. Esther Johnson was Stella, fourteen years
younger than Swift, Esther Vanhomrigh was Vanessa, twenty-two
years younger, and their relationship to Swift was a fraught one. The
indignation of two younger women directed at an older man prefigures Earwicker's encounter with the two (saucy?) girls in the Park.
The fact that here they are not just saucy but 'sosie' sisters – French
sosie ('twin'), Modern Greek *sósias* ('double'); two girls with one given
name – evokes Earwicker's self-obsessed, mirror-loving, and guiltily
desired daughter Issy. The fact that they are 'sosie sesthers wroth' reveals that before they were two they were three, namely Susannah
(Susi), Esther, and Ruth, biblical heroines of tales once again involving the desire of old men for young girls (Campbell and Robinson
1961, 30).

The 'sosie sesthers' (limiting ourselves initially just to Susannah and Esther and returning later to Ruth) undergo a number of interesting transformations in their transposition into other languages. In du Bouchet's French, they thus become 'les susisthœurs,' in a briskly efficient conflation of 'Susi,' 'Esther,' and English 'sisters' doubled by French *sœurs* ('sisters'). For Lavergne, they are merely 'les doubles sœurs' ('the sisterly doubles'). In Wilcock's Italian, they are 'le sosisorelle,' conflating Italian *sosia* ('double') and *sorelle* ('sisters'), including Susannah but abandoning Esther to her fate, while Schenoni's 'le sosie sesterelle' more imaginatively manages to include not only both biblical ladies as well as echoes of English *sisters* and Italian *sorelle*, but also a hint of Italian *stelle* ('stars'), reminding readers that one of Swift's Esthers became a Stella, a name derived from the Latin *stella* ('star').

In Pozanco's Spanish, the sisters become 'las me(s)mas hermanas,' sisters (*hermanas*) who are both silly (*memas*) and both the same (*las mismas*). For Victoria, they are just 'hermanas sosias' ('sosie sisters'). In Portuguese, Lourenço has them merely as 'ambasirmans,' literally both (*ambas*) sisters (*irmãs*), while for Schüler they are 'as tristes esthernes,' conflating English *sisters*, Esther, though sad (*triste*) rather than sosie, and German *Sterne* ('stars'), recalling once again the passage of Swift's first Esther to Stella – and possibly also reminding readers that the name *Esther* may itself derive from the Persian *stara* ('star') (Hanks et al. 2002, 752). Pagán's Galician version has 'esters irmás isosi,' succinctly referring to 'those sisters' (*estas irmás*) 'so sosie' (*si sosi*), Ester and Susi, and hinting at their status as avatars of Issy.

In German, three versions adopt quite similar solutions: Beck has 'das doppelte schwestherchen,' literally 'the doubled little sister,' including Esther; Rathjen has 'sosie Schwesthern,' doubled sisters (*Schwestern*) including both Susi and Esther; and Schrödter, likewise including both, has a pair of 'Susillings-schwEsthern,' sisters who are now twins (*Zwilling*, 'twin'). Jauslin's 'schickseste Geschwester' evokes a single sister (*Schwester*) named Ester as one of a pair of siblings (*Geschwister*), while describing them both as elegant (German *schick*) and, shifting now to Swift's Esthers rather than the biblical Esther, non-Jewish (Yiddish *shikse*, 'non-Jewish girl'). In Dutch, Bindervoet and Henkes have 'sosie zwesthers,' conflating Esther and *zusters* ('sisters').

The fact that these sisters were 'wroth with twone nathandjoe' also gives rise to some interesting translatorial issues. To begin with, the Ruth who is likewise 'wroth' needs to find some suitable accommodation. She finds it, however, only in a small minority of the versions under consideration. Du Bouchet's 'déruthé' conflates Ruth and the French verb *dérouter* ('to lead astray, confuse'); Pagán's 'aborrutheran' combines Ruth and the Galician verb *aborrecer* ('to annoy'); Schrödter's 'wRüthend' wraps Ruth in the German present participle *wütend* ('furious'); and Bindervoet and Henkes's 'pruttelig' conflates Ruth and the Dutch adjective *pruttelig* ('grumbling, grumpy'). Other than in these four versions, Ruth must resign herself to remaining lost among the alien corn.

The term 'wroth' translates variously in other versions into Lavergne's 's'étaient en colère' ('were angry with'), Wilcock's 'si erano imbronciate' ('had grown surly'), Schenoni's 's'erano adirate' ('had got angry'), Victoria's 'iracundas' ('enraged, wrathful'), and Lourenço's 'estavam iradas' ('were angry'). Beck, Jauslin, and Rathjen likewise employ three different expressions for being angry: 'zornig,' 'ergrimmt,' and 'zürnten' respectively. A few versions introduce more idiosyncratic touches. Pozanco's 'se habían ... encolorizado' combines Spanish *encolerizado* ('had become angry') and *colorado* ('were blushing'). Victoria's supplementary Spanish 'fueron envueltas [& escritas]' suggests a reading of 'wroth' as implying both 'wrapped' ('envueltas') and 'written' ('escritas'). Schüler's '[se] tinham dilaceradoo,' the additional final vowel implying 'they were not just torn apart (*dilacerado*) but more (-*o*) than torn apart,' makes suggestive use of the Portuguese verb *dilacerar* ('to lacerate, to rend asunder') to recall the wording of Swift's epitaph, describing his last resting place (shared with Stella) as the only one 'ubi saeva indignatio ulterius cor lacerare nequit' ('where savage indignation can tear his heart no further').

'Twone nathandjoe' is of course Swift, father-surrogate for the two girls, as 'two-in-one Wise Nathan and Chaste Joseph,' a Jonathan 'split in two and turned head over heels by his two young-girl loves, Stella and Vanessa,' as Campbell and Robinson put it (1961, 30). 'Nathandjoe' undergoes only minimal change for several of our translators, becoming a 'natangiò' for Wilcock and Schenoni and a 'Joe Nathan' for Lavergne and Pozanco, while 'twone' is rendered by various linguistic combinations of *two* and *one*. He emerges, more interestingly, as 'leur doublempair Nathanjoe' for du Bouchet, a Dublin *père* at once singular and a pair; as a 'doblum nathanjo' for Lourenço, likewise at once a Dubliner and doubled; and as a 'nathandeãojo' for Schüler, a 'nathandjo' revealed in passing as also, like Swift, holding the office of dean (Portuguese *deão*).

We may conclude by turning finally to two particularly idiosyncratic rewritings of Joyce's text. The most extravagant of all the versions considered of the phrase 'were sosie sesthers wroth with twone nathandjoe' is certainly Elizondo's Spanish rendering, which humorously builds on the coincidence that in Venezuela, as Elizondo remarks in a footnote (1992, 159n17), the term *nanatajo* denotes a particular kind of natural fibre used to weave mats. The resulting transposition of Joyce's text is 'a lo largo de la rutha en que susuenan las lianas de nanathajo con que tejen las estheras,' literally 'along the route where one can hear the rustling sound of the *nanatajo* vines used for weaving mats.' Elizondo incorporates Ruth in 'rutha' (*ruta*, 'route'), conflates Susannah, *sonar* ('to sound, to be heard') and *susurrar* ('to rustle') in 'susuenan,' conceals Esther in 'estheras' (*estera*, 'mat'), and rearranges Jonathan among the *nanatajo* vines in 'nanathajo.'

Stündel's German version of the same phrase is almost equally extravagant, though in an entirely different key. In this rendering, 'wahren soßische Schwustern mit zweins Nathanjöl geschrüben,' where 'wahren' conflates *waren* ('were') and *wahr* ('true,' suggesting 'in all truth'), 'soßische Schwustern' evokes Susannah, Esther, and sisters (*Schwestern*) in a humorously self-reflective jumble (*Wust*) of meanings, while a faintly discernible *Stern* ('star') once again reflects the possible etymological relationship between the names *Stella* and *Esther*. Joyce's 'twone' is rendered by 'zweins' (*zwei-eins*), while 'Nathandjoe' is nonetheless transposed into an unambiguously singular 'Nathanjöl,' more obviously a variation on *Nathanael* than on the etymologically related *Jonathan*.[1]

Idiosyncratically, 'wroth' is rendered by 'geschrüben,' a vowel-shifted variation on German *geschrieben* ('written'), reading 'wroth' as suggesting 'wrote' and ignoring both Ruth and any suggestion of anger. Even more idiosyncratically, an entirely unexpected layer of culinary meanings is imposed on the whole phrase: the 'soßische Schwustern' are not only sosie but flavoured with *Soße* ('sauce'), 'Nathanjöl' contributes *Öl* ('oil') as well, and 'geschrüben' generously includes a complementary (and complimentary) serving of *Rüben* ('turnips').

Little enough of Joyce remains in Stündel's culinarily enhanced transposition – and very little indeed in Elizondo's determinedly South American relocalization. The extremes of translatorial licence involved in both versions, however, especially in the latter, are once again strongly reminiscent of the semantic liberties Joyce himself took

---

1 The name *Jonathan* derives (Hanks et al. 2002, 794) from Hebrew *yonatan, yehonathan* ('gift of God': cf. *Nathaniel, Theodore, Bogdan*). *Nathan* derives from Hebrew *Natan* ('given').

in his versions of excerpts from *Anna Livia Plurabelle* (to which we shall return in a later chapter).

[5]   *Rot a peck of pa's malt had Jhem or Shen brewed by arclight*

du Bouchet (French, 1962): Et mie Jhem ou Shaun, sous volts arctiques, lampé le malt palternel

Lavergne (French, 1982): Onc mais n'avaient Jhem ni Shem brassé de becquée le malte paternel sous l'arcastre solaire

Wilcock (Italian, 1961): Né a luce d'arco avevano Giem o Shem distillato un gallone del malto paterno,

Schenoni (Italian, 1982): Rutta un poco del malto di pa' Jhem o Shen avevano fatto fermentare con luce d'arco

Elizondo (Spanish, 1992): pudre un pito con malta la cerveza del viejo que Sem y Cam habían caldeado a la luz de lampararea,

Pozanco (Spanish, 1993): Ni un cuartillo de la cerveza paterna habían fermentado Jhem ni Shem bajo la achispada bóveda

Victoria (Spanish, 2009): [Al] Pudrir una pizca de la malta de 'pá había Jhem o Shen hecho cerveza por luzarco

Lourenço (Portuguese, 1968): Jhem ou Shem apodreceram um pinto da bebida do pai preparada à luz de um candelabro oval

Schüler (Portuguese, 2003): Barrica nenhuma de maltescocês tinham Jhem ou Shen fermentado à luz iriada darco

Pagán (Galician, 2000): Ven un cuartillo da cervexa de papá elaboraran Jhem ou Shen à luz de arco

Beck (German, 1989): Kein peck von papas malz hatten Jhem oder Shen bei archuslicht verbraut

Jauslin (German, 1989): Ein verbeultes Viertelscheffel von Papas Malz hatten Jhem oder Shen im Regenbogenlicht gebraut

Rathjen (German, 1989): Nücht einen Viertelscheffel von Pas Malz hatte Jhem oder Shen bis zum Boginnlicht gebraut

Schrödter (German, 1989): Vernicht einen Packen von Paps Malz hatten Jhem oder Shen unter einem arch de luminiere gebraut

Stündel (German, 1993): Einen verrotteten Haufen von Pas Malz
   hatten Jhem oder Shem bei BogenLicht gebraut

Bindervoet and Henkes (Dutch, 2002): Nocht had Jhem of Shen bij
   arklicht een pikkig vaatje pa's tanig malt gebrouwen

We may once again take as our starting point Joyce's explanation to
Harriet Weaver of November 1926: 'Noah planted the vine and was
drunk / John Jameson is the greatest Dublin distiller / Arthur Guinness
[is the greatest Dublin] brewer.' Our text here returns under the influence of alcohol to the conflict between fathers and sons and the associated castration motif – sons suggested as at least potentially conspiring
against their father, at once Earwicker and the biblical Noah, who, intoxicated, is treated disrespectfully, perhaps even sexually assaulted,
by his son Ham (Genesis 9:20–7).

   'Rot a peck of pa's malt had Jhem or Shen brewed by arclight' can be
read as referring to Noah himself as not yet having begun his brewing
activities: 'Jhemorshen' suggests an appropriately inebriated trisyllabic
Irish pronunciation of 'Jameson,' referring to John Jameson and Sons,
Dublin's largest distiller, seen as a worthy descendant of Noah the first
brewmaster. The phrase can also be read as suggesting that neither of
his two sons, Jhem or Shen, had infringed on their father's monopoly
– but that is very likely what an offending son with a guilty conscience
would protest in the first place. 'Rot a peck' is not a drop, damn the
drop, but also, suggesting an implied Freudian slip, reflects the fact that
malt liquor is distilled from barley germinated ('rotted') in water. 'Rot'
for 'not' is echoed by 'pa's,' evoking French *pas* ('not'). The ambiguity
as to who the brewer (or distiller) may or may not have been is reflected
by the ambiguity as to the amount 'brewed' or not brewed: a peck is a
liquid measure equivalent to sixteen pints and thus a considerable
amount, but a peck is also not more than a small bird would ingest, so
a very small amount indeed. 'Jhem or Shen,' hesitating between singu-
larity and plurality, also anticipates the sibling rivalry of Shem and
Shaun, and Jhem/Shem and Shen/Shaun as potential brewers suggest
in turn the lordly brothers Iveagh and Ardilaun of the house of
Guinness, Dublin's largest brewer. The alcohol-producing activities we
are considering here take place (or don't) 'by arclight,' thus at once
within a well-lit ark (Noah's, for example), and/or by lamplight produced by an electric arc, and/or by the light of the rainbow (French
arc-en-ciel).

Some of our translators, to begin with, seem to display significant uncertainty as to the identity and/or the number of the individuals involved. Joyce's Jhem and Shen remain unchanged in the majority of the versions considered, but in others they metamorphose variously into Jhem and Shaun (du Bouchet) or the biblical Shem and Ham in the Spanish versions of those names, Sem and Cam (Elizondo). For several translators in other languages, moreover, they become, suggesting a single individual rather than a pair, a rhyming Jhem or Shem (Lavergne, Pozanco, Lourenço, Stündel), and the same change is also variously naturalized in Italian as Giem or Shem (Wilcock), in Russian as Čhem or Šem (Volokhonsky), and in Polish as Drzim or Szim (Królikowski).

Our translators as a group rise manfully, if with divergent results, to the challenge of 'rot a peck.' Most versions seem convinced by the innocence of the might-have-been bootleg brewers. In Lavergne's French, they have never ever (*oncques mais*) brewed, not even 'by the least little bit' (*de becquée*), any of the paternal product. 'Not even a pint' ('ni un cuartillo'), 'not a pint' ('ven un cuartillo'), 'not even a gallon' ('né ... un gallone'), 'not a single barrel' ('barrica nenhuma'), not even 'a little bitty barrel' ('een pikkig vaatje'), Pozanco's Spanish, Pagán's Galician, Wilcock's Italian, Schüler's Portuguese, and Bindervoet and Henkes's Dutch rather less convincingly concur in an ascending sequence of doubt. Joyce's 'rot' becomes Schenoni's Italian *rutta* (literally 'belch'), appropriate for the alcoholic context, while for Elizondo the amount brewed conflates *pudre* ('rot') and *no vale un pito* ('it's not worth a straw'), in fact 'un pito con malta,' literally 'a malted straw.' 'Not a peck' ('kein peck'), Beck chimes in interlingually; 'not a quarter-bushel' ('nücht einen Viertelscheffel'), Rathjen agrees, though since a very indeterminate German *Scheffel* can vary in liquid quantity from roughly thirty to roughly three hundred litres, the confirmation is rather less than convincing. Schrödter's 'vernicht einen Packen' conflates *nicht* ('not') and *vernichten* ('to destroy') to assure us that no single peck, pack (*Pack*), or pile (*Packen*) of anything at all was ever involved.

Not all versions are equally convinced. Jauslin's German has it that they (or he) brewed 'ein verbeultes Viertelscheffel,' literally 'a dented quarter-bushel'; Stündel's German holds that they (or he) brewed 'einen verrotteten Haufen' ('a rotted heap') of malt; and in both cases, as in Joyce's original, readers are invited to decide whether the statement is to be considered a confirmation or a denial of their guilt or his industry. Lourenço's Portuguese holds, confusedly, that through some odd process and for some even odder reason they actually 'rotted' (*apodrecer*, 'to rot') at least a pint of their father's beverage: 'apodreceram um pinto da bebida do pai.' Victoria's Spanish, however, has no doubt that '[al] pudrir una pizca de la malta' ('when a tiny amount of the malt had rotted'), one or other of the erring pair did indeed brew beer. Whether the beverage in question was whiskey or beer remains a debated point: several versions are quite specific that it was beer (Elizondo, Pozanco, Pagán), others leave it merely as unspecified malt liquor (Schenoni, Beck, Rathjen, Schrödter), while Schüler is convinced, inexplicably, that it was Scotch whisky ('maltescocês') rather than Jameson's good Irish whiskey.

The (possible) act of brewing (or distilling) 'by arclight' takes place in Dutch, for Bindervoet and Henkes, 'bij arklicht,' namely by whatever light is available in an ark. For several other translators it happens variously, and less restrictedly, 'a luce d'arco' (Wilcock), 'con luce d'arco' (Schenoni), 'à luz de arco' (Pagán), or 'por luzarco' (Victoria), all including 'light' and elements of 'arc, arch, ark,' as well as oblique references to the rainbow that will put in an appearance in the next clause of Joyce's text. Lavergne adopts 'sous l'arcastre solaire,' playing on French *arc* ('arc, arch'), *arc-en-ciel* ('rainbow'), *astre* ('star'), and *solair* ('solar') to suggest something like 'under the celestial arch of the solar rainbow.' Pozanco's Spanish 'bajo la achispada bóveda' refers somewhat obscurely to activities taking place 'under the tipsy (*achispada*) arch (*bóveda*),' presumably the rainbow, with the transferred epithet 'achispada' possibly suggesting a humorously translingual 'well lit up.' Schrödter's German version opts for 'unter einem arch de luminiere,' turning to French to suggest an activity under an arch (*arche*) of light (*lumière*), whether of the rainbow or as if in a mine (*minière*), illuminated by a miner's light (*lampe de mineur*). In Portuguese, Schüler's 'à luz iriada darco,' playing translingually on light and (English) *dark*, involves the 'shimmering light (*luz iriada*)' of either an *arco* ('arc') or an *arco-íris* ('rainbow'), while Lourenço's 'à luz de um candelabro oval,' literally 'by the light of an arched (*oval*) candelabra,' appears to refer primarily to a somewhat utilitarian rainbow.

In German, Jauslin's 'im Regenbogenlicht' is unambiguously 'by the light of the rainbow (*Regenbogen*),' while Stündel's 'bei Bogen-Licht' allows itself to be read as referring primarily either to an arc light (*Bogenlampe*) or, once again, to the light of the rainbow. Two other German versions add further complexities. Rathjen's 'bis zum Boginn-licht' once again implies an arc light (*Bogenlampe*) but also suggests that the brewing activities had (or had not) continued until (*bis zu*) the light (*Licht*) of a new dawn, a new beginning (*Beginn*), as symbolized by the rainbow (*Regenbogen*). Beck's 'bei archuslicht' rather more elegantly conflates Latin *arcus* ('bow'), Greek *arkhē* ('beginning'), and German *Licht* ('light') to very similar effect.

More idiosyncratic versions, finally, are provided by Elizondo in Spanish and du Bouchet in French. Elizondo's 'a la luz de lampararea,' conflating Spanish *lámpara* ('lamp, light'), *lampa* ('shovel for grain'), *lamprea* ('lamprey eel'), *amparar* ('to seek shelter'), *parar* ('to prepare'), and *área* ('area'), seems to have his brewer(s) shovelling malt in a sheltered area presumably designated for such preparatory activities and illuminated by the redirected energy of an electric eel. In the world of *Finnegans Wake,* the mundane facts that a lamprey eel is not an electric eel and that neither one is actually an eel at all are of course less important than the electric illumination provided by the spark of an unexpected and exhilarating verbal play. Du Bouchet, for his part, defends 'Jhem or Shaun' against quite a different charge than illicit brewing: 'Et mie Jhem ou Shaun, sous volts arctiques, lampé le malt palternel.' Whether they engaged in brewing or not, they certainly did not (*ne ... mie*, 'not at all'), whether by the light of a lamp (*lampe*) or not, guzzle (*lamper*, 'to gulp down') quantities of the paternal (*paternel*) beverage, whether both at once or turn and turn about (*alterner*, 'to take in turn'), whether under 'arctic volts' ('volts arctiques') or voltaic arcs (*arcs voltaïques*).

[6]   *and rory end to the regginbrow was to be seen ringsome on*
       the aquaface.

du Bouchet (French, 1962): et de l'arc-en-cil l'irroré se pouvait à la
    ronde boire sur l'aquaface.

Lavergne (French, 1982): et l'on voyait la queue rugissante d'un
    arc-en-cil encerner le quai de Ringsend

Wilcock (Italian, 1961): né il roriadoso estremo dell'altobaleno
    regisplendeva girigiocoso sull'acquispecchio.

Schenoni (Italian, 1982): e una rorida fine al regginbaleno si doveva
    ancora vedere ringsull'acquafaccia.

Elizondo (Spanish, 1992): hacia el último extremo del sarkoliris visto
    anulosamente sobre la caragua.

Pozanco (Spanish, 1993): y ya se veían los anillos de la juguetonaco-
    la del arco iris sobre el aquaface.

Victoria (Spanish, 2009): y al final del [puente] rory el arco iris [cejarreina] estaba para ser vistos algunosanillos sobre la caragua.

Lourenço (Portuguese, 1968): e paroriente o arquiris podia ser visto sob a forma de um anel sobre a aquaface.

Schüler (Portuguese, 2003): e a chuvosa-pestana brilhava em anel à tona d'aquaface.

Pagán (Galician, 2000): e xa ser via o roridante cabo do arco da cella formando aneis na aquaface.

Beck (German, 1989): unds taurote end vom regenbrowgen konnt man ringsam sehn auf dem aquaface.

Jauslin (German, 1989): und das Spektakelende der Regginbrühe war ringelklingelnd im Wassergesicht zu besichtigen.

Rathjen (German, 1989): und rötaurig Ende zum Gegenbrauen war allherund zu sehen auf der Aquafratz.

Schrödter (German, 1989): und das vertaummte Ende zum Regginbraugen war rgsomm auf dem Euangesicht zu sehen.

Stündel (German, 1993): und das rohrie Ende des ReckenBockens zeigte sich ringsum auf dem SchnappsGesicht

Bindervoet and Henkes (Dutch, 2002): en was aan de roriënt ringsom op het watergezicht de reigenbrauw te zien.

Campbell and Robinson read the phrase 'and rory end to the regginbrow was to be seen' as meaning 'and toward the orient the rainbow was to be seen' (1961, 31). Such interpretive confidence is somewhat undermined by Joyce's comment to Harriet Weaver: 'rory = Irish = red / rory = Latin, roridus = dewy / At the rainbow's end are dew and the colour red: bloody end to the lie in Anglo-Irish = no lie.' For all that 'rory' is not, strictly speaking, the Irish for *red*, Joyce's comment supports the reading that just as 'rot a peck' suggests 'damn the drop, not a drop' in the previous clause, so 'rory end' here suggests that, at least for the time being, 'damn the end of any rainbow was to be seen.' Alternatively, however, if we take 'rory' as indeed meaning red, and since red is the outermost colour of the rainbow, the rainbow's end (like its beginning) can usually be expected to be 'rory.'

Tindall suggests that 'rory' and 'reggin' refer to the contending opposites Rory (hero) and Regan (villain) in Samuel Lover's popular novel

Rory O'More: A National Romance (1837), thus anticipating the fraternal rivalry of Shem and Shaun (1996, 50). Campbell and Robinson take a different approach, reminding us that after the waters of the biblical Flood recede, the Lord tells Noah that the rainbow is a symbol of a divine covenant that he will never again reduce the world to chaos (Genesis 9:12–16). They accordingly suggest that 'rory' connotes Rory O'Connor, 'who was High King of Ireland when the royal brow of the conqueror, Henry II, came up over the eastern horizon. This brow was the beginning of a new age, as was the rainbow in the time of Noah' (1961, 31). Whether or not one is happy to agree with this characterization of Henry II's beneficent role in Irish history, the Irish *Ruairí*, from which the anglicized form *Rory* derives, does indeed contain the element *rua*, meaning 'red' (Hanks et al. 2002, 857).

The terms 'regginbrow' and 'ringsome,' meanwhile, as Joyce also observed to Harriet Weaver, play on two German words, *Regenbogen* ('rainbow') and *ringsum* ('all around'). Readers are free (though not, of course, obliged) to see Joyce's use of German here as a whimsical anticipation of the arrival, likewise from the east, of the eighteenth-century Hanoverians (and their equally German successors of the House of Saxe-Coburg-Gotha after 1901) who would eventually and inevitably follow the twelfth-century Normans. The 'aquaface' is the face of the waters of primordial chaos on which, in Genesis 1:2, the formative spirit of God moved. Less solemnly, as joking Joyce also suggested to Weaver, 'when all vegetation is covered by the flood there are no eyebrows on the face of the Waterworld.'

In French, we find two very different interpretations of all this. For du Bouchet, 'de l'arc-en-cil l'irroré se pouvait à la ronde boire sur l'aquaface,' where 'l'irroré,' echoing 'rory,' conflates *orée* ('edge') and the negative prefix *ir-*, suggesting 'the non-edge' with more than an accompanying hint of Iris, rainbow goddess and messenger of the gods; where this 'non-edge' of the 'arc-en-cil,' at once suggesting rainbow (*arc-en-ciel*), eyelash (*cil*), and, by propinquity, brow (*sourcil*) could not only be seen (*se pouvait voir*) all around ('à la ronde') but, given the alcoholic context, could also be drunk in (*se pouvait boire*) at one's leisure. For Lavergne, 'l'on voyait la queue rugissante d'un arc-en-cil encerner le quai de Ringsend,' where 'la queue rugissante' suggests the at-once 'roary' (*rugissant*, 'roaring') and 'reddening' (*rougissant*, 'growing red, blushing') end (*queue*, 'tail') of a once again eyebrowed rainbow ('arc-en-cil'), this time, with remarkable specificity, 'surrounding' (*en-cerner*, 'to make a ring around') the pier at Ringsend. Employing the name of a particular coastal Dublin locality, Ringsend, to play on 'ringsome' is a good example of one of Lavergne's less effective translatorial strategies, namely an often excessive tendency to localize in Irish terms – geographically and / or historically – where possible, though not always where their appropriateness is immediately obvious. (What is considered appropriate, of course, may vary widely from reader to reader.)

Italian likewise offers two versions. For Wilcock, who takes 'rory' to imply a primarily negative adjective, 'né il roriadoso estremo dell'altobaleno regisplendeva girigiocoso sull'acquispecchio,' which is to say, more or less, 'nor was the dewy-edged (*rorido*, "dewy"; *oriado*, "edged") end (*estremo*) of the rainbow (*arcobaleno*) on high (*alto*, "high") royally (*regio*, "royal") resplendent (*risplendere*, "to shine") in a playful (*giocoso*) ring (*giro*) on the mirror (*specchio*) of the waters (*acque*).' Schenoni, on the other hand, with 'una rorida fine al regginbaleno si doveva ancora vedere ringsull'acquafaccia,' conflates 'rory' and *rorido* ('dewy') in describing the end (*fine*) of a translated rainbow (*arcobaleno*) that still contains a translingual trace ('reggin-') of its origins and could still be seen 'ringsull'acquafaccia,' all around (German *rings* and *ringsum*) on the face (*faccia*) of the water (*acqua*).

Spanish offers three readings. Elizondo's version continues his statement in the prevous clause that Sem and Cam's brewing activities (if any such existed) had taken place in lighting conditions that in some undefined way extend 'to the far end' ('hacia el último extremo') of the rainbow ('del sarkoliris') that is visible (*visto*, 'seen') in the form of a ring ('anulosamente') on the waterface ('sobre la caragua'). Elizondo's rainbow is also an enhanced one, a 'sarkoliris,' conflating *arcoiris* ('rainbow'), *círculo* ('circle, ring'), and, unexpectedly, Greek *sárx, sarko-* ('body'), suggesting 'the rainbow, embodied in a ring,' with that ring then appropriately repeated (*anuloso*, 'ringshaped') on the face (*cara*) of the water (*agua*). Pozanco's version more simply reports that 'ya se veían los anillos de la juguetona cola del arco iris sobre el aquaface,' literally 'the rings (*anillos*) of the playful (*juguetón*) end (*cola*, "tail") of the rainbow were to be seen on the aquaface.' Victoria reports in quite similar vein that 'al final del [puente] rory el arco iris [cejarreina] estaba para ser vistos algunosanillos sobre la caragua,' roughly 'at the end of the rory [bridge], the rainbow, were to be seen some rings on the waterface,' where 'some rings' ('algunosanillos') is a punningly reversed 'ringsome.' A parenthetical insertion annotates the 'arco iris' ('rainbow') as 'cejarreina,' evoking the original 'regginbrow' with a combination of *ceja* ('eyebrow') and *reina* ('queen'), the latter, perhaps once again recalling Iris, messenger of the gods, playing simultaneously on Latin *regina* ('queen'), German *Regen*, and English *rain*.

In Portuguese, Lourenço, closely following Campbell and Robinson, relates in straightforward terms that 'paroriente o arquiris podia ser visto sob a forma de um anel sobre a aquaface'; thus 'to the east (*par oriente*) the rainbow (*arco-íris*) could be seen in the form of a ring (*anel*) on the aquaface,' with 'paroriente' echoing the original 'rory end.' Schüler prefers the formulation 'a chuvosa-pestana brilhava em anel à tona d'aquaface,' suggesting that the rainbow 'was shining (*brilhava*) in a ring (*anel*) on the surface (*tona*) of the aquaface.' Schüler's rainbow, weeping in the rain, is circumscribed as a 'chuvosa-pestana,' literally a 'rainy (*chuvosa*) eyelash (*pestana*),' a rather cumbersome rendering of the original 'regginbrow.' Pagán's Galician version has 'e xa ser via o roridante cabo do arco da cella formando aneis na aquaface,' roughly 'and already (*xa*) the end (*cabo*) of the rainbow, becoming dewy (*roridante*), could be seen again (*se revia*), forming rings (*aneis*) on the aquaface.' In this rendering, the 'regginbrow' becomes an 'arco da cella,' a conflation of *arco-celeste* ('rainbow') and the arch of an eyebrow (*cella*). Intriguingly, the phrase 'ser via,' while readable as 'could be seen again' (*se revia*) could also be read as 'nobody saw,' with *ser* ('person') being used in a negative sense, similar to French *personne* ('nobody').

Among German versions, Beck opts for 'unds taurote end vom regenbrowgen konnt man ringsam sehn auf dem aquaface,' roughly 'and one could see the dew-red (*Tau*, "dew"; *rot*, "red") end of the rainbow like a ring (*ringsam*) on the aquaface,' where the rainbow now combines German *Regenbogen* and English *brow*. Jauslin is less restrained, with 'und das Spektakelende der Regginbrühe war ringelklingelnd im Wassergesicht zu besichtigen,' which suggests, approximately, that 'the spectacular end of the regginbrew (*Brühe*, "brew") could be observed ringlet-ringing on the face (*Gesicht*) of the water.' The German *Spektakel* ('spectacle') includes the sense of 'hullabaloo, uproar,' and thus does duty here for 'rory'; Joyce's 'regginbrow' becomes a 'regginbrew,' continuing the alcohol theme; and 'ringelklingelnd' contains the German noun *Ring* ('ring') as in *Ringel* ('ringlet') and the English verb *ring* by means of the German verb *klingeln* ('to ring'). Rathjen's complex version, 'und rötaurig Ende zum Gegenbrauen war allherund zu sehen auf der Aquafratz,' renders 'rory' as 'rötaurig,' combining *Röte* ('redness, glow, blush') and *Tau* ('dew'); 'regginbrow' now becomes 'Gegenbrauen,' combining the preposition *gegen* ('against, counter-'), the noun *Braue* ('eyebrow'), and the verb *brauen* ('to brew'), once again continuing the alcohol theme; and this alcoholic counterbrow can be seen, round (*rund*) and all around (*allherum*), on the distorted face (*Fratze*, 'grotesque face, grimace') of the water. In Dutch, meanwhile, Bindervoet and Henkes opt for 'en was aan de roriënt ringsom op het watergezicht de reigen-brauw te zien,' a relatively straightforward suggestion that 'to the east the rainbow could be seen, ring-like on the face (*gezicht*) of the water,' where 'aan de roriënt' combines 'rory' and *aan de oriënt* ('to the east'), while 'reigenbrauw' conflates *regenboog* ('rainbow'), *brauw* ('brow'), *brouwen* ('to brew'), and, perhaps as a result of the latter activity, also *rei* ('dance').

Two German renderings, finally, are more idiosyncratic than most. Stündel's version, 'und das rohrie Ende des ReckenBockens zeigte sich ringsum auf dem SchnappsGesicht,' raising the alcohol content to new heights, performs purely orthographic variations on 'rory' and *Regenbogen* before finding the latter reflected on a no doubt highly co-loured 'drinker's face,' the reading deriving presumably, if scarcely logically, from the *aqua* in aquavit, a type of schnapps. Schrödter's rendering is considerably more complex, if no less idiosyncratic: 'und das vertaummte Ende zum Regginbraugen war rgsomm auf dem Euangesicht zu sehen.' Here 'rory end' is rendered as 'das vertaum-mte Ende,' combining *Tau* ('dew') and *verdammt* ('damned'), evidently construing 'rory' as negative, thus 'damn the dewy end was to be seen.' The 'regginbrow,' as 'Regginbraugen,' now also includes *Braue* ('brow'), *Regenbogen* ('rainbow'), and once again, the verb *brauen* ('to brew'), while 'ringsome' is cryptically rendered, perhaps suggesting either a pronunciation distorted by alcohol or the distortion of a reflec-tion in water, as 'rgsomm.' Finally, intriguingly, 'aquaface' becomes 'Euangesicht,' combining German *Angesicht* ('face') and Greek *euánge-los* ('messenger of good news'). The implication here, significantly different in tone from that suggested by any other version considered so far, appears to be an invocation of the message of hope delivered to Noah by the Lord after the Flood: a movement from the implied opening German *verdammt* ('damned') via the Latin *aqua* that, while referring to the waters of chaos, can nonetheless also be read in a Wakean context as containing within itself (*aq-ua*) a Greek *eu-* ('good'), namely the good news (Greek *euangélion*) symbolized by the rainbow of Genesis.

PART THREE

Rivering Waters

6 Tales Told

A particularly intriguing aspect of comparing translations of *Anna Livia Plurabelle* is the fact that Joyce himself was significantly involved in at least two of them – each of which, even more interestingly, is now available in two different versions. The primary French version is the *Nouvelle Revue Française* translation published in 1931 (Beckett and Joyce 1931), but an earlier version of this, prepared by Alfred Péron and Samuel Beckett in 1930 though not separately published until 1985 (Péron and Beckett 1985), is also available for comparison.[1] The primary Italian version is now agreed to be the translation prepared by Joyce and Nino Frank in 1938 but not published until 1979 (Joyce and Frank 1979), likewise inviting comparison with the revised version of that translation by Ettore Settanni, published in 1940 in a form apparently designed to avert possible recriminations in Mussolini's Italy (Joyce and Settanni 1940). Joyce also seems to have given at least his general stamp of approval to a German version prepared by Georg Goyert that was completed in 1933, partially published after the Second World War in 1946, and published in full only in 1970 (Goyert 1946, 1970).[2]

---

1 On the relationship between the Péron and Beckett rendering and that of Beckett and Joyce, see Quigley (2004). The present chapter includes a much expanded version of an earlier discussion in my book *Polyglot Joyce: Fictions of Translation* (2005).

2 Of these, both French and both Italian versions are based on the 1928 edition of *Anna Livia Plurabelle*, while the German version is based on the 1930 edition (Reichert and Senn 1970, 165). All the remaining translations from which excerpts are quoted below are based on the final version that appeared in *Finnegans Wake* in 1939. The wording of the brief excerpts from Joyce's English examined here are identical in all three of these editions.

A primary focus of interest for students of Joyce in translation has been, as already mentioned, that Joyce, especially in the Italian version but also to some degree in the French, emerges as being much less interested in producing a translation aiming at fidelity to the original than in providing, as one scholar phrases it, 'a similarity of reading experience even at the expense of semantic equivalence' (Bosinelli 1998a, 195). Convincingly argued claims have therefore been made that the Italian and (if perhaps to a lesser extent) the French renditions should more properly be regarded as autonomous parallel texts, as re-creations rather than as translations in any traditional sense.[3] In the three very brief excerpts we examine in this chapter we shall be able, for reasons of space, to look at only one or two examples of Joyce's deliberate departures (especially in Italian, but also in French) from his original text. The details of Joyce's practice as translator per se, however, are not our primary concern here, but rather the comparison of Joyce's versions as translator with those of other translators in the production of a transtextual *Anna Livia Plurabelle* as represented by these few sentences.

Anna Livia Plurabelle, as Joyce famously wrote to Harriet Weaver on 7 March 1924, 'is a chattering dialogue across the river by two washerwomen who as night falls become a tree and a stone. The river is named Anna Liffey' (*L* 1:213). The river is thus also ALP, and the washerwomen (who will eventually emerge also as aspects of ALP, the river talking to itself) are discussing her affairs (in all senses of the word) as well as washing her dirty linen (in all senses of the word). Her consort, Humphrey Chimpden Earwicker, alias HCE, never far away and at least equally productive of dirty linen, enters the washerwomen's eager dialogue within the first few lines as the 'old chap,' his identity discreetly concealed as a disguised 'old cheb' and simultaneously revealed by the first three letters of the distorted version, *CHE* standing in (as on many other occasions) for *HCE*.

To the extent that one can identify narrative lines, the opening sentences are (also) concerned with some indeterminate act of real or imagined wrongdoing on HCE's part in the Phoenix Park. ALP's centrality is already reflected in the typographical delta formed by the opening

---

3 Discussions of the specific issues involved in translating *Anna Livia Plurabelle* include Aubert (1967), Senn (1967b, 1998), Risset (1973), Lobner (1986, 1994), Bosinelli (1996, 1998a, 1998b, 2000, 2001), Eco (1996), Ferrer and Aubert (1998), García Tortosa (1998), Milesi (1998), Szczerbowski (2000), and Zanotti (2004).

lines of the chapter: her symbol throughout *Finnegans Wake* is the upper-case Greek delta, representing (topsy-turvy) the female genitalia as well as a river mouth (and much else). It is typical of the pervasive blurring of identities in *Finnegans Wake*, including (or especially) the identities of ALP and HCE, that if the text of *Anna Livia Plurabelle* begins with the river's delta, the remainder would thus 'logically' have to represent the open sea – and thus be representative of HCE rather than ALP.[4] The two washerwomen on their opposing banks will likewise blur towards the end of the episode, as night falls, not only into aspects of ALP herself but also into tree and stone, emanations of ALP *and* HCE respectively. Tree and stone are also emanations of Shem and Shaun, the twin sons of ALP and HCE, not only the warring products of their union, but also, combined, a Tristan ('tree-stone') lusting (à la HCE) after his Iseult (à la ALP) in the all too seductive shape of Issy, sister to Shem and Shaun, daughter to HCE and ALP.

O/tell me all about/Anna Livia! I want to hear all/about Anna Livia.
Well, you know Anna Livia? Yes, of course, we all know Anna Livia.

(FW 196.1–4)

Péron and Beckett (French, 1985 / 1996): Ô dis-moi tout d'Anna Livia! Je veux tout savoir d'Anna Livia. Eh bien, tu connais Anna Livia? Évidemment, tout le monde connaît Anna Livia.

Beckett and Joyce (French, 1931 / 1996): O, dis-moi tout d'Anna Livie! Je veux tout savoir d'Anna Livie! Eh bien! tu connais Anna Livie? Bien sûr tout le monde connaît Anna Livie.

Butor (French, 1948): O / Dites-moi tout à propos / d'Anna Livia! Je veux tout entendre / à propos d'Anna Livia. Bien vous connaissez Anna Livia? Oui bien sûr nous connaissons tous Anna Livia.

Lavergne (French, 1982): O / Tellus, dis-moi tout sur / Anna Livia! Je veux tout savoir d'Anna Livia! / Mais connais tu Anna Livia? Oui, bien sûr, nous connaissons tous, Anna Livia.

---

4 Brendan O Hehir similarly notes (1965, 165) that in Irish the term *alp* means, inter alia, 'a protuberance, a huge lump, a high mountain' – attributes, that is to say, consistently evocative of HCE rather than ALP.

Joyce and Frank (Italian, 1979 / 1996): Raccontami di Anna Livia. Tutto sapere vo' di Anna Livia. Beh, conosci Anna Livia? Altro che, conosciamo tutte Anna Livia!

Joyce and Settanni (Italian, 1940): Raccontami di Anna Livia. Tutto vo' sapere di Anna Livia. Beh, la conosci Anna Livia? Altro che, conosciamo tutte Anna Livia!

Wilcock (Italian, 1961): Oh / raccontami tutto di / Anna Livia! Voglio sapere tutto / di Anna Livia. Dunque, conosci Anna Livia? Ma sí, certo, noi tutte conosciamo Anna Livia.

Schenoni (Italian, 1996): O / dimmi tutto di / Anna Livia! Voglio sentire tutto / di Anna Livia. Be', conosci Anna Livia? Sí, certo, Anna Livia la conosciamo tutti.

García Tortosa (Spanish, 1992): O / dímelo to de / Anna Livia! Quiero oirlo to / de Anna Livia. Bueno, conoces a Anna Livia? Sí, claro, tol mundo conoce a Anna Livia.

Pozanco (Spanish, 1993): ¡Oh, / cuéntamelo todo / Anna Livia! Quiero saberlo todo / de Anna Livia. Porque sabéis quién es Anna Livia, ¿no? Claro que sí; todos sabemos quién es Anna Livia.

Aixàs (Catalan, 2004): Ω / Explica-ho tot / d'Anna Livia! Ho vull saber tot / d'Anna Livia. ¿Bé, coneixes Anna Livia, oi? Si, és clar. / Tots coneixem a l'Anna Livia.

Campos (Portuguese, 1962): Ah / fala-me de / Ana Lívia! Quero ouvir tudo / sôbre Ana Lívia. Bem, você conhece Ana Lívia? Mas claro, todo mundo.

Schüler (Portuguese, 2003): O / Conta-me tudo sobre / Ana Lívia! Quero ouvir tudo / sobre Ana Lívia. Bem, conheces Ana Lívia? Açai, claro, todos conhecemos Ana Lívia.

Amarante (Portuguese, 2009): O / Me conta tudo sobre / Anna Livia! Quero saber tudo / sobre Anna Livia. Bom, conheces Anna Livia? Claro que sim, todo mundo conhece Anna Livia.

Antip (Romanian, 1996): O / spune-mi totul despre Anna Livia! Vreau să aud totul despre Anna Livia. Ei, o ştii pe Anna Livia? Da, sigur, o ştim cu toatele pe Anna Livia.

Goyert (German, 1970): Oh! Erzähle mir alles über Anna Livia! Alles will ich von Anna Livia wissen! Du kennst doch Anna Livia? Aber natürlich, wir alle kennen Anna Livia.

Hildesheimer (German, 1970): O / sag mir alles von / Anna Livia! Ich muß alles hören / von Anna Livia. Na, ihr kennt Anna Livia? Aber ja, wir alle kennen Anna Livia.

Wollschläger (German, 1970): O / erzähl mir alles von / Anna Livia! Ich will alles hören / von Anna Livia. Ach, du kennst Anna Livia? Ja doch, klar, wir alle kennen Anna Livia.

Stündel (German, 1993): Eau / sag mir alles über / Anna Livia! Ich will alles über / Anna Livia wissen. Also, kennt ihr Anna Livia? Ja freilich, wir alle kennen Anna Livia.

Bindervoet and Henkes (Dutch, 2002): O / vertel me alles over / Anna Livia! Ik wil alles horen / over Anna Livia. Nou, je kent Anna Livia? Ja natuuurlijk, Anna Livia kennen we allemaal.

Grut (Swedish, 2001): Å / berätta allt om / Anna Livia! Jag vill höra allt / om Anna Livia. Känner du Anna Livia? Så klart, gör vi alla.

Weatherall et al. (Czech, 1932 / 1996): Ó / pověz mi všechno / o Anně Livii! Chci slyšet všechno / o Anně Livii! Nu tak, znáš Annu Livii? / Ovšem, všichni známe Annu Livii.

Słomczyński (Polish, 1985): O / mów mi wszystko / o Annie Livii! / Chcę słyszeć wszystko / o Annie Livii. No cóz, znasz Annę Livię? Tak, oczywiście, wszyscy znamy Annę Livię.

Belyaev (Russian, 2000): O / rasskaži mne vcё pro / Annu Liviju! Hoču uslyšat' vcё pro / Annu Liviju. Ty čto že, znaeš' Annu Liviju? Eščё by, vce my znaem Annu Liviju.

Bíró (Hungarian, 1992): Ó / mondj el mindent Anna / Líviáról! Mindent tudni akarok Anna Líviáról. Hát te ismered Anna Líviát? – Persze, mindenki ismeri Anna Líviát.

The multilingual multiplication of voices is particularly appropriate in this context, eager as our translated washerwomen are for gossip, preferably scandalous, and to tell and be told 'all about' the flibbertigibbet ALP and the reprehensible HCE. 'O' is both French *eau* ('water') and

Greek omega, both associated with ALP (as with Molly Bloom), as well as a symbol of female sexuality and fertility. The name *Anna Livia* appears on old maps, a corruption of the Latin *Amnis Livia* (river Liffey) but evocative also of the Irish *Abha na Life* (river Liffey), which in turn, and invitingly, looks as if it should be referring to the Heraclitean 'river of life.' (Etymologically, at least, it is doing nothing of the sort: *Life*, pronounced approximately like its English variant 'Liffey,' is an entirely unrelated place name – but only, of course, if one accepts that *Finnegans Wake* allows for the concept of unrelatedness in the first place.)

The typographical delta formed by the opening lines, suggesting a river mouth, was restricted to two lines ('O / tell me all about') in the 1928 and 1930 editions; the third line was introduced only when the text of *Anna Livia Plurabelle* reappeared in 1939 with slight textual modifications as the eighth chapter of *Finnegans Wake*. Almost all our translators who worked with the 1939 version of the text retain the three-line introductory structure, exceptions being Antip in Romanian, who limits her introduction to just one line ('O'), and Bíró in Hungarian, who is content with two lines. Those who worked with the 1928 or 1930 text, however – including Joyce himself – uniformly, with just one exception, ignore the introductory typographical delta altogether. The exception is the 1932 Czech version of Weatherall, Procházka, and Hoffmeister, which, at least in the 1996 edition, improves the shining hour with an expanded four-line opening delta, followed by a new paragraph.

The suggestion of ALP as omega and mother goddess is replicated in all versions that begin with 'O' or, less elegantly, 'Oh' (thus Wilcock, Goyert, Pozanco), or even 'Ω' (thus Aixàs). Péron and Beckett's 'Ô,' though not repeated in the subsequent Beckett and Joyce version, succeeds also, by means of the strategically placed circumflex, in suggesting the delta. Campos's 'Ah,' abandoning the generic French *eau* ('water') for the specific French river Aa, suggests both the delta (intimated by the shape of the capital *A*) and *A* for ALP, as well as, serendipitously, the Sumerian *a* ('water'). Grut's Swedish 'Å,' even more ingeniously, manages to incorporate ALP's own initial, the (diacritical) *O*, the delta suggested by an upper-case *A*, the Swedish *å* ('river'), the French river Aa, and the Sumerian *a* ('water'). Stündel's 'Eau' has been criticized (Drews 1993, 153; 1998, 430) as reductive, which it indisputably is – but it also underlines one particularly interesting dimension: the water itself is invited to tell all about Anna Livia, reminding us that the two washerwomen are also a dual manifestation of ALP and that the entire episode is therefore also (and reminiscent of Molly Bloom) an implied soliloquy. We may note that Pozanco's perhaps inadvertent omission of the Spanish preposition *de* ('about') in his second line, as if addressing Anna Livia herself, temporarily achieves exactly the same effect.

Joyce's English is at obvious pains to locate the opening 'O' exactly; it is therefore all the more noticeable that in Italian, Joyce and Frank as well as Joyce and Settanni simply omit it altogether, cavalierly opting instead for the more urgent rhythm of an unadorned 'Raccontami di Anna Livia' ('Tell me about Anna Livia'). García Tortosa's Spanish achieves a similar sense of urgency with 'díme lo to,' where 'to' is both a colloquial contraction of *todo* ('all') and an urgent interjection meaning 'come on!' (García Tortosa 1998, 209). Campos, we notice, adopts a much less urgent Portuguese 'fala-me de Ana Livia' ('speak to me of Anna Livia').

There is a division, indeed, between those voices who ask to be 'spoken' to and those who ask to be 'told' about Anna Livia: the former are in the majority (and include Beckett and Joyce); the latter, asking more urgently and more specifically for a narrative account, for the story of what happened, include Joyce and Frank's version, and also those of Goyert, Wilcock, Wollschläger, and Pozanco. Similarly, there is certainly a difference between 'hearing' everything (as in Joyce's English) and 'knowing' everything about Anna Livia, and here our translators split into two almost equal groups. As for Anna Livia herself, she remains essentially unchanged in all versions, with the single significant exception of Beckett and Joyce, which goes to some pains to remind us that Anna Livia is also 'Anna Livie,' the river of life (French *la vie*) itself, perhaps not entirely to be disassociated from the Irish *uisce beatha*, the 'water of life,' otherwise whiskey.

These lines so far, as we notice, are in plain English, not 'Wakean.' With four exceptions, all our translators (including the French and Italian Joyces) likewise translate without Wakean distortions or embellishment. The exceptions are Stündel's 'Eau' and Aixàs's 'Ω,' as already discussed; Lavergne's 'O Tellus, dis-moi tout sur Anna Livia,' opportunistically (and translingually) invoking the earth mother Gea Tellus in mock epic style to 'tell us' all about her affairs as Anna Livia, the river of rivers; and Campos's naturalization of 'Anna' to a more Portuguese if equally palindromic 'Ana,' succinctly conflating in the process Turkish *ana* ('mother') and the Irish mother goddess Ana, tutelary deity, under an alternative form of her name, of the mythological Tuatha Dé Danann, the 'people of the goddess Dana' (O Hehir 1965, 164).

Two further sentences in plain English follow in this segment, concluding the ritualized fourfold invocation of the name of Anna Livia, and again they remain similarly undistorted in their various translated forms. The question 'Well, you know Anna Livia?' might initially seem to be purely rhetorical in Joyce's original, serving merely to heighten narrative anticipation. It is duly left in this form by the majority of the translations. But of course we *don't* know Anna Livia, whose essence is her mutability and indefinability. Two or three of our translators therefore not inappropriately phrase the question as truly interrogative rather than rhetorical: Stündel's straightforward 'Also, kennt ihr Anna Livia?' ('So, do you know Anna Livia?') for example, or Pozanco's 'Porque sabéis quién es Anna Livia, ¿no?' ('For you do know who Anna Livia is, don't you?'). Pozanco's washerwomen are perhaps more distanced in their relationship to Anna Livia than most, for the second accordingly answers, 'Claro que sí; todos sabemos quién es Anna Livia' ('Yes, of course, we all know who Anna Livia is'). Knowing 'who Anna Livia is,' however, is not the same as knowing 'Anna Livia,' which is the washerwoman's response in all other translations.

And who exactly is the 'we' in 'we all know Anna Livia'? Joyce and Frank, Joyce and Settanni, and Wilcock – Italian versions in all cases – are the only ones to specify, for example, that 'we' is feminine: 'conosciamo tutt*e*,' 'noi tutt*e* conosciamo.' All others, including the French Beckett and Joyce, are indeterminate as to whom the washerwoman speaks for. By the same token, transtextual uncertainties also already begin to emerge as to how many addressees are involved: most versions have an unambiguously singular addressee, as Joyce's original seems to call for, but three are equally unambiguously plural (Hildesheimer's and Stündel's German 'ihr,' Pozanco's Spanish 'sabéis'). Butor's French 'vous,' a form of address appropriate for either a plural or a formally addressed singular interlocutor, is usefully ambivalent.

Anna Livia Plurabelle is celebrated for containing the (usually disguised) names of more than one thousand rivers and assorted waterways: Grut, in the notes to his Swedish translation, actually counts (and lists) no fewer than 1,022 (2001, 33–7). The first word of our opening sentence, with its 'O' readable as French *eau* ('water'), opens a series of references to rivers and to water in general. The aqueous implications of the first word, as we have seen, are replicated, with occasional adjustments, in the great majority of versions. The implied reference to water in Joyce's interjection 'well,' meanwhile, just a few words later, disappears without trace in all translations except Wollschläger's, whose German interjection *ach* may or may not serve to remind his readers that there are several German and Austrian rivers of the names Ach and Ache, echoing across the centuries the Old High German *aha* ('water, river'). Dublin's Liffey is of course central in all versions, and the opening invitation to 'tell me all about' Anna Livia contributes references to the Indian river Tel, the Ugandan river Alla, and the South American Abou.

Almost all versions considered here contribute rivers, streams, and other water references not to be found in the original text – and they do so with particular enthusiasm in these opening lines. Péron and Beckett's 'tu connais Anna Livia?' evokes the Japanese Onna River, while the response, 'Évidemment' contributes the Swiss river Emme. The Onna reappears, unsurprisingly, in all three of the other French versions. Joyce's English 'Yes, of course' invokes the course of any river, but Joyce and Frank's Italian succeeds with the invitation 'Raccontami' ('tell me') in evoking the Raccoon River of Iowa, the Welsh Teme, and the English Thames (in Italian *Tamigi*). The declaration that 'Tutto sapere vo' di Anna Livia' ('I want to know all about Anna Livia') contributes the Sape River of the Solomon Islands, and the following question and response, 'Beh, conosci Anna Livia? Altro che' ('Well, you know Anna Livia? Yes, of course'), adds the river Behy of County Kerry, the Japanese Ono, and the English Roch. The variation 'Beh, la conosci Anna Livia?' ('Well, you know Anna Livia?') in Joyce and Settanni contributes the Philippine Laco instead of the English Roch. Wilcock's variation 'Dunque conosci Anna Livia?'('Well, you know Anna Livia?') adds the river Dun of County Antrim and various English rivers of the same name, while Schenoni's 'Voglio sentire tutto' ('I want to hear all') contributes the Scottish river Tirry, and his 'Sí, certo' ('Yes, of course') suggests the English river Irt.

In Spanish, García Tortosa's 'dímelo to de Anna Livia!' ('Tell me all about Anna Livia') evokes the English river Mel and the Australian Todd; 'Bueno' ('Well') contributes the Chilean Río Bueno; and 'tol mundo conoce' ('everybody knows') hints at the Slovenian Tolminka. García Tortosa also notes (1998, 209) that his Spanish 'tol mundo' is both a colloquial contraction for *todo el mundo* ('everyone') and a gesture towards the Yiddish *tol* ('valley'), thus extending the water imagery by hinting at the world as a biblical valley of tears. Aixàs's Catalan 'Explica-ho tot ... Ho vull saber tot' ('tell about it all ... I want to know it all') twice invokes the Chinese noun *ho* ('river'), while '¿Bé, coneixes Anna Livia, oi?' ('Well, you know Anna Livia, right?') gestures towards the Scottish river Oich, and 'Tots coneixem a l'Anna Livia' ('We all know Anna Livia') adds the also Scottish Allan Water.

Campos's Portuguese 'fala-me de Ana Livia' ('speak to me of Anna Livia') allows the incorporation of references to the African river Fala and the Syrian river Alameda; his 'Quero ouvir tudo' ('I want to hear all') evokes the French river Ouvèze; and his 'Bem' ('Well') and 'claro' ('of course') add the Australian Bemm and the Brazilian Rio Claro. Amarante's Portuguese 'Quero saber tudo' ('I want to know all') provides another oblique glance at the Croatian river Save, while her substitution of 'Bom' ('Well') for Campos's 'Bem' evokes the Sudanese river Boma. Schüler's idiosyncratic Portuguese rendering of 'Yes, of course' as 'Açaí' not only plays on Portuguese *ah sim* ('ah yes') and French *assez* ('enough already') but introduces a double water reference: the *açaí* palm is native to the wetlands of the Amazon basin, while its name in the local Tupian language, *iwasa'i*, is reported by Wikipedia as referring to its fruit that literally 'cries water.' Antip's Romanian 'Vreau să aud totul' ('I want to hear all') includes the French *eau* ('water') as well as a reference to the French river Aude, while her 'o ştim cu toatele' ('we all know') reminds us once again of the Indian river Tel.

German contributes relatively few new fluvial references, but Goyert's 'Alles will ich von Anna Livia wissen!' ('I want to know all about Anna Livia') evokes the English river Wissey; Hildesheimer's 'Na, ihr kennt Anna Livia?' ('Well, you know Anna Livia?') contributes the English river Kent; and Stündel's 'Ja freilich' ('Yes, of course') adds the Scottish waterway Allt an Eilich. Bindervoet and Henkes's Dutch 'vertel me alles' ('tell me all') evokes the English Ver, the Indian Tel, the Ugandan Alla, and the German Aller, while 'Ja natuuurlijk, Anna Livia kennen we allemaal' ('Yes, of course, we all know Anna Livia') contributes the eastern European Tur, the English Ure, the Ugandan Alla, the German Aller, and the Belgian Maalbek, a stream that runs through Brussels. Grut's Swedish assurance, 'Så klart' ('yes, of course'), that 'vi alla' ('we all') know Anna Livia evokes the Swedish river Klar as well as gesturing once again towards the German river Aller and the Ugandan Alla. Eastern European languages also contribute to the fluvial flow. Weatherall's 'Nu tak' ('Well') adds the Japanese Nuta River, while Belyaev's Russian 'rasskaži mne vcë' ('tell me all') adds the Serbian Raška. Bíró's Hungarian 'mondj el mindent' ('tell me all') contributes the Elm River of Illinois and the German Inde; while 'Mindent tudni akarok Anna Líviáról' ('I want to hear all about Anna Livia') adds the English Tud and the Indian Karo; and 'Persze' (Yes, of course') gives us Manitoba's Persse Lake.

The precise geographical location of these and other waterways, meanwhile, though interesting in its own right, is (or at any rate appears to be) essentially irrelevant, since the main role of the multiple river references is to function as fluvial representatives and emanations of Anna Livia, the river of all rivers, whose name is also ceremonially recalled no fewer than four times in each of twenty-two of the twenty-five versions considered. Even the three exceptions, Campos, Grut, and Aixàs, have her name echo three rather than four times in each case.

That name also reminds us once again that even in the case of a foreign language of which one is almost entirely ignorant, occasional glimpses may be caught of intriguing interlingual modulations of the Joycean text. In Czech, for example, Anna Livia, acquiring new alphabetical plurabilities, translates unchanged as 'Anna Livia' in the nominative case, but appears, perhaps rather disconcertingly for a nonnative reader, as 'Annu Livii' and 'Anně Livii' in oblique cases, while undergoing corresponding changes to 'Annu Liviju' in Russian, to 'Annę Livię' and 'Annie Livii' in Polish, and even to 'Anna Líviáról' and 'Anna Líviát' in Hungarian, in the case of all four languages thus felicitously (and quite independently of the individual translators involved) reflecting ALP's shape-changing riverine mutability.

Well, you know, when the old cheb went futt and did what you know.
(FW 196.6–7)

Péron and Beckett (French, 1985 / 1996): Alors, tu sais, quand le vieux gaillarda fit krach et fit ce que tu sais.

Beckett and Joyce (French, 1931 / 1996): Alors, tu sais, quand le vieux gaillarda fit krach et fit ce que tu sais.

Butor (French, 1948): Vous savez quand le vieux type devint futt et fit ce que vous savez.

Lavergne (French, 1982): Non tu sais lorsque le vieux, et crac, fit ce que tu sais.

Joyce and Frank (Italian, 1979 / 1996): Beh, sai quando il messercalzone andò in rovuma e fe' ciò che fe'?

Joyce and Settanni (Italian, 1940): Beh, sai allorché il messercalzone andò in rovuma e fe' ciò che fe'?

Wilcock (Italian, 1961): Dunque, sai, quando il vecchio perse la bussola e fece quel che sai.

Schenoni (Italian, 1996): Be' sai quando il vecchio chebscalzone fece foutsco e combinò quello che sai.

García Tortosa (Spanish, 1992): Bueno, ya sabes lo del viejo calandrajo ganforro que hizo lo que sabes.

Pozanco (Spanish, 1993): Ya sabes, cuando el viejo anduvo riorriendo, se mojó e hizo lo que hizo.

Aixàs (Catalan, 2004): Bé, saps quan el vellot es tornà boig i féu el que ja saps?

Campos (Portuguese, 1962): Ora, você sabe, quando aquêle malandro fêz baque e fêz o que você sabe.

Schüler (Portuguese, 2003): Bem, sabes, quando o velho velhaco fez fiasco e fez o que fez.

Amarante (Portuguese, 2009): Bem, sabes, quando o velho foolgado fallou e fez o que sabes.

Antip (Romanian, 1996): Păi, ştii, când pezevenghiul de babalâc a luat-o razna şi a făcut ce ştii.

Goyert (German, 1970): Na, du weißt doch, als der alte Holdrio hopps ging und tat, was du weißt.

Hildesheimer (German, 1970): Na, du weißt, als der alte Kjärl fehltrat und tat, was du weißt.

Wollschläger (German, 1970): Also, du weißt doch, wie der alte Sack futtsch ging und tat, was du weißt.

Stündel (German, 1993): Also, du weist doch noch, als der alte KNaabbe fotzging und das tat, was du weißt.

Bindervoet and Henkes (Dutch, 2002): Nou, weet je nog, diem khabbir met z'n ongein en toen hij je weet wel wat deed.

Grut (Swedish, 2001): Du vet när gubbstrunten fick fnatt och gjorde det där, du vet.

Weatherall et al. (Czech, 1932 / 1996): Tak tedy víš, jak se ten starej chlop zjančil a co proved.

Słomczyński (Polish, 1985): Nocóż, wiesz, kiedy ten stary kiep futtknął się i zrobił to, co wiesz.

Bíró (Hungarian, 1992): Hát tudod, mikor az ura, az a vén kos kilett
   és azt a tudodmit csinálta.

From stories about ALP, we quickly turn to stories about HCE. The language, once again, is essentially standard English. To go 'futt' or 'phutt'
variously suggests fizzling out like a damp firework, suffering a short
circuit, blowing a fuse, going bust, losing it – some or all of which HCE
here reportedly does, or might have done if given the chance, or perhaps
just consciously or subconsciously fantasizes doing. What exactly his
alleged failing was, or is, or might have been, however, is never unambiguously revealed, though there are strong suggestions at various
points that voyeurism of some kind may (or might) at least have been
involved, perhaps along the lines of Leopold Bloom's self-satisfying activities in 'Nausicaa.' Joyce's English sentence begins and ends with 'you
know': the issue, in other words, is less that HCE did what he did (if he
did) than that he 'did what you know,' which is 'you know what,' whatever it is you think you know – where 'you,' of course, includes the reader as well as the washerwomen. What we know can quickly become
what he did, however: in Pozanco's Spanish, HCE 'hizo lo que hizo,' in
Schüler's Portuguese he 'fez o que fez,' just as in Joyce and Frank's and
Joyce and Settanni's Italian, where he likewise 'fe' ciò che fe',' where in
all cases he did not do 'what you know' but rather 'what he did.' It may
just be seeing things, meanwhile, to discover HCE himself hidden in the
formula 'fe' ciò *che* fe',' as well as in the small but perhaps not insignificant change from Joyce and Frank's 'quando' ('when') to Joyce and
Settanni's 'allor*ché*' ('when').
   Many good stories begin with an introductory 'well,' and this one is
no exception, reminding us in passing that we are still in a chapter
awash in water references. HCE makes his entrance as an 'old cheb,' an
appearance accompanied by that of the Cheb, a river in what is now the
Czech Republic. The Cheb thus does double duty, not only standing in
for a concealed and perhaps voyeuristic HCE but also providing another fluvial reference to ALP. The old cheb in question, meanwhile,
reveals himself transtextually as an old chap of many parts. For Péron
and Beckett as well as for Beckett and Joyce he is a 'gaillarda,' a 'dirty
old man' who is apparently still a 'strapping character' (French *gail-
lard*), doubtless with a taste for *gaillardises* ('dirty stories, dirty jokes').
Fritz Senn sees the Swiss-German noun *Cheib* potentially present in
'the old cheb,' meaning approximately 'the old bugger' (1967a, 108–9)
– though 'the dirty old shagger' would be closer to Hiberno-English

idiom. Apart from that, perhaps the old cheb isn't entirely as bad as he is made out to be, at least for some of our translators: Butor's 'le vieux type,' Wilcock's 'il vecchio,' Lavergne's 'le vieux,' Pozanco's 'el viejo,' Aixàs's 'el vellot,' Wollschläger's 'der alte Sack,' and Stündel's 'der alte KNaabbe' are in all cases, linguistically at least, just a harmless 'old chap.' Perhaps he is even unjustly maligned: for Hildesheimer he is 'der alte Kjärl,' a possibly disreputable old fellow (German *Kerl*), but nonetheless revealing Scandinavian roots that may even suggest the inherited nobility of an earl (Norwegian *jarl*).

Less charitable opinions are also readily to hand, however. For Joyce and Frank as for Joyce and Settanni he is 'il messercalzone,' invoking both *calzoni* ('trousers') and *calzare* ('to try something on'), and thus suggesting something like 'Mister Trousers,' perhaps hinting at trouser-related misdemeanours. For Goyert he is 'der alte Holdrio' ('the old rake'), for Campos 'aquêle malandro' ('that good-for-nothing'), for Schüler 'o velho velhaco' ('the old crook'), for Amarante he is a 'velho foolgado' – a translingual 'old fool' who is also a 'lazy old devil' (*folgado*) – for Słomczyński he is just 'ten stary kiep' ('the old fool'), for García Tortosa he is 'el viejo calandrajo ganforro' ('the ragged old rogue'), for Grut he is a 'gubbstrunt' ('an old good-for-nothing'), and for Antip he is a 'pezevenghiul de babalâc,' not just an 'old crock' (*babalâc*) but one who is living off immoral earnings (Turkish *pezevengi*, 'pimp').' For Schenoni he is 'il vecchio chebscalzone' (suggesting something like 'the old tramp'), having now kept his trousers but lost his shoes, by way of the adjective *scalzo* ('shoeless, discalced').

The river Cheb also still flows in Schenoni's version, we note, and Goyert allows his old rake, that notorious 'Holdrio,' to evoke also a Spanish *río* ('river'). Stündel's 'der alte KNaabbe' invokes the German river Naab. Weatherall's 'ten starej chlop' has 'the old chap' (*ten starej chlap*) accompanied by the river Lop of Pakistan. Bindervoet and Henkes remodel him as an old *khabbir* ('chap, fellow') with a touch of the boor (*Kaffer*) about him, his identity suggested by the letters *KHI*, this version's Dutch equivalent of *CHE*, a rearranged set of the initials *HCE*. More specifically, he is described as 'diem khabbir met z'n ongein,' roughly 'the fellow involved in a funny business (*ongein*) of some sort,' a rendering that offers a comfortable home to four separate rivers from near and far: the Dutch Diem, the Laotian Kha, the Australian Birrie, and the Dutch Gein.

The specific water reference in Joyce's opening 'well' disappears in all versions examined here. Interestingly, however, two different compensatory strategies, not necessarily intended in all cases, can be identified in the Romance languages. First, Joyce's 'you know' is rendered in French by 'vous savez' (Butor), in Spanish by 'sabes' (García Tortosa, Pozanco), in Portuguese by 'você sabe' (Campos) and 'sabes' (Schüler, Amarante), each of these choices unremarkable except that each allows a reference to the Croatian river Sava, known in German as the Save. Second, Joyce's suggestion that the old cheb did 'what you know' is rendered in Italian as 'quel che sai' (Wilcock) and 'quello che sai' (Schenoni), each of which, though again quite unremarkable, allows a translingual reference to the German *Quelle* ('spring, well').

Whatever the details of his disreputable character may be, HCE goes 'futt,' an event marked by the simultaneous appearance of the South American river Futa. He also succeeds in going transtextually 'futt' in a satisfying plurality of ways. The story for Goyert is that he 'hopps ging,' for Wollschläger that he 'futtsch ging'; he likewise 'fece foutsco' for Schenoni and 'devint futt' for Butor, behaving in all cases, that is to say, just as indeterminately as in Joyce's original, though the implication in Butor (clearer in the French text than in the English) that he may either have gone a bit crazy (French *fou*) or else been involved in some sexual misadventure (French *foutre*, 'to fuck') offers at least some additional information. At any rate, he seems to be well and truly *foutu* ('done for').

Some translations prefer to draw a veil of indeterminate decency over what he may have been up to. Lavergne's French thus limits itself to hinting obliquely that 'le vieux, et crac, fit ce que tu sais' ('the old fellow, bang, just like that, did what you know'). Others have their own theories. In Pozanco's Spanish he 'anduvo riorriendo, se mojó e hizo lo que hizo' – roughly 'he was laughing (*riendo*) and playing about down by the river (*río*), got himself all wet (*se mojó*), and did what he did.' For Wilcock he 'perse la bussola' ('lost his bearings'), while for Campos he 'fêz baque' ('went bang, took a bad fall'), for Schüler he 'fez fiasco' ('came a cropper'), for Antip he 'a luat-o razna' ('went astray'), and for Aixàs he simply 'es tornà boig' ('went crazy'). More specifically, he 'andò in rovuma' for Joyce and Frank, which suggests with exemplary compactness that he went to the dogs (*andò in rovina*), suffered a bad fall (*rovina*) like Tim Finnegan, came to his ruin (*rovina*), that all of this was connected in some unspecified way with a bush (*rovo*) of some sort, and that a stream of some sort was also involved, as conveniently represented by the Rovuma River of Mozambique. Hildesheimer's German knows only that he 'fehltrat' ('took a false step'), but Stündel's is all too gleefully clear that he 'fotzging,' the inclusion of the vulgar term for female genitals *Fotze* narrowing the area of doubt as to the general nature of his perceived offence. Meanwhile, Péron and Beckett seem to take a surprisingly different view of the matter, as do Beckett and Joyce: HCE's problems may in fact have been primarily market-related, for in both of these versions he 'fit krach' ('went bust'), ostensibly adding financial disaster (French *krach*) to whatever other woes he may have had – and adding the French river Krach to our collection of waterways.

> *Or whatever it was they threed to make out he thried to two in the Fiendish park.* (FW 196.9–11)

Péron and Beckett (French, 1985 / 1996): Ou quel quel que fût le tréfleuve qu'il aurait trouvé dans le parc de l'Inphernix.

Beckett and Joyce (French, 1931 / 1996): Ou quelque fut le tréfleuve que le triplepatte qu'on dit qu'il trouva dans le parc de l'Inphernix.

Lavergne (French, 1982): Ou quoi que ce fût que l'on essaya de découvrir qu'il ait bien pu faire à Fiendish Park.

Joyce and Frank (Italian, 1979 / 1996): O cosa mai fece bifronte o triforo in quel'infenice di porco nastro?

Joyce and Settanni (Italian, 1940): O cosa mai fece bifronte o triforo in quell'infenice di porco nastro?

Wilcock (Italian, 1961): Ma non so bene che cosa dicono che egli abbia fatto a quelle due in quell'infenice parco.

Schenoni (Italian, 1996): O qualunque cosa fosse che hanno trescato di affermare che tontò con quei due nel Fistolpark.

García Tortosa (Spanish, 1992): O lo que tresaran soltar que intrestó doser en el Parque Findio.

Pozanco (Spanish, 1993): Fuese lo que fuese lo que intentasen descubrir que les hiciera a aquellas dos en Phoenix Park.

Aixàs (Catalan, 2004): O fos el que fos que intentaren traspunxar que temptegés fer al parc Fiendish.

Campos (Portuguese, 1962): Ou que diabo foi que trentaram duescobrir que êle tresandou fazendo no parque de Duendix.

Schüler (Portuguese, 2003): O que é que Tefé que tresandaram a
  descobrir o que ele doisdou de fazer no Fuscoix Parque.

Amarante (Portuguese, 2009): Seja lá o que quer que tenha sido
  eles teentaram doiscifrar o que ele trestou fazer no parque
  Fiendish.

Antip (Romanian, 1996): Sau cum naiba îi spune la ce au tăiat ei firul
  în trei să priceapă că a încercat el în doi în parcul Necurat.

Goyert (German, 1970): Oder was alles sie ihm zu beweisen sich
  erdreisten, was er in Pfuinix-Park zu entzweien versuchte.

Hildesheimer (German, 1970): Oder was das wohl war, was die Drei
  sich erdachten, was den Zweien er tat, da im Viechspark.

Wollschläger (German, 1970): Also was denn auch ilmer sie ausdrifteln wollten, daß er's bezwockt hätt im Faunix-Park.

Stündel (German, 1993): Oder was war es bloiß ach, was die Draige
  sich ausdachten, was er mit den Zwaithgen im Föhlnix Park
  versyrchda.

Bindervoet and Henkes (Dutch, 2002): Of tweet niet wat drie
  trachtten te zien wat hij triochtte te duon in het Vreeslix Park.

Grut (Swedish, 2001): Eller vad tre nu påstred han försöktu sig två i
  Fiendix Park.

Weatherall et al. (Czech, 1932 / 1996): Tak at' už to bylo, co chtělo,
  co se lidi potrojčili nadělat z toho, co on se podvojil udělat v
  Čertovce.

Słomczyński (Polish, 1985): Mów, o czym po padło, co im się troiło z
  tego, co wtroił tym dwóm w Pieklix parku.

Bíró (Hungarian, 1992): – Hogy mi a csuda vót, amit megpróbáltak
  kitudni, hogy mit próbált a Fujnix parkba.

Whatever it was that HCE did or did not do or might have done if given
a chance, the report of it gives rise to the most complex utterance we
have encountered so far in *Anna Livia Plurabelle*, producing a significant
scatter of multilingual renderings even though its immediate surface
meaning appears to be relatively clear: 'or whatever it was they tried to
make out he tried to do in the Fiendish park.'

The 'Fiendish park' is of course a humorous distortion of the Phoenix Park, the fictional location of HCE's fall from grace, whatever form that may or might have taken. The English name of the park derives from that of a residence named The Phoenix, built by one Sir Edward Fisher about 1615 on the site of the future Magazine Fort. The property was later greatly extended to form a viceregal demesne and deer park, and by 1700 it was already known as the Phoenix Park. The association of the phoenix and the park is etymologically spurious, as it happens, for the name chosen for Sir Edward's residence is merely a serendipitous corruption of an earlier Irish place name involving the term *fionnuisce* ('clear water'), referring to a natural well of clear water that once existed near the present Zoological Gardens (de Courcy 1996, 297–8).

Spurious or not, however, the phoenix's mythological connotations enable it to function both as a symbol of death and of resurrection, a recurring theme in *Finnegans Wake*, and also as a broad hint that HCE's alleged misdemeanour may have involved risings and fallings of a more earthy nature. At any rate, the location is perfectly suited to this chapter of Joyce's text: the titular Finn (again) is a variation on the Old Irish *find*, Modern Irish *fionn* ('white, fair, clear'), and this chapter is all about *uisce* ('water'). Tim Finnegan, for his part, we may remember, was happily resurrected after being inadvertently sprinkled with *uisce* of a more potent sort, namely *uisce beatha*, the 'water of life,' otherwise good Irish whiskey.

One possible version of HCE's misdemeanour that readers of *Finnegans Wake* are at liberty to reconstruct is that he ill-advisedly seized an opportunity to spy on two girls surreptitiously relieving themselves in the park (and thus also contributing to the general water level of the chapter). Whether he 'tried to do' anything further is unclear. Whatever he did, he himself was possibly observed doing so by three soldiers, who at any rate seem to have subsequently spread various colourful versions of the story around Dublin. One piece of 'evidence' for this particular version of the story is the present sentence fragment, with its pronounced play on the numbers three and two: 'Or whatever it was they threed to make out he thried to two,' which seems, on closer examination, also to imply 'whatever the three in the trees tried to make out he tried to do to the two of them.'

The two girls and three soldiers may be read as corresponding to the five members of Earwicker's own family: mother and daughter as the watched, father and sons as the voyeuristic watchers (Tindall 1959, 241). Alternatively, the two temptresses can be read as two versions of his daughter Issy, who suffers from (and enjoys) a split personality, while the three soldiers can be read as his sons Shem and Shaun individually and, as a joint threat to a father all too uneasily conscious of the passing years, combined. One possible pictorial source of the whole incident, meanwhile, as has been variously observed, is the Dublin city coat of arms, which shows two demure maidens holding aloft olive branches of peace while three warlike escutcheoned castles burst impetuously into flame. As in the best detective stories, both the evidence and the reactions to it become even more ramified when we consult our multilingual witnesses.

Five of our translators feel the need to state the issue in plain language. Lavergne's version, reduced from Wakean to plain French, seems to be picking its words very carefully and avoids any reference either to the three watchers or the two watched: 'Ou quoi que ce fût que l'on essaya de découvrir qu'il ait bien pu faire' ('Or whatever it might be they tried to establish he may have done'). Aixàs's Catalan version likewise avoids these details: 'O fos el que fos que intentaren traspunxar que temptegés fer al parc Fiendish' ('Or whatever it was they intended to spread about that he attempted to do in the Fiendish park'). Wilcock's rendering, also in plain Italian, omits any reference to the three possible watchers but includes the two girls: 'Ma non so bene che cosa dicono che egli abbia fatto a quelle due' ('But I don't rightly know what they say he did to those two'). Pozanco's version makes a similar choice, once again in plain and very carefully phrased Spanish: 'Fuese lo que fuese lo que intentasen descubrir que les hiciera a aquellas dos' ('Whatever it may have been they tried to maintain he did to those two'). Hildesheimer's 'Oder was das wohl war, was die Drei sich erdachten, was den Zweien er tat' ('Or whatever it was that the three of them worked out that he did to the two of them') is equally plain German but is the first version so far to include plain reference to the 'three' as well as the 'two' – while invoking in passing the German river Oder.

Other versions are couched in what one might call moderate transtextual Wakean. Goyert's version likewise invokes the German Oder: 'Oder was alles sie ihm zu beweisen sich erdreisten, was er ... zu entzweien versuchte' translates as 'or whatever they were being bold enough to claim he tried to break asunder,' where 'sich erdreisten' ('being bold enough') and 'zu entzweien' ('to break asunder'), both ordinary German phrases, manage also to include references respectively to *drei* ('three') and *zwei* ('two'). Wollschläger's 'Also was denn auch ilmer sie ausdrifteln wollten, daß er's bezwockt hätt' translates roughly as 'or whatever it was they wanted to cobble together that he intended to do,' where the phrase *was auch immer* ('whatever') is made to act as host for the German river Ilm, the verb *austüfteln* ('to cobble together') is made to incorporate a dialect form *dri* ('three'), and 'bezwockt' is a combination of *bezweckt* ('intended') and a colloquial *zwo* ('two').

Schenoni's 'O qualunque cosa fosse che hanno trescato di affermare che tontò con quei due' translates as something like 'or whatever it was the three of them tried to insinuate he foolishly tried to do with those two,' where *trescato* implies both 'to intrigue' (*trescare*) and 'three' (*tre*), and *tontò* implies both 'tried' (*tentò*) and 'foolishly' (*tonto*). Once again, whether intentionally or not, supplementary water references are provided in some of the versions in Romance languages: Joyce's 'whatever' is rendered in French as a stuttering 'quel quel' (Péron and Beckett) or 'quelque' (Beckett and Joyce); the phrase 'the Fiendish park' is preceded in Italian by a demonstrative 'quel'' (Joyce and Frank) or 'quell'' (Joyce and Settanni); and the stuttering phrase 'to two' is likewise preceded in Italian by a demonstrative 'quelle' (Wilcock) – choices once again quite unremarkable, but allowing in each case a translingual reference to the German *Quelle* ('spring, well').

Three Portuguese versions adopt roughly similar strategies, with roughly similar results. Campos's 'Ou que diabo foi que trentaram duescobrir que êle tresandou fazendo' translates as something like 'or whatever the devil the rotten thing was they tried to claim he gave offence by trying to do,' where 'trentaram' includes *tentar* ('to try'), *três* ('three'), and the English river Trent; 'duescobrir' conflates *descobrir* ('discover, reveal, claim') and the Italian *due* ('two'); and 'tresandou' includes *três* once again as well as the verb *tresandar*, which means both 'to upset, to disturb, to give offence' and 'to stink.' Schüler's 'O que é que Tefé que tresandaram a descobrir o que ele doisdou de fazer' translates roughly similarly as 'or whatever the devil (German *was Teufel*, 'what the devil') nasty plan the three (*três*) of them had (*tresandar*) to reveal (*descobrir*) what he decided (*decidir*) to do to the two (*dois*).' Amarante's 'Seja lá o que quer que tenha sido eles teentaram doiscifrar o que ele trestou fazer' likewise translates approximately as 'Let it be whatever it may have been they tried to make out (*decifrar*, 'to decipher') he tried (*tratar*, 'to try') to do,' with references to both the three ('trestou') and the two ('doiscifrar'). García Tortosa's Spanish rendering, 'O lo que tresaran soltar que intrestó doser,' works along more compressed lines, translatable as 'or whatever they settled on giving out that he was interested in trying to do to the two of them,' where 'tresaran' includes *transar* ('to allow, concede, settle on') and *tres* ('three'); 'intrestó' conflates *tres* ('three'), *intentó* ('tried'), and *interés* ('interest'); and 'doser' conflates *dos* ('two') and *hacer* ('to do').

Stündel's 'Oder was war es bloiß ach, was die Draige sich ausdachten, was er mit den Zwaithgen ... versyrchda' has the reasonably clear surface meaning of 'or what was it then that the three of them made out that he had tried to do with the two.' As well as the German Oder once again, three far-flung river names also appear in Stündel's version – the generic German-language Ach, the Algerian Dra, and the New Zealand Waitiki, the latter two also including references to *drei* ('three') and *zwei* ('two') – while 'versyrchda' includes *versuchte* ('tried') as well as invoking the Central Asian Syr Darya (Persian *daryō*, 'river'). Bindervoet and Henkes's Dutch 'Of tweet niet wat drie trachtten te zien wat hij triochtte te duon' translates roughly as 'I don't know what the three (*drie*) of them were trying to see that he was trying to do,' where 'tweet' conflates *ik weet* ('I know') and *twee* ('two'), 'triochtte' conflates Dutch *trachten* ('to try') and English *trio*, and 'te duon' conflates Dutch *doen* ('to do') and English *duo*. Grut's Swedish 'Eller vad tre nu påstred han försöktu sig två' wonders 'what three (*tre*) now maintained he tried his hand at doing to two,' where 'påstred' conflates *påstå* ('to maintain') and *tre* ('three') and 'försöktu sig två' conflates *försöka sig på* ('to try one's hand at') and *två* ('two'), as well as changing the regular past-tense verb ending -*te* into a -*tu* that likewise evokes the English *two*.

Four versions differ quite radically from all the others. Péron and Beckett's 'Ou quel quel que fût le tréfleuve qu'il aurait trouvé' departs from Joyce's original with something like 'or what whatever the triple stream or three-leaved clover was that he was supposed to have found,' where the initial 'quel quel que' provides an example of HCE's stutter, employed throughout *Finnegans Wake* as a reference to the latter's guilty conscience, and the *tré*- of 'tréfleuve' suggests a three-fold element. There now also appears to be the hint of a reference to St Patrick, whose reputation, now beyond reproach, was also once subject to rumour, and to the three-leaved clover (*trèfle*) or shamrock he reportedly used to demonstrate the unity of the Trinity. But 'tréfleuve' is at least as much 'fleuve' ('river') as 'trèfle' ('clover'), so we do still seem after all to be talking also about the less strictly theological concerns of HCE and the forbidden 'river' (or rivers) he may have peeked at in the park.

Beckett and Joyce, based on Péron and Beckett, provides a version even less amenable to linear translation: 'Ou quelque fut le tréfleuve que le triplepatte qu'on dit qu'il trouva.' One possible reading of this would be 'or whatever the triple stream or three-leaved clover or triple whatever it was they say he found.' The new term 'triplepatte' further stresses the threefold element, gestures towards a wholly indeterminate *patte* ('paw, hand, leg, foot') whose owner or owners (not to mention relevance) we can only guess at, and once again suggests tongue in cheek (with both 'tréfleuve' and '-patte') the unlikely identity of the much maligned HCE and a sainted precursor. Perhaps the parallel is all too pat, however, for HCE's guilty conscience still appears to play a noticeable role in the stuttering 'quelque ... que ... qu' ... qu'' that runs through the Beckett and Joyce version. Péron and Beckett together with Beckett and Joyce (unlike Lavergne, Wilcock, and Pozanco, as we have seen) both seem to lose sight of the two girls (if that's what they were) in favour of the three soldiers (if that's what they were) – or perhaps there were even three girls and *trois fleuves*. Joyce and Frank as well as Joyce and Settanni reintroduce both groups with the same very crisp formulation that once again deviates markedly, but differently and indeterminately, from the original of *Finnegans Wake*: 'O cosa mai fece bifronte o triforo.' The first phrase, 'o cosa mai fece,' simply means 'or whatever it was he did'; the second plays much more polyvalently on the Italian architectural terms *bifronte* ('double-fronted') and *triforo* ('having three openings, three lights') to suggest HCE's two-faced behaviour relating to two girls as observed from three vantage points.

The location of Earwicker's fall from grace in the 'Fiendish park,' meanwhile, underlines the irredeemably (or perhaps just exaggeratedly) diabolical nature of his putative offence. The multilingual translations of the name provide a transtextual extension of the text in several directions. Of our translators, Pozanco, preferring real-world geography to onomastic fantasy, simply places the event in the Phoenix Park, while Lavergne, Aixàs, and Amarante opt for an untranslated 'Fiendish.' Grut's 'Fiendix' park suggests it as a place where one might well encounter an enemy (Swedish *fiende*) – or perhaps even three. For García Tortosa it is 'el Parque Findio,' a name (hinting in passing at the German river Inde) that temporarily dispenses with the phoenix (Spanish *fénix*) while nonetheless invoking its 'outlandish' origins as *indio* ('Indian, foreign') and identifying HCE with Finn, once also considered by some Celtic scholars to have foreign origins. For Schüler, it is not surprising that dark deeds take place in a 'Fuscoix Parque,' Portuguese *fusco* meaning 'dark, dusky,' while for Bindervoet and Henkes, the 'Vreeslix Park' is a 'frightful' (*vreselijk*) place, a place of 'fear' (*vrees*).

The 'infernal' location, invitingly recalling Don Juan's eventual fate, is stressed by Péron and Beckett as well as by Beckett and Joyce, each of them electing for 'le parc de l'Inphernix,' combining phoenix and inferno. Schenoni's version is in similar mode with 'Fistolpark,' courtesy of an obsolete Italian expression *fistolo* ('fiend, devil') that also suggests an oblique reference to the Polish river Vistula. For Campos it is rather the 'parque de Duendix,' where the phoenix (Portuguese *fénix*) doubles as a *duende* ('ghost, spook, hobgoblin') as well as referring once again to the two girls (Italian *due*, 'two') who became the object of Earwicker's attentions. For Wilcock, likewise, the 'infenice parco' evokes both the Italian *fenice* ('phoenix') and *infelice* ('unfortunate'), while also invoking the Indian river Feni.

Joyce and Frank along with Joyce and Settanni opt for a similar solution, 'quel'infenice di porco nastro' and 'quell'infenice di porco nastro' respectively ('that unfortunate phoenix park of ours'), but rearrange *parco nostro* ('our park') into 'porco nastro,' which not only invokes the Italian river Orco but also roundly characterizes *pater-noster*-HCE's offence as that of a *porco* ('pig, swine'). Three German voices agree unanimously as to his swinish behaviour: for Goyert the park is the 'Pfuinix-Park,' with the phoenix accompanied by a German *pfui*, a conventional exclamation of disgust; for Wollschläger it is the 'Faunix-Park,' with the phoenix lasciviously accompanied by a sex-obsessed satyr (German *Faun*), a complementary hint of County Derry's river Faughan and a translingual reminder (English *faun*) that the Phoenix Park was once a deer park; and for Hildesheimer it is simply the 'Viechspark' ('Swinish Park'), with the phoenix metamorphosed into a *Viech* ('swine, dirty animal'), a German colloquialism reserved for those who commit disgusting acts.

For Stündel, the 'Föhlnix Park' is revealed as a pronouncedly Freudian site: 'Föhlnix,' while revealing a thinly disguised German *Phönix* ('phoenix') and gesturing towards Fohl Creek, Idaho, also contains barely concealed interlingual suggestions (as if the German verb *fühlen* were really the English verb *feel*) both of a minatory '*fühl nichts*' ('don't feel anything') and a permissive '*fühl Nix*' ('feel nymph'), a German *Nixe* ('water nymph') not being entirely out of place either in a park named for water or in a chapter awash in it. Bíró's Hungarian 'a Fujnix parkba' echoes the distaste expressed by Goyert's German 'Pfuinix-Park.'

Three eastern European renderings see things in a more determinedly diabolical light. Antip's Romanian version, the opening 'sau' ('or') of which allows glimpses of both the eastern European river Sau and the

Indian river Sāu, has Earwicker's dark deed take place in 'parcul Necurat,' the unclean park, the term *necurat* ('unclean') one traditionally used in euphemistic and apotropaic reference to witches and vampires. Weatherall's Czech version sees it taking place 'v Čertovce,' literally 'in the park of the devil (*Čertova*),' a transcultural reference that includes not only the Phoenix Park in Dublin but also the small park on Kampa Island in central Prague, formed at the confluence of the Vltava River and a tributary, the Čertovka or 'Devil's Brook.' Washerwomen traditionally gathered on the Čertovka, originally a millrace, to wash their laundry, taking advantage of its several flour mill wheels. Słomczyński's Polish 'w Pieklix parķu,' finally, not only characterizes the park as 'infernal' (*piekło*, 'inferno') but also mischievously evokes Earwicker's falling prey to the not unproblematic translingual combination of 'peeks' and 'leaks.'

Looking at the opening sentences specifically of *Anna Livia Plurabelle*, as we have seen, has the additional interest that we can compare, on a line-by-line and word-by-word basis, Joyce's practice as translator with that of his subsequent fellow translators. Within the limited scope of our very brief textual sample here, it emerges quite clearly that Joyce's choices as translator are sometimes similar to those of other translators – and sometimes, exercising an author's privilege, very different indeed. Discussions of his involvement in both the French version and more particularly the Italian version of *Anna Livia Plurabelle* strongly suggest that Joyce saw the exercise of translating his own text not so much as an opportunity simply to replicate his original in a different linguistic context but as an opportunity to *extend* that text by confronting it with a parallel version that is at times almost exactly coincident, at times radically deviant, and always, for readers willing to take the trouble, potentially both complementary and interrogative. Joyce's practice as translator of his own work, in short, evokes in exemplary form both the concept and the practice of transtextual reading.

the rivering waters of   (FW 216.4)

Since *Anna Livia Plurabelle* is obsessively concerned with the ritualistic invocation of river names, it is interesting, in conclusion, to compare the number of rivers invoked by Joyce and by his multilingual translators in the three brief excerpts examined here.

Joyce's original, as we have seen, invokes just six altogether in addition to the Liffey: the Indian Tel, the Ugandan Alla, the German

Aller, the South American Abou, the Czech Cheb, and the South American Futa.

Our translators (including Joyce himself) cumulatively invoke more than seventy rivers altogether, namely, in the sequence in which they are mentioned above: the German Ach, the Austrian Ache, the Indian Tel, the English Roch, the French Aa, the African Fala, the Croatian Save, the French Aude, the German Aller, the Ugandan Alla, the Japanese Onna, the Swiss Emme, the Raccoon River of Iowa, the Welsh Teme, the English Thames, the Sape River of the Solomon Islands, the Japanese Ono, the Behy of County Kerry, the Philippine Laco, the Dun of County Antrim, the Scottish Tirry, the English Irt, the English Mel, the Australian Todd, the Chilean Río Bueno, the Slovenian Tolminka, the Scottish Oich, the Scottish Allan Water, the Syrian Alameda, the French Ouvèze, the Australian Bemm, the Brazilian Rio Claro, the Sudanese Boma, the English Wissey, the English Kent, the Scottish Allt an Eilich, the English Ver, the eastern European Tur, the English Ure, the Belgian Maalbek, the Swedish Klar, the Japanese Nuta, the Serbian Raška, the Elm River of Illinois, the German Inde, the English Tud, the Indian Karo, Manitoba's Persse Lake, the Czech Cheb, the South American Futa, the German Naab, the Pakistani Lop, the Dutch Diem, the Laotian Kha, the Australian Birrie, the Dutch Gein, the African Rovuma, the French Krach, the eastern European Sau, the Indian Sāu, the Czech Čertovka, the German Oder, the German Ilm, the English Trent, the Algerian Dra, the New Zealand Waitiki, the Central Asian Syr, the German Inde, the Polish Vistula, the Indian Feni, the Italian Orco, the Irish Faughan, and the American Fohl Creek. One feels that Joyce would have more than enthusiastically approved.

7 Opinions Voiced

A central topic of the two washerwomen at the ford, as they enthusiastically wash the family's dirty linen in public, is the shameful delinquency of the reprehensible HCE. We will limit ourselves over the next few pages to a very select anthology of just a few of their preliminary opinions and comments – investigating how these opinions and comments survive their multilingual transformation, becoming in the process the views of washerwomen at once the same and entirely different concerning an HCE likewise both still the same and entirely different. We shall once again have the opportunity to compare the strategies employed in Joyce's own renderings and in those of later translators. We shall also have the opportunity once again to witness the continuing introduction of new rivers and streams and lakes of all kinds from all corners of the world, swelling and varying the initial flood unleashed by Joyce and reminding us that while the many-voiced washerwomen's immediate topic may be the delinquencies of HCE, the fluvial context of which they too are part always involves the uninterrupted presence of ALP.

He's an awful old reppe.   (FW 196.11)

Péron and Beckett (French, 1985 / 1996): C'est un beau salaud.

Beckett and Joyce (French, 1931 / 1996): C'est un beau saalaud!

Lavergne (French, 1982): Il a une affreuse vieille réputation.

Joyce and Frank (Italian, 1979 / 1996): Oibò, quel lughero malandrone!

Schenoni (Italian, 1996): É una vecchia orribile repceanaglia.

García Tortosa (Spanish, 1992): Es un viejo carona asqueroso.

Aixàs (Catalan, 2004): És un maleït vell grapejador.

Schüler (Portuguese, 2003): Trata-se de piolhento pilontra.

Amarante (Portuguese, 2009): É um grandessíssimo velhaco.

Antip (Romanian, 1996): E un hodorog scârbos.

Goyert (German, 1970): ein ganz dreckiger Lümmel

Hildesheimer (German, 1969 / 1970): Durchtriebener Schurke!

Wollschläger (German, 1970): ein greißlicher alter Wüstling

Stündel (German, 1993): Er ist ein schrecklicher alter Peeniger.

Bindervoet and Henkes (Dutch, 2002): 't Is een saramacase raudauner.

Grut (Swedish, 2001): En skitgubbe är han.

Weatherall et al. (Czech, 1932 / 1996): Je to starej rapl, až hrůza!

Słomczyński (Polish, 1985): To straszny stary dren.

The overt meaning here, summing up most of the other comments expressed, is quite clear: HCE is totally depraved, an awful old reprobate
– a characteristic with little to excuse it except that mention of it permits
incorporation of the German river Repe and the French river Reppe.

For Péron and Beckett, the 'awful old reppe' is 'un beau salaud,'
a 'right bastard (*salaud*),' a sentiment echoed by Beckett and Joyce but
making the reference to the German river Saale more obvious ('saalaud')
by doubling a vowel. Lavergne, while gesturing towards the Swiss river Reuss and the English river Ouse, concurs, if surprisingly mildly,
that he has 'une affreuse vieille réputation,' a 'terrible old reputation.'
Joyce and Frank's Italian goes to more elaborate lengths with 'Oibò,
quel lughero malandrone!,' roughly 'For shame (*oibò*), what a dismal
(*lugubre*) ruffian (*malandrino*)!,' simultaneously invoking for good measure three foreign rivers, the Ibo of the Philippines, the Welsh Lugg,
and the American Andro. Schenoni's Italian is no less outspoken: he is
'una vecchia orribile repceanaglia,' roughly 'a horrible wretched old
scoundrel,' where the combined epithet performs well beyond the call

of duty in conflating Italian *recere* ('to retch'), English *wretch*, and Italian *canaglia* ('scoundrel'), as well as maintaining the original references to the Repe and the Reppe rivers, adding the Scottish Orr and the English Rib, and hinting at the Latvian Cena.

For García Tortosa, our hero is 'un viejo carona asqueroso,' which suggests 'a filthy (*asqueroso*), stinking old toe-rag,' this particular accolade achieved by resort to the Spanish noun *carona*, which not only provides referential access to the Scottish Carron, Venezuelan Caroní, and Romanian Rona rivers, but, according to my thickest Spanish dictionary, also denotes 'the padding of a saddle next to the animal's back,' and thus thoroughly and odoriferously sweat-soaked. For Aixàs, in Catalan, he is 'un maleït vell grapejador,' a 'damned old groper,' a dirty old man with roving hands. In Portuguese, for Schüler, he is a 'piolhento pilontra,' an unpromising combination of *piolho* ('louse') and *violento* ('violent, furious'), suggesting a furious old louse while invoking the Mexican river Pilon; while for Amarante, evoking in passing the North American Río Grande, he is 'um grandessíssimo velhaco,' one of the very greatest (*grandíssimo*) old (*velho*) crooks (*velhaco*) ever seen. In Antip's Romanian, invoking the Nigerian river Odo and hinting at the French Arbois, he is 'un hodorog scârbos,' physically degenerated as a result of his heinous propensities into a 'disgusting (*scârbos*) old dodderer (*hodorog*).'

His detractors are no less reluctant to voice their opinions in German. He is 'ein ganz dreckiger Lümmel,' a 'really dirty blackguard' for Goyert; a 'durchtriebener Schurke,' a 'crafty (*durchtrieben*) scoundrel (*Schurke*)' for Hildesheimer; a 'greißlicher alter Wüstling,' an 'abominable (*grässlich*), hoary (*greis*) old lecher (*Wüstling*)' for Wollschläger; a 'schrecklicher alter Peeniger,' an 'awful old tramp (*Penner*) and tormentor (*Peiniger*)' for Stündel, who also includes a passing reference to the German river Peene. Nor do other versions hold back. For Bindervoet and Henkes he is a 'saramacase raudauner,' a 'rough (German *rauh*), raucous (Dutch *rauw*) troublemaker (German *Radau machen*, "to make trouble")' who can only be described as 'saramacase,' which, invoking the South American Saramacca River, might be taken to suggest a wild man from the depths of the rain forest.

His ill repute crosses linguistic, national, and cultural borders: in Weatherall's Czech, he is a 'starej rapl, až hrůza,' an 'old madman (*rapl*), an absolute horror (*hrůza*)'; in Słomczyński's Polish, he is a 'straszny stary dren,' a 'dreadful (*straszny*) old sewer (*dren*).' Grut's Swedish is exemplarily succinct and unambiguous: he is a 'skitgubbe,' an 'old shit' (*skit*, 'shit'; *gubbe*, 'old man'). It is fair to say, indeed, that for our collective translators he is the very model of a paragon of awfulness.

duddurty devil   (FW 196.15)

Péron and Beckett (French, 1985 / 1996): le misérable

Beckett and Joyce (French, 1931 / 1996): le mymyserable

Lavergne (French, 1982): ce vieux cochon

Joyce and Frank (Italian, 1979 / 1996): Lordo balordo

Schenoni (Italian, 1996): quel duddondino di darteggiante diavolo!

García Tortosa (Spanish, 1992): dudublercodriante

Aixàs (Catalan, 2004): Menyspreableporcpervés

Schüler (Portuguese, 2003): esse diacho sujo

Amarante (Portuguese, 2009): suujeito suujo

Antip (Romanian, 1996): diavolul pututuros

Goyert (German, 1970): son lausiges Luder

Hildesheimer (German, 1969 / 1970): der ddreckige Deibel

Wollschläger (German, 1970): der dreckeckige Debbel

Stündel (German, 1993): deedreckige Deviling

Bindervoet and Henkes (Dutch, 2002): den dommelse does

Grut (Swedish, 2001): den grisen

Weatherall et al. (Czech, 1932 / 1996): ten čuňácký čert

Słomczyński (Polish, 1985): ten prutney diabeł

The less than adulatory chorus continues for 'duddurty devil,' all too easily identified by his guilty stammer and the implied initials of 'dear dirty Dublin,' while four separate rivers from far and near are called upon to bear witness: the Dirty Devil River of Utah, the English river Duddon (as sung by Wordsworth), the Alaskan Dudd Creek, and the Russian river Uda.

Several versions limit themselves to more or less vituperative comment on our hero, with or without associated fluvial references. Péron and Beckett's French rendering, 'le misérable' ('the wretch'), thus adopts a minimalist approach that nonetheless allows access to three new rivers, the Czech Iser, the German Isar, and the French Isère. The Beckett and Joyce version, 'le mymyserable,' agrees with the assessment of HCE's character, identifying it with a stuttering 'mymy-' and adding a reference to the Franco-Belgian river Yser. Joyce and Frank's Italian 'Lordo balordo' considers him both 'dirty' (*lordo*) and 'stupid' (*balordo*), while contributing references to the Canadian Lord River and the Australian Ord River. García Tortosa's Spanish 'dudublercodriante' likewise evokes our hero's stuttering and suggests the presence of Dublin and a Dublin drunkard (*odre*) as well as at least five separate rivers: the French Doubs, the Lerr of County Kildare, the Serbian Drina, the Canadian Codroy, and the Polish Odra.

Different versions reveal different degrees of vilification. Goyert's relatively mild German rendering, 'son lausiges Luder,' refers merely to a 'lousy creep' (*Luder*). Lavergne's French 'ce vieux cochon' more emphatically considers our man an 'old swine.' In Grut's Swedish 'den grisen,' he is likewise a 'pig' (*gris*), an opinion also invoking the Haitian Grise River. For Amarante's Portuguese, he is a 'suujeito suujo,' a decidedly dirty (*sujo*) character (*sujeito*), the lengthened vowels emphasizing his awfulness. Aixàs's sesquipedalian 'Menyspreableporcpervés' goes considerably further in Catalan, suggesting that he is a 'contemptible (*menyspreable*) pig (*porc*) pervert.'

Other versions make a point of emphasizing our lamentable hero's allegedly diabolical qualities. In Polish, Słomczyński's 'ten prutney diabeł' considers him a 'dirty (*brudny*) devil (*diabeł*)' while referring to the Ukrainian river Prut. Weatherall's Czech 'ten čuňácký čert' considers him a 'swinish (*čuňě*, 'pig') devil (*čert*)' while referring to the Čertovka, or Devil's Brook waterway of Prague. In Schüler's Portuguese, he is a 'diacho sujo,' a 'dirty (*sujo*) devil (*diacho*),' the variation on *diabo* ('devil') allowing access to the German river Ach. Antip's Romanian goes further in condemning this 'diavolul pututuros,' this 'stinking (*pututuros*) devil (*diavol*),' betrayed once again by a guilty stammer ('-tutu-') that also signals supplementary access to the Australian Tuross River.

Still other versions place importance on retaining the triple-*d* echo of 'dear dirty Dublin.' Schenoni's bravura Italian 'quel duddondino di darteggiante diavolo' does so with style, summoning up a highly energetic (*dardeggiante*, 'darting') devil (*diavolo*) while equally energetically evoking in the process not only the English river Duddon, but also

Scottish, English, Canadian, and Russian rivers Don, the English river Dart, and various North American Egg Rivers. Three German versions opt for roughly similar strategies in order to achieve the desired triple *d*. Hildesheimer's 'der ddreckige Deibel' employs a strategic stammer and the dialect form *Deibel* ('devil'). Wollschläger's 'der dreckeckige Debbel' suggests a 'dirty (*dreckig*), impudent (*keck*) devil,' the alternative dialect form *Debbel* also suggesting that while our hero may or may not be feeble-minded (*debil*), any sense of common decency he may have is certainly at a very low ebb (*Ebbe*, 'low tide'). Stündel's 'deedreckige Deviling' once again offers us a dirty (*dreckig*) devil, while evoking the Welsh and Scottish rivers Dee, the Irish river Devlin, and Dublin itself as a diabolical location. In Dutch, finally, Bindervoet and Henkes's 'den dommelse does' achieves the triple *d* in a surprisingly mild assessment of our delinquent's character, combining *dom* ('stupid'), *dommelen* ('to doze'), and *does* ('poodle') not only to evoke the Dutch river Dommel but to suggest that HCE is just a 'dumb dozy dog.'

And how long was he under loch and neagh?   (FW 196.19–20)

Péron and Beckett (French, 1985 / 1996): Hélac! sombien de cachot sans bourger?

Beckett and Joyce (French, 1931 / 1996): Combien resta-t-il au bloch et sous nlefs?

Lavergne French (1982): Et combien de temps resta-t-il enfoui sous clé à double-tour?

Joyce and Frank (Italian, 1979 / 1996): E quanto rimase dai frati Branca?

Schenoni (Italian, 1996): E per quanto tempo è stato sotto loughiave e neaghratura?

García Tortosa (Spanish, 1992): Y cuánto tiempo bañolas a piedra y lodo?

Aixàs (Catalan, 2004): Quant temps va estar a la trena?

Schüler (Portuguese, 2003): E quanto tempo jouve lugnegado debaixo do lago?

Amarante (Portuguese, 2009): E quanto tempo ele ficou trancafiado no lago?

Antip (Romanian, 1996): Şi cât a zăcut la propreală în udeală?

Goyert (German, 1970): wie lang saß er im Loch, mit dem Boden als See

Hildesheimer (German, 1969 / 1970): Und wie lang war er unter Schlucht und Regen?

Wollschläger (German, 1970): Und wie lang saß er hinter Schloch und Neaghal?

Stündel (German, 1993): huonter Shoaloß und Ryegel

Bindervoet and Henkes (Dutch, 2002): En hoe lang loch hij in de lek achter sloe en kendel?

Grut (Swedish, 2001): Och hur länge var han under lago väta?

Weatherall et al. (Czech, 1932 / 1996): A jak dlouho bručel v kase?

Słomczyński (Polish, 1985): I jak długo był w lochu u nich?

At a surface level, the question here is clearly just how long this paragon of depravity must have spent (or should have spent) under lock and key for his criminal activities – ideally, for example, buried deep under Lough Neagh, the largest lake in Ireland. The particular location is suggestive of indefinitely extended incarceration, for Lough Neagh was once held to offer access to the Celtic underworld. Indeed the Old Irish name, *Loch nEchach* ('the lake of Eochu'), referred to one of the lords of that underworld, Eochu (Bishop 1986, 462) – whose name is related to Old Irish *ech* ('horse'), thus by happy coincidence clearly anticipating ECH, alias HCE.

Péron and Beckett's 'Hélac! sombien de cachot sans bourger?' opens with an interjection that conflates a pseudo-sympathetic *hélas* ('alas') and, appropriately, a French *lac* ('lake'), then proceeds to conflate *combien de cachot sans bouger?* ('how much jail time without parole?') and a series of river references to the French Somme, various North American waterways named Cache River and Cache Creek, and the Belgian Our. Beckett and Joyce wonder instead how long our hero unwillingly spent 'au bloch et sous nlefs,' suggesting 'under lock and key,' conflating French *à bloc* ('raring to go'), German *Loch* ('prison, clink'), and English *loch* and *lock*, before combining *sous clé* ('locked up') and *nef* ('ship),' the latter usually pronounced /nef/, but here, in a good cause, as /ne/, a reasonable rhyme for 'Neagh.' The French rivers Aube ('au b-') and

Saône ('sous n-') are recruited in passing. Lavergne's 'Et combien de temps resta-t-il enfoui sous clé à double-tour?' resorts to standard French to enquire how long our resident reprobate was 'buried' (*enfoui*) behind or under a double-locked door.

Changing tack somewhat, and evoking the Água Branca River of Brazil, Joyce and Frank's Italian 'E quanto rimase dai frati Branca?' wonders how long our hero remained (*rimanere*, 'to remain') in the custody of the police, colloquially designated 'the Brothers Grab' (*brancar*, 'to seize, grab, arrest'). Schenoni's Italian rendering returns to the more specific query as to how long he spent 'sotto loughiave e neaghratura,' conflating *sotto chiave* ('under lock and key') and *ferratura* ('clamped in irons') as well as Lough Neagh and, not to be fluvially outdone, the Serra Negra River of Brazil.

In Spanish, García Tortosa's 'Y cuánto tiempo bañolas a piedra y lodo?' wants to know, while evoking the Spanish Lake Bañolas, how long he was cooling his heels (*bañar*, 'to bathe') shut up behind behind an impenetrable wall of stone (*piedra*) and mortar (*lodo*, 'mud'). In Catalan, Aixàs's 'Quant temps va estar a la trena?' summons up the Canadian Ena River and wishes to know how long he was wrapped in chains (*a la trena*). In Portuguese, Schüler's 'E quanto tempo jouve lugnegado debaixo do lago?' enquires, while invoking the Canadian Jouve and French Ouvèze rivers, how long our delinquent lay drunk (*estar na chuva*, 'to be caught in the rain, to be drunk') and in the dark (*luznegado*, 'denied light') beneath the lake identified in passing ('lugneg-') as Lough Neagh. Also in Portuguese, Amarante wonders how long he 'ficou trancafiado no lago,' stayed (*ficou*) in the lake (*lago*); that is to say, 'locked up' (*trancado*) but fully 'alert' (*afiado*) thanks to the presence of the Ghanaian river Fia.

Among our German translators, Goyert has no difficulty in summoning up Lake Constance (German *Bodensee*) while wondering how long our man spent in the loch in the clink (*im Loch*), where the ground (*Boden*) and the lake (*See*) were the same. All three other German renderings share a strategy involving the idiomatic phrase *hinter Schloß und Riegel* ('under lock and key'). Hildesheimer's 'unter Schlucht und Regen' literally means 'under gorge (*Schlucht*) and rain (*Regen*)' but invokes the German Schluchsee lake and the German river Regen; Wollschläger's otherwise meaningless 'hinter Schloch und Neaghal' conceals and reveals our Lough Neagh; and Stündel's 'huonter Shoaloß und Ryegel' offers a hiding place for the Tasmanian Huon River, the Canadian Shoal River, and the Irish and English Rye Rivers.

Bindervoet and Henkes's Dutch similarly ponders 'hoe lang loch hij in de lek achter sloe en kendel?,' clearly suggesting at a surface level 'how long did he lie in the lake under lock and key?,' but where 'loch' conflates Dutch *lag* ('lay'), English *loch*, and the Australian Loch River; 'lek' conflates English *lake* and the Dutch Lek River; and 'achter sloe en kendel' conflates the idiomatic phrase *achter slot en grendel* ('under lock and key') and the Dutch Sloe and Kendel Rivers. Grut's Swedish, finally, considers how long our man was 'under lago väta,' ostensibly suggesting 'under low water,' but where 'lago' conflates Swedish *låg* ('low') and Italian *lago* ('lake'), and 'väta' combines Swedish *väta* ('wet'), *vatten* ('water'), and the likewise Swedish Lake Vättern, allowing us to think of our wetly bedraggled delinquent as deeply submerged under the chilly waters of Lake Vättern, one of the two largest lakes in Sweden – and one that in legend shares something of the otherworldly aura of Lough Neagh, being a notorious gathering place of forest spirits, trolls, and gnomes (*vättar*).

the roughty old rappe   (FW 196.24)

Péron and Beckett (French, 1985 / 1996): le vieux polisson

Beckett and Joyce (French, 1931 / 1996): ce vieux rot de canail

Lavergne (French, 1982): c'est bien dur pour lui allez!

Joyce and Frank (Italian, 1979 / 1996): che carogna

Schenoni (Italian, 1996): la rozza vecchia repceanaglia

García Tortosa (Spanish, 1992): sobado estrupador!

Aixàs (Catalan, 2004): Maleït bordegàs

Schüler (Portuguese, 2003): O rude raptor!

Amarante (Portuguese, 2009): O, rude raptor!

Goyert (German, 1970): der rülpsende Raufboldrüpel

Hildesheimer (German, 1969 / 1970): getrübener Hurke

Wollschläger (German, 1970): dieser zootige olle Notzürchter

Stündel (German, 1993): dieser wickerlde holle Scourke

Bindervoet and Henkes (Dutch, 2002): wat een rakase rauser

Grut (Swedish, 2001): Den mucho lymmeln!

Weatherall et al. (Czech, 1932 / 1996): ten starý proudník

Słomczyński (Polish, 1985): ruski stary rappcio

Translators who had risen enthusiastically to the suggestion that 'He's an awful old reppe' (*FW* 196.11) are given another chance to flex their linguistic muscles along similarly vituperative lines. The overt meaning is clear: HCE is indeed a right old rep. A *rep* is a reprobate; a *rip* is a worthless, dissolute fellow (*OED*), though more usually applied in Ireland to a woman rather than a man; a *rap*, as used by Swift in the *Drapier's Letters*, is a bad or counterfeit coin (*OED*): none of these epithets redounds to the credit of the egregious HCE, who, for his part, may or may not care a rap. 'Roughty' includes 'right' – HCE as a 'right old rep' – and 'raughty' (rhyming with 'naughty' and defined by the *OED* as 'fine, splendid, jolly, etc.') as well as 'rough,' while evoking in passing the Rough River of Kentucky, the Roughty River of County Kerry, the French river Reppe again, the German Rappach (*Ach*, 'river'), and by fluvial extension the Scottish Rappach Water.

Limiting ourselves largely to the additional rivers summoned up by our multilingual group of translators, we find that 'the roughty old rappe' acts as a catalyst for the following. Péron and Beckett's 'le vieux polisson,' where a French *polisson* is a 'dirty old scoundrel,' gives us the Italian Po, Chinese Li, and French Isson. Beckett and Joyce's 'vieux rot de canail,' playing on *rot* ('belch') and *canaille* ('scoundrel'), gives us the German Rot, Indonesian Anai, and Egyptian Nile. Lavergne's 'c'est bien dur pour lui allez!' ('Hey, it must be tough for him!') contributes the French Allier. Joyce and Frank's Italian 'che carogna,' giving us CHE as well as *che carogna* ('what a swine'), also gives us the Scottish Carron and the Venezuelan Caroní once again. Schenoni's Italian 'la rozza vecchia repceanaglia,' characterizing HCE as a crude (*rozzo*) old wretch, adds to our list the Ukrainian Roza River as well as a repeated invocation of the German Repe and French Reppe, the Scottish Orr and the English Rib, and a hint of the Latvian Cena.

García Tortosa's Spanish 'sobado estrupador' even hints at rape (Italian *stupro*) as one of our delinquent's crimes, while extravagantly contributing the Sudanese Sobat, the Russian Ob, the Nigerian Oba, the Canadian Oba, the Ukrainian Strupa, the Russian Upa, and the French Adour. Aixàs's Catalan 'maleït bordegàs,' dismissing him as a damned (*maleït*) idiot (*bordegàs*), adds the Russian Alei, English Leith, Australian Ord, and Spanish Ega. Schüler's Portuguese 'O rude raptor!' ('the impudent predator!') and Amarante's 'O, rude raptor!' ('O, impudent predator!') give us the Alaskan Rude, Romanian Ruda, and another hint of the German Rappach.

In German, Goyert's 'der rülpsende Raufboldrüpel,' seeing our dubious hero as a ruffian (*Raufbold*) and a blackguard (*Rüpel*) who has now even added belching (*rülpsen*) in public to his multiple delinquencies, contributes the Scottish Ruel, the Romanian Bold, and the Belgian Rupel. Hildesheimer's 'getrübener Hurke,' suggesting a shiftless (*getrieben*) rogue (*Schurke*) and, other things being equal, a restless whore (*Hure*), adds the Indian Uben River. Wollschläger's 'dieser zootige olle Notzürchter' finds the filthy (*zotig*) old man guilty or at least capable of rape (*Notzucht*), while adding Lake Zurich, the Zürchersee, to our list. Stündel's 'dieser wickerlde holle Scourke' likewise considers him (identified as '-er wicker') a wicked old (*olle*) rogue (*Schurke*), while contributing the Scottish Wick, the German Elde, the Indian Adda Holle, and the Belgian Our.

In Dutch, Bindervoet and Henkes's 'wat een rakase rauser' considers him a rogue (*rakker*) and a troublemaker (*rauzen*, 'to kick up a row'), while adding the Central African Kasai as well as the historical Italian river Auser. Grut's Swedish 'Den mucho lymmeln!' forces the great (Spanish *mucho*) blackguard (*lymmel*) to contribute the English Uck, Chinese Ho, and English Lyme. Weatherall's Czech 'ten starý proudník,' suggesting something like 'the old river (*proud*) rat,' adds the Scottish Oude, while Słomczyński's Polish 'ruski stary rappcio,' dismissing him as not only an old reprobate but also, and by apparent implication even worse, a Russian, gives us the North American Russian River as well as the German Rappach once again.

Reeve Gootch was right and Reeve Drughad was sinistrous.   (FW 197.1)

Péron and Beckett (French, 1985 / 1996): Rive gauche était droite et rive druite était sinistre.

Beckett and Joyce (French, 1931 / 1996): Sbire Kauche était droit mais Sbire Troyt senestre.

Lavergne (French, 1982): Sa Rive Gauche était dans le droit chemin mais sa Rive Droite était bien sinistre.

Joyce and Frank (Italian, 1979 / 1996): Ha regiona Ciulli, e Piesse pure, che le prove dirotte non mancano mica.

Schenoni (Italian, 1996): La reeva gàuccia era retta e la reeva druatta era sinistra.

García Tortosa (Spanish, 1992): Golilla Ledra vera a derecho y Golilla Godo vera a siniestro!

Pozanco (Spanish, 1993): La rive gauche was right et la rive droite sinistrous!

Aixàs (Catalan, 2004): La rive gauche era dretera i la rive droite sinistra.

Schüler (Portuguese, 2003): O Rio Esquerdo fluía direito, mas o Direito era sinistro.

Amarante (Portuguese, 2009): A Margem Esquerda era direita e o Direito era sinistro!

Antip (Romanian, 1996): Popa Pileală avea dreptate iar Popa Amețitu era sinistru!

Goyert (German, 1970): Uferzier war im Recht, sein Rival doch sinister.

Hildesheimer (German, 1969 / 1970): Riff gauche war im Recht, und Riff droite war ihm schlechter.

Wollschläger (German, 1970): Vogt Gootch war im Rechts und Vogt Drughad Sinister.

Stündel (German, 1993): Die reesede Banak war im Recht und die lauanke Banak war lenakisch.

Bindervoet and Henkes (Dutch, 2002): Sherrive Koosje had bij het rechtse eind en Sherrive Droggerd was sinister!

Grut (Swedish, 2001): Vänsla handen var recht och högra helt för gauche!

Weatherall et al. (Czech, 1932 / 1996): Levý Sváh se popravil a Pravý Sváh se polevil!

Słomczyński (Polish, 1985): Rzekał to raz Gucz prawy i rzekał Drugihad to na odlewy!

Yet another of our man's multifarious failings, as vigorously identified by the rigorous washerwomen, appears to be that he is incapable of telling right from wrong, or indeed, if it comes to that, right from left. This particular failing is once again expressed in fluvial terms.

HCE here stands specifically accused that 'Reeve Gootch was right and Reeve Drughad was sinistrous.' The charge, as read, may be understood either as personal (one person was right and another was less to be trusted) or as complicatedly fluvial (a left bank was right and a right bank was left) or, of course, both. 'Reeve' combines a French *rive* ('riverbank') and the English title of a local official, a reeve. 'Gootch' ostensibly provides this official with a surname, while simultaneously combining French *gauche* ('left') and offering a possible hint of the Canadian Goose River. 'Reeve Drughad' is both a second named official and combines French *droit* ('right'), Irish *droichead* ('bridge'), and the waters of the Irish Drogheda Bay and the Canadian Drogheda Lake. The rightness of the left bank is left undistorted, but the leftness of the right is 'sinistrous,' the archaic English term suggesting 'inauspicious' as well as playing the literal meaning of Latin *sinister* ('left') against its standard English meaning. For an Irish ear, used to horrific accounts of Cromwell's criminal Irish campaign of the 1600s, any suggestion of Drogheda evokes the butchery of war, while hooch and drugs appear to be a contributory factor of the hostilities hinted at here.

The two 'reeves' may also be taken as referring to HCE's warring sons, the rival twins Shem and Shaun. Specifically, Reeve Gootch and Reeve Drughad refer to Shem and Shaun respectively if we think we are talking about the *rive gauche* and *rive droite* of the Seine – but to Shaun and Shem respectively if we think we are talking about the left and right banks of the Liffey, for, as has been pointed out, Shem is associated with the south side of both the Liffey (right bank) and the Seine (left bank, *rive gauche*) and Shaun correspondingly with the north side of both the Liffey (left bank) and the Seine (right bank, *rive droite*), while the two together, Reeve Gootch and Reeve Drughad combined, add up to HCE, 'who as the city itself combines the often opposite characteristics of his twin sons' (Mink 1978, xxiv).

For Péron and Beckett's 'Rive gauche était droite et rive druite était sinistre,' the context is primarily fluvial, with the *rive gauche* right but the *rive droite*, though allowing a passing reference to the Vietnamese Rui River, nonetheless unambiguously 'sinister.' For Beckett and Joyce, in a play on linguistic rather than martial opposition, namely that of voiced and unvoiced stops, Reeve Gootch and Reeve Drughad become 'Sbire Kauche' and 'Sbire Troyt.' 'Sbire' combines the colloquial French *sbire* ('thuggish policeman'), the standard French *spire* ('swirl'), as of water, and the Rhodesian river Biri, while 'Kauche' combines French *gauche* and, appropriately in the context of the nocturnal world of the *Wake*, the suggested beginning of a *cauchemar* ('nightmare'). 'Troyt' is not only *droit* but evokes in passing the 'strait' (*détroit*) and narrow Detroit River of North America, while gesturing in passing towards the wars between Greeks and Trojans. As in the original, 'droit' is undistorted, but modern French *sinistre* becomes Old French *senestre*, emphasizing the rivalry theme by the use of the technical heraldic term for features on the left of a shield – the shield bearer's left, that is to say, while for an opponent the same features are on the right (O'Shea 1986, 130).

In Italian, however, Joyce and Frank appear to ignore the riverbanks altogether, opting instead for a completely rewritten 'Ha regiona Ciulli, e Piesse pure, che le prove dirotte non mancano mica,' which appears to suggest, obscurely, that 'Ciulli is right (*ha ragione*), and so is Piesse, that direct proofs (*prove dirette*) are not at all lacking,' but *ragione* ('reason') and *regione* ('region') are conflated, as are *diretto* ('direct') and *dirotto* ('copious') and perhaps *piovere a dirotto* ('raining cats and dogs'). References to a spate of rivers, including the Swiss Giona, Indian Ull, German Esse, English Ure, and Dutch Rotte, as well as to the Mica Dam of British Columbia, are detectable but do little to lighten the darkness. The riverbanks are unambiguously central in several other renderings, however. Schenoni's Italian 'La reeva gàuccia era retta e la reeva druatta era sinistra' produces a sort of pidgin Italian version of Joyce's original. In Spanish, Pozanco's 'La rive gauche was right et la rive droite sinistrous!' manages to include no word of Spanish. In Catalan, Aixàs's 'La rive gauche era dretera i la rive droite sinistra' likewise focuses exclusively on French riverbanks, as does Lavergne's French, which attempts a normalizing explanation: 'his Left Bank was on the right path but his Right Bank was quite sinister.' In Portuguese, Schüler's 'O Rio Esquerdo fluía direito, mas o Direito era sinistro' prefers rivers to riverbanks: his 'Rio Esquerdo' ('left river') flows to the right (*direito*) while the right, or perhaps the law (*direito*) that governs such flows, is sinister. Amarante's 'A Margem Esquerda era direita e o Direito era sinistro!' adds a new note in referring to a feminine 'left bank' (*margem esquerda*) that was 'right' (*direita*) but to a masculine law (*direito*) that, far from being right (*direito*), is in fact sinister.

Other versions prefer to focus on the reeves rather than the *rives*. Goyert's German, omitting the pseudo-onomastic 'Gootch' and 'Drughad' altogether, translates 'Reeve' into an 'Uferzier,' combining a German *Ufer* ('riverbank') and a military *Offizier* ('officer') who was 'im Recht,' which is to say, both *im Recht* ('in the right') and *ihm recht* ('okay by him'), while 'sein Rival' ('his rival' and Latin *riva*, 'riverbank') was frankly 'sinister.' Hildesheimer's 'Riff' combines a tranquil French *rive* and a threatening German *Riff* ('reef'). The onomastic potential of 'Riff gauche' and 'Riff droite' is once again abandoned (as indicated by the lack of capital letters), while the former is once again 'im Recht' and the latter 'war ihm schlechter,' playing now on the combined phrases *ihm war schlecht* ('he felt sick') and *schlecht und recht* ('after a fashion'). Wollschläger retains an anthropomorphosed 'Gootch' and 'Drughad,' both now unambiguously holders of the office of *Vogt* ('reeve'), the banks of the river evoked by the trilingual pun involving German *Vogt*, English *reeve*, and French *rive*. Vogt Gootch, 'im Rechts,' was now not only *ihm recht* ('okay by him') and *im Recht* ('in the right'), as in the case of both Goyert and Hildesheimer, but also *ihm rechts* ('to his right'), while Vogt Drughad was 'Sinister,' his sinister propensities emphasized and nominalized by virtue of the unexpected capital letter. Standard German grammar, indeed, would suggest that he is not just sinister but 'a Sinister' by profession, as it were, even by right.

Stündel's German, while opting for baroque exuberance, holds that the issue is riverbanks rather than public position, and emphasizes the matter by importing four new rivers. Reversing in passing the order of left and right, 'die reesede Banak' suggests 'the right bank,' with 'reesede' combining German *rechte* ('right') and the American Reese River and 'Banak' apparently forcing the also American Kanab Creek likewise into reverse in order to suggest an English 'bank,' while 'lauanke' combines German *linke* ('left') and the Indian river Laua. Abandoning the chiastic structure of the original, Stündel's right bank is now 'im Recht' ('in the right'), while his left bank is 'lenakisch,' awkwardly combining the German adjective *linkisch* ('awkward'), the German river Lenne, and the Russian river Lena.

Further versions add further complications. In Dutch, Bindervoet and Henkes's 'Sherrive Koosje had bij het rechtse eind en Sherrive Droggerd was sinister!' conflates an English *sheriff* and a French *rive*, renaming the pair in accordance with Dutch phonetics. Sherrive Koosje has things 'right' (*bij het rechte eind*) as well as 'on the right' (*rechts*), may prefer his diet kosher (*koosjer*), and introduces the German river Oos. Sherrive Droggerd, who was sinister, seems to have little else to recommend him. Grut's Swedish 'Vänsla handen var recht och högra helt för gauche!' abandons sheriffs, reeves, and *rives* alike for 'the left hand' (*vänster handen*), which was not only 'right' (German *recht*) but also 'popular' (*vänsäll*) as a result of its ingratiating ways (*vänslas*, 'to caress'), while the right (*höger*) was entirely (*helt*) on the left (French *gauche*) and presumably correspondingly less popular.

Among eastern European languages, Weatherall's Czech 'Levý Sváh se popravil a Pravý Sváh se polevil!' refers to a left (*levý*) bank (*svah*) that, for whatever reason, apparently got very excited (*se popravit*, 'to become electrified') and a right (*pravý*) bank (*svah*) that apparently remained calm (*polevit*, 'to ease off'). In each case, *svah* ('bank') is conflated with the Slovak river Váh, and the associated verbs add the Italian river Po, the Ghanaian river Pra, and the Slovak river Poprad. Antip's Romanian 'Popa Pileală avea dreptate iar Popa Ameţitu era sinistru!' introduces a new and idiosyncratic note with a pair of clerical gentlemen (*popă*, 'priest') who clearly share Tim Finnegan's love of the liquor, a Father Hooch (*pileală*, 'hooch') whose opinion 'was right' (*avea dreptate*), and a Father Tipsy (*ameţit*, 'tipsy') who was 'sinistru.' In each case, adding water to their chosen beverage, their clerical title is conflated with the Italian Po and the Romanian Pop and Popa rivers.

The most idiosyncratic version of all, however, is certainly García Tortosa's Spanish rendering, which is, as usual, of considerable complexity – 'Golilla Ledra vera a derecho y Golilla Godo vera a siniestro!' – and has very little to do with riverbanks, though evoking three separate rivers. *Golilla* is a colloquial Spanish term for a magistrate (based on the ruffed collar or *golilla* traditionally worn), and the title as used here incorporates a doubled reference to the Indian river Gola. Our Golilla Ledra's name, in addition to suggesting the African river Dra, is an hispanicized version of the French *le droit* ('the law, what is right and just'), an appropriate field of interest for a magistrate. Golilla Ledra should therefore correspond to Joyce's Reeve Drughad, but we find that instead of being 'sinistrous,' he in fact 'vera a derecho' or 'veers to the right,' conflating 'to the right-hand side' and 'to what is right and just.' His counterpart, Golilla Godo, meanwhile, has a name that evokes the Nigerian river Odo, while suggesting that its owner is of blood so noble (*ser godo*, 'to be of noble blood') and so ancient that it is perhaps even originally Gothic (*godo*). Since the name, humorously also suggesting the Irishman Samuel Beckett's French *En attendant Godot*, is clearly based on the French *gauche*, Golilla Godo should therefore correspond to Joyce's Reeve Gootch, but instead of consequently being 'right' as we might expect, he in fact 'vera a siniestro,' which conflates veering to 'the left-hand side' (*siniestra*) and veering towards a 'vicious' (*siniestro*) 'depravity' (*siniestro*). The invented verb 'vera' ('veers'), finally, conflates the normal Spanish verb *virar* ('to veer'), the Latin noun *vera* ('the things that are true'), and the Spanish noun *vera* ('edge, border'), suggesting the fine line that must always be walked, whether by magistrates or by others, between what is right and what is wrong. Our delinquent hero HCE might profitably have heeded the admonition.

the famous eld duke alien   (*FW* 197.3–4)

Péron and Beckett (French, 1985 / 1996): le vieux deuc alien célèbre

Beckett and Joyce (French, 1931 / 1996): le vieux deuc alien célèbre

Lavergne (French, 1982): Ce fameux duc échu de l'étranger, tout imbu de son Elbe

Joyce and Frank (Italian, 1979 / 1996): il degno duca Lione

Schenoni (Italian, 1996): il famoso elduca alieno

García Tortosa (Spanish, 1992): el gran de yerro de uca a lion

Aixàs (Catalan, 2004): el famós vell duc Howth

Schüler (Portuguese, 2003): o famoso duque, o velho da estranja

Amarante (Portuguese, 2009): o famoso velho duque estrangeiro

Antip (Romanian, 1996): vestitul duce bătrân venetic

Goyert (German, 1970): der famose alte Monarch

Hildesheimer (German, 1969 / 1970): dieser deukältische Herzögler

Wollschläger (German, 1970): der femmeuse olle Don Kallion

Stündel (German, 1993): der falmöse eeldere Hexzog exzohtikus

Bindervoet and Henkes (Dutch, 2002): dien fameuze owen knar van een duke ellejan

Grut (Swedish, 2001): den gamle asatoken

Weatherall et al. (Czech, 1932 / 1996): ten starý slavný vévoda z Tramtárie

Słomczyński (Polish, 1985): ten sławny djukon obcy

Yet another of HCE's shortcomings is his ridiculous conviction of his own importance in the scheme of things. As our washerwomen comment, with jaundiced eye, 'he used to hold his head as high as a howeth, the famous eld duke alien, with a hump of grandeur on him like a walking wiesel rat' (*FW* 197.3–4). For some readers, the phrase 'the famous eld duke' may evoke the English children's rhyme 'The Grand Old Duke of York,' with its mocking reference to military incompetence: 'he had ten thousand men; / He led them up to the top of the hill, / And he led them down again.' The 'eld duke' suggests a faint hint of *eldritch* ('weird, unnatural') as well as *old*, while co-opting the German river Elde, and an *alien* is one who, like HCE in many people's estimation, belongs elsewhere.

The 'duke alien' is also the Deucalion of Greek mythology, the legendary equivalent of Noah: Deucalion and his wife, having built an ark on the advice of his father Prometheus, were the sole survivors of a flood unleashed on the impious Pelasgians by an angry Zeus. Landing on the shores of Thessaly, they eventually, following the gods' instructions, produced a new and purer race, the Greeks. The name *Deucalion* (Greek *Deukalíōn*) is believed to combine the elements 'new wine' and 'sailor' – from *deúkos*, a variant of *gleúkos* ('sweet new wine') and *halieús* ('sailor') (Graves 1960, 2:388). Deucalion thus also shares with Noah the combination of wine and water, since the sailor Noah was also held to be the inventor of wine. The combination (with an appropriate Irish substitution for wine) is also an appropriate one for HCE, a publican by trade and an imputed arrival from overseas by origin.

Péron and Beckett share a French version with Beckett and Joyce, 'le vieux deuc alien célèbre,' where 'deuc alien' conflates the *duc* ('duke') and a French Deucalion. Joyce and Frank's Italian, 'il degno duca Lione,' gives us an Italian Deucalione masquerading as a worthy (*degno*) duke (*duca*) named *Lione*, the latter also the Italian name of the French city of Lyons and thus emphasizing his foreignness. Schenoni's 'il famoso elduca alieno' retains the reference to the German Elde while recasting the Italian Deucalione as a '-duca alieno,' confirming his alien if still ducal status. Hildesheimer's rendering, 'dieser deukältische Herzögler,' ignoring age and fame, turns a seafaring German Deukalion into a Celtic (*keltisch*) duke (*Herzog*) approaching (*herziehen*), perhaps belatedly (*Nachzügler*, 'late arrival'), shores that are presumably Irish rather than Greek.

Several renderings simply ignore Deucalion altogether, however. Aixàs's Catalan version, 'el famós vell duc Howth,' invents a new Irish duchy in referring to 'the famous old Duke Howth.' In Portuguese, Schüler's 'o famoso duque, o velho da estranja' speaks much less specifically of a famous but anonymous duke, an old man (*velho*) from foreign parts (*estranja*), while Amarante is similarly unspecific with 'o famoso velho duque estrangeiro,' a famous old foreign (*estrangeiro*) duke. Antip's Romanian 'vestitul duce bătrân venetic' likewise refers to the same famous (*vestit*) but anonymous old (*bătrân*) alien (*venetic*) duke (*duce*). Goyert's German version, 'der famose alte Monarch,' elevates our hero to the realms of royalty rather than mere nobility, once again ignoring Deucalion while allowing mention of the Indian Mona River. Słomczyński's Polish 'ten sławny djukon obcy' refers to a famous (*sławny*) and alien (*obcy*) 'djukon,' the latter (invented) term conflating an English *duke* and the far distant Canadian Yukon River, while *obcy* allows for further access to the Russian river Ob. Weatherall's Czech, 'ten starý slavný vévoda z Tramtárie,' more expansively refers to an old (*starý*) and famous (*slavný*) duke (*vévoda*) from Tramtária, the latter place name a Czech expression for an unspecified remote location, giving us a famous but anonymous old Slavic duke from far away, a noble what's-his-name from who knows where.

Three versions, meanwhile, seize on Joyce's 'famous' to suggest suspicious doubts as to our alien duke's sexual identity. Wollschläger's 'der femmeuse olle Don Kallion' associates him overtly with HCE (alias Don Dom Dombdomb), emphasizes his foreignness by giving him a Spanish title ('Don') and a Greek name (Greek *kallíōn*, 'more beautiful'), and raises French doubts as to his sexual orientation, 'femmeuse' including *femme* as well as echoing 'famous.' This formulation allows fluvial access to the French-Belgian-Dutch river Meuse and several Don Rivers as well as the Kalindi and various Kali Rivers of India. Bindervoet and Henkes's Dutch version, 'dien fameuze owen knar van een duke ellejan,' refers to a famous 'old geezer' (*ouwe knar*) of a 'duke ellejan,' a Dutch Deukalion whose claims to fame appear to include his unusual height (*elle*, 'ell, yard'; *jan*, 'giant'). Joyce's 'famous' is rendered as 'fameuze' rather than the normal Dutch *beroemd*, thus agreeing with Wollschläger's 'femmeuse' and likewise referring to the Meuse. The description of the duke as an 'owen knar' draws on the anglicized version of the Irish *abhainn* ('river'), and 'duke ellejan' provides access to the Breton river Ellé, while hinting heavily at the gendered implications of the French pronoun *elle* ('she'). The theme of sexual identity is taken up with customary radical excess in Stündel's 'der falmöse eeldere Hexzog exzohtikus,' where the now once again anonymous duke is not just 'eld' but 'eelder,' not just old (*alt*) but older (*älter*); he may be famous, but he is also 'pale and wan' (*fahl*) and equipped with female genitals (*Möse*, 'cunt'); he is not only a duke (*Herzog*) but a cross-gendered old hag of a witch (*Hexe*), and while he may be an exotic alien (*Exot*), he has a frankly filthy (*zotig*) mind, excessively addicted to the dirty joke (*Zote*). This less than flattering assessment is accompanied by fluvial reference to the Ukrainian Alma, French Meuse, German Elde, and South African Hex rivers.

Three final versions arrive at solutions almost equally extravagant, if presented in quite different keys. Lavergne's expanded rendering, 'Ce fameux duc échu de l'étranger, tout imbu de son Elbe,' in speaking of a famous foreign duke who is *échu* ('expired, overdue'), elevates our hero from ducal to imperial dignity: an ECH who, clearly past his sell-by date, is 'tout imbu de son Elbe,' at once thoroughly soaked (*imbibé*) by the German river Elbe, drunk (*imbibé*), and, suddenly revealed as none other than Napoleon, obsessed (*imbu*) with the Italian island of Elba (French *Elbe*). García Tortosa's Spanish rendering, 'el gran de yerro de uca a lion,' is phrased in terms of a cryptic crossword clue involving neither duke nor emperor but, more exotically, a Turkish dey, as rulers of Algiers under the Ottoman Empire were called: 'a great (*gran*) ruler (*dey*), a foreign grandee (*grande*), I wander (*yerro*), perhaps in error (*yerro*), from *uca* to *lion*,' with the final four words, 'de uca a lion,' giving us the required answer, namely a Spanish Deucalión. Grut's succinct Swedish version, finally, 'den gamle asatoken,' while invoking the Japanese Asato and Alaskan Tok Rivers, ignores Deucalion altogether in favour of a play on the fact that the Swedish noun *as* can designate either an animal carcase or a god, one of the *Æsir* of Old Norse mythology. The result is a distinctly unflattering characterization of our hapless Dublin Deucalion as a decrepit old (*gammal*) fool (*tok*) who seems to think himself a godlike hero.

And his derry's own drawl and his corksown blather and his doubling stutter and his gullaway swank. (FW 197.4–6)

Péron and Beckett (French, 1985 / 1996); Beckett and Joyce (French, 1931 / 1996): Et sa voix qu'il traîne derryère chaque phrase de sa bouche onflée de mots corquets et tous ses bégaiements à dublintente, le farceur qu'il est sans égalouégaux.

Lavergne (French, 1982): Son parler nonchalant de Derry, ses scottises et blagues de Cork Town, son bégaiement à double entente de Dublin, et son épate de Galway.

Joyce and Frank (Italian, 1979 / 1996): Un ghigno derriso del corcontento, ma chiazze galve dal cervel debolino.

Schenoni (Italian, 1996): E il suo decantato accento di derrycante, le sue chiacchiere da còrkido, la sua balbuzie doppintese e il suo pavoneggiarsi da galwayocco.

García Tortosa (Spanish, 1992): Y su deje de derry y su corkney perora y su double tartaja y su calawaymetías.

Aixàs (Catalan, 2004): I el seu xerroteig derrinià tan particular, lent i afectat, i la seva fatxenderia dublinesa.

Schüler (Portuguese, 2003): Com seu arrastado falar derryano, seu blablablá corkiano, seu gaguejar dublinense e sua afetação gulla way ana.

Amarante (Portuguese, 2009): E o seu típico sotaque derryense e sua fala corketípica e sua gagueira duplinense e seu comportamento galowayense.

Antip (Romanian, 1996): Şi bâiguielile lui lâlâite şi aiurelile lui beţivăneşti şi bâlbâielile lui poticnite şi făloşenia lui de găgăuţă.

Goyert (German, 1970): Und seine Belfastreden und sein vercorkstes Geplapper und sein Dublsinn-Gestotter und sein Galliwog-Stolz.

Hildesheimer (German, 1969 / 1970): Und sein gedänt Derryliktchen und sein corkiger Schwatz und sein doppeltes Stotter und sein Gallwegsgestellz.

Wollschläger (German, 1970): Und sein derryg Gestammel und corkig Gequatsch und sein Tumblingsgestotter und Gallwehsgelatsch!

Stündel (German, 1993): Und mit derry ihm eigenen learmigen lennesamen Spreechweise und seiner vercorribsten Schwarzeelstern und seinem dappelinnten Gestourtter und gallwegishim Geflynker.

Bindervoet and Henkes (Dutch, 2002): En zijn lijzige derrisch en zijn ontkorkte gewauwel en zijn verdublinde gestotter en zijn gallawaaiig gesnoef.

Grut (Swedish, 2001): Och hans derriton och corkade snack och dubblinstamstam och galwayskrävel.

Weatherall et al. (Czech, 1932 / 1996): Slova dřel na jazyce, jako to
dělají v Dřevnici, koktal, jako by byl z Kokořína, dublíroval slova
po dublansku a válel hlásky po valašsku.

Słomczyński (Polish, 1985): A jego derrydymały, gdy odkorkował
bełtkot, a to jego doubeltowe jąkanie jak świański gullasz.

HCE's public behaviour, finally, is reportedly just as deplorable as his
personal failures. His egregious speaking manner as public figure, for
example, is described in terms of high disapproval involving the four
corners of Ireland – north, south, east, and west – and the four prov-
inces – Ulster, Munster, Leinster, and Connacht – as represented respectively by the cities of Derry, Cork, Dublin, and Galway. All four, as
cities, refer primarily to HCE as master builder, while the names of all
four also provide complementary fluvial reference to ALP, for County
Wicklow boasts a river Derry, and the other three place names derive
respectively from the Irish *Corcaigh* ('swampy place'), *Duibhlinn* ('black
pool'), and *Gaillimh* ('stony river'). The repeated 'own' once again
evokes the common anglicized element in Irish river names, *owen* (Irish
abhainn, 'river'). HCE's devil's own drawl becomes a 'derry's own
drawl,' and since opposites attract, a devil's own drawl evokes a god's
own blather, and blather, notoriously, is nowhere more at home than in
Cork (close neighbour to Blarney Castle).[1] His stuttering duplicity is
already well known in Dublin, and his fraudulent airs and swanking
graces would no doubt equip him to gull Galway too if he so chose. The
term 'gullaway' also reminds us once again not only of his status as
suspected foreigner (Irish *gall*) and interloper from far away, but also of
the universally shared desire that this particular *gall* should indeed just
'go away.'

For Péron and Beckett and (adopted word for word) for Beckett and
Joyce, HCE's voice drawls and drags (*traîne*) in French after every
phrase, with 'derryère' doing double duty for *derrière* ('after') and the
city of Derry. Each phrase falls from a 'bouche onflée de mots corquets,'
from a 'mouth crammed (*enflée*) with cajoling (*coquet*) words,' where the
city of Cork can be found lurking not only in 'mots corquets' but also in
the phrase 'bouche onflée,' since a French *bouchon* is literally a 'cork' for

---

1 Stanislaus Joyce writes of his father, a Corkman, that when drunk he had 'in an
   unusual degree that low, voluble abusiveness characteristic of the Cork people'
   (1971, 5). Corkonians may or may not agree with this characterization.

a bottle. HCE's 'bégaiements' ('stutterings') are both literally 'double meaning' (*à double entente*) and associated ('à dublin-') with Dublin, this evidence of his duplicity confirming him as the matchless joker (*farceur*) he is universally agreed to be. The phrase 'sans égalouégaux' (*sans égal ou égaux*, 'without equal or equals') conveniently incorporates an approximate French pronunciation ('-galoué-') of Galway as well as ('-gaux') of an English *go*, as in the devout wish, in French as in English, that he should once and for all just go away, back to where he came from and should ideally have stayed. Lavergne's less complex French rendering refers to HCE's offhand (*nonchalant*) Derry dialect (*parler*) that essentially says nothing at all (*non-chalant*), his typically Irish (Latin *Scottus*) Cork stupidities (*sottises*) and blarney (*blague*), his double-meaning (*à double entente*) Dublin stuttering (*bégaiement*) and his Galway swagger (*épate*), duplicitly, in view of his obviously foreign origins, emulating ('-pat-') the typical patter of a genuine home-grown Irish Paddy.

In Italian, the Joyce and Frank version completely ignores our hero's oral delivery, choosing to focus instead on his equally unprepossessing facial appearance. We thus hear of his irritating sneer (*ghigno*), where 'derriso' does duty for both *derisivo* ('derisive') and Derry, a sneer presumably the product of a 'corcontento,' a perversely contented Cork ('corc-') heart (*core*), but accompanied by unsightly blotches (*chiazza*, 'stain') resulting from drunken (*albo*, 'drunk') misbehaviour in some riverbed (*alveo*) in Galway ('galve') and that are caused ultimately by a 'cervel debolino,' a brain (*cervello*) made feeble (*debole*) by the rigours of life in a feeble-minded Dublin. Schenoni's Italian, however, returns to matters of oral presentation and public behaviour, focusing on his Derry accent ('derrycante'), both singsong (*decantare*, 'to sing praises') and never-ending (*ricantare*, 'to sing again'), his unending gossipy anecdotes (*chiacchiera*, 'gossip') 'da còrkido,' from Cork or from hell (*Orco*) as his hearers decide, his doubling (*doppio*, 'double') stutter (*balbuzie*) that seems to imply secret Dublin meanings (*intesa*, 'secret agreement'), and his peacock (*pavone*) strutting about like a 'galwayocco,' a great Galway scoundrel (*galeotto*).

García Tortosa's Spanish rendering finds just as little to approve of in a Derry accent (*dejo*) that suffers from slovenliness (*dejo*) and laziness (*dejar*, 'to let it be'), his holding forth (*perorar*) in a Cork accent that (unaccountably) sounds like cockney, his stuttering (*tartajear*, 'to stutter') Dublin doublespeak, and his ear-piercing (*calar*, 'to pierce') Galway gibberish (*galimatías*) and low slang (*caló*). The reference to ear-piercing volume, we may notice, establishes a cross reference to HCE as Persse ('pierce') O'Reilly that is found neither in Joyce's original nor in any other version. In Catalan, meanwhile, Aixàs's rendering confines itself for unspecified reasons to verbal peculiarites relating to Derry and Dublin, omitting any reference to Cork or Galway. The tone of castigation is considerably reduced, the focus being on peculiarity: our hero's Derry accent is described as a high-pitched squeak (*xerroteig*) that also manages to be slow (*lent*), affected (*afectat*), and entirely peculiar (*particular*), while his Dublin delivery is characterized by swaggering bluster (*fatxenderia*), a quality, we notice, that is associated in Joyce's original with Galway rather than Dublin.

In Portuguese, Schüler refers to his drawled out (*arrastado*) Derry speech (*falar*), his nonsensical Cork blather (*blablablá*), his Dublin stutter (*gaguejar*), and his 'gulla way' affectation (*afetação*), while Amarante speaks of his typical (*típico*) Derry accent (*sotaque derryense*), his way of speaking (*fala*) that is likewise typical of Cork (*corketípica*), his doubling (*duplo*) Dublin stutter (*gagueira*), and his cock-of-the-walk behaviour (*comportamento*), strutting like a Galway (*galowayense*) rooster (*galo*). In Romanian, meanwhile, Antip dispenses with any echo of any of the four cities involved, merely referring instead to a set of generic linguistic and behavioural shortcomings: his stammering mumble (*bâigui*, 'to stammer'; *lâlâi*, 'to mumble'), his drunken nonsense (*aiureli*, 'to talk nonsense'; *betie*, 'drunkenness'), his incomprehensible stuttering (*bâlbâi*, 'to stutter'; *poticni*, 'blundering'), and his idiotic boasting (*făloşenia*, 'boasting'; *găgăuţă*, 'idiot').

Our four German renderings offer a range of relatively interesting effects. Goyert's version draws attention to the miscreant's 'booming' (*belfern*) 'public speeches' (*Festreden*) as delivered not in Derry but in Belfast ('belf-'), not to mention his Cork 'babbling' (*Geplapper*) that is totally 'screwed up' (*verkorkst*), or his Dublin 'stutter' (*Gestotter*) that is nothing but *Doppelsinn* ('double meaning'), or his Galway swagger (*Stolz*, 'pride') that is as ridiculous as it would be in a child's golliwog doll. Hildesheimer's 'Derryliktchen' suggests a 'dereliction' unsuccessfully concealed, whether by the use of a Derry dialect (*Dialekt*) that is both long drawn-out (*gedehnt*) and, reflecting the delinquent's Scandinavian origins, foreign-sounding (*Däne*, 'Dane'), or by Cork chatter (*Schwatz*) more appropriately kept 'corked' (*korkig*), or by a 'double' (*doppelt*) stutter, or by language both 'stilted' (*gestelzt*) and 'caustic' (*gallig*) that would turn the rocky road to Galway into a 'Gallweg,' a road (*Weg*) full of resentment and bad temper (*Galle*). Wollschläger's miscreant, with his continual stammer (*Gestammel*), uses language that is both coarse (*derb*) and dirty (*dreckig*) as well as redolent of Derry, or else he utters a string of nonsense (*Gequatsch*) again better kept 'corked' (*korkig*), whether in a 'Tumbling' Dublin stutter (*Gestotter*) that falls over itself (*tummeln*) in its haste, or alternatively in a lazy dragging delivery (*latschen*, 'to slouch') full of 'gall' (*Galle*) and 'woe' (*Weh*).

Stündel's version, finally, constitutes something of a tour de force in managing to include reference to no fewer than ten separate rivers. His reworking of the standard German phrasing *mit der ihm eigenen lärmigen, langsamen Sprechweise* ('in his own peculiar loud and slow delivery') nods not only to the city of Derry but also variously to the Irish river Derry, the British river Leam, and the German rivers Lenne and Spree. Joyce's 'his corksown blather' is rendered highly idiosyncratically as 'seiner vercorribsten Schwarzeelstern,' where the invented adjective 'vercorribst' contains just a faint hint of a Cork that is *verkorkst* ('all screwed up') and a much more obvious reference to the Irish river Corrib, on which not Cork but Galway stands. 'Schwarzeelstern,' meanwhile, refers to the German river Schwarze Elster, a tributary of the Elbe, whose unusual name literally means 'black magpie' and is paralleled by that of a sister river, the Weisse Elster ('white magpie'). Its surprising appearance here may be due to 'blather' suggesting *black*, leading to German *schwarz*. 'His doubling stutter' is transformed into 'seinem dappelinnten Gestourtter,' incorporating several North American Apple Rivers into a Dublin marked by doubled consonants and inserting the British river Stour into his 'stutter' (*Gestotter*). Reference to his 'gallwegishim Geflynker,' finally, introduces the Russian river Ishim into the Irish city of Galway ('gallweg-') and the Fly River of faraway Papua New Guinea into the dubious tales full of resentful bitterness (*Galle*) with which his listeners are regularly regaled (*flunkern*, 'to spin a yarn').

Bindervoet and Henkes's Dutch version identifies our man's drawling (*lijzig*) delivery from the muck (*derrie*) of Derry, his drivelling rigmarole (*gewauwel*) uncorked (*ontkurken*, 'to uncork') from Cork, his doubling (*verdubbelen*, 'to double') Dublin stuttering (*gestotter*), and his windy (*waaien*, 'to blow in the wind') Galway bragging crammed with gall (*gal*). The term *gesnoef* ('bragging') allows fluvial access to the Scottish and English Noe Rivers. Grut's Swedish, finally, makes reference in slightly less negative terms than most to our hero's 'derriton,' his tone of voice (*ton*) characteristic of Derry, his stupid (*korkad*) gossip (*snack*) from Cork, his 'dubblinstamstam' that conflates *dubbel*

('double'), Dublin, and a doubled *stamma* ('to stutter'), as well as to his
Galway blustering and bragging (*skrävel*).

the rivering waters of   (FW 216.4)

We may conclude by once again comparing the number of rivers and
waterways invoked by Joyce and by his multilingual translators respectively in the few brief passages that we have examined here from little
more than a single page of *Anna Livia Plurabelle*.

Joyce himself invokes at least seventeen: the German Repe, the
French Reppe, the Dirty Devil River of Utah, the English Duddon,
the Alaskan Dudd Creek, the Russian Uda, the Irish Lough Neagh,
the Rough River of Kentucky, the Roughty River of County Kerry, the
German Rappach, the Scottish Rappach Water, the French Seine, the
Canadian Goose River, the Irish Drogheda Bay, the Canadian Drogheda
Lake, the German Elde, and the Irish Derry.

His translators, in the twenty or so versions considered in this chapter, collectively invoke more than 150 altogether. More obsessive readers may be interested in the complete listing, as follows, in the sequence
in which they are mentioned above: the Swiss Reuss, the English Ouse,
the Philippine Ibo, the Welsh Lugg, the American Andro, the German
Repe, the French Reppe, the Scottish Orr, the English Rib, the Latvian
Cena, the Scottish Carron, the Venezuelan Caroní, the Romanian Rona,
the Mexican Pilon, the American Río Grande, the Nigerian Odo, the
French Arbois, the German Peene, the South American Saramacca, the
Czech Iser, German Isar, French Isère, and Belgian Yser, the Canadian
Lord River and Australian Ord River, the English Duddon, the Scottish,
English, Canadian, and Russian rivers Don, the English Dart, various
North American Egg Rivers, the French Doubs, the Irish Lerr, the
Serbian Drina, the Canadian Codroy, the Polish Odra, the German Ach,
the Australian Tuross, the Welsh and Scottish rivers Dee, the Irish
Devlin, the Dutch Dommel, the Haitian Grise, the Czech Čertovka, the
Romanian Prut, the French Somme, various North American Cache
Rivers and Cache Creeks, the Belgian Our, the French Aube, the French
Saône, the Brazilian Água Branca and Serra Negra, the Catalan Lake
Bañolas, the Canadian Ena and Jouve, the French Ouvèze, the Ghanaian
Fia, the Irish Lough Neagh, the German Bodensee and Schluchsee
lakes, the German Regen, the Tasmanian Huon River, the Canadian
Shoal River, the Irish and English Rye Rivers, the Australian Loch, the
Dutch Lek, Sloe, and Kendel, the Swedish Lake Vättern, the Italian Po,

the Chinese Li, the French Isson, the German Rot, the Indonesian Anai, the Egyptian Nile, the French Allier, the Scottish Carron, the Venezuelan Caroní, the Ukrainian Roza, the Scottish Orr, the English Rib, the Latvian Cena, the Russian Ob, Nigerian and Canadian rivers Oba, the Sudanese Sobat, Ukrainian Strupa, Russian Upa, French Adour, Russian Alei, English Leith, Spanish Ega, Alaskan Rude, Romanian Ruda, Scottish Ruel, Romanian Bold River, Belgian Rupel, Indian Uben, Swiss Lake Zürich, Scottish Wick River, German Elde, Indian Adda Holle, Belgian Our, Central African Kasai, the no longer existent Italian Auser River, the English Uck, Chinese Ho, English Lyme, Scottish Oude, the North American Russian River, the French Seine, the Vietnamese Rui, the Rhodesian Biri, the American Detroit River, the American Reese River and Kanab Creek, the Indian Laua, the German Lenne, the Russian Lena, the German Oos, the Slovak river Poprad, the Ghanaian river Pra, the Indian Gola, the African Dra, the Romanian Pop and Popa, the German Elbe, the Indian Mona, the Indian Kalindi and various Kali Rivers, the South African Hex, the French-Belgian-Dutch Meuse, the French Elle, the Japanese Asato, the Alaskan Tok, the Canadian Yukon, the Irish Derry, the British Leam, the German Spree, the Irish Corrib, the German Schwarze Elster, various North American Apple Rivers, the British Stour, the Russian Ishim, the Fly River of Papua New Guinea, and the Scottish and English Noe Rivers. Joyce's translators, it is surely fair to say, rise as a group with enormous enthusiasm to the challenge of providing ALP, the river of rivers, with an appropriate retinue of 'rivering waters of, hitherandthithering waters of' (FW 216.4–5).

PART FOUR

Naming Names

8 Here Comes Everybody

The protagonist of *Finnegans Wake* is called by many different names in constantly changing narrative contexts, but is very frequently identified, as we have seen, by the initials *HCE* or some permutation of them (*HEC*, *ECH*, *CHE*, and so on). Sometimes the initials are those of a character or pseudo-character (such as Humphrey Chimpden Earwicker, Huges Caput Earlyfowler, or Haroun Childeric Eggeberth), sometimes they occur as a sequence of initials in phrases whose relevance may be fairly obvious (such as 'this man of hod, cement and edifices') or considerably less so (such as 'Heinz cans everywhere'). *Finnegans Wake* can be read as the text of a monstrously proliferating dream or series of dreams, in which the dreamer-narrator as HCE plays a starring role. In that capacity, 'HCE is also everybody (including Joyce) and his dream the dream of all men' (Tindall 1959, 264). For some readers, the dream, the text, *is* HCE and his initials a reflection of Christ's *HoC Est enim corpus meum* ('This is my body'), as lettered in illuminated medieval manuscripts. The similarity between the formulas *HCE* and *IHS* has also not gone unnoticed.

This is far from saying that HCE in all his manifestations has a great deal in common with Christ, though in some of his manifestations he certainly does. For as Joyce scholars have long since demonstrated, HCE can be read as both a macrocosmic father of all men and conflation of all heroes through history ('Here Comes Everybody') and simultaneously as a microcosmic man in the street, specifically a decidedly harassed publican in the Dublin suburb of Chapelizod with a guilty conscience and a persistent thirst. We never achieve certainty as to the reason or reasons for Humphrey Chimpden Earwicker's guilty conscience, but he undoubtedly has one, is a fallen man just as Adam was a fallen man. The boundary between macrocosm and microcosm is entirely permeable, and transitions between the two are both fluid and continuous. HCE is omnipresent in the *Wake*, and readers have found that presence signalled by a thousand or more variations on his initials.

As for the specific set of initials, there is some general agreement among Joyce scholars that HCE ultimately owes his initials to the British politician Hugh Culling Eardley Childers (1827–96), a Member of Parliament and one-time Secretary for War. Childers became embroiled in several highly publicized political affairs, including especially one involving the *HMS Captain*, a ship whose construction he had ordered to proceed despite professional advice to the contrary, which almost immediately sank (drowning his own son in the process), and the blame for which disaster he very ungallantly attempted to shift to his officials. Towards the end of his career he was uncharitably lampooned for his combination of corpulence and self-importance as 'Here Comes Everybody Childers' and 'H.C.E.' (Curran 1968, 86; Glasheen 1977, 56). Childers also had Irish connections – and specifically with Howth: his younger cousin Robert Erskine Childers (1870–1922), who spent his boyhood in County Wicklow and first achieved fame as a novelist with *The Riddle of the Sands* (1903), used his private yacht *Asgard* to smuggle a cargo of rifles and ammunition for the Irish Volunteers from Hamburg into Howth harbour in 1914, winning further fame among Irish Republicans. (He was subsequently executed by Free State forces in 1922, during the Irish Civil War.) In a case of life (and initials) splendidly imitating art, another cousin, Erskine Hamilton Childers (1905–74), son of Robert Erskine Childers, was to become the fourth president of Ireland in the 1970s.

Much more could be (and has been and will undoubtedly continue to be) said about Humphrey Chimpden Earwicker, but we will limit ourselves in the present context to following for a while the transtextual onomastic fortunes of HCE as variously referred to in Joyce's text. We shall follow the order in which references occur in the text.

Howth Castle and Environs   (FW 3.3)

Like Leopold Bloom, likewise no stranger to Howth, whose first name is that of an Austrian emperor and whose family name was changed from the Hungarian, HCE is a foreigner by blood. Linguistically, *Howth* is Danish, *Castle* is English, *Environs* is French. This first variation on HCE's name thus links him to three different sets of invaders of Ireland: the ninth-century Vikings; the twelfth-century Normans (since Howth Castle was built by the Norman adventurer Sir Almeric Tristram); and their immediate and long-lived successors, the English. The phrase not only associates HCE by implication with a position of power and leadership; it also already anticipates the theme of an older man losing his wife to a younger rival. According to Fenian tradition, Howth was one of the locations used as a hiding place by the young lovers Diarmuid and Gráinne as they fled the vengeance of the aging leader Finn mac Cumhaill, whose promised wife Gráinne had abandoned him for his trusted follower Diarmuid Ó Duibhne. We have already seen how this particular phrase has been rendered in several languages.

Bygmester Finnegan, of the Stuttering Hand   (*FW* 4.18)

du Bouchet (French, 1962): Dignemestre Finnegan, de Mainbègue

Lavergne (French, 1982): Finnegan le Constructeur, stathouder de sa main

Schenoni (Italian, 1982): Bygmester Finnegan, della Stuttering Hand

Pozanco (Spanish, 1993): El gran maestre Finnegan, el de la estatud-eresca mano

Schüler (Portuguese, 2003): O Bygmester Finnegan, o Mão-Gaga

Beck (German, 1989): Großbaumeister Finnegan, freier maurer von der Stottrigen Hand

Jauslin (German, 1989): Großpygmaester Finnegan, Freierndmaurer von der stotternden Hand

Stündel (German, 1993): BaugerMeister Finnegan, von der Schlotternden Hand

Bindervoet and Henkes (Dutch, 2002): Bygmestor Finnegan, van de Stotterende Hand

Volokhonsky (Russian, 2000): Gruzmajster Finnegan, iz Kistej Zaiki

One of the earliest references to our hero identifies him – 'Finnegan, erse solid man' (*FW* 3.20–1) – with the bibulous builder's labourer of the music-hall song 'Finnegan's Wake,' whose drunken fall from a ladder prefigures HCE's own fall from grace. Less than a page later,

Finnegan becomes 'Bygmester Finnegan, of the Stuttering Hand,' a 'big mister' as befits the giant Finn he also will turn out to be and a master builder (Danish *bygmester*) who builds Dublin city, his 'stuttering hand' an indication at once of his rapid and untiring brick-laying, his alcoholic shakes, and his additional qualification in the matter of erections, not just as master builder but also as masturbator.

Joyce's 'Bygmester' overtly invokes Ibsen's play *Bygmester Solness* (1892), translated as *The Master Builder*, whose protagonist, the architect Halvard Solness, attempting to construct a house with the tallest tower in town, finally completes the tower only to fall to his death from it. Finnegan's title remains unchanged in Schenoni's Italian and Schüler's Portuguese. It is rendered respectfully in French, both in Lavergne's straight-faced 'Finnegan le Constructeur' ('the Builder'), as in a modern job description, and in du Bouchet's ironically medievalized 'Dignemestre Finnegan,' a title combining *digne* ('worthy') and an archaizing *mestre*, modern *maître* ('master'). Pozanco's Spanish refers with equally great respect to 'El gran maestre Finnegan' ('the grand master'), while Volokhonsky's Russian 'Gruzmajster' characterizes our hero as a German *Großmeister* ('grand master') who bears a heavy burden (Russian *gruz*, 'load'), as in the hod carried by Tim Finnegan to rise in the world. Beck's German has him as a 'Großbaumeister' ('grand master builder') responsible for a construction site (*Großbaustelle*), while Jauslin describes him considerably more ambiguously as a 'Großpygmaester,' a grand master (*Großmeister*) indeed, but one who, far from being a giant among men, turns out, by oblique courtesy of the Danish *bygge* ('to build'), to be in fact a pygmy (*Pygmäe*), presumably as regards his moral stature. Beck sees him as a 'freier maurer,' a 'free mason,' independent rather than indentured, while for Jauslin he is in fact a 'Freierndmaurer,' an institutional member of the Freemasons (*Freimaurer*) too fond for his own good of alcoholic celebrations (*feiern*, 'to celebrate'), a failing that contributes at least one reason for the stuttering hand.

Two other versions take less charitable views. In Stündel's German, our hero is a 'BaugerMeister,' conflating German *Baumeister* ('master builder'), Danish *bygge* ('to build'), and German *Bauer*, the latter clearly in its derogatory sense of 'bumpkin, yokel.' In Bindervoet and Henkes's Dutch, even less charitably, he is a 'Bygmestor,' an appellation (differing from Joyce's English by only one vowel) that conflates Danish *bygmester* ('master builder'), Dutch *bouwmeester* ('architect'), and, gesturing towards the insect world that Earwicker's name also evokes, Dutch *mesttor* ('dung beetle'). A big mess, in short.

As for the 'stuttering hand,' Schenoni's Italian treats it as a title of honour become a family name, 'della Stuttering Hand.' Du Bouchet also treats it as if it were an inherited title from a noble past, in this case a French 'de Mainbègue' (*main*, 'hand'; *bègue*, 'stuttering'). Lavergne's French sees the 'stuttering hand' as further confirmation of Finnegan's high social standing, as 'stathouder de sa main,' one who has achieved the position of stadtholder or lieutenant general purely on his own merits. Pozanco's Spanish is in enthusiastic agreement: Finnegan is 'el de la estatuderesca mano,' he whose hand (*mano*) is that of a stadthold- er (*estatúder*).

Other versions are more doubtful about him. In Dutch, in Bindervoet and Henkes's 'van de Stotterende Hand,' the verb *stotteren* can mean both 'to stutter' and 'to falter,' the latter raising the spectre of our hero's alcoholic overindulgence once again. Schüler's Portuguese epithet 'o Mão-Gaga' suggests not only a hand (*mão*) that is *gago* ('stuttering') but a possessor of that hand who is *gagá* ('senile, gaga'). Volokhonsky's Russian epithet 'iz Kistej Zaiki' concentrates on a technical detail of the matter at hand, noting that the stuttering (*zaika*) is actually less a matter of the hand than of the wrist (*kist'*). Stündel's German epithet 'von der Schlotternden Hand' suggests an enthusiastic assessment based on simi- lar, if hardly flattering, considerations: though the hand may 'tremble' or 'shake' (*schlottern*) rather than 'stutter' (*stottern*), the impressive result produced is reminiscent of nothing short of a 'chimney stack' (*Schlot*).

this man of hod, cement and edifices   (FW 4.26)

Lavergne (French, 1982): cet homme d'oiseau, de ciment et dédifices

Schenoni (Italian, 1982): quest'uomo di hsparviero, cemento ed edifici

Schüler (Portuguese, 2003): esse biscateiro de deus, cimento e mitifícios

Beck (German, 1989): dieser mann von hucke, cement und erbau- lichkeiten

Jauslin (German, 1989): der Mann aus Hucken, Cement und Erb- bautem

Stündel (German, 1993): der Mann Hottes, Cements und Ebäudes

Bindervoet and Henkes (Dutch, 2002): deze man van hop, kalkse- ment en inbouwwerken

HCE's hidden presence in the sad tale of Tim Finnegan's fall is quickly manifested in the initials of the phrase 'hod, cement and edifices.' Two German versions have relatively little difficulty in replicating them: Beck's HCE is a man of *Hucke* (an obsolete term for a load carried on the back), *Cement* (a now obsolete spelling for standard German *Zement*), and 'erbaulichkeiten,' which ironically conflates *Baulichkeiten* ('buildings') and the adjective *erbaulich* ('edifying, uplifting'); Jauslin adopts a very similar strategy with 'Hucken, Cement und Erbbautem,' the final conflation involving *Erbautes* ('something built') and *Erbbauer*, a term normally denoting a farmer (*Bauer*) with a hereditary right (*Erbe*, 'inheritance') to his property, but here punning on both *bauen* ('to build') and *Bauer* ('bumpkin') to suggest a bumpkin builder with hereditary rights to his highly personalized constructions.

Three of the other translations deal with the initial challenge by rather more adventurous adjustments to the normal behaviour of their respective languages. Lavergne's French takes advantage of an 'homme' ('man') rather than a 'oiseau' ('hod'), has no difficulty with 'ciment' ('cement'), and only a missing apostrophe prevents his 'dédifices' (conflating *dédier*, 'to dedicate,' and *édifices*) from completing the trio of initials. Schenoni's Italian has no difficulty with 'cemento ed edifici,' but finds an *h* (a letter that rarely occurs initially in Italian) only by humorously prefixing an honorary (and unspeakable) one to 'sparviero' ('hod'). Both French and Italian, it may be noticed, acquire a supplementary avian overtone here that is quite missing in the original, since French *oiseau* means not only 'hod' but also 'bird,' while Italian *sparviero* means not only 'hod' but also, more specifically, 'sparrow hawk.' A transtextual reading might suspect a parodic invocation here of the Holy Spirit (often represented pictorially as a dove, if hardly as a hawk) in view of the underlying 'man of God' reference – a reading perhaps a little too academic for some tastes, but as it happens, Italian *sparviero* also means an academic 'mortar-board.' Stündel's German rather cavalierly turns the standard phrase *Mann Gottes* ('man of God') into a 'Mann Hottes,' a man perhaps more familiar with horses (*hott*, 'giddy up'), re-spells the usual German *Zement* as 'Cement,' and deprives the word *Gebäude* ('building, edifice') of its initial altogether.

The Bindervoet and Henkes Dutch version approaches the matter more radically by changing the 'man of hod' into a 'man van hop,' invoking both a 'man of hope' (Dutch *hoop*) and a 'man of hops' (Dutch *hop*), the latter helping to explain once again why Tim Finnegan suffers his fall. The initial *k* that the Dutch translators, as we have seen already, use throughout for HCE's *c* is provided by 'kalksement' ('limestone cement'), and the initial *i* that similarly replaces *e* throughout is provided by edifices that are as yet unfinished, 'inbouwwerken' designating buildings under construction (*in bouw*), or in more specifically Joycean terms, 'works in progress.' Schüler's Portuguese rendering ignores the presence of HCE's initials but not that of HCE himself, translating our 'man of hod' as a mere 'odd-job man' (*biscateiro*) but simultaneously as an 'odd-job man of God' (*de deus*) who uses both *cimento* ('cement') and imagination for his 'mitifícios,' constructions that share the nature of real-world *edifícios* ('buildings') and those of *mito* ('myth').

Haroun Childeric Eggeberth   (*FW* 4.32)

Lavergne (French, 1982): Haroun Childéric Eudebert

du Bouchet (French, 2003): Haroun Childéric Egobert

Schenoni (Italian, 1982): Haroun Childeric Eggeberth

Pozanco (Spanish, 1993): Haroum Childeric Eggeberth

Schüler (Portuguese, 2003): Haroun Criancerrico Euevoberto

Beck (German, 1989): Harun Childerich Eggeburt

Jauslin (German, 1989): Herrein Chinderich Eisenbarth

Stündel (German, 1993): Harun Cinderlich Eggebärt

Bindervoet and Henkes (Dutch, 2002): Haroen Kilderik Iggeberth

Volokhonsky (Russian, 2000): Urun Čil'derik Negbert

Far from being merely a builder's labourer with a taste for the tipple and no head for heights, or even a master builder with significant constructions to his credit (or discredit), HCE is early revealed as also having a bloodline that includes the heights of medieval royalty: Haroun al-Rashid was a celebrated eighth-century caliph of Baghdad, Childeric was the name of three Merovingian kings of the Franks, and Ecgberht or Egbert was a ninth-century king of the West Saxons. 'Haroun Childeric Eggeberth,' with its supplementary resonances of harems and children and eggs and birth, survives unscathed and untranslated in Schenoni's Italian and with only minimal (and perhaps inadvertent) modification in Pozanco's Spanish. The Dutch translators discreetly reshape him as 'Haroen Kilderik Iggeberth' in accordance with Dutch spelling conventions and the need for their chosen initials.

Lavergne's French 'Haroun Childéric Eudebert' respects HCE's Arabian and Merovingian credentials but rejects his Saxon lineage in dethroning 'Eggeberth' in favour of 'Eudebert,' decorating a historical Eudes, ninth-century king of the Western Franks, with the linguistically appropriate West Germanic epithet *berht* ('bright') while retaining a reference to humpty-dumpty French eggs (*oeufs*, pronounced exactly like *eu-*). André du Bouchet's French similarly casts doubts on HCE's Saxon bloodline, bluntly suggesting that he was less an 'Eggeberth' than an 'Egobert.' Beck's German 'Eggeburt' implies a translingual suggestion that he was in fact (à la Humpty Dumpty, perhaps) born (*Geburt*, 'birth') from an egg. Jauslin's German version, 'Herrein Chinderich Eisenbarth,' dispenses with all historical echoes, suggesting instead that HCE may actually be a female ruler (*Herrin*) rather than a male (*Herr*), and that she or he is furthermore blessed with many children (*kinderreich*) and related to the comic protagonist of a humorous German folk song for children, 'Doktor Eisenbart,' whose remedies are usually far worse than the original ailment.

Stündel's German transforms Childeric – whose name was originally based on the Germanic elements *hild* ('battle') and *rīc* ('power') – by renaming him 'Cinderlich,' accurately (if quite unreasonably) translating what appears to be the English 'child' by the German *Kind*, modifying the initial as required, and for good measure casting ungenerous doubt on Childeric's political astuteness by suggesting that his activities may in fact have been merely 'childlike' (*kindlich*) and his political ambitions more fit for children (*Kinder*). Eggeberth meanwhile undergoes a radical sex change in order to 'give birth' (*gebären*) as Eggebärt. Schüler's Portuguese is similarly unimpressed by Childeric's credentials, dubbing him 'Criancerrico' instead, thus likewise suggesting that he was merely a child (*criança*), even if a rich one (*rico*). Eggeberth also receives a fairly thorough but more positive makeover at Schüler's hands, becoming a 'Euevoberto' instead, his new onomastic combination of Greek *eu-* ('good'), Spanish *huevo* ('egg'), and Italian *evo* ('historical age') hopefully suggesting that he might well be a thoroughly good egg, exactly the right sort of chap to bring nations together and introduce a bright new historical age. Volokhonsky's Russian version, on the other hand, 'Urun Čil'derik Negbert,' is far less hopeful, with 'Urun' associated not with the caliph Haroun, who is normally known as *Harún* in Russian, but only with actual or anticipated 'losses' (*urón*) of an unspecified nature, while 'Negbert' strongly suggests that our hero, here also deprived of his distinctive initials, is actually nothing short of a reprobate (*negódnik*) and a scoundrel (*negodjáj*).

Wassaily Booslaeugh of Riesengeborg   (*FW* 5.5–6)

du Bouchet (French, 1962): Wassouly Whiskgand de Rincegebourg

du Bouchet (French, 2003): Wassaouly Whiskygand de Rincegebourg

Lavergne (French, 1982): Georges Grosboeuf de Grandgousier

Schenoni (Italian, 1982): Wassaily Booslaeugh di Riesengeborg

Pozanco (Spanish, 1993): Wassaily Booslaegh de Riesegeborg

Schüler (Portuguese, 2003): Aquoso Pinguço Serragigante

Pagán (Galician, 2000): Wassaily Booslaeugh de Riesengeborg

Beck (German, 1989): Wassüfflij Boosegelagh vom Riesengeburg

Jauslin (German, 1989): Wartseglich PichelstEiner vom Riesengeboerg

Stündel (German, 1993): Wasserli Buskläff vom RiesenGeborge

Bindervoet and Henkes (Dutch, 2002): Schnappsili Foezljajev Vandenriesengeborge

Volokhonsky (Russian, 2000): Vassajli Buslaev fon Rizengeborg

HCE's further appellation 'Wassaily Booslaeugh of Riesengeborg' invokes Vasilii Buslaev, hero of the twelfth-century Russian Novgorod epic cycle, who has been described as a sort of Russian Finn mac Cumhaill (Škrabánek 1973, 42). The name *Vasilii* derives, appropriately for the standing of the Russian hero, from Greek *basileios* ('royal'). Joyce's 'Wassaily,' however, ignores these regal overtones in favour of incorporating the English drinking salutation *wassail* ('your health!'), which originally derived from Middle English *wæes hæil* ('be healthy!') but later came to be applied also to the liquor occasioning it and eventually to carousal in general.

The bibulous implications of Joyce's coinage are strongly supported by 'Booslaeugh,' for while the name *Buslaev* is a variant of *Boguslav* ('glory to God'), the Russian noun *buslai* means 'fallen man, drunkard' (Škrabánek 1973, 42). English *booze*, Middle Dutch *busen* ('to drink immoderately'), modern Dutch *boos* ('angry, evil, malicious'), and English *laugh* are all arguably present. Some readers might also detect Irish *laoch* ('warrior'), characterizing our hero as a 'booze-warrior,' a hard man for the drink – and HCE as tavern-keeper will indeed turn out to be one of his own best customers.

As for 'Riesengeborg,' HCE as Finn is a giant (German *Riese*), whom Joyce, following a once-popular theory (O Hehir 1967, 421; MacKillop 1986, 40), found to be of conveniently Scandinavian origins, and Old Norse *borg* denotes variously 'a small dome-shaped hill; a stronghold, fortification, castle; a fortified town, city' (Zoëga 1910, 63). Small hills (and Howth Head has an altitude of less than six hundred feet) can equally conveniently be exaggerated into mountains (German *Gebirge*) where necessary – even inflated into the central European *Riesengebirge* or Giant Mountains. It need hardly be said that 'Riesengeborg,' a hill, castle, and city associated with this hard-drinking hero of foreign extraction, also combines Howth and Dublin.

Schenoni and Pagán simply leave Joyce's version of the name unchanged, while Pozanco's 'Booslaegh' for 'Booslaeugh,' possibly an inadvertent change, makes HCE in this particular manifestation less prone to drunken laughter. Volokhonsky's Russian version, 'Vassajli Buslaev fon Rizengeborg,' dismisses the implications of 'Booslaeugh' altogether in favour of identifying the Russian literary model, Vasilii Buslaev, any bibulous tendencies the latter may have had discreetly indicated by the conflation of 'Vasilii' and *wassail*. Lavergne's French variation, on the other hand, adopts an entirely different strategy and abandons all Russian overtones, substituting a completely different formula, 'Georges Grosboeuf de Grandgousier,' characterizing our hero, though still a foreigner, as English and a beef-eater courtesy of St George, and as French and an alliterative fat glutton (*goûter*, 'to taste, to enjoy'; *gosier*, 'throat') courtesy of Rabelais. While Lavergne's hero may not be entirely averse to an occasional tipple, he evidently prefers eating to alcohol.

Other translators rise with enthusiasm to the alcoholic challenge. In French, du Bouchet even provides two versions, 'Wassouly Whiskgand' and 'Wassaouly Whiskygand,' where the former includes *soûl* and the latter *saoul*, both meaning 'drunk.' The earlier 'Whiskgand' may be a typographical error for the latter 'Whiskygand,' which admirably conflates French *vice* ('vice'), Scotch *whisky* (or Irish *whiskey*, to individual taste), and a French pronunciation of Greek *gigant-* ('giant'). French *vice* suggests not only our hero's general depravity but casts doubt on his status as giant, hinting that he is actually only a stand-in for the real thing, a mere 'vice-giant.' As to 'Rincegebourg,' the rinsing (French *rincer*) of used glasses is a constantly repeated chore for a tavern-keeper in a small town (French *bourg*).

Two of three German versions are in no doubt at all as to our hero's capacity for alcoholic consumption. Beck's 'Wassüfflij Boosegelagh vom Riesengeburg' invokes German *süffeln* ('to tipple'), English *booze* and German *Gelage* ('carousal'), while Jauslin's 'Wartseglich PichelstEiner vom Riesengeboerg' suggests a toper (German *picheln*, 'to booze') for whom alcohol is like (*gleich*) mother's milk (*Warze*, 'nipple'). Stündel's 'Wasserli Buskläff vom RiesenGeborge,' however, finds water (*Wasser*) rather than wassail before rediscovering the booze in 'Buskläff,' which also suggests convivial yelps (*kläffen*, 'to yelp') of laughter ('-läff'). The three accompanying variations on Joyce's 'Riesengeborg' give alternative access to a castle (*Burg*) and to mountains both singular (*Berg*) and plural (*Gebirge*).

Bindervoet and Henkes's Dutch rendering, 'Schnappsili Foezljajev Vandenriesengeborge,' invokes a serious Dutch ('Vanden-') drunkard of Germano-Slavic extraction, with 'Schnappsili' accentuating his foreignness by having him drink German *Schnaps* rather than Dutch *snaps*, and 'Foezljajev' suggesting an undiscriminating taste for cheap liquor (Dutch *foezl*, 'fusel') of any sort. Schüler's Portuguese 'Aquoso Pinguço Serragigante,' finally, has our hero still associated with giants and mountain ranges (Portuguese *serra*, 'mountain range'; *gigante*, 'giant, gigantic'), but now also, much more abstemiously, with water in large quantities (Latin *aquosus*, 'abounding in water') – Schüler, like Stündel, having evidently extracted German *Wasser* ('water') from Joyce's alcoholic 'Wassaily.' Our giant's foreign origins are now Latin, and his tastes seem to run neither to whiskey nor cheap brandy but rather to rum (Portuguese *pinga*, 'rum').

Mister Finn, you're going to be Mister Finnagain! (FW 5.9–10)

du Bouchet (French, 1962): Messire Finn, vas être Finn négant

Lavergne (French, 1982): Maître Finn, vous aurez l'air Finn encore!

Schenoni (Italian, 1982): Mister Finn, stai per diventare Mister Finnagain!

Pozanco (Spanish, 1993): Mister Finn, ¡vais a emular a Mister Finn McCumbal!

Schüler (Portuguese, 2003): Mister Finn, o senhor será Mister Refinnado!

Pagán (Galician, 2000): Señor Finn, seredes de novo o señor Finnlan-grán!

Beck (German, 1989): Herr Finn, sie werden bald Herr Finnüber sein!

Jauslin (German, 1989): Mister Finn, bist dabei dein Muster zu finnagieren!

Stündel (German, 1993): Meister Finn, du bist dabei, Meister Finnagain zu werden!

Bindervoet and Henkes (Dutch, 2002): Meneer Finn, u wordt Meneer Finnegein!

The tipsy hod-carrier Finnegan falls and rises again, dies and is resurrected through the miraculous agency of whiskey. The legendary Finn also dies, as all men die, and in various versions of his legend he will come back to life again when Ireland's need once again requires his presence: now departed and no longer Finn, he will yet one day be Finn again. It is of course grist to Joyce's mill that the name *Finnegan* actually sounds more or less like 'Finn again' in English. Even the Irish name *Ó Fionnagáin*, of which *Finnegan* is an anglicization, looks as if it should also mean 'Fionn (or Finn) again,' even if it does not – the name actually meaning 'descendant of *Fionnagán*,' where the personal name, derived from *fionn* ('fair'), means 'fair-haired' (Cottle 1978, 139).

Here, however, Joyce's 'Mister Finn' is indeed going to be 'Mister Finnagain.' Our Mister Finn retains his name unchanged in all ten versions considered here, though his title is variously adjusted. Several versions stay with 'Mister Finn': thus Schenoni in Italian, Pozanco in Spanish, Schüler in Portuguese, and Jauslin in German, even though this appellation is of course a foreign body in all four languages. Other versions employ archaic titles: thus du Bouchet's 'Messire Finn' and Lavergne's 'Maître Finn' in French and Stündel's 'Meister Finn' in German, the latter two referring rather to the status as 'master' (French *maître*, German *Meister*) not of Finn but of Bygmester Finnegan. Pagán's Galician 'Señor Finn,' Beck's German 'Herr Finn,' and Bindervoet and

YBP Library Services

O'NEILL, PATRICK.

IMPOSSIBLE JOYCE: FINNEGANS WAKES.

                              Cloth   322 P.
TORONTO: UNIV OF TORONTO PRESS, 2013

AUTH: QUEEN'S UNIVERSITY. STUDY OF APPROACHES TO
TRANSLATING FINNEGAN'S WAKE.

   ISBN 1442646438   **Library PO#** GENERAL APPROVAL

		List	60.00	USD
5461 UNIV OF TEXAS/SAN ANTONIO		**Disc**	17.0%	
App. Date 5/07/14 ENG.APR.e 6108-11	**Net**	49.80	USD

SUBJ: JOYCE, JAMES, 1882-1941. FINNEGANS WAKE.

CLASS PR6019   DEWEY# 823.912   LEVEL ADV-AC

YBP Library Services

O'NEILL, PATRICK.

IMPOSSIBLE JOYCE: FINNEGANS WAKES.

                              Cloth   322 P.
TORONTO: UNIV OF TORONTO PRESS, 2013

AUTH: QUEEN'S UNIVERSITY. STUDY OF APPROACHES TO
TRANSLATING FINNEGAN'S WAKE.

   ISBN 1442646438   **Library PO#** GENERAL APPROVAL

		List	60.00	USD
5461 UNIV OF TEXAS/SAN ANTONIO		**Disc**	17.0%	
App. Date 5/07/14 ENG.APR.e 6108-11	**Net**	49.80	USD

SUBJ: JOYCE, JAMES, 1882-1941. FINNEGANS WAKE.

CLASS PR6019   DEWEY# 823.912   LEVEL ADV-AC

Henkes's Dutch 'Meneer Finn' opt, more neutrally, merely for modern equivalents of Joyce's 'Mister' in their respective languages.

'Mister Finnagain,' as might be expected, appears in coats of distinctly divers colours. Schenoni's Italian Finn and (surprisingly soberly) Stündel's German Finn are both going to be an untranslated 'Finnagain.' In Dutch, Bindervoet and Henkes alter only a single vowel in having their Finn about to become 'Finnegein' instead, promising 'lots of fun' (*gein*) at that gentleman's wake. In French, du Bouchet's Finn is going to be 'Finn négant' (literally 'negating Finn'), suggesting resurrection by 'negating' (*négant*) any 'end' (*fin*), while Lavergne's Finn is assured that 'vous aurez l'air Finn encore' ('you're going to be looking fine [*fin*] and Finn again'). In Spanish, Pozanco's Finn is going to 'imitate' (*emular*) one 'Mister Finn McCumbal,' fallen multiply victim to inadequate proofreading. Schüler's Portuguese Finn is promised a future as 'Refinnado,' a Finn not only redivivus but also suitably 'refined' (*refinado*).

Three versions attempt, with varying degrees of success, more overtly adventurous solutions. Pagán's Galician Finn will be once again ('de novo') a 'señor Finnlangrán,' not only a Finn who is 'great' (*grán*) but one who is also a Finn from Finland (*Finlándia*). Beck's German Finn is soon going to be a 'Finnüber,' which is to say, on the one hand a super-Finn (*Über-Finn*) but on the other, more doubtfully, one who is possibly already *hinüber* ('over and done with'). Jauslin's German version, finally, 'Mister Finn, bist dabei dein Muster zu finnagieren,' is constructed on a pair of puns involving, first, English 'mister' and German *Muster* ('model, pattern') and, second, the German verbs *fingieren* ('to fabricate') and *agieren* ('to play the part of somebody'), resulting in a Finn who is going to fabricate the model of his own future, unspecified, by acting the part of somebody else, likewise unspecified but apparently ('finnag-') not entirely unrelated.

Humphrey Chimpden   (FW 30.2)

Lavergne (French, 1982): Humphrey Chimpden

Schenoni (Italian, 1982): Humphrey Chimpden

Pozanco (Spanish, 1993): Humphrey Chimpden

Schüler (Portuguese, 2003): Humphredo Corcovado

Pagán (Galician, 2000): Humphrey Chimpden

Rathjen (German, 1989): Humphrey Chimpden

Stoltefuß (German, 1989): Humphrey Chimpden

Stündel (German, 1993): Hamphri Chimpden

Bindervoet and Henkes (Dutch, 2002): Humfried Kimpanszoon

Belyaev (Russian, 2000): Hamfri Čimpden

The name by which our hero is most commonly known, *Humphrey Chimpden Earwicker*, puts in a partial first appearance ('Humphrey Chimpden') only thirty pages into the *Wake*, its remainder ('Earwicker') mentioned only after a further three pages.

The name *Humphrey* has several interlinked resonances for readers. Cottle (1978, 190) lists it as a normarized Germanic name possibly combining the elements 'giant' (*hūne*) and 'peace' (*frid*). More recently, Hanks and others (2002, 310, 782) list it as composed rather of the Germanic elements *hūn* ('bear cub') and *frid* ('peace'). The onomastic connection with a giant is of course appropriate for one of HCE's main avatars, Joyce's version of Finn, while the connection with a bear once again underlines HCE's animality. The Germanic *hūn*, meanwhile, in due course became the Middle High German *hiune*, which originally meant both 'Hun' and 'Hungarian,' offering an intertextual nod to that other Joycean character of Hungarian (if scarcely Hunnish) origin, Leopold Bloom. The Irish name *Amhlaoibh* is also conventionally (though arbitrarily) anglicized as 'Humphrey' (Hanks et al. 2002, 782). *Amhlaoibh* /ˈauliːv/, in turn, is derived from the Norse *Óláfr*, thus also providing an appropriately Scandinavian link, since Earwicker will be presented as a descendant of Norse Vikings. Strengthening that link, the founding of the Norse city of Dublin is traditionally attributed to one Óláfr hvít, otherwise Olaf the White.

Meanwhile, the *hump* in *Humphrey* reminds us of Humpty Dumpty, who likewise had a great fall. Humpty Dumpty also tells Alice that his name refers to his shape, which may remind us of HCE's 'hump of grandeur' (*FW* 197.3–4), which in turn, for some readers at least, may be seen as the visual burden of his guilt (Glasheen 1977, 175). Then there is the verb *to hump*, which includes among its meanings 'to carry' – a hod, for example, as in the case of Tim Finnegan, or a barrel, as in the case of Mr Porter, tavern-keeper. Finally, *to hump* is colloquially 'to have sexual intercourse with' (Partridge 1972, 468), and such matters also occupy our Humphrey's thoughts more than a little.

The name causes relatively little initial excitement in our group of translators, however, who for the most part simply replicate it. There are four exceptions. Schüler's Portuguese 'Humphredo' gives the name a more Latinate colouring while retaining Humphrey's hump. Bindervoet and Henkes's Dutch takes the opportunity to stress our hero's peaceful nature – giant or not, bear or not – by renaming him 'Humfried,' thus foregrounding the original Germanic *frid* ('peace'). Stündel's German translation rather more interestingly renames him 'Hamphri,' not only in an apparent attempt to approximate the English pronunciation, but also associating the unspecified sexual offences of HCE with those of the biblical Ham, son of Noah and recipient of a paternal curse rather than a blessing. Belyaev's 'Hamfri,' the most complex version of the four, conflates a Russian transliteration of 'Humphrey,' a reference to the biblical Ham (also known in Russian as 'Ham') once again, and a correspondingly censorious Russian *ham* ('cad, boor'). Humphrey's hump, we notice, disappears in the Dutch, German, and Russian renderings alike.

The earliest draft (August 1923) of what became the second chapter (I.ii) of *Finnegans Wake* has HCE's name as 'Humphrey Coxon,' which latter originally meant 'son of Cock,' a personal given name that died out during the late Middle Ages and whose sexual connotations are clearly appropriate for HCE. *Coxon* would also have underlined his qualities as a leader of men: a 'coxswain' (an earlier spelling of which is 'coxon') is a steersman, a man at the helm; etymologically, a cox-swain is the 'swain' or man in charge of a 'cock' or ship's boat, thus strictly speaking a 'cockswain' – again not at all inappropriate for HCE's reputed sexual adventures. The Old English *cocc*, furthermore, also meant 'hillock,' likewise appropriately for HCE's role (Hanks et al. 2002, 134).

In subsequent drafts, however, 'Coxon' becomes 'Chimpden,' and within three pages of its first appearance 'Chimpden' is relegated from surname to middle name in favour of 'Earwicker' (*FW* 33.30). The invented 'CHimpdEn,' of course, has the advantage over 'Coxon' of containing the formula CHE *en abyme*. It also gestures more comically than does 'Coxon' towards HCE's reprehensibly animal nature, preparing the way for the insect reference of 'Earwicker.' A chimp or chimpanzee is an African ape, and the Turkish suffix *-den* ('of, from') even makes HCE a humorously Darwinian descendant of the species. A den, meanwhile, is the lair of a wild beast, and HCE's postulated animality is underlined even by the fact that his public house is situated in

Chapelizod, a village whose name is often popularly pronounced in Ireland (and was indeed written on some older maps) as 'Chapelizard.'

Eight of ten translators in this case are content to remain with Joyce's 'Chimpden' – the Russian 'Čimpden' is merely a transliteration – but two attempt more adventurous solutions. Bindervoet and Henkes thus opt for 'Kimpanszoon,' which conflates the Dutch for 'chimpanzee' (*chimpansee*) and 'son' (*zoon*) in order to leave no doubt as to HCE's Darwinian ancestors. Schüler's Portuguese adopts a quite different strategy, essentially ignoring 'Chimpden' in favour of 'Corcovado,' which literally means 'hunchback' (*corcova*, 'hump') and thus refers more obviously to 'Humphrey' than to 'Chimpden.'

Here Comes Everybody   (*FW* 32.18)

Lavergne (French, 1982): Here Comes Everybody

Schenoni (Italian, 1982): Hecco Cheviene Evognuno

Pozanco (Spanish, 1993): *Here Comes Everybody*

Schüler (Portuguese, 2003): o Homem a Caminho Está

Pagán (Galician, 2000): o Home Chega Eiqui

Rathjen (German, 1989): Hier Commet Edermann

Stoltefuß (German, 1989): Hier Commt Er, jedermann

Stündel (German, 1993): Hier Commt Einjeder

Bindervoet and Henkes (Dutch, 2002): Hier Komt Iedereen

HCE as 'Here Comes Everybody' appears unchanged (and thus made foreign for target-language readers) in Lavergne's French and (italicized as a foreign body) in Pozanco's Spanish. He is translated relatively neutrally in three German versions as Stündel's 'Hier Commt Einjeder' (*ein jeder*, 'everybody'), Rathjen's 'Hier Commet Edermann' (*jedermann*, 'everybody'), and Stoltefuß's 'Hier Commt Er, jedermann' ('Here he comes, everybody') and likewise in Dutch as 'Hier Komt Iedereen' (*iedereen*, 'everybody'), all four cases employing linguistic sleight of hand in the matter of initials. Alberte Pagán's Galician version celebrates the coming of HCE in the phrase 'o Home Chega Eiqui,' literally 'Here comes the man, here comes mankind,' and Schüler's Portuguese finds itself in agreement that 'o Homem a Caminho Está,' literally 'the man (or mankind) is under way.' Schenoni's Italian goes furthest in its enthusiasm: 'Hecco Cheviene Evognuno,' literally 'behold (*ecco*) that (*che*) everybody (*ognuno*) through the ages (*evo*) is coming (*viene*).' We may note that Schenoni celebrates HCE's promised coming by not only replicating the phrasal initials HCE but also, in tribute to our hero's shape-shifting ubiquity, presenting two complementary sets of variations, HEC in *hecco* and CHE in *che*.

H.C. *Earwicker*   (FW 33.30)

Lavergne (French, 1982): H.C. Earwicker

Schenoni (Italian, 1982): H.C. Earwicker

Schüler (Portuguese, 2003): H.C. Elecrainha

Pagán (Galician, 2000): H.C. Earwicker

Rathjen (German, 1989): H.C. Earwicker

Stoltefuß (German, 1989): H.C. Ehrwicker ·

Stündel (German, 1993): H.C. Earwicker

Bindervoet and Henkes (Dutch, 2002): H.K. Ierwicker

As in the case of 'Humphrey,' and to a lesser extent 'Chimpden,' the name 'Earwicker' has rich possibilities in the context of *Finnegans Wake*. Appearances to the contrary, perhaps, the name is not a Joycean invention but rather a Joycean *objet trouvé*. Cottle lists the names *Earwaker* and *Earwicker* as both deriving from an Old English designation of an ancestor as a 'wild-boar (*ēofor*) watchman (*wæccan*, "to watch"; *wacor*, "watchful, vigilant")' (1978, 124; cf. Hanks et al. 2002, 189). The suggestion has occasionally been voiced that the entire course of Western culture sometimes seems to have been just a dry run for *Finnegans Wake*. In Fenian legend, for example, the youthful warrior Diarmuid, tricked into eloping against his better judgment with Finn's betrothed Gráinne, is eventually killed by a magic boar. Finn, who could have helped him, fails to do so, thus choosing to remain, as if he were called *Earwicker*, simply a 'boar-watcher.'

According to Ellmann, Joyce made the happy discovery of the name *Earwicker* during a family holiday in the summer of 1923 in the seaside town of Bognor, in Sussex, where he spent his time working 'with passion' (1982, 554) on the very early stages of what would eventually become *Finnegans Wake*. On an outing to the nearby village of Sidlesham, near Chichester, he discovered the existence of a family rejoicing in the name of Earwicker, who reportedly pronounced the name 'Erricker' (Hart 1968a, 21–2) – and we may note that Hanks and others give *Earwaker* as the primary name, with both *Earwicker* and *Erricker* as variant forms (2002, 189). Among its many other virtues, the name so pronounced allowed Joyce a glancing reference to the Old Norse name *Eiríkr* ('Eric'), while in its written form, it provided access to the Old Norse *vík* ('inlet, bay'), suggesting *víkingr* ('sea-rover, pirate, viking'), thus in both cases helping to authenticate Earwicker's Scandinavian origins. As pronounced, it could be heard as a reminder that to 'err' is all too human; as written, it captured the *ear-* in the name of Hugh Culling Eardley Childers. Since Old English *wīc* meant a 'town' or 'hamlet,' a 'wicker' could quite logically mean someone who lived in such a place. By the same logic, an *Earwicker* could certainly mean an inhabitant of Ireland, an 'Eirewicker' (*FW* 593.3). Or again, more specifically, 'Ear suggests Eire and wicker suggests Ford of the Hurdles (made of wickerwork) or Dublin; hence Earwicker could mean a dweller (wicker) in Dublin, Ireland' (Tindall 1996, 65). By the same token, an earwicker could also mean an ear dweller, and thus, at least in popular belief, an earwig. An earwig is an insect, the word *insect* rearranges the letters of the word *incest*, and the nature of Earwicker's regard for his daughter seems to be distinctly problematic. And so on.

Our hero is first given his proper bourgeois appellation, complete with initials, in the present passage. The name survives intact in French, Italian, Galician, and two of three German versions, but metamorphoses in Stoltefuß's German into 'H.C. Ehrwicker,' suggesting that HCE is both a man of honour (*Ehre*) and a resident of Ireland, the German *Ehre* approximating the pronunciation of the Irish *Éire*. The name changes in Bindervoet and Henkes's Dutch into 'H.K. Ierwicker,' the change from an initial *e* to *i* in 'Ierwicker' taking advantage of the fact that Dutch *ier* not only approximates the pronunciation of English *ear* but, serendipitously, also means 'Irishman.' In Portuguese, meanwhile, the initials HCE remain, but Earwicker changes his name to 'Elecrainha,' a telescoping of *ele* ('he') and *lacrainha* ('earwig'), 'an earwig he.'

human, erring and condonable   (*FW* 58.19)

Lavergne (French, 1982): humaine erreur est pardonnable

Schenoni (Italian, 1982): humana, errante e condonabile

Schüler (Portuguese, 2003): humano, errante e condenável

Stündel (German, 1993): human, ehring und ceihungsfähig

Bindervoet and Henkes (Dutch, 2002): humaan, ingebrekebeen en kwijtgescholden

To err is human, we are told, and HCE as Earwicker is evidently all too human – but since forgiveness is divine, he too is presumably at least theoretically forgivable and his offences (whatever they may be) perhaps condonable. This comforting doctrinal point leads to some serious disagreement among our small group of translators, however. Lavergne's French is convinced of the assurance in general terms – 'humaine erreur est pardonnable' ('human error is pardonable') – but perhaps rather less so in the specific case of HCE, who, a victim of a not uninteresting Freudian slip, passes all unrecognized by Lavergne, even in the transparently thin disguise of HEC. Schenoni, however, recognizes him clearly and concedes charitably (and literally) that he is indeed (if momentarily feminized) 'humana, errante e condonabile.' Stündel is quite ambivalent about the whole thing, conceding that HCE as HEC may indeed be 'human,' but raises the question of whether a specific variant of his 'ehring' behaviour involved an *Ehering* ('wedding ring') and thus perhaps marital infidelity, in which case Stündel, juggling initials once again, wavers between finding him *zeihungsfähig* ('accusable') or *verzeihungsfähig* ('pardonable, condonable'). In Dutch, Bindervoet and Henkes are subject to no such doubts, for though admitting that he is a complete bungler (*brekebeen*) and certainly subject to an occasional failing (*gebrek*), possibly extending even to house-breaking (*inbreken*), they nonetheless state their charitable belief that he is not just forgivable but, all too *humaan* as he is, has in fact already been forgiven (*kwijtgescholden*). Not so Schüler in Portuguese, however, who, far from making any moral allowances for HCE, *humano* or not, finds him and his offences not at all condonable but in fact *condenável* ('reprehensible').

Huges Caput Earlyfouler   (*FW* 197.8)

Péron and Beckett (French, 1985 / 1996): Huges Caput Earlyfowler

Beckett and Joyce (French, 1931 / 1996): Hughes Caput Earlyfowler

Lavergne (French, 1982): Hugues Caput Earlyfouler

Joyce and Frank (Italian, 1979 / 1996): Hugo Capeto L'Eccellatore

Schenoni (Italian, 1996): Hugo Capeto l'Eccellatore

García Tortosa (Spanish, 1992): Huges Caputes Enciernes

Pozanco (Spanish, 1993): Hugo Capito Excetrero

Aixàs (Catalan, 2004): Huges Caput Earlyfouler

Schüler (Portuguese, 2003): Huges Caput Eadesonra

Amarante (Portuguese, 2009): Huges Caput Earlyfouler

Goyert (German, 1970): Huges Caput Earlyfowler

Hildesheimer (German, 1970): Hüno Caput Erstvögler

Wollschläger (German, 1970): Huges Cappes Eiligvögler

Stündel (German, 1993): Hugo Capütt ÄrschtFöckler

Bindervoet and Henkes (Dutch, 2002): Hugues Kaput Iepelijmer

Grut (Swedish, 2001): Huge Caput Earlyfouler

Słomczyński (Polish, 1985): Huges Caput Ejżeświntuch

Weatherall et al. (Czech, 1932 / 1996): Honza Cápek Eštěshnilý

In the opening pages of the eighth chapter (I.viii) of *Finnegans Wake*, originally published as *Anna Livia Plurabelle*, attention shifts back to HCE's noble and indeed royal bloodlines. HCE, of huge renown, is now recognized as the legitimate descendant if not indeed the bodily reincarnation of two famous tenth-century monarchs, French and German respectively: Hugues (or Hugh) Capet was king of France and ancestor of a long line of French monarchs; Henry the Fowler (Heinrich der Vogler), so named for his passion for falconry, was king of Germany and ancestor of a long line of German emperors. HCE's British onomastic forebear H.C.E. Childers, as we have seen, bore the given name *Hugh*. And the 'Huges Caput' is also the huge head (otherwise Howth) of the sleeping giant Finn MacCool, whose Irish name, Finn mac Cumhaill, literally means 'Fair One (*finn*), son (*mac*) of Champion (*cumhall*).'

HCE's illustrious forebears, however, cannot disguise the embarrassing fact that the appellation *Huges Caput Earlyfouler* is also suggestive of a huge and all too enthusiastic erection (Latin *caput*, 'head') followed by an all too premature ejaculation (German *kaputt*, 'finished, over and done with'). In the riverine context of *Anna Livia Plurabelle*, 'Huges' also invokes the Hughes River in Manitoba, while 'Earlyfouler' does the same for Lake Earl in California and Fowlers Bay in South Australia. The context of *Anna Livia Plurabelle* also involves a considerably increased number of translators – including, as we have already seen, Joyce himself.

Several of our translators are content to leave Huges Caput Earlyfouler essentially to his own devices, Aixàs in Catalan and Amarante in Portuguese, for example, merely repeating the name without variation. Grut adjusts 'Huges' to a Swedish *Hugo* inflected by the English adjective *huge*. Lavergne in French and Bindervoet and Henkes in Dutch normalize 'Huges' to a French 'Hugues,' allowing access in both cases to the Scottish river Ugie, while Beckett and Joyce adjust it to 'Hughes,' thus invoking instead the Hughes River of Virginia. Weatherall's Czech version normalizes 'Huges' in quite a different direction, namely to Czech 'Honza,' the equivalent of 'Johnny.' Rather surprisingly, Péron and Beckett along with Beckett and Joyce tactfully adjust 'Earlyfouler' to a more respectable 'Earlyfowler,' as does Goyert in German. Pozanco's Spanish 'Hugo Capito Excetrero' has a Hugo 'understood' (Italian *capito*) as a 'former' ('Ex-') fowler (*cetrero*, 'falconer'), not to mention various other things (*et cetera*).

Joyce and Frank's Italian not only ignores any possible sexual shortcomings involved but treats our hero with great respect, elevating him to 'Hugo Capeto L'Eccellatore,' thus both restoring an Italianized Hugo to his Capetian origins (*Capeto*) and recognizing him as one who excels (*eccellere*), whether as a fowler (*uccellatore*) or otherwise. Schenoni's Italian follows suit. García Tortosa's Spanish version, 'Huges Caputes Enciernes,' while invoking the Irish river Erne, places less emphasis on past glory than on future promise, with our hero now not only sporting a bullfighter's cloak (*capote*) but winning all the tricks at cards (*dar capote*), a blossoming (*en cierne*, 'in blossom') star of the bullring and the casino alike.

Others are considerably less respectful, particularly in German. Hildesheimer's German recognizes HCE, renamed 'Hüno,' as no doubt a one-time giant (*Hüne*) of a man, but one who is now *kaputt* ('finished'), possibly as a result of his exhausting propagatory efforts as father (*erst*, 'first') of all fuckers (*Vögler*, as opposed to *Vogler*). Wollschläger's German confirms the propagatory efforts of 'Huges Cappes Eiligvögler' as well as the fact that his ejaculations are speedy (*eilig*), while casting serious doubts on his intelligence, 'Cappes' conflating Latin *caput* ('head') and German *Kappes* ('cabbage'). Stündel's German further suggests, in tortured orthography, that 'Hugo Capütt ÄrschtFöckler' favours specialized sexual practices, in that his no doubt laudable efforts not only came before all others (*ärscht* as a colloquial South German pronunciation of *erst*, 'first') but also came from behind (*Arsch*, 'arse'). Schüler's Portuguese renames him 'Huges Caput Eadesonra,' bluntly stating the comprehensive dishonour (*desonra*) with which he has managed to cover himself. Bindervoet and Henkes's 'Hugues Kaput Iepelijmer,' adjusting for initials, leaves our hero's derelictions unspecified while invoking two rivers, the Belgian Ieperlee and the Dutch river Ij, perhaps reminding some readers at least of the obscure but apparently fluvial events allegedly witnessed in the Phoenix Park.

her erring cheef   (*FW* 198.12)

Péron and Beckett (French, 1985 / 1996): son maître égaré

Beckett and Joyce (French, 1931 / 1996): Herr aarand chief

Lavergne (French, 1982): *herr erring cheef*

Joyce and Frank (Italian, 1979 / 1996): al capo reone

Schenoni (Italian, 1996): il hsuo erroante chef

García Tortosa (Spanish, 1992): su percebo preboste

Aixàs (Catalan, 2004): al seu mascle erràtic

Schüler (Portuguese, 2003): seu Arenque-chefe

Amarante (Portuguese, 2009): seu comandante transgressor

Goyert (German, 1970): zu ihrem Herring

Hildesheimer (German, 1970): dem Herrn Chef zu Erin

Wollschläger (German, 1970): ihres Ehringels Häubling und Chef-Chelif

Stündel (German, 1993): ihrem erinschen Chef

Bindervoet and Henkes (Dutch, 2002): haar indewarre kroonheer

Grut (Swedish, 2001): Hennes Chiefande Ergo

Słomczyński (Polish, 1985): jej hultaja ech cheełpliwca

Small wonder that HCE's wife and others might think of him as 'her erring cheef,' the CHE of 'cheef' as well as the HEC initials of the phrase establishing his identity beyond all reasonable doubt, however much he might try to disguise it. Surprisingly, the initials disappear in both Péron and Beckett's 'son maître égaré' and in Beckett and Joyce's 'Herr aarand chief,' the former translating literally as 'her master gone astray,' while the latter chooses to play instead on German *Herr* and the Swiss river Aar in characterizing a chief both arrant and errant. Lavergne's *'herr erring cheef'* rescues both sets of initials by the relatively simple expedient of leaving the phrase untranslated while likewise incorporating a German *Herr* in order to suggest a 'cheef' who errs not once but (at least) twice.

Joyce and Frank's Italian also blithely ignores the original double set of initials with 'al capo reone,' preferring instead to combine *capo* ('chief'), *re* ('king'), and *capone* ('blockhead') in order to transform 'her erring cheef' into 'her chief and blockhead king.' Two other translators also ignore the presence of HCE's initials, Aixàs referring in Catalan merely to an erring 'male' (*mascle*), Amarante in Portuguese to an erring 'leader' (*comandante*). Schenoni's Italian, while nodding to Colorado's Roan Creek, manages to rescue both sets with 'il hsuo erroante chef' ('her erring chief'), if only by the humorous expedient of prefixing an entirely gratuitous *h* to the adjective *suo* ('her').

Two German versions choose to make explicit the implied reference to Charles Stewart Parnell, known to his multitude of supporters as the Chief, who rose to heights of political power as 'the uncrowned king of Ireland' only to suffer a humiliating fall as the result of what popular opinion professed to see as moral impropriety. Hildesheimer accordingly renders 'her erring cheef' as 'dem Herrn Chef zu Erin,' literally 'the chief of Erin,' while Stündel, though ignoring the initials, adopts a similar strategy with 'ihrem erinschen Chef,' literally 'her Erin chief.'

Several versions choose to perform flauntedly extravagant verbal gymnastics on this relatively uncomplicated phrase. Goyert's German rendering, 'zu ihrem Herring,' concisely conflates German *Herr* and English *erring*, while the English *herring* clearly, if oddly, resonates in the background. Even more oddly, Schüler's Portuguese 'seu

Arenque-chefe' quite literally refers to a (capitalized) 'herring' (*arenque*) chief. More oddly still, García Tortosa's exquisitely tortured Spanish rendering, 'su percebo preboste,' translates 'cheef' as, literally, 'provost' (*preboste*) and 'erring' by a conflation of *percibo* ('I perceive') and *percebe* ('barnacle goose'), seizing the opportunity to 'perceive' ALP to be none other than Nora Barnacle. Wollschläger's rather gratuitously inflated German version, 'ihres Ehringels Häubling und Chef-Chelif,' while achieving no fewer than three sets of initials (a feat otherwise achieved only by Słomczyński's Polish 'jej hultaja ech cheełpliwca'), transforms 'erring' into a reference to a wedding ring (*Ehering*), while 'cheef' is doubly rendered by conflations of, first, German *Häuptling* ('chief') and the French river Aube and, second, German *Chef* ('chief') and the Algerian river Chélif – the latter with a faint suggestion (*chez* 'lif') of a chief 'on the Liffey.' Bindervoet and Henkes's Dutch rendering, 'haar indewarre kroonheer,' while invoking the German river Inde, elevates the erring 'cheef,' in the interests of identifying appropriate initials, into a 'royal master' (*kroonheer*) who has blundered badly (*in de war brengen*, 'to make a mess of things'). Grut's Swedish version, finally, 'Hennes Chiefande Ergo,' combines an invented Anglo-Swedish verb *chiefa* ('to act as chief, to guide'), the Swedish noun *ande* ('spirit'), and, standing in for 'erring,' the Latin adverb *ergo* ('therefore') to arrive by a devious route at a distinctly dubious characterization in this particular context of HCE as 'her guiding spirit therefore.'

Her Chuff Exsquire   (*FW* 205.22)

Lavergne (French, 1982): Her Chuff Exsquire

Schenoni (Italian, 1996): il Hsuo Chúggticone Esquire

Schenoni (Italian, 2001): il Hdilei Ciufciuffolone Esquire

García Tortosa (Spanish, 1992): Cuento hace que contento exgentilea!

Aixàs (Catalan, 2004): Her Chuff Exsquire

Schüler (Portuguese, 2003): Herr Chato Exnobre

Amarante (Portuguese, 2009): Homo Camponês Excudeiro

Goyert (German, 1970): Her Chuff Esquire

Hildesheimer (German, 1969 / 1970): den Herrn, den Chaib, den Erhabenen

Wollschläger (German, 1970): Herrn Chuff Exsquire

Stündel (German, 1993): Hirrem Chlampicheln Exquisiehten

Bindervoet and Henkes (Dutch, 2002): Haar Kweledelgewezen Inzijnschikkelijkheid

Grut (Swedish, 2001): Hennes Chefiga Esquire

Słomczyński (Polish, 1985): w Hnią Cham Exsquire

Weatherall et al. (Czech, 1932 / 1996): jejího Hrožně Chmurného Exrytíře

The appellation 'Her Chuff Exsquire' is appropriate for HCE both as shapeshifter and as fallen man. A 'chuff' (Middle English *chuffe*), as defined by the *OED*, is 'a rude coarse churlish fellow'; 'chuff' as an adjective, however, can mean variously 'morose, churlish' or 'chubby' or 'happy.' While the title *esquire* would technically qualify HCE as a gentleman, the prefix *ex-* promptly deprives him of that presumptive standing. Two of our translators (Lavergne in French, Aixàs in Catalan) are content to retain Joyce's formulation untouched. Wollschläger achieves a disproportionately effective result for a minimal change by merely altering the English 'Her' to the German 'Herrn,' the accusative case of *Herr* ('Mr'). His 'Herrn Chuff Exsquire' takes advantage of the fact that *Mr* and *Esquire* are not used together in English: the fact that HCE is now an 'exsquire' is therefore emphasized by the use of the ostensibly honorific *Herr*. Schüler's Portuguese uses the German *Herr* to similarly ironic effect with 'Herr Chato Exnobre,' where *chato* means 'rude, boring' and *nobre* is 'noble' – thus 'Mr Rude Formerly-Noble.' Amarante's Portuguese transforms him into a member of the species 'Homo Camponês Excudeiro,' defining him as a *camponês* ('countryman, farmer') who no longer has any claim to the title *escudeiro* ('squire').

Some more charitably inclined translators allow HCE to retain his (possible) original status: in Goyert's German all is forgiven and HCE is 'Her Chuff Esquire' all over again. Grut's Swedish goes even further and declares him 'Hennes Chefiga Esquire,' generously restoring him also to his rank of *chef* ('chief'). Schenoni's two Italian versions, 'il Hsuo Chúggticone Esquire' and 'il Hdilei Ciufciuffolone,' once again making strategic use of a prefixed *h*, similarly allow him to retain his civilian honours, though characterizing him in the earlier version as a donkey (*ciuco*) and in the later as a stuttering ('Ciufciuff-') and unkempt buffoon (*ciuffone*, 'person with long untidy hair').

Others, however, are outspokenly uncharitable. Bindervoet and Henkes, for example, go to positively baroque lengths in grandiloquently renaming their Dutch HKI as 'Haar Kweledelgewezen Inzijnschikkelijkheid,' where 'Haar' includes both Dutch *haar* ('her') and German *Herr* ('Mr'), 'Kweledelgewezen' suggests someone who has been (*gewezen*) noble (*edel*) from, capturing a water reference, the very beginning (*kwel*, 'well, source') and is consequently well pleased with both himself (*in zijn schik zijn*, 'to be pleased with oneself') and his advanced degree of general obligingness (*schikkelijkheid*). García Tortosa's Spanish remarks of no one in particular (but pointedly retaining HCE's initials) that 'cuento hace que contento exgentilea,' thus acidly suggesting that 'it always generates gossip (*hacer un cuento*, 'to make a story') when someone is happy (*contento*) to quit the ranks of the genteel (*gentil*).' Two German translators prefer greater bluntness, resorting to open abuse. Stündel's German refers scornfully to 'Hirrem Chlampicheln Exquisiehten,' where 'Hirrem' includes *ihrem* ('her') and *Herr*, 'Chlampicheln' includes both a de-initialized *schlampig* ('slovenly') and *picheln* ('to go boozing'), and 'Exquisiehten' includes *Exquisit* ('dandy, fop') while making 'Ex-' do double duty, thus amounting altogether to 'her slovenly, boozing dandy that was.' Hildesheimer's German is equally scornful and even more pointed, referring to 'den Herrn, den Chaib, den Erhabenen,' or, as one might say in Dublin, 'the high and mighty (*erhaben*, 'exalted') gentleman (*Herr*) – and dirty shagger (Swiss German *Cheib*).'

like any Etrurian Catholic Heathen   (FW 215.20)

Ogden (Basic English, 1932 / 1996): like Etrurian Catholics of hated religion

Beckett and Joyce (French, 1931 / 1996): comme tout Etrusque Catholot Hérétique

Lavergne (French, 1982): *Etrurian Catholic Heathen*

Schenoni (Italian, 1996): come qualsiasi Etrusco Cattolico Hpagano

García Tortosa (Spanish, 1992): como cualquier Etrusco Católico Hereje

Pozanco (Spanish, 1993): como cualquier Herético Católico Etrurio

Aixàs (Catalan, 2004): com qualsevol Etrusc Catòlic, Escèptic

Schüler (Portuguese, 2003): como qualquer Etrúrio Católico Herético

Amarante (Portuguese, 2009): como qualquer Etrusco Católico Herege

Goyert (German, 1970): wie jeder Etrurisch Catholische Heide

Hildesheimer (German, 1969 / 1970): wie irgendein Etrurisch Catholischer Heide

Wollschläger (German, 1970): wie jeder Etrurisch Catholische Heide

Stündel (German, 1993): wie so ein Errtruskisch Catholischer Heide

Bindervoet and Henkes (Dutch, 2002): als die ierstebeste Italo-Etrurische Katholieke Heiden

Grut (Swedish, 2001): Etruriskt Catolsk Hedning

Słomczyński (Polish, 1985): jak każdy inny Etruski Catolicki Heretyk

Weatherall et al. (Czech, 1932 / 1996): jako kterýkoli Etruhrský Civilní Heretik

Unsurprisingly, doubts are also expressed as to the orthodoxy of HCE's (or ECH's) religious beliefs, behaving as he allegedly does like 'any Etrurian Catholic Heathen,' which is to say, like neither a good Catholic nor an honest heathen – behaviour typical of the unreliability to be expected of a shifty foreigner from the ends of the earth. The Etrurians appear to be singled out for this rather thankless role as allowing for the inclusion of both an appropriate initial and (in this river-obsessed chapter) reference to both the German river Ruhr and the English river Truro.

Lavergne contents himself with Joyce's original formulation, and several other translators render the phrase quite literally – thus Goyert, Hildesheimer, Wollschläger, and Grut. Beckett and Joyce's French, we notice, refers not to a heathen but to a heretic ('Hérétique'), and this definitional distinction is also followed by the Spanish, Portuguese, Czech, and Polish translators, all of whom consider either that HCE is a heretic rather than a heathen, or that being a heathen actually constitutes heresy. Stündel, along similar lines, emphasizes the doctrinal error of ECH's ways by inscribing the English verb *to err* into the German adjective *Etruskisch* ('Etruscan') in his formulation 'Errtruskisch.' Aixàs, on the other hand, is more liberally inclined to see him (even if momentarily deprived of his initials) as less a heathen or a heretic than merely an agnostic (*escèptic*). Bindervoet and Henkes, in pursuit of the initials IKH, specify that their Etrurians are 'Italo-Etrurisch,' but by way of compensation also emphasize the Irish connection by rendering the innocuous term 'any' as 'die ierstebeste,' conflating the Dutch phrase *de eerste de beste* ('the first to come along') and the adjective *iers* ('Irish'). Intriguingly, Ogden's Basic English version, 'like Etrurian Catholics of hated religion,' deviates most markedly from Joyce's original – and seems to do so, suggesting that 'Etrurian Catholics' are ipso facto either heathens or heretics, from a decidedly non-ecumenical standpoint.

HCE's inability to decide between one doctrinal direction and another is transtextually mirrored by our translators' inability to decide whether it is a matter of 'Etrurians' or 'Etruscans' – the latter label once again introduced by Beckett and Joyce's 'comme tout Etrusque Catholot Hérétique.' Schenoni, García Tortosa, Aixàs, Amarante, Stündel, and Słomczyński all follow Beckett and Joyce in opting for Etruscans, a choice that allows fluvial access to the Spanish Rus, the Canadian Ruscom, and the Welsh Usk rather than to the Ruhr or the Truro, while all other versions follow Joyce's original English preference for Etrurians. Weatherall's Czech version emphasizes more obviously than most the presence of the German Ruhr in 'Etruhrský Civilní Heretik' – a rendering in which misguided religion also gives way to misguided politics, 'civil' (*civilní*) heresy being substituted for what, by implication, is religious heresy. Joyce's original phrase might of course conceivably also be taken as meaning, more broadly, 'like any Italian Catholic, which is to say, like a heathen.' None of our translators chooses to replicate (or invent) any such slanderous aspersion. With one exception (Aixàs), HCE's initials are retained in one combination or another by all versions considered.

Haveth Childers Everywhere   (FW 535.34)

Lavergne (French, 1982): *Haveth Childers Everywhere*

Schüler (Portuguese, 2003): Há Chorões Entodaparte

Stündel (German, 1993): Habes Cindler Euberall

Bindervoet and Henkes (Dutch, 2002): Hebbet Kinders Inallehoek-
    enengaten

HCE's sexual mores are clearly deplorable, and the predictable result is that he 'Haveth Childers Everywhere.' The nineteenth-century Irish political leader Daniel O'Connell (1775–1847), celebrated as the Liberator for his efforts on behalf of Catholic Emancipation, notoriously enjoyed a similar reputation both for his sexual energy and for his widespread progeny – or, in the doubly pluralized Dublin colloquialism, *childers*. The colloquialism of course also recalls the name of H.C.E. Childers once again. Moreover, since 'Haveth' can be read as also evoking *Hoved* ('head'), the Danish name for Howth, 'Childers' also provides a reference to the Howth gunrunning expedition of Erskine Childers in 1914.

Lavergne is once again content with Joyce's original formulation. Schüler's Portuguese reports that our hero indeed 'has squalling children (*chorões*; from *chorar*, 'to cry') everywhere (*en toda parte*).' Bindervoet and Henkes confirm that HCE, alias HKI, 'Hebbet Kinders Inallehoekenengaten' ('hath children in every hole and corner') their multiplicity, signalled by Joyce's double plural *childers*, confirmed not by a standard Dutch plural *kinderen* ('children') but by a corresponding double German plural *Kinders*. Stündel's German, humorously adjusted for initials, likewise confirms the existence of children (*Kinder*) of all ages, including tiny ones (*Kindlein*), everywhere (*überall*). Joyce's 'Haveth' for standard English *has* or *hath* is paralleled by Bindervoet and Henkes's 'Hebbet' for standard Dutch *heeft* and by Stündel's 'Habes' (Latin *habes*, 'you have') for German *hat* – neither translation, however, managing to replicate the suggested reference to Howth.

Heinz cans everywhere   (FW 581.5)

Lavergne (French, 1982): Hun Ci Erre

Schüler (Portuguese, 2003): Henrique caminha em-tudo

Stündel (German, 1993): Heinz cann eberall

Bindervoet and Henkes (Dutch, 2002): Heinz Krachtvoer Inblik

HCE, to his many detractors (who on numerous occasions clearly include himself), appears in many cases as little better than street litter, a threat to public health and safety, not to mention aesthetics, that should be carted off somewhere for dumping. Bindervoet and Henkes appear to be bothered primarily on aesthetic and environmental grounds, their

'Heinz Krachtvoer Inblik' firmly associating the objectionable litter with HKI while simultaneously deploring the ubiquity of Heinz 'power-fodder' (*kracht*, 'power'; *voer*, 'fodder') cans (*blik*, 'tin') left lying around in full view (*blik*, 'glance, look') of all. (The H.J. Heinz Company had begun its eventually worldwide operations in Pittsburgh in 1869.) Lavergne, however, elevates the potential threat to apocalyptic dimensions, possibly seeing HCE's Scandinavian origins and Hungarian onomastic connections as sufficient reason for evoking marauding tribes of modern vandals from the east, with his solemn warning that 'the Hun wanders (*erre*) here (*ici*), the Hun is afoot.' Schüler for his part sees neither garbage nor threats, but only one further confirmation that our ubiquitous hero, momentarily renamed for Portuguese consumption from *Heinz* via *Heinrich* to *Henrique*, is present and under way (*caminha*) in everything (*em-tudo*), be it for good or for bad.

Stündel, however, astutely seeing through a message ostensibly involving merely abandoned soup cans, has little difficulty in deciphering a coded comment on the sexual potency of a hitherto unmentioned Heinz, identified once again by tortured German initials as our hero in deep disguise. As Stündel sees it, perhaps remembering the etymology of the name *Earwicker*, our Heinz not only has the sexual energy of a wild boar (*Eber*) but is accustomed to putting that energy into enthusiastic action anywhere he can (*kann*) and anywhere and everywhere (*überall*) he may want to – 'Heinz,' in short, 'can do it anywhere.' Our beleaguered hero would no doubt appreciate the implied vote of confidence.

9 ALPs Allonymous

As in the case of HCE, we will limit ourselves in this chapter to following the comparative interlinguistic fortunes of ALP, Anna Livia Plurabelle – 'Anna was, Livia is, Plurabelle's to be' (*FW* 215.24) – as exemplified by a number of variations on her name, her acrostic presence in the text, and selected other references to her. Our coverage, once again, will of course be merely suggestive rather than exhaustive.

If HCE represents the city of Dublin, ALP represents the river Liffey, on which the city, a much later arrival, was eventually built. During the early Middle Ages the Liffey, estimated to have been as much as four times the size of the present river and liable to sudden devastating flash floods, is recorded under the earlier name *An Ruirthech* ('the tempestuous one'). Later it acquired its modern Irish name from the plain through which it flowed before reaching what is now Dublin. That plain (mainly in what is now County Kildare) was called *Magh Life* /ma'li.fə/ ('the plain of *Life*'), possibly involving a variation on *Magh Luibhe* /ma'li.və/ ('the plain of herbs, the fertile plain'), and the river thus eventually acquired the name *Abhainn na Life* /au.in.ne.'li.fə/, 'the river (*abhainn*) of *Life.*' Since *luibh* /liv/ can mean 'leaf' as well as 'herb, grass, plant,' the name *Abhainn na Life* might also be taken as meaning either 'Herb River' or 'Leaf River.' 'Whatever about the accuracy of this etymology, it seems clearly evident that James Joyce accepted it' (O Hehir 1967, 392), as when we find ALP 'leafy speafing' (*FW* 619.20).

By the early nineteenth century the Irish name was often rendered in English as *Anna Liffey* – and is several times so used in *Ulysses* (e.g., *U* 12.647). Some forty other variations on the name have also been recorded. Some include the Irish word for 'river' (*abhainn*) or some corruption of it, as in *Abhainn Liphthe, Avon Liffey, Avenlif, Amliffy,* and *Anliffe.* The form *Liffe* was also used alone, as were variants such as *Liphi, Lyffye* – and a Latinized *Amnis Livia* (de Courcy 1996, 228). Joyce took the form *Anna Livia* as the name of his heroine. (His daughter Lucia, born in 1907, had received the full name *Anna Lucia Joyce.*)

Anna is very advantageously connected both etymologically and on-omastically. Brendan O Hehir, to begin with, provides a supplementary aquatic connection, noting that *anna* in Irish place names is frequently also an anglicization of the Irish *eanach* /'anəx/ ('marsh, fen') – which derives from the Old Irish *an,* Middle Irish *ean,* meaning 'water' (1965; 1967, 355–6). The Old Irish and Middle Irish forms derive in turn from a proto-Celtic **an* ('swamp, water, river') that is found, for example, in the modern name of the Spanish river Guadiana, where it is tauto-logically combined – as if anticipating *Finnegans Wake* – with the Arabic *wadi,* also meaning 'river.' It may or may not be a coincidence – if it makes any sense at all to speak of coincidences in *Finnegans Wake* – and it is certainly serendipitous that *Anna* begins and ends with *a,* and that Sumerian *a* also means 'water.' *Anna* is of course also a palindrome, readable in either direction – and the Liffey is a tidal river for several miles inland, thus also flowing in either direction at different times.

In another register, *Anna* also invokes the Celtic goddess Ana, whose name is based on the Old Irish *ana* ('riches, plenty, prosperity') and who is otherwise known as Anu or Danu, the goddess of fecundity and mother of the Irish gods, the *Tuatha Dé Danann* or 'People of the god-dess Danu.'[1] Moving further afield, we find a variant of Anna's name present in the ancient Middle East in that of the Persian water goddess, *Anahita* or *Anaitis,* and doubly present in that of the Hurrian mother goddess, *Hannahannas. Anna* serendipitously allows also for supple-mentary etymological access to Turkish *anā* and *anne* and Hungarian *anya,* all meaning 'mother,' as well as to Sanskrit *anna* ('food, suste-nance'), Sumerian *an* ('sky, heavens'), Hebrew *anan* ('cloud'), Indonesian *anak* ('young'), Greek *ana* ('back again, anew'), and even Czech *ano* (meaning 'yes,' à la Molly Bloom) – not to mention the American Ana River in the state of Oregon and the Santa Ana River of Southern California. The fact that ALP sometimes appears as a tiny little person – 'He addle liddle phifie Annie ugged the little craythur' (*FW* 4.28–9)

---

1   See MacCana (1970, 85); Green (1992, 30); Gibson (2005, 53).

– reflects both the geographical fact of the Liffey's beginnings as a tiny spring in the Wicklow mountains and the purely etymological fact that Sanskrit *ána* and the related Hindi *ānā* and Punjabi *ānnā* all mean 'small' (Onions 1966, 38).

Onomastically, *Anna* is the Greek form of the Hebrew *Hannah*, usually taken to mean 'God has been gracious to me' (Hanks et al. 2002, 776). In Ireland, moreover, the names *Anna* and *Hannah* have long been employed as anglicized versions of the otherwise unrelated Irish *Áine*, meaning 'radiance, splendour, brilliance.' In the Fenian tales, Áine, the daughter of the king of Scotland, refuses to sleep with any man but Finn mac Cumhaill and in due course becomes the mother of his two sons (Ó Corráin and Maguire 1990, 19–20), just as HCE and ALP produce the two warring siblings Shem and Shaun. There is even a link to Nora Joyce: the Anglo-Norman name *Honora* was borrowed in early Irish as *Onóra*, later frequently anglicized as *Nora*, but in Ulster, where the accent shifted to the first syllable, also as *Hannah* (Ó Corráin and Maguire 1990, 150).

The second element of ALP's name, meanwhile, *Livia*, suggested itself on at least one level, we are told (Ellmann 1982, 5–6), from the luxuriantly flowing hair of Italo Svevo's wife Livia, evoking for Joyce the sensuously luxuriant flow of the feminized Liffey. *Livia* also happily facilitates the interlingual pun on Irish *Life* and English *life*, allowing the Liffey to double as a source of the 'water of life,' promising (as in Revelations 32:1) spiritual salvation through Christian baptism. More transient happiness is promised by that other 'water of life,' spirituous rather than spiritual, called *uisce beatha* in Irish and rendered in English as 'whiskey' (with or without water as preferred). Since the city of Dublin was founded on the Liffey by ninth-century Scandinavians, it is also appropriate that *Livia* additionally promises life (though not necessarily whiskey) in each of the three major Scandinavian languages (Danish *Liv*, Norwegian *liv*, Swedish *liv* all, like Old Norse *líf*, meaning 'life').

ALP is finally *Plurabelle*, suggesting a combination of plurality and beauty (French *belle*, 'beautiful'), while evoking *en passant* the English Ure, Russian Ura, Japanese Abe, Australian Bell, and French Ellé rivers. ALP conflates many identities, many beauties, many femininities conjoined – not to mention many tributaries and many rivers, both Irish and worldwide. Brendan O Hehir suggested the presence in *Plurabelle* of the Old Irish *bile*, a term used for a sacred tree and thus also intimating the essential sacrality of Anna Livia (1965, 160). One might add that a further and transferred meaning of *bile* in Old Irish was 'hero,' thus suggesting the irreducible interrelatedness of ALP and HCE. Lavergne ingeniously notes (1982, 214n20) that the suffix *-anna* is a plural marker (one of several) in Irish, thus already introducing the notion of ALP's plurality. It has also been observed that the philosopher Giambattista Vico, referring to military undertakings historically sanctioned by the church, uses the phrase *pia et pura bella* as meaning 'holy wars,' which thus also succeeds in evoking the rivalry of ALP's two sons, Shem and Shaun, who also function at various points as the opposing banks of the Liffey. Vico's Latin, where *bella* is the plural of *bellum* ('war'), also allows for the punning suggestion of an Italian *pia e pura bella*, where plural 'holy wars' give way to a singular 'pious and chaste beauty' named Anna Livia Plurabelle. The degree to which both her piety and her chastity are open to question need not detain us here.

As for the acronym *ALP*, as Stuart Gilbert has long since pointed out, the Semitic root *alp* (meaning 'ox,' a possession once regarded as a primary necessity for survival) is the root of the first letter, *aleph*, of both the Phoenician and Hebrew alphabets and the corresponding first letter of the Greek alphabet, *alpha* (Gilbert 1930 / 1955, 112). The Sanskrit *alpa-*, meanwhile, means 'small' (Buck 1988, 880–1), once again recalling ALP's fluvial origins as a trickling mountain stream. The Greek noun *alphós* means 'whiteness,' and the name of the Greek river (and river god) *Alpheios* means 'whitish,' both of which we may wish to see as a chromatic response to the name of the city, *Dublin*, as we have already noticed, deriving from the Irish *duibhlinn*, literally 'black (*dubh*) pool (*linn*),' and thus onomastically linked to the river it stands on. ALP also suggests Coleridge's 'Alph, the sacred river,' which in the Joycean context channels underground for hundreds of pages through the 'caverns measureless to man' of *Finnegans Wake*, Joyce's 'stately pleasure dome' in Xanadu – which serendipitously shares its final syllable with Dublin's first.[2]

The inextricable interdependability of ALP and HCE, finally, is etymologically reinforced by the fact that while ALP is associated with rivers and HCE with mountains, an *alp* in English refers to a mountain, and the same is true of an *alp* (literally 'mountain') in Irish (Dinneen 1927). Furthermore, while the Irish Ana or Anu was the goddess of

---

2 *Xanadu*, we are told, is an anglicization of the Chinese *Shàngdū*, 'upper (*shàng*) capital (*dū*)' (Schinz 1996, 286).

fertility and mother of the other gods, the Sumerian Anu was the god of the heavens and father of the other gods.

> *He addle liddle phifie Annie ugged the little craythur*   (FW 4.28–9)

Lavergne (French, 1982): L'avait un'tite phifée Annie, petite craieture qu'il ograit.

Schenoni (Italian, 1982): Lui e la aliata lìddela phogliettina Annie ci marcivano con la lìttela cicchettatura.

Pozanco (Spanish, 1993): Y a la pequeña Annie dejó pasmada.

Schüler (Portuguese, 2003): Tinha a linda, purinha, gatinha a fina e fophA niña, treme-papou a creiarthurinha.

Beck (German, 1989): Er hat a lieschen phein Anna kost das süße metchen.

Jauslin (German, 1989): Er has'de lüdde phiffze Annie beschmutzfingert die winzige Krabbe.

Stündel (German, 1993): Er addelte lütte phiffich Annie, eckelte sich vor der kleinen Krähatour.

Bindervoet and Henkes (Dutch, 2002): Die adde luddel pfeivie Annie knuftut peuterneutje.

One of the earliest occurrences of ALP's acronymic presence occurs with the information that HCE 'addle liddle phifie Annie ugged the little craythur,' the surface meaning of which at least initially seems clear enough: 'he had a little wifey, Annie, and he hugged the little creature.' The cuddlesome cuteness of this diminutive child-wife is emphasized by the near-repetition of 'liddle' and 'little.' As is well known among Joyce scholars, the adjective 'liddle' also invokes another little girl whose initials are a permutation of those of ALP, namely Alice Pleasance Liddell, the ten-year-old Alice who so fascinated the story-spinning Oxford don Charles Lutwidge Dodgson, alias Lewis Carroll – who, incidentally, also played with acrostics in celebrating his young girl friends Alice and Isa. Why HCE might be 'addled' is left unspecified, but one may assume that his 'liddle' companion had something to do with it.

The reference to the *Alice* books also establishes at least two other connections between ALP and HCE. First, our Humphrey owes his 'hump' inter alia to Lewis Carroll's Humpty Dumpty, who likewise had a great fall. Second, the reference to ALP's diminutive stature relative to the (sometimes) giant HCE punningly invokes the fact that the 'Big Liddell' was the name humorously given by generations of British students to the canonic *Greek-English Lexicon* (1843) compiled by H.G. Liddell and Robert Scott, of whom the former, as it happens, was Alice's father. The main element of linguistic instability in the phrase is the expression 'ugged,' which on the surface implies 'hugged,' but which also involves an uneasy relationship with the obsolete English verb *to ug*, which means 'to loathe' (*OED*). The expression 'craythur,' in the context, is humorous Hiberno-English for *creature*.

All eight of our translators succeed in retaining ALP's acronymic presence, though *ALP* is rearranged to *LPA* by Lavergne ('L'avait un'tite phifée Annie'), Pozanco ('la pequeña Annie'), and Jauslin ('lüdde phiffze Annie'). For Lavergne, the 'phifie' Annie becomes a 'phifée,' suggesting an English 'wifey' with a touch of the French 'fairy' (*fée*) about her; the 'little craythur' becomes a 'petite craieture,' conflating *créature* ('creature') and *craie* ('chalk'), and 'ugged' becomes 'ograit,' combining the French *ogre* ('ogre') and the English *ogle*, leaving us with the suggestion of a great ogre ogling a tiny fairy-like creature white as chalk with fear. Stündel's German Annie, very much to the contrary, is less fairy-like than 'phiffich,' suggesting *pfiffig* ('precocious'), and HCE now frankly 'disgusted' (*ekelte sich*) with the little creature (*Kreatur*) and her incessant 'crowing' (*krähen*, 'to crow'). In Jauslin's German, 'Er has'de lüdde phiffze Annie beschmutzfingert die winzige Krabbe,' sexual connotations are much closer to the surface: HCE (almost) hates (*hasst*) the precocious (*pfiffig*) 'liddle' ('lüdde') Annie, the 'little shrimp' (*Krabbe*) whom he desires (*begehrt*) and loves to run his fingers over (*befingert*), though uneasily aware that his doing so sullies (*beschmutzt*) them both. Pozanco, for his part, is not at all sure what is going on, other than that HCE, whatever he was up to, left little Annie 'stunned' (*pasmada*) – and the translator, one might suspect, in like condition.

Alcohol plays a significant role in several renderings. For Beck, HCE has 'a lieschen phein,' the 'Lieschen fein' ('pretty little Lizzy') of a German children's rhyme temporarily standing in for ALP; 'Anna kost das süße metchen,' which is to say that he both kisses (*küsst*) the sweet little girl (*Mädchen*) and tastes (*kostet*) the sweetly alcoholic mead (*Met*). For Bindervoet and Henkes, HCE had a little 'pfeivie' who combined the qualities of an English 'wifey' and a now Dutch 'fairy' (*fee*), and he 'cuddled' (*knuffelen*) both the 'tiny tot' (*peuter*) that was Annie and with equal enthusiasm a tiny 'tot' (*neutje*) of liquor – in other words, in good burlesque Hiberno-English, a 'drop o' the craythur.'

Schüler's Portuguese, playing on rhyming diminutives, takes the alcoholic reference considerably further: HCE now turns out to have once had a 'lovely' (*linda*), 'innocent' (*pura*) 'little kitten' (*gata*), a 'delicate' (*fina*) and 'cute' (*fofa*) 'little girl' (Spanish *niña*), but he both feared (*tremer*) and cheated (*papar*) on the poor little creature (*criaturinha*) and, ogre that he was, eventually resolved the issue in orthodox cannibal fashion by simply eating her right up (*papar*, 'to eat'). However, though identified as ALP both by the initials of the first words in the sequence – 'a linda, purinha' – and the capitalized final letter of 'fophA,' the poor little creature, promoting as she does the benefits of having an -*arthur*-inside a *criatura*, reveals herself also, very much in the spirit of *Alice in Wonderland*, as having on this occasion been in fact nothing more (or indeed less) all along than a small Guinness, a beverage produced to general applause in Dublin since 1759 under the name of Arthur Guinness and Sons.

Schenoni's Italian version, in quite a different key, is particularly interesting in its overtones of moral and physical depravity on HCE's part. While Bindervoet and Henkes adumbrate the possibility in referring to Annie as 'luddel' rather than the standard Dutch *luttel* ('little'), Schenoni's 'la aliata lìddela ... Annie,' characterizing little Annie as fluttery and flighty (*aliare*, 'to flutter, fly, flit'), more obviously retains an interlingual play on the original 'liddle' and thus provide its readers with target-language access to the complex of Alice references present in the original. For Schenoni, indeed, Annie is HCE's 'phogliettina,' a highly suggestive combination of *mogliettina* ('wifey') and *figlia* ('daughter') that anticipates the fraught relationship of HCE and his daughter Issy that will later be multiply and multifariously intimated. Alcohol is advanced as playing a degenerative role here too, for both HCE and his flighty little Annie ('lui e la aliata ... Annie'), we are informed, were in fact in a genuinely bad way, morally corrupt and physically wasted (all of these meanings present in the verb *marcire*) because of the 'lìttela cicchettatura,' the interlingual adjective 'lìttela' hinting darkly once again at the Alice connection and the portmanteau noun 'cicchettatura' at once concealing and revealing not only a poor little *creatura* ('creature, child') but also what was perhaps the root cause of such depravity (actual, fantasized, or feared), namely a *cicchetto*, a nice 'glass of brandy.'

In the name of Annah the Allmaziful, the Everliving, the Bringer of
Plurabilities, haloed be her eve, her singtime sung, her rill be run,
unhemmed as it is uneven! (FW 104.1–3)

Lavergne (French, 1982): Au nom d'Annah Miséricordieuse, éternelle. Dispensatrice de Plurabilités, bénie soit son heure, chantée son histoire, coulé son fleuve, sans fin, sans égal.

Wilcock (Italian, 1961): In nome di Annah l'Onnivolgente, la Sempiterna, la Portatrice di Plurabilità, cantificata sia la sua eva, il suo corso percorso, tanto libero quanto capriccioso!

Schenoni (Italian, 2001): Nel nome di Annah Agnimazicordiosa, Sempreviva, Latrice di Plurabilità, aureolificato sia il suo eva-nome, venia il suo vegno, sia ratta la sua riolontà così in gelo come in guerra!

Schüler (Portuguese, 2003): Em nome de Annah a Allmissassombrosa, a Sempreviva, a Portadora de Plurabilidades, sanctificada seja sua evigília, venha o reino de seu canto, ritmem suas rumas sem peias assim na terra como no céu!

Stündel (German, 1993): Im Namen von Annah, der Allmächtlicken, der Ewiglebenden, der Bringerin der Plurabellitäten, gehailogt sei ihr Edbend, ihr SingZeit sang, ihr Rinnsal rinne, ungehemd wie es umhymnisch ist!

Bindervoet and Henkes (Dutch, 2002): In de naam van Annah de Almhartige, de Immerlevende, de Brengster van Plurabiliteiten, allerheilig worde haar vloed, haar kozingtijd kome, heer ril vervliede, uit waarden evanals in de dommel!

If ALP turns out to be merely ridiculous in some ways, in others she is close to (or even entirely) divine, reminding us that the Celts were only one ancient people who saw major rivers as earthly manifestations of a divine mother.

Suras, or individual sections of the Islamic Koran, as has variously been pointed out, begin with the ritual formula 'In the name of Allah, the Merciful, the Compassionate.' Here the male Arabic *Allah* ('God') becomes the female 'Annah,' suggesting primarily the Turkish *anā* ('mother'). The Christian Lord's Prayer ('Hallowed be Thy name, Thy kingdom come, Thy will be done on earth as it is in Heaven') becomes a Lady's Prayer, the expression 'haloed' suggesting moreover not only the Lord's Prayer, addressed to God the Father, but the Hail Mary, addressed to the Mother of God. Annah, meanwhile, is not only an all-merciful Alma Mater but also one who is 'allmaziful,' pluriform and unpredictable as in the always multiple possibilities of a maze, present in the Liffey ('Everliving') but also by implication even in the distant waters of the Amazon, present now as in olden times (Turkish *mazi*, 'past') and times to come.

Annah 'the Allmaziful' is reduced and normalized to being merely 'Miséricordieuse' ('merciful') in Lavergne's French. The Dutch translators think of her as 'de Almhartige,' an Alma Mater who is both *almachtig* ('almighty') and *barmhartig* ('merciful'). In Schüler's Portuguese, she is 'a Allmissassombrosa,' the 'amazing' (*assombrosa*) Alma Mater ('missus'). Two Italian translators see her in two quite different lights. For Wilcock she is 'l'Onnivolgente,' combining *onnipotente* ('omnipotent') and *volgente* ('rolling on'), while for Schenoni she is 'Agnimazicordiosa,' combining *Anna, ogni* ('all'), *misericordiosa* ('merciful'), and the translingual suggestion of the plural possibilities of a maze. Stündel's German, referring to her as 'der Allmächtlicken,' goes its own way, combining in her the qualities of being both *allmächtig* ('almighty') and *allnächtlich*, flowing on incessantly, 'night after night.'

'The Everliving,' with its suggestion of the Liffey, evokes little divergence of response among our translators, with no response going beyond the strictly literal. Annah is 'éternelle' in French, 'la Sempiterna' (Wilcock) and 'Sempreviva' (Schenoni) in Italian, 'a Sempreviva' in Portuguese, 'de Immerlevende' in Dutch, and in German her name is that of 'der Ewiglebenden.' Other than Stündel's faint anticipation of its presence in his rendition of the preceding phrase, no reference to the Liffey survives.

Annah as 'Bringer of Plurabilities' is rendered in the singular – 'plurability' – in both Italian versions, Wilcock with 'Portatrice di Plurabilità,' Schenoni with 'Latrice di Plurabilità,' where *portatrice* and *latrice* both mean 'bearer,' with *latrice* in addition introducing a suggestion of *latría* ('divine service'). All four other versions are in agreement that Annah's 'plurabilities' are indeed plural. Schüler's Portuguese 'Portadora de Plurabilidades' is a 'bearer of plurabilities,' while Bindervoet and Henkes likewise have a parallel Dutch 'Brengster van Plurabiliteiten.' For Lavergne, Annah is not just a 'bringer' or 'bearer' but rather a more actively engaged 'Dispensatrice de Plurabilités,' literally a 'dispenser' of plurabilities, while Stündel's German sees her as a 'Bringerin der Plurabellitäten,' a bringer of both plurabilities and beauties.

The next four phrases present translators with a double difficulty, namely how to retain an appropriate degree of fidelity to Joyce's text while simultaneously echoing or at least evoking in their respective languages the parody of the Lord's Prayer.

'Haloed be her eve' echoes the phrase 'hallowed be Thy name' while simultaneously evoking a sunset over the Liffey, establishing a relationship between Annah and Eve, the mother of all mankind, and, by means of the echo of the Hail Mary, suggesting a relationship also with Mary, the Mother of God. In Italian, the equivalent of 'hallowed be Thy name' is usually 'sia santificato il tuo nome.' Wilcock's rendering 'cantificata sia la sua eva' combines the Italian *santificata* ('hallowed') and the verb *cantare* ('to sing') – thus anticipating the next phrase to come – while successfully retaining the reference both to Eve and to the Hail Mary, since Italian *Eva* reversed is the first word of that prayer's Latin title, Ave Maria. Schenoni's 'aureolificato sia il suo evanome' evokes the biblical text more obliquely, translating 'haloed' more literally with his 'aureolificato' and thus also retaining the reference to a sunset over the river, while combining 'Eve' and 'name' in the expression 'evanome.' Schüler's 'sanctificada seja sua evigília' stays close to the standard Portuguese wording of the Lord's Prayer, 'santificado seja o vosso nome.' His version thus translates 'hallowed' rather than 'haloed,' abandoning any reference to a sunset. His translation of 'eve' as 'evigília' successfully retains the double sense of *Eva* and *vigília* ('vigilance'), suggesting a biblical 'evening watch.'

The German wording of the prayer, 'geheiligt werde dein Name,' is retained only obliquely in Stündel's 'gehailogt sei ihr Edbend,' where, as is often the case in Stündel's renderings, the alteration of vowels from *geheiligt* to 'gehailogt' appears random rather than functional, though some readers might possibly feel justified in seeing the element '-hail-' as a translingual reference to the English Hail Mary. His 'Edbend' even more obliquely evokes Eve by combining German *Abend* ('evening') and an *Eden* whose orthographically fractured state might be read as reflecting the unfortunate results of Eve's biblical temptation of Adam. Two renderings, meanwhile, abandon almost all the overtones of both Joyce's and the respective biblical texts. Lavergne's 'bénie soit son heure' (literally 'blessed be her hour') at best only very faintly echoes the French biblical text 'que ton nom soit sanctifié,' while introducing the concept of liturgical hours in rendering Joyce's 'eve' as 'heure.' The Dutch translators maintain a similar distance from the Dutch wording of the prayer, 'geheiligd zij Uw naam' and abandon any reference to either of the senses of 'eve' in their version, 'allerheilig worde haar vloed' (literally 'all holy be her flood').

'Her singtime sung' parodically echoes 'Thy kingdom come.' This time it is Schenoni rather than Wilcock who achieves a stronger correspondence between Joyce's text and the Italian 'venga il tuo regno.' Wilcock, in fact, rather minimally allows his inclusion of the verb *cantare* ('to sing') in his translation of the previous phrase to do justice here as well, while Schenoni's 'venia il suo vegno' suggests her coming (*venuto*) as constituting a new kingdom (*regno*) based on 'forgiveness' (*venia*). Schüler likewise stays close to the Portuguese biblical wording 'venha a nós o vosso reino' with his 'venha o reino de seu canto' (literally 'may the kingdom of her song come') while arguably staying less close to Joyce's text, which seems to call rather for the singing of liturgical hours. Bindervoet and Henkes play on the Dutch biblical wording 'Uw rijk kome' with 'haar kozingtijd kome,' where 'kozingtijd' suggests both *koninkrijk* (an alternative expression for 'kingdom') and a time (*tijd*) for 'cuddling' (*kozen*). Once again, two versions abandon any attempt to reproduce the relevant biblical echoes. Lavergne's 'chantée son histoire' ignores the biblical 'que ton règne vienne' in favour of, literally, 'her story sung.' Stündel similarly ignores the standard German 'uns zukomme dein Reich' in favour of another reference to liturgical hours, 'ihr SingZeit sang' ('her song-time sang').

'Her rill be run' echoes 'Thy will be done,' while including an English 'rill' or rivulet. To begin with Italian once again, Wilcock ignores altogether the biblical 'sia fatta la tua volontà' in favour of the purely riverine 'il suo corso percorso' (literally 'her course traversed'), while Schenoni achieves an almost exact echo of the prayer with his 'sia ratta la sua riolontà,' where *riolontà* combines *rio* ('stream') and *volontà* ('will'), and the adjective *ratta* (playing on the past participle *fatta*, 'done') literally means 'swift.' Lavergne's French adopts a similar choice to that of Wilcock, ignoring the biblical 'que ta volonté soit faite' in favour of 'coulé son fleuve' (literally 'her river run'). Stündel likewise ignores 'dein Wille geschehe' with 'ihr Rinnsal rinne' ('may her rivulet flow'). Bindervoet and Henkes allude to the Dutch 'Uw wil geschiede' with their version 'heer ril vervliede,' literally 'may her rill glide on,' combining *vlieden* ('to flee, fly, fleet') and *vervloeien* ('to flow away') as well as *haar* ('her') and, appropriately for the context, *de Heer* ('the Lord'). Schüler, meanwhile, chooses this time also to ignore the

Portuguese wording 'seja feita a vossa vontade' for a decidedly idio-syncratic 'ritmem suas rumas sem peias,' where *ruma* is a carter's cry to a horse ('giddy-up!') but also includes *rua* ('street, way'), *peia* is a 'fetter' for a horse, and *ritmar* implies 'to maintain a rhythm,' the combination thus suggesting, roughly, 'may her wishes flow without impediment.'

The phrase 'unhemmed as it is uneven,' finally, echoes 'on earth as it is in heaven,' though now apparently referring in Joyce's text not only to the irregular course of the river but to the river as a roughly fin-ished fluvial garment. Again, our two Italian translators choose dif-ferent paths. Wilcock ignores the biblical 'come in cielo così in terra' in his 'tanto libero quanto capriccioso' (literally 'as free as it is fanciful'). Schenoni, on the other hand, succeeds once again in a achieving a clear echo of the prayer with his 'così in gelo come in guerra,' even if at the expense of cheerfully departing from Joyce, suggesting 'in freezing cold (*gelo*) as in the heat of war (*guerra*).' Schüler, with his 'assim na terra como no céu,' goes further, ignoring Joyce altogether in favour of quoting the Portuguese biblical text exactly, if parodically. Lavergne goes even further still, abandoning not only the biblical 'sur la terre comme au ciel' but Joyce too in his version 'sans fin, sans égal' ('with-out end, without equal'). Bindervoet and Henkes achieve a close echo of the biblical 'op aarde zoals in de hemel' with their appropriately flu-vial 'uit waarden evanals in de dommel,' literally 'out of polders (*waard*, 'polder') as into the Dommel,' the latter a minor Dutch river. Stündel chooses to ignore the biblical 'auf Erden, so wie auch im Himmel' in favour of 'ungehemd wie es umhymnisch ist,' where 'ungehemd' con-flates *ungehemmt* ('unrestrained') and a proposed riverine garment (*Hemd*, 'shirt') and 'umhymnisch' suggests the sound of 'hymns all around,' multilingual hymns of praise, as it might be, to a macrotextual Annah, allmaziful across translations and languages.

Amnis Limina Permanent   (*FW* 153.2)

Lavergne (French, 1982): Amnis Limina Permanent

Schenoni (Italian, 2001): Amnis Limina Permanent

Schüler (Portuguese, 2003): Amnis Liminina Permanent

Rathjen (German, 1989): *Amnis Limina Permanent*

Stündel (German, 1993): aine limitierte Permanenz

Bindervoet and Henkes (Dutch, 2002): Amnis Limina Permanent

Occasionally, one or two translators will see possibilities in a phrase that others overlook – or deliberately choose to ignore. Casting ALP as 'Amnis Limina Permanent' allows her to function as her own motto, so to speak, the Latin phrase meaning, literally, 'the banks of the river endure.' Four of six versions here leave the phrase untranslated, retaining Joyce's Latin original, presumably on the entirely defensible grounds that materials in languages other than English (or 'English') should not be translated. Two other translators choose quite different responses. Schüler's version alters Joyce's 'Limina' ('banks') little more than minimally to 'Liminina,' but manages in doing so to embed the Portuguese verb *ninar* ('to sing to sleep') and evoke the image of ALP the river singing her children (the banks of the river) to sleep. Stündel opts for an entirely different approach, retaining ALP's initials by only slightly altering German *eine* to an identically pronounced 'aine,' but choosing to alter the phrase itself completely rather than making any attempt to translate it. His alternative 'aine limitierte Permanenz' (literally 'a limited permanence') represents in principle a highly dubious strategy for a translator, but in our specifically transtextual context offers a not inappropriate and certainly salutary reminder that neither rivers nor banks nor any other natural phenomena have any unlimited claim to permanence.

Sabrine asthore   (*FW* 197.21)

Péron and Beckett (French, 1985 / 1996): la chère Sabine saumarée

Beckett and Joyce (French, 1931 / 1996): sa Sabrine saumoureuse

Lavergne (French, 1982): l'enlèvement des Sabines et le duo d'Astarté

Joyce and Frank (Italian, 1979 / 1996): Sabrinettuccia la fringuellina

Schenoni (Italian, 2001): Sabrina carasthore

García Tortosa (Spanish, 1992): Sabrina corilla

Aixàs (Catalan, 2004): Estimada Sabrina

Schüler (Portuguese, 2003): a querida Sabina

Amarante (Portuguese, 2009): Sabrina amaratriz

Goyert (German, 1970): seine Sabrine

Hildesheimer (German, 1970): sein Sabrinchen

Wollschläger (German, 1970): Sabrine an der Küßte

Stündel (German, 1993): Sabrina Leafling

Bindervoet and Henkes (Dutch, 2002): 't Sabeise chonteke

Grut (Swedish, 2001): sabrinskevis

Słomczyński (Polish, 1985): Sabrinę astoretkę

Weatherall et al. (Czech, 1932 / 1996): Sabinku

Chapter I.viii, otherwise *Anna Livia Plurabelle*, is famous, as we have already seen, for its evocation of the names of more than a thousand rivers worldwide, all of them functioning as an aspect of Anna Livia Plurabelle, the mother of all rivers. Here the reference to ALP as 'Sabrine' evokes the English river Severn (whose modern name derives from the Romano-Celtic *Sabrina*), the Russian river Savran, and the Scottish river Brin, while 'asthore' evokes the Indian river Astor. The expression *asthore* is also an anglicization of the Irish term of endearment *a stóir* ('my treasure, my darling'). The phrase 'Sabrine asthore' thus simultaneously evokes two popular Irish songs, 'Eileen Aroon' (Irish *a rúin*, 'my darling') and 'Savourneen deelish' (Irish *'s a mhúirnín dílis*, 'and my own dear darling').

Our translators (of whom, in a chapter always a favourite with translators, there is now a considerably increased number) rise to this particular challenge in a variety of ways. Beckett and Joyce's 'Sabrine saumoureuse' features both a loving lady (*amoureuse*) and an evocation of the eastern European river Sau (also known as the Sava), the Indian River Sāu, and the Far Eastern Russian river Amur. In Goyert's German we have a restrained 'seine Sabrine' ('his Sabrine'), with just a hint of the French river Seine, in Hildesheimer's German a more obviously affectionate 'sein Sabrinchen' ('his little Sabrine'), while in Joyce and Frank's exuberant Italian we encounter a baroque 'Sabrinettuccia la fringuellina,' a Sabrina affectionately subjected not only to a double diminutive – from *Sabrina* to *Sabrinetta* to *Sabrinettuccia* – but characterized in similarly diminutive terms as a cute little songbird, and specifically, if we insist on ornithological precision, as a little 'chaffinch' (*fringuello*).

Wollschläger's German, reading 'asthore' as primarily involving a pun on *ashore*, renders the endearment as 'Sabrine an der Küßte,' playing on a combination of the phrase *an der Küste* ('on the shore') and *Kuss* ('kiss'). García Tortosa's Spanish favours 'Sabrina corilla' – combining *corola* ('petals'), *río* ('river'), and the diminutive suffix *-illa* – and Aixàs's Catalan 'Estimada Sabrina' ('dear Sabrina'), both changing 'Sabrine' to a more Hispanic 'Sabrina' in the process. Amarante's Portuguese prefers a 'Sabrina amaratriz,' combining *amar* ('to love'), *amaro* ('bitter'), separate meanings of the verb *amarar* implying both a personal 'flooded by grief' and a riverine 'flooded by water,' and, for good measure, veiled references to the Scottish river Amar and the Bangladeshi river Atrai.

Two translators (both of whom also prefer the form *Sabrina*) play more overtly on the term 'asthore': Schenoni's 'Sabrina carasthore' combines the Italian *cara* ('dear') and the original 'asthore,' while hinting at the Caragh River of County Kerry and the Caras River of Romania; Stündel's 'Sabrina Leafling' punningly combines the German *Liebling* ('darling') and the English *leaf*, conjuring up the Liffey while referring simultaneously to the North American Leaf River and the Scottish river Ling. Grut's Swedish pursues a more obscure solution with 'sabrinskevis,' which seems to imply a complexly flibbertigibbet Sabrine at once 'wrong-headed' (*skev*) and 'wise' (*vis*) while evoking the Angolan Keve River. The Scottish Brin continues to flow in all these versions, and the river Abra of the Philippines can be faintly distinguished in the background.

Several versions, meanwhile, prefer to focus on an implied reference to the Sabine women of Roman legendary history, kidnapped by the Romans to provide mothers for their children but proving themselves to be peacemakers between the warring male sides. Péron and Beckett's 'chère Sabine saumarée' plays with a variety of aquatic references, including French *marée* ('tide'), *amarrer* ('to moor'), and *sous-marin* ('submarine') as well as evoking the eastern European Sau and the Indian Sāu once again and introducing the American Sabine River. Schüler's Portuguese speaks with sober restraint merely of 'a querida Sabina' ('the dear Sabine') and Weatherall's Czech of a 'Sabinku' ('little Sabina') – though, sober or not, Schüler also manages to suggest an oblique reference to the river Eridanos of Greek mythology as well as to the Sabine, while Weatherall provides a reference to the Nepalese river Inku. All of the Sabine versions abandon the Scottish Brin for the Zimbabwean Sabi.

Two of the Sabine versions adopt distinctly adventurous solutions. Lavergne's French goes further than anyone might reasonably have been expected to do in invoking Roman quasi-history for the first word and Phoenician mythology for the second in his preference for 'l'enlèvement des Sabines et le duo d'Astarté' ('the abduction of the Sabine women and the duo of Astarte'). The arcane latter reference may relate to the fact that Astarte, a Semitic fertility goddess later adopted by the Greeks as Aphrodite, was sometimes portrayed together with the virgin war goddess Anat. While many readers would consider Lavergne's version to depart far too radically from Joyce's text, we may note that it is one of only three (the others being Schenoni's and Słomczyński's) to retain the original reference to the Indian Astor River – Słomczyński's Polish 'Sabrinę astoretkę' likewise combining the river Astor and the goddess Astarte in her Hebrew guise as Ashtoreth. Bindervoet and Henkes, finally, mischievously prompted no doubt by the 'ass' at once concealed and revealed in 'asthore,' go entirely their own merry way with "t Sabeise chonteke,' admiring the 'cute little Sabine (*sabijnse*) bottom (*kont*)' of the lady in question, with an accompanying bravura fanfare of echoes (Dutch *echo*, as in '-e cho-') of no fewer than ten far-flung rivers and lakes: the Zimbabwean Sabi, the American Sabine, the Chinese Abei, the Ethiopian Abay, the Chinese Bei, the Indian Beas, the English Ise, Tasmania's Echo Lake, the Siberian river Chona, and Lake Teke of Kazakhstan.

Annona, gebroren aroostokrat Nivia   (*FW* 199.34)

Péron and Beckett (French, 1985 / 1996): Annona, née aroostuckra-
tiquement Nivia

Beckett and Joyce (French, 1931 / 1996): Annona née aroostucra-
tiquement Nivia

Lavergne (French, 1982): Annona, aristocratiquement née Nivia

Joyce and Frank (Italian, 1979 / 1996): Annona genata arusticrata
Nivea

Schenoni (Italian, 2001): Annona, gebrorenata aroostookratica Nivia

García Tortosa (Spanish, 1992): Annona, gebrotada areostokroática
Nivia

Aixàs (Catalan, 2004): Annona, la que es crià aristòcrata Nivia

Schüler (Portuguese, 2003): Annona, de nascimento aristocrata,
Nívia

Amarante (Portuguese, 2009): Annona, nata aroostokrat Nivia

Goyert (German, 1970): Annona aristokratzig gebrorene Nivia

Hildesheimer (German, 1970): Sanda Annona, gebrorene Nivea

Wollschläger (German, 1970): Annone, gegorene Nivia, Arußtokratin

Stündel (German, 1993): Annona, gebojana Nivea, arostookratische Dochtder

Bindervoet and Henkes (Dutch, 2002): Annona, borne arostookraat Nivia

Grut (Swedish, 2001): Annona, vonfödd Nivia

Słomczyński (Polish, 1985): Annona, ugebrorendzona arystokurka Nivia

Weatherall et al. (Czech, 1932 / 1996): Arnona, rožděná aroštikratka Nivia

ALP as 'Annona, gebroren aroostokrat Nivia,' is transformed momentarily into Annona, the Roman goddess of the harvest, whose name is based on the Latin noun *annona* ('the year's produce'). The Roman goddess Annona is thus closely related functionally to the Irish goddess Ana, whose name, as we have seen, is based on the Irish *ana* ('riches, plenty, prosperity'). The name *Annona*, moreover, also evokes the Celtic suffix -*ona* ('great'), which typically connotes divinity, as in *Matrona* ('Great Mother'). In our context, *Annona* is therefore 'Anna, the great goddess,' multiply deified. Our Annona's origins are international: the implied *geboren* suggests German, while 'aroostokrat' suggests aristocratic Russian origins. Her accompanying train of rivers, meanwhile, includes the Scottish Annan, the Spanish Ebro, the American Aroostook, the French Nive, the English Neve, and the Spanish Navia, as well as the American Lake Nona of Florida. The name *Nivia* permits the Latin *nivea* ('snow-covered') to substitute for 'Livia,' the oblique suggestion of a high mountain also invoking HCE once again.

With two exceptions, all the versions cited retain the name *Annona* unchanged: Wollschläger's 'Annone' merely gives the name a more typically German ending, while Weatherall's Czech 'Arnona' introduces an additional fluvial reference, this time to the Italian river Arno. The name *Nivia* likewise remains largely unchanged, though Joyce and Frank, Hildesheimer, and Stündel all alter it to the Latin 'Nivea,' thus permitting access to the French river Nive and the English river Ive. Lavergne leaves 'Nivia' unaltered, but in a footnote idiosyncratically associates Nivia with Niamh, daughter of the king of Tír na nÓg, the land of youth. *Finnegans Wake* can more than comfortably accommodate idiosyncracy, however: first, the Old Irish adjective *niamh* /'niːəv/ ('shining, brilliant') is a not at all unreasonable transposition of Latin *nivea* ('snow-covered'); second, in the Fenian tales, as we have seen, Áine, beloved of Finn mac Cumhaill, has a name also meaning 'radiance, splendour, brilliance'; and third, Niamh, beloved of Oisín, likewise in the Fenian tales, is called *Niamh Cinn Óir* ('Niamh of the Golden Hair'), reminding us of Joyce's association of Anna Livia and the flowing hair of Livia Schmitz.

Some versions attempt to retain the river Ebro in their rendering of 'gebroren,' and some do not. Péron and Beckett along with Beckett and Joyce are surprisingly restrained with a plain river-free French 'née' ('born'). Goyert and Hildesheimer have no difficulty with just leaving it alone in German, other than adding an appropriate declensional ending; Wollschläger, however, abandoning the Ebro, chooses to pun instead on German *gegoren* (literally 'fermented'), while Stündel, playing on a colloquial Berlin pronunciation of *geboren* as *gebojan*, likewise abandons the Spanish Ebro but substitutes in compensation the Albanian Bojana and the Irish Boyne. García Tortosa employs 'gebrotada,' retaining the Ebro, combining the original 'gebroren' and a Spanish *brotada* ('issued, appeared'). Both Schenoni and Słomczyński also opt for a somewhat similar solution, the former with 'gebrorenata,' suffixing an Italian *nata* ('born'), the latter with 'ugebrorendzona,' conflating 'gebroren' and Polish *urodzona* ('born'). Joyce and Frank's Italian 'genata' preserves the Germanic *ge-*, combining it with a double Italian rendering of 'born,' *genita* and *nata*. Other translators capitulate and content themselves with substituting the standard vocabulary term for 'born' in the relevant language.

Annona's birth as an alleged 'aroostokrat' leads to a more varied range of solutions. Some versions merely report her ostensibly 'aristocratic' origins (Lavergne, Schüler, Aixàs), while most others choose to stay close to Joyce's original neologism and its riverine reference by devising a similarly structured variant. Among the more interesting versions, Goyert's German has her 'aristokratzig,' combining *aristokratisch* ('aristocratic') and *kratzig* ('scratchy') to produce a high-class lady with a sharp temper and nails to match. For García Tortosa she is 'areostokroática' and thus of a similarly indomitable cast of mind, an *aristócrata* ('aristocrat') with skills clearly 'warlike' (Greek *areios*), but whose Slavic origins now emerge as not Russian at all but rather as Croatian (Spanish *croata*). In Grut's Swedish she appears instead to be of German aristocratic origins, for she is now 'Annona, vonfödd Nivia,' which is to say, 'born (Swedish *född*) with the (German) particle of nobility *von*,' while related to the English river Avon. In Hildesheimer's German, finally, it is quite unimportant whether she was of aristocratic birth or not and what her origins may have been: what is important is her subsequent (or at least fully deserved) canonization as 'Sanda Annona,' her new ecclesiastical title combining Italian and Spanish *santa* ('saint'). It goes without saying that as such she is, of course, the patron saint of rivers, and her title thus appropriately also contains a trinity of attendant Sanda Rivers, which can be found flowing variously in Iceland, Kenya, and the Philippines.

Anna-na-Poghue   (*FW* 203.36)

Lavergne (French, 1982): Anna-na-Poghue

Schenoni (Italian, 2001): Anna-na-Poghue

García Tortosa (Spanish, 1992): Anna-da-Poga

Aixàs (Catalan, 2004): Anna Pogue

Schüler (Portuguese, 2003): Arna-na-Ponga

Amarante (Portuguese, 2009): Anna-na-Poghue

Goyert (German, 1970): Anna-na-Poghue

Hildesheimer (German, 1970): Anna-na-Pokuss

Wollschläger (German, 1970): Anna-na-Poghue

Stündel (German, 1993): Anna-nah-Påckes

Bindervoet and Henkes (Dutch, 2002): Anna-na-Poghue

Grut (Swedish, 2001): Anna-na-Poghue

Słomczyński (Polish, 1985): Anny-na-Poghue

Weatherall et al. (Czech, 1932 / 1996): Anny-na-Poli

The reference to ALP as 'Anna-na-Poghue' evokes the nineteenth-century Irish dramatist Dion Boucicault's popular melodrama *Arrah-na-Pogue, or The Wicklow Wedding* (1864). Arrah-na-Pogue, the heroine of the piece, whose name suggests an anglicization of an Irish *Ara na póige* ('Arrah of the kiss'), wins her sobriquet as a result of the dramatic occasion on which (shades of Molly Bloom's seed cake) she successfully passes her unjustly imprisoned foster-brother a mouth-to-mouth written message in the course of a kiss (Irish *póg*), following which they all, naturally and in due course, live happily ever after. (The name *Arrah*, incidentally, is Boucicault's invention and is unconnected with the name *Nora*, despite occasional suggestions to the contrary among Joyce scholars.) 'Anna-na-Poghue' may be understood as similarly meaning *Anna na póige* ('Anna of the kiss') or, if the activity in question occurred on more than one occasion, *Anna na bpóg* ('Anna of the kisses') (O Hehir 1967, 360). In Joyce's 'Poghue' rather than 'Pogue,' moreover, Anna is supplemented by the Sudanese river Hu – and indeed, for the more obsessive investigator, by the Chinese noun *hú* ('lake').

Several of our translators, more than half, take the easy way out and merely replicate Joyce's formulation more or less exactly. Weatherall's very early Czech version, however, interestingly opts for 'Anny-na-Poli' instead, possibly on the assumption that nothing, kisses included, can ever exceed the pleasure – *vedere Napoli e poi mori*, 'see Naples and die' – of at least once seeing the fabled Bay of Naples. Hildesheimer, on the other hand, chooses 'Anna-na-Pokuss,' which has far less to do with Naples than with Leopold Bloom's osculatory preferences (German *Kuss*, 'kiss,' and *Popo*, 'bottom'), with a supplementary composite echo of chamber pots, the Italian river Po, and assorted hocus pocus. Schüler, eschewing osculation, concentrates instead on riverine possibilities with his preferred choice, 'Arna-na-Ponga,' which manages to include the river Arna in Denmark, another river of the same name in India, a suggestion of the Italian Arno, and a fourth river, the Naponga, in far-away Zambia. García Tortosa's Spanish 'Anna-da-Poga' suggests that Anna does indeed give (Spanish *da*, 'gives') kisses (Irish *póga*, 'kisses'), even if possibly meaning nothing at all (*nada*) by them. Stündel's German 'Anna-nah-Påckes,' finally, while referring in passing to the Pack River of Idaho, suggested as being quite close by (German *nah*, 'near'), rejects kissing but sceptically suggests by the use of the non-German grapheme *å* (generating the pronunciation /ˈpokəs/) that there may indeed be a strong element of unspecified hocus pocus in play.

Annushka Lutetiavitch Pufflovah   (*FW* 207.8–9)

Lavergne (French, 1982): Annushka Lutetiavitch Pufflovah

Wilcock (Italian, 1961): Annushka Lutetiavitch Pafflova

Schenoni (Italian, 2001): Annushka Lutetiavitch Pufflovah

García Tortosa (Spanish, 1992): Anushka Luteciavich Pauborla

Pozanco (Spanish, 1993): Annushka Lutetiavitch Pufflovah

Aixàs (Catalan, 2004): Annushka Lutetiavitch Pufflovah

Schüler (Portuguese, 2003): Annushka Lutetiavitch Pufflovah

Amarante (Portuguese, 2009): Annushka Lutetiavitch Pufflovah

Goyert (German, 1970): Annuschka Lutetiavitch Pufflovah

Hildesheimer (German, 1970): Annuschka Lätiziowitsch Puffliewa

Wollschläger (German, 1970): Annushka Lutetiawitsch Pufflovah

Stündel (German, 1993): Annuschka Lutetiawitch Puffklowahr

Bindervoet and Henkes (Dutch, 2002): Annoesjka Lutetiavitsj
    Pufflovah

Grut (Swedish, 2001): Anjusjka Lutetiavitj Pustlova

Słomczyński (Polish, 1985): Annusszka Lutecjawicz Puwlowa

Weatherall et al. (Czech, 1932 / 1996): Anuška Luteriovna Pufflova

ALP operating as Annushka Lutetiavitch Pufflovah is most obviously
associated with Anna Pavlovna Pavlova (1881–1931), Joyce's close con-
temporary and the most celebrated ballerina of her day, who, born
Russian, charmed Paris as well as London and New York in the course of
a brilliant career. *Annushka* is a Slavic pet form of *Anna*, a diminutive, as
opposed to the augmentative *Annona* already encountered. Despite the
diminutive, the fact that Anush is the mother of dragons in Armenian
mythology may be read as suggesting a lady not to be tampered with
lightly. The quasi-male quasi-patronymic *Lutetiavitch* (where one might
expect the quasi-female *Lutetiovna*) is initially reminiscent of Leopold
Paula Bloom's feminine middle name and might seem to raise some
doubts as to Annushka's complete femininity, but it simultaneously clas-
sifies her as both a bewitching Parisienne and a Parisian witch, *Lutetia*
being the Romano-Celtic name for the settlement that later became Paris.

ALP's aquatic associations are very much in evidence. *Annushka*,
stressed on the first syllable, combines the Old Irish *an* (a near-
homophone of the English name *Ann*), meaning 'water,' and a close

approximation of the Modern Irish *uisce*, also meaning 'water'; stressed on the second syllable, it evokes a whole body of water, namely Minnesota's Nushka Lake. *Lutetiavitch* contains a glancing reference to the French river Tech, and the place name *Lutetia* seems to contain both the Latin *luteus* ('muddy') and a Celtic element **luto-* or **luco-*, meaning 'marsh' (Whatmough 1970, 2:512). *Pufflovah*, beyond the obvious play on *Pavlova*, and references in passing to the Lova River of Papua New Guinea and the Váh River of Slovakia, reflects the fact that all successful ballerinas need to be endowed with a lot of puff (breath, stamina) as well as depending on puffs (favourable reviews). That *Puff* means 'brothel' in informal German usage adds an interesting note, and further questions of sexual identity are raised by the suggestion of 'puff lover,' the slang term *puff* to denote a male homosexual having been in use since the 1870s (Partridge 1972, 730).

All sixteen of our translations succeed without obvious difficulty in retaining ALP's acrostic initials. 'Annushka' either remains unchanged (as in the majority of cases) or undergoes nothing more than minor orthographic surgery: Spanish 'Anushka' (García Tortosa), German 'Annuschka' (Goyert, Hildesheimer, Stündel), Swedish 'Anjusjka' (Grut), Dutch 'Annoesjka' (Bindervoet and Henkes), Czech 'Anuška' (Weatherall), Polish 'Annusszka' (Słomczyński). The same is true, again in the majority of cases, for 'Lutetiavitch,' but there are some interesting variations. Weatherall's Czech, for example, preferring a more normalized and more normally gendered patronymic, changes it to 'Luteriovna' (literally 'daughter of Luther'), providing an unexpected German Protestant lineage for our heroine as well as a glancing and likewise unexpected reference to southern Ontario's Luther Marsh wetlands. Hildesheimer's German, playing on gendered names, prefers 'Lätiziowitsch,' literally 'son of Laetitius,' a Latin name whose feminine form, *Laetitia* or *Letitia* ('joyful'), is far more common, whether in German or in English. While Hildesheimer and Wollschläger both use the spelling '-witsch' that is standard for the German transliteration of Russian names, Stündel prefers '-witch,' thus foregrounding the potential complementary presence of an English *witch*.

As for 'Pufflovah,' the majority decision is again either to leave the name unchanged or to alter it only minimally in accordance with the orthographical conventions of the relevant language (Weatherall's Czech 'Pufflova' or Słomczyński's Polish 'Puwlowa,' for example). Wilcock's Italian 'Pafflova' brings the name somewhat closer to that of the historical Anna Pavlova, though ungallantly suggesting – with a 'bang' (*paf!*) – that our Annushka was rather too fat (*paffuta*). Hildesheimer's German 'Puffliewa' moves the name further away from *Pavlova* while simultaneously evoking a French *fleuve* ('river'). Grut, apparently worried about his Anjusjka's stamina, moves further still with his 'Pustlova,' based on the Swedish noun *pust* ('puff, bellows'). Marching determinedly to his own drummer, Stündel transforms Joyce's 'Pufflovah' into 'Puffklowahr,' gleefully seizing the opportunity to include the German nouns *Puff* ('brothel') and *Klo* ('toilet, washroom') as well as a reference to the German river Ahr. Marching with equal determination but to a very different tune, García Tortosa plumbs Spanish lexicographical depths (and includes another aquatic reference) with his 'Pauborla,' which combines *paúl* ('marsh, bog'), *borla* ('doctor's hood'), and the phrase *tomar la borla* ('to graduate') to suggest our Annushka, not inappropriately, as being not only a successful graduate of a Wicklow bog but also a riverine relative of the French Pau and Aube as well as the German Orla.

Ah, but she was the queer old skeowsha anyhow, Anna Livia, trinkettoes!
(FW 215.12–13)

Ogden (Basic English, 1932 / 1996): Ah, but she was a strange little old woman, anyhow, Anna Livia, with drops from her toes.

Beckett and Joyce (French, 1931 / 1996): mais quelle drôle de drôlesse quand même qu'Anna Livie petontintamahr.

Lavergne (French, 1982): Ah, mais c'était quand même une drôle de Squaw-sha, cette Anna Livia, tu peux m'en croire!

Joyce and Frank (Italian, 1979 / 1996): era una stramba duenna, quell'Anna Livia, zampolona.

Schenoni (Italian, 2001): Ah, ma lei era la strana vecchia skeowshamìca adognimodo, Anna Livia, trinkentamente!

García Tortosa (Spanish, 1992): Ah, pero ella era esa extraña entrañable rapaza, Anna Livia, piesapelusca!

Pozanco (Spanish, 1993): Ah, pero era una vieja amiga a pesar de todo, Anna Livia.

Aixàs (Catalan, 2004): Ah però, que quedi clar, ella era una estranya bastarda, Anna Livia, peusenjoiada!

Schüler (Portuguese, 2003): Ah, mas era, apesar de tudo, uma velhamiga bem exquisita, Ana Lívia nos trinques!

Amarante (Portuguese, 2009): Ah, mas apesar de tudo ela era a estranha velhamica, Anna Livia, adedornada!

Antip (Romanian, 1996): Ah, dar Anna Livia a fost, oricum, o bătrână muiere bizară.

Goyert (German, 1970): Ache, eine seltsame alte Skeowsha war sie doch, die Anna Livia, die klinkerzehe.

Hildesheimer (German, 1970): Ach, war doch eine silsame alte Huttzel, wie auch immer, Anna Livia, Flitterzehe

Wollschläger (German, 1970): Ah, aber jedenfalls war sie ja doch die komische alte Skeowsha, Anna Livia, Glitterzeh!

Stündel (German, 1993): Arch, aber sie war irgendwie eine komische alte Freundin, Anna Livia, SchmuckZehe!

Bindervoet and Henkes (Dutch, 2002): Ah, maar ze was en raar oud squawtsje toch, Anna Livia, met haar kleinpodieën!

Grut (Swedish, 2001): Men ett särligt kvinnostycke var hon ändå, Anna Livia Nippertå!

Słomczyński (Polish, 1985): Ach, lecz była dziwną starą zdzirą, Anna Livia, dzwonkopalca!

Weatherall et al. (Czech, 1932 / 1996): Ej, ale byla to dviná potvůrka, Anna Livia, parádiprstá.

We may conclude with the washerwomen's backhanded summary that Anna Livia, all things considered, 'was the queer old skeowsha anyhow.' 'Skeowsha' is a metathesized variant of the humorously affectionate Hiberno-English *segocia* ('comrade, friend, fellow, creature'), of undetermined origin, whose rearranged spelling here allows for similarly rearranged references to various Esk Rivers (the name related to Irish *uisce*, 'water') in Britain and elsewhere as well as the Ow River of County Wicklow, the Sha River of China, and two Shaw Rivers of Australia. The epithet 'trinkettoes' suggests dancing twinkletoes, trinkets, rings on her fingers, bells on her toes, and refers in passing to the river Ketto of Gambia. Even the opening 'ah, but' manages to refer to the river Abu of Ghana.

'The queer old skeowsha' evokes a wide range of responses. In Ogden's Basic English, she is 'a strange little old woman'; for Beckett and Joyce, more colourfully, a 'drôle de drôlesse' ('a really funny old biddy'). Joyce and Frank's Italian considers her 'una stramba duenna' ('a queer old lady'), taking the opportunity to invoke the river Amba of Russia, two other rivers of the same name in India and Nigeria, and the Italian river Enna. In García Tortosa's Spanish, she is an 'extraña entrañable rapaza,' a 'strange (*extraña*), affectionate (*entrañable*) girl. (*rapaza*),' a less old and less odd figure than in most other versions, while Pozanco's Spanish has her as merely 'una vieja amiga' ('an old dear'). Rather more robustly, Aixàs's Catalan considers her 'una estranya bastarda' ('a strange old bastard'). The two Portuguese translators agree with each other: for Schüler, she is 'uma velhamiga bem exquisita' ('a very strange old dear'), for Amarante an 'estranha velhamica' ('a strange old dear'), in both cases discreetly evoking the English Ham River. In Antip's Romanian, she is likewise a 'bătrână muiere bizară' ('a peculiar old woman'). Among German versions, Hildesheimer describes her as 'eine silsame alte Huttzel,' a 'strange (*seltsam*) little old woman (*Hutzel*),' referring in so doing to the Swiss river Sihl ('silsam') and the Hutt River of New Zealand, while for Stündel she is just 'eine komische alte Freundin' ('a funny, friendly old dear'). Grut's Swedish speaks for all in considering her 'ett särligt kvinnostycke,' a 'strange (*särling*) kind of a woman (*kvinnostycke*).'

Several translators are either frankly puzzled by Joyce's 'skeowsha' or reluctant to abandon it in view of the spate of rivers it evokes, or perhaps both. Lavergne's French thus considers Anna 'une drôle de Squaw-sha,' literally 'a funny old squaw-sha,' contributing an unexpected North American touch: the word *squaw* derives from the Massachusetts Indian *squa* ('woman') (Onions 1966, 859), a term rarely heard in the immediate environs of the Liffey. Bindervoet and Henkes's Dutch likewise considers Anna 'en raar oud squawtsje' ('a rare little old squaw'). Two German translators capitulate and simply adopt Joyce's term unchanged: Anna is 'eine seltsame alte Skeowsha' for Goyert, a 'komische alte Skeowsha' for Wollschläger, in both cases a 'funny old skeowsha.' Schenoni's Italian combines Joyce's 'skeowsha' and the noun *amica* ('friend') in finding Anna a 'strana vecchia skeowshamìca,' a 'strange old skeowsha-dear.' The opening 'ah,' meanwhile, gives Goyert an opportunity ('Ache') to evoke the Austrian river Ache, while Stündel ('Arch') seizes the chance to evoke likewise the Austrian and German Ach Rivers – and, since it would clearly be a shame to squander such an opportunity, also a supernumerary German *Arsch* ('arse').

As for Anna Livia's 'trinkettoes,' Ogden sees it as meaning 'with drops from her toes,' the drops presumably sparkling in sunshine. Beckett and Joyce's French refers in a linguistic fireworks display to 'Anna Livie petontintamahr,' combining her *peton* ('tiny foot, footsy-wootsy') and the resulting publicity *tintamarre* ('racket, ballyhoo') it allegedly evokes as well as a nod to the Austrian river Mahr and the German river Ahr. Joyce and Frank evoke an 'Anna Livia, zampolona,' combining *zampa* ('tiny paw') and a nod to the Italian river Olona. Schenoni's Italian 'Anna Livia, trinkentamente' combines English *trinket*, German *trinken* ('to drink'), the English rivers Kent and Tame, and the African river Ntem. García Tortosa's 'Anna Livia, piesapelusca' combines Spanish *pelusa* ('down, floss') and the Welsh river Usk (a name related once again to Irish *uisce*, 'water') to produce a flossy-footed riverine Anna Livia. Aixàs's Catalan 'Anna Livia, peusenjoiada' is 'foot-bejewelled' (*peu*, 'foot'; *joia*, 'jewel'). Schüler's Portuguese Anna turns out to have been a nice old dear 'nos trinques' ('in her cups, when she had a drink taken'), with no report on how she might have behaved under other conditions. Amarante's Portuguese Anna is 'adedornada,' with her 'toes (*dedo*, 'toe') adorned (*adornada*).'

Among German translators, there is close agreement. Goyert's Anna is 'die klinkerzehe' ('jingletoes'), where *Klinker* ('clinker') evokes toes (*Zehe*, 'toe') that *klingen* ('ring, jingle') – as well as the Link River of Oregon; Hildesheimer's Anna is 'Flitterzehe' ('spangletoes'), with toes covered in *Flitter* ('sequins, spangles'); Wollschläger's is 'Glitterzeh' ('glittertoes') with toes that *glitzern* ('glitter, twinkle'); and Stündel's is 'SchmuckZehe' ('jewel-toes'). Grut's Swedish Anna is 'Nippertå' ('trinket-toes'), courtesy of *nipper* ('trinkets') and *tå* ('toe'). In Dutch, Bindervoet and Henkes have 'Anna Livia, met haar kleinpodieën,' an Anna with toes (*teen*, 'toe') covered ·in jewels (*kleinood*, 'jewel, trinket') and evoking the Italian river Po. Two translators simply abandon the struggle, Pozanco in Spanish and Antip in Romanian offering no translation at all of 'trinkettoes.' Lavergne, for his part, sidesteps the issue, merely assuring the reader, who by now surely needs no more assurance on the matter anyway, that when it comes to Anna's oddness, 'tu peux m'en croire' ('you can take my word for it'). When it comes to her cumulative transtextual oddness, readers will certainly have no need for any further assurance.

10 Dear Dirty Dublin

As part of his early attempt to explain to Harriet Weaver some of the logic of the extraordinary undertaking that would become *Finnegans Wake*, Joyce wrote in November 1926 that 'some of the words at the beginning are hybrid Danish-English. Dublin is a city founded by Vikings' (*L* 1:213). Prior to its fortification by the Vikings, early medieval Dublin grew up around two neighbouring settlements on the river Liffey, *Áth Cliath* and *Duibhlinn*. The former centred on an ancient and strategically important ford, near the present site of the Four Courts, made of hurdles, or interwoven branches, across the river, and *Baile Átha Cliath* – 'the town (*baile*) of the ford (*áth*) of hurdles (*cliath*)' – is still the official name of the city in Irish. The nearby *Duibhlinn*, a monastic settlement, was named for a 'black (*dubh*) pool (*linn*)' near the confluence of the Liffey and the Poddle, further downstream. The Vikings called the city they began to fortify in the year 841 by the existing Irish name of the latter settlement, recasting it in Old Norse phonetics as *Dyflin*. By the tenth century the Norse kingdom of Dublin, known to the Scandinavians as *Dyflinnarskiri* ('Dublinshire'), stretched some seventy miles along the Irish east coast from Skerries in the north to Arklow in the south and inland along and around the Liffey valley to Leixlip, about ten miles inland (de Courcy 1996, 136).

The city of Dublin is inextricably linked in *Finnegans Wake* with both HCE and ALP and they with it, and that triple interconnection will be evident throughout this chapter, devoted to the transtextual representation of what that wild Irish girl Lady Morgan liked to call 'dear dirty Dublin.' To begin with, it is worth repeating that the founding of Scandinavian Dublin is traditionally attributed to the Norwegian Óláfr hvítr, who in due course, about the year 853, became its first Norse king. The Irish Gaelic form of *Óláfr*, anglicized as *Olaf*, is, as we have seen, *Amhlaoibh* – which in turn is traditionally (though quite arbitrarily) anglicized as *Humphrey*. The Old Norse name *Óláfr hvítr* means 'Olaf the White,' the byname thus providing an onomastic link to two of HCE's principal avatars, Finn and Finnegan: the name *Finn*, as we have seen, derives from the Old Irish *find*, meaning 'fair' or 'white,' while *Finnegan* is an anglicization of the Irish *Ó Fionnagáin* ('descendant of *Fionnagán*,' the personal name meaning 'fair-haired').

But the name *Óláfr* also provides an unexpected link to ALP, deriving as it does from a combination of the Old Norse elements *anu* ('ancestor') and *leifr* ('heir, descendant') (Hanks et al. 2002, 837). For while Old Norse *anu* means 'ancestor,' Old Irish *anu* means 'wealth, abundance' and became, as we have seen, the name of the mother goddess who was later called *Ana* and as such is one avatar among many of Anna Livia Plurabelle. The byname *hvítr* ('white'), meanwhile, provides an onomastic link not only, as we have seen, to HCE as Finn (Old Irish *find*, 'white') but also to ALP, whose three-letter acronym may also be discerned – at least in English transliteration – in the Greek *alphós* ('whiteness'). As if in anticipation of *Finnegans Wake*, moreover, the Old Norse adjective *hvítr* ('white') present in its founder's name also evokes the Old Irish adjective *dub*, Modern Irish *dubh* ('black'), contained in the name of the city founded, Dublin.

So This Is Dyoublong?   (*FW* 13.4–5)

du Bouchet (French, 1962): Dieublingue

Lavergne (French, 1982): Dieublingue

Schenoni (Italian, 1982): Doblungo

Pozanco (Spanish, 1993): Dublín

Schüler (Portuguese, 2003): Dublíngua

Stündel (German, 1993): Dubelienrst

Bindervoet and Henkes (Dutch, 2002): Dubballeen

In 1927 the Irish journalist and man of letters M.J. MacManus, soon to become the literary editor of the *Irish Press*, took satiric aim in a book entitled *So This Is Dublin* at James Joyce and all his newfangled works and pomps. Parodying MacManus's title, Joyce's 'Dyoublong,' focused on the issue of belonging, as in the case of HCE (not to mention Joyce himself), undergoes some interesting variations at the hands of its translators. Pozanco's Spanish, for example, simply cuts through the wordplay and its associated implications and restores the literal meaning of 'Dyoublong' as 'Dublín,' with an appropriate Spanish accent. Two French versions, by du Bouchet and Lavergne, see the issue of belonging as involving primarily issues relating to 'God' (*dieu*) and 'language' (Latin *lingua*), twin shibboleths of the tribe. Schüler pays less attention to possible religious issues than to those of language, and his 'Dublíngua' combines a Portuguese *Dublim* /du'blĩ/ ('Dublin') and *língua* ('language'). Schenoni's 'Doblungo' combines Italian *dóppio* ('double') and *lungo*, which can mean 'long' or 'at great length,' or, appropriately for a city built on the Liffey and demonstrating a high regard for the merits of whiskey, 'diluted with water.' Bindervoet and Henkes, opting for 'Dubballeen,' focus in existential mode on the duplicity of the city instead, inevitably *dubbel* ('double'), and the isolation of the individual, inevitably *alleen* ('alone'). Stündel's 'Dubelienrst' suggests a cryptic reference to the title of *Dubliners* as well as conflating the German *Dublin erst* ('only Dublin') and an idiosyncratic *du berlinerst* ('you're speaking Berlin dialect'), further suggesting that the issue of belonging and exclusion is by no means confined to Dublin and that one person's Dublin may be another's Berlin.

Hyde and Cheek, Edenberry, Dubblenn, WC   (*FW* 66.17–18)

Lavergne (French, 1982): Hyde and Cheek, Edenberry, Dubblenn, WC

Schenoni (Italian, 1982): Hyde and Cheek, Edenberry, Dubblenn, WC

Schüler (Portuguese, 2003): Guarda e Busca, Edenossementópolis polis, Dubelém, WC

Stündel (German, 1993): Heide und Chick, Edenberri, Dubblänn, WC

Bindervoet and Henkes (Dutch, 2002): Hiero Kijkdan, Ieveransburgh, Dubblenn, WC

The city bisected by a river can metamorphose on occasion from Dublin to Paris or London or Budapest (*FW* 199.7–9). The address – containing the acrostic initials *HCE* – to which ALP's letter defending her husband's reputation is sent conjoins three of the capital cities of the British Isles, though each of them is here also just one more face of Dublin. 'Edenberry' suggests Edinburgh, but also a Dublin doubling as a new Eden – since in Basque, once held to be the language spoken by Adam and Eve, *berry* means 'new.' As has variously been observed, moreover, *Finnegans Wake* begins on Merchant's Quay (with Adam and Eve's) and ends downstream in 'Edenborough' (*FW* 29.35), a reflection of the fact that Eden Quay and Burgh Quay are opposite each other on the Liffey. 'Dubblenn' is evidently Dublin, but also, echoing the cheeky hide-and-seek motif, 'double *n*' or 'N.N.' or *nomen nescio* ('name unknown'). 'WC' refers both to West Central London and to the Irish-all-too-Irish latrine that is also called Dublin. The motif of doubling and duplicity is emphasized by the double *r*, the double *b*, the double *n*, and the letter name *double u* – as it is by the name 'Hyde and Cheek,' which plays simultaneously on 'hide and seek,' hiding and peeping, and the two faces of Dr Jekyll and Mr Hyde.

Both Lavergne and Schenoni simply retain Joyce's formulation. Stündel's 'Heide und Chick' may perhaps be read as suggesting that HCE is a *Heide* ('pagan') without the advantages of a religious upbringing and therefore not above taking advantage of a young girl (a 'chick'), given a suitably lonely place (*Heide*, 'moorland'). The motif of doubling is graphically increased by the doubled dot of the umlaut in 'Dubblänn,' with the ending '-länn' – a variant of *land* ('land, province') that occurs frequently in Swedish place names – suggesting a Scandinavian extension of a Dublin founded by Scandinavians. Bindervoet and Henkes, as usual rendering the initials *HCE* by their chosen *HKI*, alter 'Hyde and Cheek' to 'Hiero Kijkdan,' a Greek *hieros* ('holy') unexpectedly elevating HKI to sainthood, though his ostensible sanctity is somewhat undermined by the fact that Dutch *kijken*, as in 'Kijkdan,' means 'to have a peep,' which advice the sainted sinner of Scandinavian origin (Swedish *dan*, 'Dane') already appears to have followed all too enthusiastically. The new Eden of 'Edenberry,' meanwhile, is transformed under the tutelage of the sainted HKI and with the assistance of the Dutch *ijveren* ('to be industrious') into a thoroughly modern 'Ieveransburgh,' a hive of industry. *Laborare*, after all, *est orare*: to work is to pray.

Schüler, finally, ignoring HCE's initials, transforms 'Hyde and Cheek' into a Portuguese 'Guarda e Busca,' literally 'Hide and Seek.' The gentlemen so named are now, it emerges, residents of 'Edenossementópolis polis,' a name that brings us graphically back to Bygmester Finnegan and his erections, architectural and otherwise. For 'Edenossementópolis polis' is a new 'Eden' that is also (*ou*, 'or') a city (Greek *polis*), doubling all the time ('-polis polis') as a result of the continued industrious use by its citizens – introduced by a parodic Portuguese pronunciation of the Swiss term for a citizen, *Eidgenosse* – of both *cimento* ('cement') and *sêmen* ('semen'). The city in question is now called 'Dubelém,' substituting a 'double *m*' for a double *n*, since a Portuguese 'Dublin' is properly called *Dublim*, but also, since this particular 'Dubelém' is clearly a city capable of producing a new saviour, including the hopeful further designation *Belém* ('Bethlehem'). In geographical rather than biblical terms, and still doubling all the time, Dublin on the Liffey is conflated with the Brazilian city of Belém on the Amazon, named for the biblical Bethlehem.

Humphrey's fordofhurdlestown   (*FW* 203.6–7)

Lavergne (French, 1982): le Gué des Haies de Humphrey

García Tortosa (Spanish, 1992): villalosvadosdevallas de Humphrey

Aixàs (Catalan, 2004): les ciutats emmurallades de Humphrey

Schüler (Portuguese, 2003): Humphrey, próspera aldeia

Amarante (Portuguese, 2009): cidadevaubstáculo de Humphrey

Goyert (German, 1970): Humphreys Fordofherdlestown

Hildesheimer (German, 1969 / 1970): Humphreys Hinderfürt

Wollschläger (German, 1970): Humphreys FortvonHürdelstadt

Stündel (German, 1993): Hamfriß VorderhördelStädtchen

Bindervoet and Henkes (Dutch, 2002): Humphreys voordvanhordenstad

Grut (Swedish, 2001): Humphreys vadställstad

Słomczyński (Polish, 1985): groduznadbroduzsitowia Humphreya

Weatherall et al. (Czech, 1932 / 1996): Honzíkova Srubprutbrod

'Humphrey's fordofhurdlestown' is Dublin by its other name, *baile* ('town') *átha* ('of the ford') *cliath* ('of hurdles'). Oddly enough, several translators do not seem to catch the reference. Schüler's Portuguese, for example, speaks of 'Humphrey, próspera aldeia' (literally 'Humphrey, a flourishing village'), as if *Humphrey* were the name of the 'village.' Aixàs's Catalan version speaks of 'les ciutats emmurallades de Humphrey' ('the walled cities of Humphrey'), as if there were several cities involved, all walled. Lavergne speaks of 'le Gué des Haies de Humphrey,' literally 'Humphrey's ford (*gué*) of the hurdles (*haies*),' as if there were no town at all involved. García Tortosa's Spanish version, seduced by the musicality of its own formulation, speaks of Humphrey's 'villalosvadosdevallas,' literally 'town (*villa*) of the fords (*vado*, 'ford') of hurdles (*valla*, 'hurdle'), as if there were several fords. Grut's Swedish speaks of Humphrey's 'vadställstad' or 'town (*stad*) of the ford (*vadställe*),' as if there were no hurdles. Amarante's Portuguese speaks of Humphrey's 'cidadevaubstáculo,' or 'city (*cidade*) of the ford (*vau*) of the obstacle (*obstáculo*),' as if the hurdles were of the kind to be jumped rather than walked over.

All four German translators choose to indulge in wordplay that is not called for by the original. Goyert's 'Fordofherdlestown' retains but attempts to improve on Joyce's English by introducing 'herds' crossing over the 'hurdles.' Hildesheimer's 'Hinderfürt' is silent about the town, and suggests a 'ford' (*Furt*) that constitutes a hurdle to be negotiated, 'impeding' passage (*hindern*, 'to impede') as much as it 'leads' (*führt*) across the river. Stündel, having rendered 'Humphrey's' phonetically as 'Hamfriß,' goes on to speak of a 'VorderhördelStädtchen,' which combines a translingual 'ford' ('Vord-'), the phrase *vor der Stadt* ('outside the town'), a *Städtchen* ('little town'), and the German *Hürde* ('hurdle') with a quasi-phonetic rendering ('-hördel-') of the English *hurdle*. Wollschläger's 'FortvonHürdelstadt' accurately suggests a 'town' (*Stadt*) by a 'ford' (*Furt*) of 'hurdles' (*Hürde* 'hurdle') but also suggests the wisdom of getting 'away' (*fort*) from 'Hurdletown' (*Hürdelstadt*). Bindervoet and Henkes, finally, are alone in referring soberly and accurately to a 'voordvanhordenstad,' a 'town' (*stad*) by a 'ford' (*voorde*) of 'hurdles' (*horde*, 'hurdle'). The Dutch noun *horde*, as it happens, can mean either 'hurdle' or 'horde,' thus allowing readers who wish to do so to see hordes of people over the centuries trooping across the river over the wickerwork ford that has proved to be such a surprisingly difficult hurdle for so many of our translators.

Don Dom Dombdomb and his wee follyo! (FW 197.18)

Péron and Beckett (French, 1985 / 1996): Don Dom Dombdomb et sa p'tite fïïaut

Beckett and Joyce (French, 1931 / 1996): Dom Dom Dombdomb et elvette sa mie

Lavergne (French, 1982): Dom Dombdomb et le oui inouï de son folio

Joyce and Frank (Italian, 1979 / 1996): Don Dom Dolomuto e la piccia pazzetta

García Tortosa (Spanish, 1992): Tal Chal Chalá y su folla filena

Aixàs (Catalan, 2004): Don Dom Domdomb i el seu consegüent ploriqueig

Schüler (Portuguese, 2003): Dom Dom-dom e a sim fonia nupcial

Amarante (Portuguese, 2009): Dim Don Dombdomb e sua pequenina loucura

Goyert (German, 1970): Don, Dom, Domdomb und sein leises, flustiges Folio

Hildesheimer (German, 1969 / 1970): Don di thaka und sein flüsstrig Gefölgchen

Wollschläger (German, 1970): Don Dom Dombdomb und sein ouindsickes Follyo

Stündel (German, 1993): Don Domdie Dumpflin und sein kleinäß Gehfolgde

Bindervoet and Henkes (Dutch, 2002): Don Dom Dongdong en zijn memeltje jans

Grut (Swedish, 2001): Don Dum Dumpdump med fistligt följe

Słomczyński (Polish, 1985): Don Dom Dombdąb i jego tycie follistki

Weatherall et al. (Czech, 1932 / 1996): Don Dóm Dumdúm a jeho manýčké archibláznovství

Numerous variations occur in the *Wake* on Lady Morgan's alliterative formulation 'dear dirty Dublin.' Nor are HCE and ALP alone in boasting identifying acrostic initials, for the sequence *DDD* also occurs in a wide variety of different contexts. In the present reference we find a particularly rich combination of interactions between all three, for the phrase 'Don Dom Dombdomb' evokes Dublin in its initials, HCE in its tone, and ALP in its fluvial references.

'Don' combines a Spanish title of respect (*Don*) and invokes Russian, English, Scottish, and Canadian Don Rivers; 'Dom' combines a Portuguese title of respect (*Dom*), a dialect variant (*dom*) of Romany *rom* ('man'), and the Dutch *dom* ('foolish'). 'Domb,' doubled, is the colloquial English 'dumb, stupid,' the name of the French lake district les Dombes, near Lyon, and the Hungarian *domb* ('hill'). Following on an immediately preceding suggestion (*FW* 197.11–13) that the union of HCE and ALP may be of questionable legitimacy, the rhythm also evokes the opening chords of Wagner's wedding march from *Lohengrin* (Tindall 1996, 143). As for 'his wee follyo,' 'wee' suggests both 'small' and French *oui* à la Molly Bloom; it is also a child's expression for urine, and a 'wee folly' might suggest public urination, one possible variation of HCE's possible crime; 'follyo' hesitates between *folly*, *follower*, and *folio* (such as *Ulysses* – or *Finnegans Wake* itself) as well as suggesting the Folly River of South Carolina and the Hungarian *folyo* ('river'). The phrase as a whole can be taken as equally uncomplimentary to HCE and ALP: the 'dumbness' of the *domb* and the 'folly' of the *follyo*.

Other than Wollschläger's German, the only version to retain Joyce's original 'Don Dom Dombdomb' exactly is Péron and Beckett's French. The Beckett and Joyce rendering opts instead for 'Dom Dom Dombdomb,' casually dropping the fluvial references to the many Don Rivers. In Joyce and Frank's Italian rendering, however, 'Don Dom Dolomuto' reintroduces the Don, embellishes Wagner by two extra notes, and specifies HCE not only as a mountain range (the Dolomites) but also as being a 'fraud' (*dolo*) as well as 'dumb' (*muto*).

Of the other translators, no two agree on exactly which variations are most called for. Aixàs's 'Don Dom Domdomb,' Goyert's 'Don, Dom, Domdomb,' and Weatherall's 'Don Dóm Dumdúm' depart from the original only fairly minimally. Amarante's 'Dim Don Dombdomb' and Grut's 'Don Dum Dumpdump' contribute the English *dim* and the Swedish *dum* ('stupid) to the chorus, while Bindervoet and Henkes's 'Don Dom Dongdong' rings a change ('dongdong') on the Wagnerian motif, which has been respected, together with the *DDD* motif, by all our translators so far. Stündel's 'Don Domdie Dumpflin' extends Wagner by a beat, introduces a hint ('Domdie') of Humpty Dumpty and another ('Dumpflin') of Dublin, and augments the stupidity motif with a German *dumpf* ('dull, stupid'). Lavergne's 'Dom Dombdomb' and Schüler's 'Dom Dom-dom' abandon Wagner while retaining the initials *DDD*. The greatest deviations are Hildesheimer's 'Don di thaka,' referring somewhat unexpectedly to Ulysses, the 'gentleman (Spanish *Don*) from Ithaca' (German *Ithaka*), and García Tortosa's 'Tal Chal Chalá,' confirming that HCE is indeed *chalado* ('muddle-headed'), a Mr Muddle Muddlehead. Both Hildesheimer and García Tortosa retain the Wagnerian rhythm but, unlike others of the group, surprisingly abandon the echo of 'dear dirty Dublin.'

'His wee follyo' evokes a much greater range of responses and a quite remarkable degree of semantic scatter. We may in fact distinguish at least five groups of responses, though with a significant degree of overlapping between the groups.

A first group of responses focuses primarily on the fluvial reference suggested by the Hungarian *folyo* ('river') in 'follyo.' Péron and Beckett thus render the phrase in French as 'sa p'tite fiïaut,' conflating 'little girl' (*fillette*) and 'river' (*folyo*). Beckett and Joyce opt for 'elvette sa mie,' where 'elvette' plays on the relationship between Norwegian *elv* ('river') and Danish *elv* ('elf') as well as that between Swedish *älv* ('river') and *älva* ('elf'). Combined with the French *mie* ('sweetheart'), the phrase suggests something like 'his elfin little river sweetheart.' Hildesheimer's 'sein flüsstrig Gefölgchen' undertakes a combination of German *Fluss* ('river'), *flüstern* ('to whisper'), and *lustig* ('cheerful') as the qualities informing his *Gefolge* ('following, retinue'), personalized by the use of the diminutive (as in 'wee') *Gefölgchen*.

A second group of responses concentrates instead on the madness suggested by the possible 'folly' in 'follyo.' Joyce and Frank's Italian rendering, for example, 'la piccia pazzetta,' ignores rivers, Hungarian or otherwise, in referring to a clinging (*appiccicare*, 'to cling') little 'madwoman' (*pazza*). Wollschläger's formulation 'sein ouindsickes Follyo' retains the original 'follyo,' qualifying it by an adjectival form that combines German *winzig* ('wee, tiny'), French *oui* (à la Molly Bloom again), English *wee*, and, somewhat unexpectedly, English *sick*, adding a dark note to the 'folly' of the 'follyo.' Amarante's Portuguese opts for 'sua pequenina loucura,' literally 'his tiny (-*ina*) little (*pequena*) crazy thing (*loucura*).' Weatherall's Czech version, 'jeho manýcké archibláznovství,' uses 'manýcké' to combine *maličký* ('small') and *mánie*, while *mánie* and *bláznovství* both mean 'madness,' resulting in something like 'his mad, crazy little folly.'

A third group focuses on childish silliness rather than madness. Grut's Swedish, ignoring any fluvial reference, sees the 'wee follyo' as a 'fistligt följe,' where *fistligt* means 'piping' and *följe* means 'retinue' but also hints at *fjolla* ('silly little girl'), thus suggesting a 'silly little hanger-on twittering away.' Bindervoet and Henkes opt for 'zijn memelt-je jans,' where 'jans' plays on a provincial north German pronuncia-tion of Dutch *gans* ('goose'), and the *Memel* is the German name of the Lithuanian river Neman, suggesting something like 'his silly little goose from the bogs of Lithuania.' Aixàs's Catalan version has 'seu consegüent ploriqueig,' literally 'his crybaby (*plorar*, "to cry") follow-ing him,' the fluvial reference now supplied by tears.

A fourth group concentrates primarily on the possible 'follower' sug-gested by 'follyo.' Stündel's 'sein kleinäß Gehfolgde,' for example, has a surface meaning of 'his little following,' where *klein* ('little') is com-bined with *nass* ('wet') and *Gefolge* ('following') with *gehen* ('to go'). García Tortosa's version prefers 'su folla filena,' where 'folla' includes Spanish *folla* ('entertainment'), Italian *folla* ('crowd'), French *folle* ('cra-zy'), and Spanish *folio* ('folio'), suggesting 'his dainty (*filena*), crazy, and amusing little (*filena*) literary entourage.'

A fifth group of responses focuses instead on the reference to a book suggested by the possible 'folio' in 'follyo.' Goyert's 'sein leises, flustig-es Folio' thus combines *Fluss* ('river') and *lustig* ('cheerful') to mean approximately 'his quiet (*leise*), cheerful, fluvial folio,' German *Folio* un-ambiguously referring to a book – once again either *Ulysses* or *Finnegans Wake*. Lavergne's French, on the other hand, playing on French *oui* and *inouï* and English *wee*, chooses to employ an idiosyncratic 'le oui inouï de son folio,' literally 'the unheard of *yes* of his folio,' the folio in ques-tion identified in a footnote as *Ulysses* and the *yes* that of Molly Bloom.

One version, finally, rejects all of these strategies. Schüler's Portuguese abandons almost all the implications of the 'wee follyo' considered so far in favour of strengthening the Wagnerian echo with what he sees as primarily 'a sim fonia nupcial,' Wagner's march temporarily inflated into a 'wedding symphony' (*sinfonia*) and the symphony split ('sim fo-nia') into two parts, in order to permit the trilingual pun on Portuguese *sim* ('yes'), French *oui*, and English *wee*.

   for to ishim bonzour to her dear dubber Dan   (FW 199.13–14)

   Péron and Beckett (French, 1985 / 1996): Dan son cher paramourin

   Beckett and Joyce (French, 1931 / 1996): son cher Gouten Tage

   Lavergne (French, 1982): de la part de son cher Dublin

Joyce and Frank (Italian, 1979 / 1996): su' Rumoloremus

García Tortosa (Spanish, 1992): su divo dublio Dan

Aixàs (Catalan, 2004): seu estimat honorable Senyor

Schüler (Portuguese, 2003): seu Divo Doce Dom

Amarante (Portuguese, 2009): seu amado atrapalhado Dublinamarquês

Goyert (German, 1970): irm jieben dubber Dan

Hildesheimer (German, 1969 / 1970): ihrem turtelteuren Tauber

Wollschläger (German, 1970): ijrem deuren Drommler Dan

Stündel (German, 1993): ihrem lippen gotan Danblin

Bindervoet and Henkes (Dutch, 2002): haar duero drabber Dann

Grut (Swedish, 2001): Dan sin raske nordanman

Słomczyński (Polish, 1985): drogi dober Dan

Weatherall et al. (Czech, 1932 / 1996): svému miláčku, Dober Danu

One more implied reference to 'dear dirty Dublin' occurs when ALP is described in baby language as having a desire 'for to ishim bonzour to her dear dubber Dan.' A *dub* in colloquial Dublin usage is a native Dubliner. Dublin having been founded by Scandinavians, many native Dubliners will have some or much of the 'Dane' (Swedish *dan*) in them. According to legend, Denmark is named for an eponymous *Dan*, and the country is called *Danmark* both in Old Norse and in modern Danish. ALP's desire to wish 'bonzour' (French *bonjour*, 'good day') to her HCE is inspired by the fact that 'dubber Dan' is a close approximation to 'good day' in Slovene (*dober dan*) and both Serbian and Croatian (*dobar dan*). Multiculturalism and multilingualism are thus the order of the day in a suggested linguistic brew of English, French, Danish, and two or three Slavic languages. Some of ALP's riverine relations are also not forgotten, specifically the Russian river Ishim, the American river Dan, the Israeli river Dan, and, closer to home, nearby Lough Dan in County Wicklow.

Limiting ourselves to versions of the phrase 'her dear dubber Dan,' we discover a significant variety of responses.

One group ignores completely the triple-*d* signal of 'dear dirty Dublin.' Foremost among these are Péron and Beckett, Beckett and Joyce, and Joyce and Frank. Péron and Beckett's 'Dan son cher paramourin' limits itself to 'her dear darling Dan,' substituting an approximate rhyme for the relevant initials. Beckett and Joyce's 'son cher Gouten Tage' merely offers a humorous French mispronunciation of the German *Guten Tag* ('good day'), likewise abandoning any implied reference to Dublin, but adding references to the Chinese river Ou and the Iberian Tagus (French *Tage*). Joyce and Frank's 'su' Rumoloremus' plays on the founders of Rome instead, Romulus and Remus, while invoking the Tanzanian Umo and Kenyan Molo Rivers as well as exhorting to prayer (Latin *oremus*, 'let us pray'). Aixàs's Catalan speaks only of 'seu estimat honorable Senyor,' literally 'her dear (*estimat*) respected lord.' Amarante's version, playing on Portuguese *Dinamarca* ('Denmark') and *dinamarquês* ('Danish'), speaks of 'seu amado atrapalhado Dublinamarquês,' thus approximately 'her beloved (*amado*) but confused (*atrapalhado*) Dublin Dane' – who also turns out to be in fact a marquis (*marquês*). Grut's version, playing on Swedish *dan* ('Dane'), *Norden* ('Scandinavia'), and *man* ('man'), speaks of 'Dan sin raske nordanman,' suggesting 'her lusty (*rask*) Viking Dane.' Stündel's 'ihrem lippen gotan Danblin' provides as a surface meaning ALP's greeting, sealed with a kiss (*Lippen*, 'lips'), 'to her dear good Danblin' (*ihrem lieben guten Danblin*), with the element of foreignness strongly accentuated, however, not only by replacing the *dub* of *Dublin* by a *Dan* or 'Dane' but also by implying that her Dan may in fact have Gothic as well as Danish origins (*ihrem lieben Goten*, 'to her dear Goth').

A second group considers the triple-*d* signal essential, even at the cost in some cases of considerable simplification. García Tortosa's 'su divo dublio Dan' approximates to 'her divine Dublin Dan.' Schüler's Portuguese has her greet 'seu Divo Doce Dom,' literally 'her saintly (*divo*) sweet (*doce*) lord (*dom*),' his foreign origins ignored. Bindervoet and Henkes, playing on the Spanish river Duero and the Dutch *drab* ('sediment, river mud'), opt for 'haar duero drabber Dann,' thus roughly 'her dear (*duur*, "expensive") muddy (*drabbig*) Dann.' Wollschläger's 'ijrem deuren Drommler Dan,' changing the context significantly, speaks in baby German of 'her dear drummer Dan' (*ihrem teuren Trommler Dan*), the use of baby language and the reference to the Dutch river Dommel helping to retain the triple-*d* sequence. Słomczyński's Polish rendering, 'drogi dober Dan,' is one of the versions closest to Joyce's original, neatly conflating 'dubber Dan' and a Slovene *dober dan*.

A third group attempts a variety of compromise positions. Goyert's 'irm jieben dubber Dan' replicates the original in German baby language. Weatherall's 'svému miláčku, Dober Danu,' translates as 'to her deary (miláčku), Dober Dan.' Hildesheimer's 'ihrem turtelteuren Tauber' translates roughly as 'to her dear turtle dove,' Joyce's 'dubber' evidently evoking images of a German 'dove' (Taube), which in turn evokes a 'turtle dove' (Turteltaube), the triple-d sequence becoming a triple-t sequence in the process. Lavergne's French, finally, misreads the phrase as involving greetings sent to persons unknown 'de la part de son cher Dublin,' literally 'on behalf of her dear Dublin.'

the quaggy waag for stumbling   (FW 197.25–6)

Péron and Beckett (French, 1985 / 1996): la bourbouroute de Manquemartre

Beckett and Joyce (French, 1931 / 1996): surlaroutant viers lou capliot

Lavergne (French, 1982): un endroit bien sombre pour y faire un faux pas

Joyce and Frank (Italian, 1979 / 1996): la lunga via dell'erto

García Tortosa (Spanish, 1992): calce carruna a du clin

Aixàs (Catalan, 2004): camí llacós que duu a empentes i a rodolons a Dublín

Schüler (Portuguese, 2003): chão pantanoso, pesado pros passos

Amarante (Portuguese, 2009): o pantanoso caminho para tropeçar

Goyert (German, 1970): nach dem waagen Moor, stolperdiholper

Hildesheimer (German, 1970): ein morastiger Waag für den Stolper

Wollschläger (German, 1970): so recht ein Wehwehglein zum Stolperdihalp

Stündel (German, 1993): den steignicken Werrag nach Staptin

Bindervoet and Henkes (Dutch, 2002): in drechte struikelweg naar kromlin

Grut (Swedish, 2001): löftslott för fasafullt fall

Słomczyński (Polish, 1985): z odwaagą pośród bagien

Weatherall et al. (Czech, 1932 / 1996): klopýtaje přes váhavý váh

Finnegans Wake also contains several variations on the theme of 'the rocky road to Dublin.' The road of the well-known humorous nineteenth-century ballad of that name may preserve a memory of the ancient route called the *Slí Cualann* ('Cuala Way'), which ran from the royal site of Tara in modern County Meath to the district of Cuala in what is now County Wicklow by way of the ford of hurdles over the Liffey called *Áth Cliath* ('ford of hurdles'). It has been suggested that the *Slí Cualann* reached the ford from the north by the route now called Stoneybatter, which – since 'batter' is a very approximate anglicization of the Irish *bóthar* ('road') – may thus be the original Rocky Road (Mink 1978, 295). The route humorously described in the modern ballad, however, runs more or less at right angles to this, from Tuam in County Galway by way of Mullingar in County Westmeath to Dublin (and eventually Liverpool).

Resisting the temptation to explore transtextual variations on such competitors as 'the lucky load to Lublin' (*FW* 565.22) or 'the rollcky road adondering' (*FW* 623.24), we will reluctantly limit our explorations to just one iteration of the theme, 'the quaggy waag for stumbling,' in which the London river Quaggy, the African river Quagua, the Slovak river Waag (otherwise Váh), and the obsolete English *quag* ('bog') combine to suggest a rocky, boggy, quaggy way (German *Weg*, 'way') for stumbling towards an interlingual Dublin.

Among those versions that see the rocky road as indeed leading to Dublin, Aixàs's Catalan is direct and expansive, describing a 'boggy way (*camí llacós*) that leads, up and down (*a empentes*) and around and about (*a rodolons*), to Dublin.' Stündel prefers to think of the original rocky road rather than a quaggy road, referring thus to 'den steignicken Werrag,' where the invented adjective 'steignick' conflates *steinig* ('stony') and *steigen* ('to climb uphill') and invokes the idiomatic German phrase *ein steiniger Weg* ('a path of trial and tribulation'), avoiding the play on the Slovak Waag for one on the German river Werra, on the road to 'Staptin,' which ambitiously combines *stolpern* ('to stumble') and a Dublin almost completely submerged by the Indian river Tapti.

Bindervoet and Henkes describe a 'drechte struikelweg,' where 'drechte' combines Dutch *recht* ('straight') and *drek* ('muck'), defining a 'struikelweg' or a way where one might very well 'stumble' (*struikelen*)

on the way to 'kromlin,' the Dublin suburb of Crumlin here doing duty for the city as a whole. The Irish form of the name *Crumlin*, namely *croimghleann* ('crooked glen'), is evoked by the Dutch *krom* ('crooked'), hinting once more at the all too present possibility of straying off the straight and narrow path. García Tortosa's Spanish rendering, on the other hand, the complexity of which (here as elsewhere) more than rivals the deliberate obfuscation of the Celtic druids, goes to extraordinary lengths to avoid that path. His 'calce carruna a du clin' may possibly refer to a 'cart' (*carro*) equipped with a 'brake' (*calce*) on its way to 'du clin,' invokes in passing the English river Arun and the French river Doubs, and seems to acknowledge with a conspiratorial 'wink' (French *clin*) that the French Doubs, pronounced /du/, and the Irish city of Dublin share an etymology in the Common Celtic *dubus* ('black'). A triple-*c* sequence of initials evokes triple-*d* sequences elsewhere.

Several versions, however, more or less ignore Dublin altogether, prominent among them once more being Péron and Beckett, Beckett and Joyce, and Joyce and Frank. Péron and Beckett's 'la bourbouroute de Manquemartre' transfers the action from Dublin to Paris, and a boggy route through mire (*bourbe*) and mud (*boue*) towards a Montmartre that will turn out after all the effort to be missing (*manquer*) its martyr. Beckett and Joyce's 'surlaroutant viers lou capliot' has its wanderer wending a circuitous way along the route (*sur la route*) 'towards the capital' (*vers la capitale*) by way of the Spanish river Viar, the French rivers Viaur, Loue, and Lot, and what appears to be a cape (*cap*) but confusingly turns out to be something like an island (*ilôt*). Joyce and Frank's Italian wanderer merely undertakes a more straightforward 'lunga via dell'erto,' the 'long way up the steep (*erto*) hill (*erta*).' Lavergne, for his part, perceives only 'un endroit bien sombre' ('a very dark place') all too suitable 'pour y faire un faux pas' ('for taking a false step'). Schüler's Portuguese sees only a 'swampy (*pantanoso*) place (*chão*) where it is difficult (*pesado*) for walking (*pros passos*),' and Amarante's Portuguese likewise presents a 'swampy (*pantanoso*) way (*caminho*) for stumbling (*para tropeçar*).' The 'quaggy waag' becomes a more or less literally translated 'morastiger Waag' for Hildesheimer, who indulges in a similar play of words to Joyce, 'für den Stolper' ('for a stumble'). Wollschläger's 'ein Wehwehglein' employs children's language instead to suggest a 'little road' (*Weglein*) that might well cause a minor scrape or scratch (*Wehweh*) as a result of 'slipping and stumbling' ('Stolperdihalp').

Goyert, while retaining the river Waag and contributing a new reference to the Australian Moore River, misunderstands the action as progressing in the wrong direction, not towards Dublin but 'slipping and stumbling' (*stolperdiholper*) 'nach dem waagen Moor,' namely 'towards the moorland' that is at once *vag* ('vague, indistinct') and related to the Waag. Weatherall's Czech, meanwhile, seizing enthusiastically on the fact that the river Waag in German is the river Váh in Czech, prefers to concentrate in Slavic vein on the fate of one 'hesitating (*váhat*) indecisively (*váhavý*)' while 'stumbling (*klopýtající*)' not towards Dublin but over (*přes*) the Váh. Grut's Swedish, finally, veers even more adventurously off the beaten track, going very much its own way in replacing the 'quaggy waag for stumbling' by an alliterative 'löftslott för fasafullt fall,' which combines a *löfte* ('promise') and a *luftslott* ('castle in the air') going before (*före*) a 'fall' (*fall*) full of 'horror' (*fasa*) to produce something like 'a promising illusion going before a horrible fall.'

Having already looked in some detail in an earlier chapter at the 'Fiendish Park,' we will finish off our account of dear dirty Dublin by briefly visiting three of its outlying environs: Howth, Chapelizod, and that Irish Garden of Eden, the County Wicklow.

Hofed-ben-Edar (FW 30.11)

Lavergne (French, 1982): Hofed-ben-Edar

Schenoni (Italian, 1982): Hofed-ben-Edar

Schüler (Portuguese, 2003): Coco-bem-Quisto

Pagán (Galician, 2000): Hofed-ben-Edar

Rathjen (German, 1989): Hofed-ben-Edar

Stoltefuß (German, 1989): Hofed ben Edar

Stündel (German, 1993): Haupt-ben-Edda

Bindervoet and Henkes (Dutch, 2002): Hofed-ben-Edair

From the opening sentence, as we have already seen, HCE is associated with Howth – and Howth, of course, was not always *Howth*. The earliest recorded name is that employed by the Greek geographer Ptolemy, writing in the second century AD, who called the promontory *Adrou hérēmos* ('the solitude of Adros'), a name subsequently latinized as *Edri deserta* ('the solitude of Edrus') (Mink 1978, 345). Whether this Adros or Edrus can be identified with the Étar for whom the promontory was known in Old Irish as *Benn Étair* ('Étar's headland') is unclear, but the latter name eventually developed into the modern Irish *Binn Édair* ('Édar's headland'), explained in traditional topographical lore as being named for a pre-Celtic Tuatha Dé Danann chief allegedly buried on the hill. By some point in the ninth or tenth century, new Danish Viking settlers were calling the promontory first simply *Hofuth*, from the Old Norse *hofuth* ('head'), and later *Hoved*, from the Danish *hoved* ('head'). In the course of time and history, *Hoved*, which in Danish eventually came to be pronounced /ˈhoːðə/, in turn became meaningless, and the Danish name was corrupted by subsequent waves of invaders, Norman and English, into the present-day *Howth*.

The phrase 'Hofed-ben-Edar' plays on the linguistic abrasions and corruptions that inevitably accompany the course of history. Place (Danish *Hoved*, Irish *Binn Édair*) ostensibly becomes person ('Hofed, son of Edar') courtesy of a Hebrew *ben* ('son') that supplants the Old Irish *benn* ('mountain, headland') – just as his own sons will inevitably supplant the man-mountain HCE. The hint of Dutch *hoofd* ('head') offered by the altered spelling of *Hoved* further suggests the advent of one more wave of invaders with the late-seventeenth-century arrival of William of Orange's Dutch followers in an English cause.

The range of translated responses is narrow, but interesting in the context. Four of eight translators (Lavergne, Schenoni, Pagán, Rathjen) are content to retain Joyce's English formulation unchanged in their respective French, Italian, Galician, and German. Stoltefuß's German, by dispensing with the hyphens, underlines the status of Hofed-ben-Edar as person rather than location. Bindervoet and Henkes's Dutch, with 'Hofed-ben-Edair,' silently corrects in passing Joyce's Irish (but not necessarily his Hebrew). Stündel's 'Haupt-ben-Edda,' on the other hand, substitutes a German *Haupt* ('head') for an originally Danish *hoved*, but compensates for this by substituting for an originally Irish *Étar* or *Édar* a punning Scandinavian *Edda*, thus simultaneously evoking not only the destructive raids of the Vikings on Irish shores but also one of the highlights of Old Norse literature and culture, the collection of mythological and poetic materials first written down in Iceland during the thirteenth century. The most idiosyncratic response is certainly Schüler's humorous Portuguese version, 'Coco-bem-Quisto,' in which Portuguese *bem* ('well') trumps both the Old Irish *benn* ('headland') and the Hebrew *ben* ('son'); where 'Coco' combines Portuguese *coco* ('coconut') and *cocó* ('coiffure'), both relating to a 'head,' whether Danish or not; where *bem quisto* means 'well beloved'; and where *quisto* also means 'cyst,' both *quisto* and *cyst* deriving from the Greek *kystis* ('bladder') – resulting as the parodic sum of these interlingual wanderings in a distinctly outlandish 'Bladder-Head the Well-Beloved.' Some readers would undoubtedly have considerable difficulty with Schüler's flaunted deviation from Joyce's text here. Joyce himself, however, would almost certainly have approved.

Shop Illicit (FW 29.1)

Lavergne (French, 1982): Echoppe illicite

Schenoni (Italian, 1982): Shop Illicit

Schüler (Portuguese, 2003): Mercado Ilícito

Pagán (Galician, 2000): Chupa Ilícito

Stündel (German, 1993): Schüpp idizoot

Bindervoet and Henkes (Dutch, 2002): Kot Illiciet

If the village of Chapelizod had not already existed, Joyce would undoubtedly have had to invent it. Earwicker, a reincarnation of Finn MacCool, is a publican in Chapelizod, a village some three miles west of Dublin, situated between a weir and a bridge on the river Liffey and immediately adjacent to the 'Fiendish Park' that not only houses Finn's tumptytumtoes but also witnesses Earwicker's fall from grace. The meaning of the place name itself, as far as generations of readers were concerned, was authoritatively reported in such guides as Lewis's *Topographical Dictionary* of 1837, according to which Chapelizod 'is supposed to have derived its name from *La Belle Isode*, a daughter of one of the ancient Irish kings, who had a chapel here' (Lewis 1837, 1:320). Chapelizod also lies on both banks of the Liffey, just as the two rival brothers Shem and Shaun share incestuous fantasies of their sister (Mink 1978, 291). If all of this were not already enough, the name *Chapelizod* also contains, in addition to *Izod*, all (and only) the initials of both HCE and ALP. Often locally pronounced, finally, as if written 'Chapel Lizard' – and even appearing in this form in the first printed atlas of Ireland, Sir William Petty's *Hiberniae Delineatio* of 1685 (Mink 1978, 256) – the name also serves, to repeat a point already made, as one further suggestion of HCE's animality.

The actual origin of the name, it may be mentioned in passing, is uncertain. According to the *Placenames Database of Ireland* (www .logainm.ie), it may have originally referred simply to some local family bearing the well-documented English surname *Izod* or *Izard*. Alternatively, an early form *Chapel Isirt* suggests that it may be a corruption of an Irish *Séipéal an Disirt* ('hermitage chapel'). The association with Iseult dates back at least to the sixteenth-century Irish historian Richard Stanyhurst, whose *De rebus in Hibernia gestis* (1584) associates the name with 'la belle Isoude.' Sir Thomas Malory's *Le morte d'Arthur*, which includes a version of the story of Tristram and La Beale Iseult, had appeared almost exactly a century before, in 1485, followed by multiple reprints.

Of the numerous references in the *Wake* to a variously transmogrified Chapelizod, 'Shop Illicit' (*FW* 29.1) elicits perhaps the most interesting transtextual commentary – specifically on HCE. Joyce's English (retained without change in Schenoni's Italian) refers to the name of the village, casts some doubt on the complete legality of Earwicker's behaviour as a licensee, and hints in passing ('-ici-') at the likewise illicit character of his more than paternal interest in his nubile daughter Issy. Lavergne's French and Pagán's Galician both succeed in replicating all three of these effects. Joyce's 'Shop' becomes Lavergne's 'Echoppe,' where French *échoppe*, its first three letters evoking HCE, literally means a 'street stall,' suggesting that Earwicker's establishment may be not only illicit but a ramshackle fly-by-night affair as well. Pagán's 'Chupa' conflates Galician *chupa* ('suck'), Portuguese *chope* ('draught beer'), and Galician *chepa* ('hump'), this last once again doubly identifying the establishment as CHE / HCE's. Bindervoet and Henkes, with 'Kot Illiciet,' retain the reference to Issy ('-ici-'), but Chapelizod is less in evidence than the 'filth' (German *Kot*) of the pigsty (Dutch *kot*, 'sty') under discussion. Stündel's 'Schüpp idizoot' conflates German *Schuppen* ('low dive') and *Schoppen* ('glass of beer'), identifies Iseult ('-izoot') in the Middle High German form *Isôt*, and is silent on any illicit doings or desires, suggesting instead merely that Earwicker is an *Idiot* ('idiot') and his tavern a *Zoo* ('zoo'). Schüler adopts a different strategy with 'Mercado Ilícito,' the Portuguese *mercado ilícito* ('illicit market') suggesting not only illegal street vending, but also a broad hint that HCE might even be prepared to sell his own daughter Issy ('-íci-') into the white slave trade. An oblique commentary may also be detected on similar basely mercenary motives on the part of HCE's avatar King Mark

(Portuguese *Marco*) in merely going shopping for an Irish wife, as opposed to the overwhelming and tragic passion that will come into being
between the doomed young lovers Tristan and Iseult.

> *in county Wickenlow, garden of Erin*   (*FW* 203.1)

Lavergne (French, 1982): au Comté de Wicklow, jardin d'Erin

Schenoni (Italian, 1996): nella contea di Wickenlow, giardino d'Erin

García Tortosa (Spanish, 1992): en el condado de Wickenlow, el
   jardín de Erín

Aixàs (Catalan, 2004): en el comptat de Wickenlow, jardí de l'Edèn

Schüler (Portuguese, 2003): jardim da Irlanda, parque de Erin

Amarante (Portuguese, 2009): no condado de Wickenlow, jardim de
   Erin

Goyert (German, 1970): in der Grafschaft Wickenlow, dem Garten
   von Erin

Hildesheimer (German, 1969 / 1970): in der Grafschaft Wickenloh,
   im Garten Erin

Wollschläger (German, 1970): im Wickenlow-Lande, im Garten Erin

Stündel (German, 1993): in Lande Fickenlau, dem Garrten von
   Erinn

Bindervoet and Henkes (Dutch, 2002): graafschap Wygyngelo, hof
   van Erin

Grut (Swedish, 2001): i Wicklow len, i Erins lustgård

Słomczyński (Polish, 1985): w hrabstwie Wickenlow, ogrodzie Erynu

Weatherall et al. (Czech, 1932 / 1996): v hrabství Kratiknotu, v
   zahradě Erinu

From Dublin and its closer environs, we move in conclusion slightly
further south to the smiling fields of neighbouring County Wicklow,
traditionally known as the Garden of Ireland. The county has long been
intimately associated with Dublin, most of its eastern half having once
been part, first, of the Danish *Dyfflinarskiri* and, subsequently, of the

English Pale, centred in both cases on the city of Dublin. The establishment of the modern county of Wicklow, indeed, dates only from 1606; before that date, most of its modern territory was still part of County Dublin.

The county is also strongly associated with both HCE and ALP. The main association with HCE, other than the Earwicker-evoking *wick-* of the county's name, is that Wicklow town, like Dublin, owes its urban origins to Vikings, who at some point during the late eighth or early ninth century founded a settlement near the earlier monastic site of *Cill Mhantáin* ('Mantán's church') that they called by the Old Norse name *Vikingrlo* ('Vikings' meadow'). Since the Old Norse *lo* literally means 'swamp, marsh, low-lying meadow near water' (Price 1967, 477), the urban association with HCE is supplemented by rural association with ALP. The most obvious association with ALP is provided by the fact that the Liffey rises in the Wicklow hills – alias 'the hillydroops of Vikloefells' (*FW* 626.17) – near Kippure mountain. It was here that ALP, a 'young thin pale soft shy slim slip of a thing' (*FW* 202.27), was first violated, 'when she was barely in her tricklies' (*FW* 126.13–14), by one Michael Arklow (*FW* 203.18), whose name suggests associations with both the county itself, the town of Arklow being situated in County Wicklow, and the likewise Scandinavian founders of that town, the Old Norse name of which, *Arnkell-lo*, designated it as the meadow land (*lo*) of a Viking named *Arnkell* (Price 1967, 477).

Joyce's formulation 'Wickenlow' rather than 'Wicklow' evokes earlier versions of the county's name through history, such as *Vikingrlo*, *Vikingalo*, *Wykyngelo*, and *Wickinlowe*, and thus also the Scandinavian origins of its county town. It may furthermore, in honour of ALP, be read as gesturing to Wicken Fen, one of the best known of the Great Fens of East Anglia. The formulation 'garden of Erin' rather than the more usual 'garden of Ireland' conjures up appropriate echoes of nineteenth-century Irish Romanticism in the vein of a Lady Morgan or a Thomas Moore.

Literal translations of the phrase 'in county Wickenlow' are provided by Goyert's German, García Tortosa's Spanish, Aixàs's Catalan, Amarante's Portuguese, Schenoni's Italian, and Słomczyński's Polish. Wollschläger's German 'im Wickenlow-Lande' refers more generally to the 'land of Wickenlow,' while Bindervoet and Henkes prefer a more flauntedly archaic spelling of the historical name of the county, opting for a Dutch 'graafschap Wygyngelo.' Lavergnes's French 'au Comté de Wicklow' and Grut's Swedish 'i Wicklow len' prefer to domesticate

Joyce's 'Wickenlow' in the respective target language by using its modern name, while Schüler's Portuguese avoids any mention at all of Wicklow, referring only to the 'jardim da Irlanda, parque de Erin' ('garden of Ireland, park of Erin').

Three versions undertake to superimpose a new layer of meaning on Joyce's phrase. Hildesheimer opts for 'in der Grafschaft Wickenloh,' incorporating the German *Lohe* ('blaze'), reflecting an earlier understanding of the Danish *lo* as meaning 'fire' and thus referring to Danish beacons on the coast – which elsewhere provides food for thought in the variation 'steynish beacons on toasc' (*FW* 199.17). Weatherall's 'v hrabství Kratiknotu,' playing on Czech *knot* ('wick') and *krátit* ('to shorten'), refers to the 'county' (*hrabství*) of, literally, 'shortened wick,' a county whose 'wick' is 'low.' Stündel's 'in Lande Fickenlau' plays much more drastically with the same concept, for a wick turned low burns less brightly, offering a sexual interpretation that the German translator is only too happy to exploit: his 'Fickenlau' less than elegantly combines the verb *ficken* ('to fuck') and a suggestion of a barely 'lukewarm' (*lau*) level of performance in that activity. Joyce himself, of course, might well have approved, using as he does the element *wick-* with overt sexual connotations in various other locations in 'Fenegans Wick' (*FW* 358.23), as in the phrases 'earing his wick' (*FW* 390.5) or 'wick-in-her' (*FW* 583.31).

Joyce's 'garden of Erin' is translated quite literally by nine of our fourteen translators, if we allow for some arbitrary doubling of consonants on Stündel's part ('Garrten von Erinn' for 'Garten von Erin,' perhaps suggesting a *Garten* run wild). Hildesheimer and Wollschläger agree on the rendering 'im Garten Erin,' which on the one hand might suggest that the garden in question is actually called *Erin* – but also immediately suggests for a German-speaking reader Luther's biblical phrasing of Adam and Eve's entry 'in den Garten Eden' ('into the Garden of Eden') (Genesis 2:15). That 'Wickenlow' might be the location of the Garden of Eden is a mere hint in Joyce's version, a hint that becomes considerably stronger in these two German versions. The hint hardens into a statement of geographical fact in Aixàs's Catalan 'jardí de l'Edèn,' where the 'Fiendish Park' is now unambiguously balanced by the 'Garden of Eden.'

In the charmed world of *Finnegans Wake*, meanwhile, the garden of 'Erin' is also host not only (geographically) to the Liffey but also (linguistically) to no less a river than the Rhine, which in several European languages is called the *Rin* (Spanish, Catalan, Galician, Romanian) or the *Rín* (Icelandic). Słomczyński's Polish version of the 'ogrodzie Erynu' ('garden of Erin') accommodates the same river not only as the Frisian *Ryn* but also as the Czech and Slovak *Rýn*. Our ALP, in her riverine progress from 'young thin pale soft shy slim slip of a thing' in the Wicklow hills to 'queer old Skeowsha' as she enters Dublin Bay, manages to accumulate some very impressive international congeners in some entirely unexpected locations.

Conclusion

where in the waste is the wisdom?

(*FW* 114.20)

In William York Tindall's memorable formulation, '*Finnegans Wake* is an imitation of life. Undiscouraged by what is beyond us in life or in this book of life, we must keep on trying ... Some things will yield some meaning somehow sometime. *Finnegans Wake*, then, is the record of reality, of man's attempt to explain it, and an invitation to explain. *Finnegans Wake* is about *Finnegans Wake*' (1959, 264). The *Wake* itself offers one opinion (among various others) on its own readability, referring to 'irremovable doubts as to the whole sense of the lot, the interpretation of any phrase in the whole, the meaning of every word of a phrase so far deciphered out of it' (*FW* 117.35–118.2). If this is true of the original *Wake* (and it is, of course), it is true *a fortiori* of its collective transpositions in multilingual would-be translation, now more than ever an exponentially 'overgrown babeling' (*FW* 6.31) in 'lashons of languages' (*FW* 29.32).

The central contention of this book has been, quite simply, that one may interestingly conceive of a macrotextual *Finnegans Wake* including not only Joyce's original text but also, in principle, all its existing translations. The further assumption has been that it is also interesting to attempt to gain some limited access to this macrotext by means of a comparative reading of selected excerpts from the original text rendered into a variety of languages. The point, in principle once again, has not been to judge these would-be translations by their degree of perceived fidelity or lack of fidelity to Joyce's original. The point has been rather to examine the multifarious ways in which the text that Joyce for many years called *Work in Progress* is kept in continual multilingual progress, is extended rather than distorted by these various renderings considered collectively, even though any one of them, considered individually, is of course open in principle, if to varying degrees, to the charge of distortion.

While triumphantly impaling translators on their perceived mistakes has consequently not been any significant part of the exercise, there is nonetheless an obvious interest in considering which translations can be said to have succeeded more adequately or less adequately in the daunting task of transposing into a foreign language, even very partially, 'the hoax that joke bilked' (*FW* 511.34). The following remarks are based almost entirely on the limited number of excerpts considered. Certain broad characteristics of particular renderings nevertheless do become apparent as one compares and contrasts the solutions they propose to particular textual challenges.

It will have become apparent that would-be translations of and from *Finnegans Wake* fall into three broad categories: *explanatory* versions attempting to identify what appears to the particular translator to be at least the surface meaning of the text; *imitative* versions attempting to reproduce as faithfully as possible the play of the text, including as far as possible some rendering of its pervasively flaunted polysemy; and *competitive* versions attempting to outdo Joyce at his own game, utilizing the original text as a springboard for displays of verbal pyrotechnics whose relevance may at least occasionally be obscure. Typically, the first category tends to be overly simplistic, the third category tends to be overly complex, and the middle category attempts with varying degrees of desperation, humorous or otherwise, to adhere to more or less normal translational practice, however impossible that attempt frequently demonstrates itself to be. These categories, it need hardly be said, are found in anything like pure form only in renderings of very short passages of text; in longer renderings each of the three will certainly be found, and all three may sometimes be found even within the space of a few lines.

My own qualifications to make such judgments are of course entirely questionable – as those of any other self-appointed arbiter would be. The attempt to undertake such evaluations assumes for a start that I am fully confident as to the exact meaning of the relevant parts of Joyce's text – and the experience of repeated reading of that text by generations of readers has been to demonstrate that such certainty is always elusive.

To repeat Clive Hart's comment on 'correct' and 'incorrect' readings of Joyce's text, moreover, there may indeed be 'no such thing as an incorrect reading of *Finnegans Wake*,' given Joyce's own 'delight in the chance meanings of words, the peculiar interaction often caused by their juxtaposition, and the power of verbal circumstance' (1968b, 4, 7). The hyperbolic suggestion has occasionally been voiced, in the same vein, that if a thousand competent translators translated the *Wake* they would produce a thousand different renderings that would in principle have equal validity – which is perhaps just another way of repeating that the text is essentially untranslatable.

By and large, however, and with all due allowances made, it is probably not unfair to say, for example, that Georg Goyert's early German version in the 1930s of selected passages from *Anna Livia Plurabelle* is clearly what I am calling an explanatory translation, aiming to preserve merely a surface narrative coherence rather than striving also for multiple textual resonances (Reichert and Senn 1970, 11). The same is clearly true of the early French versions of brief excerpts by Michel Butor in the 1940s, as Butor himself was quick to acknowledge. Similarly, Juan Rodolfo Wilcock states his belief in the introduction to his 1961 collection of more substantial excerpts in Italian translation that Joyce's irreducibly polysemous text is entirely impossible to translate and freely admits that his rendering is intended only to convey some approximate sense of the general drift of it, as he understood it.

Among later efforts, Víctor Pozanco, noting that nothing he had previously attempted in his thirty years as a professional translator came anywhere close to being as difficult, readily admits that his abbreviated 1993 Spanish version of the *Wake* is much less an attempt at a translation in any normal sense than an attempt merely to 'make intelligible' (1993, 11) what he takes – not by any means always convincingly – to be the central narrative thread. Marissa Aixàs's 2004 Catalan rendering of *Anna Livia Plurabelle* likewise limits itself to a sustained attempt to recuperate what is taken, again not always entirely convincingly, to be the primary surface meaning of Joyce's text.

Even in the early years, versions appeared that can be assigned at least in large part to our second category, attempting to imitate as closely as possible the method and spirit of Joyce's text rather than merely to explain what it appeared to be 'really' saying. This is true of André du Bouchet's complex renderings in French and those of the Campos brothers in Portuguese, each of which originally appeared in the 1950s. The same holds, a decade or so later, for the two separate German renderings of *Anna Livia Plurabelle* by Wolfgang Hildesheimer and Hans Wollschläger, both of which appear, together with Georg Goyert's earlier version, in a single volume (Reichert and Senn 1970). The comparison is instructive: Goyert's version, as already suggested, is clearly explanatory; Hildesheimer's is predominantly imitative, but tends to simplify Joyce's text somewhat for the German reader; Wollschläger's is also predominantly imitative, but tends towards lesser rather than greater accessibility. A Portuguese rendering of the complete *Anna Livia Plurabelle* by Dirce Waltrick do Amarante several decades later is likewise predominantly imitative.

Our third category, involving versions that aim to out-Joyce Joyce, was flamboyantly introduced by none other than Joyce himself in the collaborative French and Italian renderings prepared under his supervision, the first of which (with Beckett and others) was published in 1931, the second (with Nino Frank, and subsequently adjusted by Ettore Settanni) in 1940. The Italian rendering, especially, makes clear Joyce's own position that a translation of the *Wake* should be not just an attempted mirror image but rather a frank and largely untrammelled continuation of it. The most interesting aspect of Joyce's renderings of his own work, as we have seen in a few examples, is his almost completely cavalier attitude to any necessity of translatorial fidelity to the original text in any normal sense. Umberto Eco points out, for example, the drastic reduction in the number of fluvial references in the Italian version: having spent almost ten years looking for many hundreds of river names to include in *Anna Livia Plurabelle*, Joyce simply 'discarded nearly nine-tenths of them' (2001, 115). So different from the original is Joyce's Italian rendering of it, indeed, that one Italian critic has stated her considered opinion that it should be considered an entirely independent text, 'the last page of great prose that Joyce left us' (Bosinelli 1998a, 197).

One later undertaking, a complete 1992 Spanish version of *Anna Livia Plurabelle* by Francisco García Tortosa and a team of collaborators, may be said to straddle two of our categories: certainly imitative in its intention, the consistency with which Joyce's methods are imitated leads to a text that easily out-Joyces Joyce on many occasions. If Goyert's rendering of *Anna Livia Plurabelle*, for example, is open to the criticism of oversimplification, García Tortosa's rendering is certainly open to criticism as being excessively complex. A number of Spanish-language reviewers observed that in relative terms, and as a result of the in-principle laudable attempt to replicate as closely as possible Joyce's textual practice, the result is actually more difficult for a Spanish-speaking reader than Joyce's original is for an English-speaking reader. While this assessment is of course debatable, the excerpts we have considered certainly bear witness to this rendering's consistently high level of challenge to the reader.

Turning our attention to complete translations of the entire *Wake*, the first to appear in any language was Philippe Lavergne's French version of 1982, which was received with general stupefaction in France and elsewhere. Opinions were of course immediately divided as to its merits – and as to the question whether such an undertaking should ever have been attempted in the first place. Lavergne's rendering is couched in essentially explanatory terms, designed to show French readers what Joyce's text is really all about. To this end, his translation is accompanied by a significant number of footnotes, many of them distinctly (and some extremely) idiosyncratic. A consistent strategy throughout is to find specific would-be explanatory references to concrete Irish places and / or persons, whose relevance, however, sometimes turns out to be very questionable, as we have had some occasion to notice. Lavergne also indisputably cuts corners and takes easy ways out on numerous occasions. While his translation, which appeared in the Joyce centenary year, certainly represented a monumental achievement and is by no means without its successes, as we have also seen, one is tempted overall to agree with one reviewer's quip that for Lavergne 'the translating of the *Wake* was indeed a labor of love, but so was the monster for Dr. Frankenstein' (Benstock and Benstock 1985, 231).

One of the most impressive complete translations so far, perhaps even the most impressive, is the Dutch version of 2002 by Erik Bindervoet and Robbert-Jan Henkes, with the original text presented on facing pages for ease of comparison. The two translators worked closely with Dutch Joyce scholars in preparing their version, provided a thirty-page appendix of suggested emendations to the original text, and claimed to have employed at least twenty-one different methods of translation (including what they describe as the approaching method, the combination method, the additive method, the other-cheek method, and so on), arguing that the numerous ways in which the *Wake* was written invite equally numerous ways of translation (van der Weide 2003, 626–7). Despite occasional extravagances, one or two of which we have noticed, this version consistently combines original, imaginative, and humorous solutions and a high degree of sensitivity to the layered complexity of Joyce's original. A notable peculiarity, as we have seen on various occasions, is the substitution of the initials *HKI* for *HCE* throughout, one obvious effect of which is to disrupt the overt relationship to H.C.E. Childers and associated textual links.

Another consistently impressive version is the Italian translation by Luigi Schenoni, which as of 2011 provided Italian readers, after almost four decades of sustained work on the translator's part, with a highly painstaking version of the first twelve chapters in a series of installments (once again with the original text on facing pages), a version whose overall quality and scrupulous attention to detail and nuance are evident. Schenoni, who had reportedly hoped to complete the entire project by 2014, to mark the seventy-fifth anniversary of the appearance of the *Wake*, died in September 2008, with the first ten of the seventeen chapters in print, two further chapters appearing posthumously in 2011. Schenoni's approach, while aiming for meticulous fidelity to Joyce's text to the degree possible, is informed throughout by a lively sense of humour. In finding the appropriate initials for HCE, for example, since *h* rarely begins a word in Italian, he has no compunction, as we have seen, about humorously prefixing a silent *h*, often comically out of place, to a standard Italian word, resulting in an outlandish combination of letters normally quite impossible in that language: thus 'hsparviero' for *sparviero* ('hod'), 'hpagano' for *pagano* ('pagan'), and the like. In each such case the Italian text self-reflexively reminds the reader that this is indeed a translation of a text that is quite untranslatable by any normal translatorial practices.

The much celebrated complete Portuguese translation by Donaldo Schüler, a professor of classics in Pôrto Alegre, Brazil, appeared in five volumes between 1999 and 2003, the final matching set printed on handmade paper with original abstract illustrations, Joyce's English text on facing pages, and very copious notes. Schüler's version is likewise one of the more impressive attempts to transpose Joyce's text into another language, but imbued with a sense of fun that in this case might arguably be seen as leading to more than occasional excesses. An interesting characteristic of this version is that on several occasions, the translator uses specifically Brazilian references instead of Irish ones to extend the international reach of the *Wake*: thus, as we have seen, 'Nossenhora d'Ohmem's' for 'Eve and Adam's,' invoking a church in São Paulo rather than on Merchant's Quay (*FW* 3.1), or 'Dubelém' for Joyce's 'Dubblenn' (*FW* 66.18), invoking the Brazilian city of Belém and the biblical town of Bethlehem as well as the Irish city of Dublin.

Whether such decisions represent valid extensions of Joyce's text or constitute unwarranted and unnecessary distortions of it is of course open to individual evaluation. They certainly make an interesting contribution to a macrotextual *Wake* – as did du Bouchet's translation of 'Eve and Adam's' to Paris with his rendering 'Évant notre Adame' (*FW* 3.1). Schüler's sense of fun can occasionally lead to distinctly extravagant results, however, as when he renders 'Persse O'Reilly' as 'Estour A. Tim Panos,' literally 'pierces (*estoura*) eardrums (*timpanos*)' (*FW* 44.24), or 'Hofed-ben-Edar' as 'Coco-bem-Quisto,' roughly 'Bladderhead the Wellbeloved' (*FW* 30.11), each of which is both clever and amusing but could certainly also be argued as distorting and damaging the overall fabric of referential allusion. As against that, however, a macrotextual *Wake* is undoubtedly flexible enough to accommodate such individual idiosyncracies – which are of course entirely reminiscent of the translatorial liberties Joyce himself had no compunction about taking. At the very least, they contribute generously to the lots of fun to be had, in whatever linguistic version, at *Finnegans Wake*.

The question of the degree to which translatorial licence and flaunted idiosyncracy can reasonably be considered appropriate is raised in exemplary fashion by Dieter Stündel's German rendering. Stündel's version, which appeared to great fanfare in 1993, with the original text on facing pages once again, was the second complete rendering of the *Wake* to appear in any European language, preceded only by Lavergne's French version. (Naoki Yanase's complete Japanese rendering appeared in two parts in 1991 and 1993 respectively.) It is without any question the most flamboyantly extravagant attempt so far, at least in any western European language, to out-Joyce Joyce, its aggressive idiosyncracy advertised already, as we have seen, by the Germano-Wakean title *Finnegans Wehg*.

Stündel's version is clearly driven by the ambition to achieve an unrelentingly self-reflexive text. When, for example, Joyce's adjective 'scraggy' (*FW* 3.5) is rendered on Stündel's opening page as 'dunn' rather than by the standard German adjective *dünn* ('thin'), the reader is put on immediate notice that 'dunn' (meaningless in standard German) both is and is not equivalent to *dünn*. A corresponding point is evidently true of all translations, Stündel's or anybody else's, in that they simultaneously are and are not equivalent to their source text – though in the case of the *Wake* the degree of equivalence is always highly debatable. The apparent intention here to keep readers continually on their interpretive toes, to prevent them from yielding to any comfortable illusion of familiarity with the text and its operations, can of course be seen as a worthy one – but to have the point made in almost every single line of every single one of 628 pages becomes extraordinarily tedious and very quickly self-defeating.

Stündel's central objective (like that of García Tortosa in his Spanish *Anna Livia Plurabelle*) is clearly to stress the irreducible foreignness, the otherness, the unreasonableness, of Joyce's text. While he succeeds extremely well in this ambition as far as his own rendering is concerned, it is highly debatable whether the cumulative result has much to do with Joyce anymore. His practice throughout certainly draws attention to the infinite malleability of language, to the tendency of language always to mean more and differently than it may initially appear to be saying. The ambition to make what is in itself a laudable point, however, translates into an obsessive need to play on words at all costs, whether warranted by Joyce's text or not. His rendering, as we have seen, has its occasional flashes of brilliance, but it is unquestionably characterized overall by a pervasive and debilitating arbitrariness. This is accompanied, moreover, by an equally arbitrary and almost obsessive tendency to invent excretory and sexual transpositions even where they are clearly entirely unmotivated by any contextual necessity.

It should of course be freely acknowledged at this point that it is a great deal easier to pontificate in a few sentences on the alleged successes and shortcomings of any one of these translations than it is to wrestle doggedly, in some cases for many years, with the formidable task of actually attempting to translate *Finnegans Wake* in the first place. The comments made here are also, as already suggested, entirely debatable; the threefold division into explanatory, imitative, and competitive renderings is at best a very blunt evaluative instrument indeed; and even to wield that imperfect instrument in any appropriate degree of detail would require one, in the unique case of *Finnegans Wake*, to consider separately the translation not just of every single sentence but of every single word contained in the more than six hundred pages of text.

Our comparative discussion of would-be translations has necessarily been limited, in that it has very largely had to exclude versions from beyond the frontiers of western European languages – including complete renderings of *Anna Livia Plurabelle* in Czech (Weatherall, Procházka, and Hoffmeister 1932), Polish (Słomczyński 1985), and Romanian (Antip 1996), as well as complete renderings of *Finnegans Wake* in Japanese (Yanase 1993) and Korean (Kim 2002). More than seventy years after the first appearance of *Finnegans Wake*, it is clear that we are now living in something close to a golden age of *Wake* translations, however theoretically fraught such endeavours may continue to be.

Strictly speaking, the *Wake* may indeed, as competent theorists have long held, simply not be truly translatable in any normal sense – but it nonetheless *has* been translated or transposed or transcreated or otherwise somehow made available, in a variety of shapes and sizes, to readers who would otherwise lack any access at all to Joyce's extraordinary text. The quip that a translation of the *Wake* may indeed be a labour of love, 'but so was the monster for Dr. Frankenstein,' holds in principle for any attempted translation of or from the *Wake*. Of those considered here, the results are in some cases undoubtedly more convincingly successful than in others, but every effort is in principle a fascinating one, and every effort contributes to the continuing and ever-expanding polyglot wake of Joyce's already extravagantly polyglot work in perennial progress, *Finnegans Wake*.

Bibliography

Joyce's works are cited parenthetically in the text by the abbreviations listed in section 1 below. The annotation 'bilingual' in section 2 (which also includes Joyce's translations of his own work) indicates that the translation is accompanied by the original text. For further details of the serial publication history of *Work in Progress* between 1924 and 1938, see Crispi and Slote (2007, 490–4).

1 Works by James Joyce

ALP   *Anna Livia Plurabelle*. 1928. Introduction by Padraic Colum. New York: Crosby Gaige. London: Faber and Faber, 1930. Corresponds to *FW* 196–216.
- *Tales Told of Shem and Shaun*. 1929. Preface by C.K. Ogden. Paris: The Black Sun Press. Corresponds to *FW* 152–9, 282–304, 414–19.
- *Haveth Childers Everywhere*. 1930. Paris: Babou and Kahane; New York: Fountain Press. Corresponds to *FW* 532–54.
- *Two Tales of Shem and Shaun*. 1932. London: Faber and Faber. Corresponds to *FW* 152–9, 414–19.
- *The Mime of Mick, Nick and the Maggies*. 1934. The Hague: The Servire Press. Corresponds to *FW* 219–59.
- *Storiella as She Is Syung*. 1937. London: Corvinus Press. Corresponds to *FW* 260–75, 304–8.
FW   *Finnegans Wake*. 1939. London: Faber and Faber; New York: Viking Press. Harmondsworth, UK: Penguin, 1999, with introduction by John Bishop.
L 1   *The Letters of James Joyce*, vol. 1. 1957. Edited by Stuart Gilbert. London: Faber; New York: Viking, 1966.
L 2 / 3   *The Letters of James Joyce*, vols. 2 and 3. 1966. Edited by Richard Ellmann. London: Faber; New York: Viking.

U *Ulysses*. 1922. Paris: Shakespeare & Co. New York: Random House, 1934. London: Bodley Head, 1936. New York: Random House / Vintage Books, 1986, edited by Hans Walter Gabler with Wolfhard Steppe and Claus Melchior.

2 Other Works

Aixàs, Marissa [Aixàs Obiols, Maria Lluïsa]. 2004. *Estudi del joc de paraules en 'Anne Livia Plurabelle': Anàlisi contrastiva de traduccions i proposta pròpia de versió*. Dissertation, Universitat Autònoma de Barcelona. Includes Catalan version of *FW* 8.8–10.24; 15.28–18.16; 182.30–186.18; 196.1–216.5.

Aixàs, Marissa. 2007. 'The Process of Transposing "Anna Livia Plurabelle" into Catalan: Some Reflections and Considerations.' In *Joyce and/in Translation*, edited by Rosa Maria Bollettieri Bosinelli and Ira Torresi, 143–8. Rome: Bulzoni Editore.

Allen, Kim. 2000. 'Beckett, Joyce, and Anna Livia: The Plurability of Translating *Finnegans Wake*.' In *Translation Perspectives XI: Beyond the Western Tradition*, edited by Marilyn Gaddis Rose, 427–35. Binghampton, NY: Center for Translation Research.

Amarante, Dirce Waltrick do. 2001. 'A terceira margem do Liffey: Uma aproximação ao *Finnegans Wake*.' Dissertação de Mestrado, Universidade Federal de Santa Catarina, Florianópolis, Brazil.

Amarante, Dirce Waltrick do. 2003a. 'A tradução antropofágica de *Finnegans Wake*.' *Cult* 6 (72): 18–20.

Amarante, Dirce Waltrick do. 2003b. 'The Language and Translation of *Finnegans Wake*.' *ABEI Journal: The Brazilian Journal of Irish Studies* 5:321–7.

Amarante, Dirce Waltrick do. 2005. 'Para as crianças de todas as idades.' *DC Cultura*, 15 January, 14–15.

Amarante, Dirce Waltrick do. 2009. *Para ler 'Finnegans Wake' de James Joyce*. São Paulo: Editora Iluminuras. Includes Portuguese version of *FW* 196.1–216.5.

Anon. 2002. 'Joyce's Monk.' *Al-Ahram Weekly Online* 583 (25 April–1 May 2002). Online.

Anon. 2003. *New Georgia Encyclopedia*. 17 December 2003. Online.

Anon. 2008. 'Oconee River.' *Wikipedia*. 31 December 2008. Online.

Anon. 2009. 'Finnegans Wake.' *Wikipedia* [Czech]. 25 March 2009. Online. Includes Czech translation of *FW* 3.1–3.

Anon. 2010. 'Finnegans Wake.' *Wikipedia* [Esperanto]. 4 March 2010. Online. Includes Esperanto translation of *FW* 3.1–3.

Antip, Felicia, trans. 1996. 'Veghea lui Finnegan: Anna Livia Plurabelle' [*ALP*: Romanian]. *Vara*, 83–8.

Atherton, J.S. 1959. *The Books at the Wake*. London: Faber and Faber.

Attridge, Derek, ed. 1990. *The Cambridge Companion to James Joyce*. Cambridge: Cambridge University Press.

Aubert, Jacques. 1965. Review (erroneously attributed to Fritz Senn) of *Finnegans Wake*, French translation by André du Bouchet (1962). *James Joyce Quarterly* 3:81–2.

Aubert, Jacques. 1967. '*Finnegans Wake*: Pour en finir avec les traductions?' *James Joyce Quarterly* 4:217–22.

Aubert, Jacques. 1969. 'Riverrun.' *Change* 11:120–30.

Aubert, Jacques. 1982. 'Un texte impossible et peu présentable: La traduction intégrale de *Finnegans Wake*.' *Le Monde* 10:23.

Aubert, Jacques, and Fritz Senn. 1985. *James Joyce*. Paris: Éditions de l'Herne.

Bartnicki, Krzysztof, trans. 2004 / 2005. '*Finneganów tren*: Bajka o Mooksie i Gripowronie' ['The Mookse and the Gripes': Polish]. *Przekładaniec* 13(2) / 14(1): 156–71. *FW* 152.4–159.23.

Beck, Harald, trans. 1986. 'Incipit opus progrediens' [*FW*, excerpt: German]. *Bargfelder Bote* 104–6 (July): 44–5. *FW* 3.1–5.29.

Beck, Harald, trans. 1987. '*Finnegans Wake* 5.29ff.' [German]. *Bargfelder Bote* 110–12 (January): 54. *FW* 5.29–7.06.

Beck, Harald, trans. 1989. 'I.1 (Der Anfang).' In Reichert and Senn 1989, 27–35. *FW* 3.1–11.28.

Beckett, Samuel, Alfred Péron, Yvan Goll, Eugène Jolas, Paul Léon, Adrienne Monnier, Philippe Soupault, and James Joyce, trans. Cited as Beckett and Joyce. 1931. 'Anna Livie Plurabelle' [*ALP*, excerpts: French]. *Nouvelle Revue Française* 19 (212): 633–46. Reprinted in Bosinelli 1996, 3–29. Corresponds to *FW* 196–201, 215–16.

Belyaev, Konstantin Aleksandrovich, trans. 2000. 'Džejms Džojs, Anna Livija Pljurabell.' *Soyuz Pisatelei*. 19 January 2000. Online. *FW* 196.1–5, 209.18–212.19.

Benstock, Bernard. 1966. Note. *A Wake Newslitter* 3(3): 61.

Benstock, Bernard. 1985. *James Joyce*. New York: Ungar.

Benstock, Shari, and Bernard Benstock. 1985. Review of *Finnegans Wake*, French translation by Philippe Lavergne (1982). *James Joyce Quarterly* 22:231.

Bergman, Peter M. 1968. *The Concise Dictionary of 26 Languages in Simultaneous Translations*. New York: New American Library / Signet.

Berresford Ellis, Peter. 1992. *Dictionary of Celtic Mythology*. New York: Oxford University Press.

Bindervoet, Erik, and Robbert-Jan Henkes, trans. 2002. *Finnegans Wake* [Dutch]. Amsterdam: Querido. Bilingual.

Bíró, Endre, trans. 1964. 'Finnegans Wake' [excerpts: Hungarian]. *Híd* 28(11): 1241–56. Includes excerpts from *FW* 8–10, 169–95, 196–216, 627–8.

Bíró, Endre, trans. 1992. *Finnegan ébredése (részletek)* [*FW*, excerpts: Hungarian]. Budapest: Holnap Kiadó. Includes excerpts from *FW* 8–10, 35, 152–9, 169–95, 196–216, 226, 261–2, 414–21, 499–501, 627–8.

Bishop, John. 1986. *Joyce's Book of the Dark: Finnegans Wake.* Madison: University of Wisconsin Press.

Blumenbach, Ulrich. 1990. 'Üb-Errsetzungen aus dem Anglo-Wakischen ins Germano-Wakische: Untersuchungen zum Problem der Übersetzbarkeit von James Joyces *Finnegans Wake*.' Wissenschaftliche Hausarbeit zur Ersten Staatsprüfung für das Amt des Studienrats. Dissertation, Berlin.

Blumenbach, Ulrich. 1998. 'A Bakhtinian Approach towards Translating *FW*.' In *Images of Joyce*, edited by Clive Hart, 2:645–9. Gerrards Cross, UK: Colin Smythe.

Bosinelli, Rosa Maria Bollettieri. 1987. 'Joyce e la traduzione: Rifacimenti italiani di *Finnegans Wake*.' *Lingua e stile* 22 (4): 515–38.

Bosinelli, Rosa Maria Bollettieri. 1990. 'Beyond Translation: Italian Re-Writings of *Finnegans Wake*.' *Joyce Studies Annual*, 142–61.

Bosinelli, Rosa Maria Bollettieri, ed. 1996. *James Joyce, Anna Livia Plurabelle*. Introduction by Umberto Eco. Scrittori tradotti da scrittori 8. Turin: Einaudi. Includes 1928 and 1939 texts; Beckett and Joyce 1931; Péron and Beckett 1985; and Schenoni 1996.

Bosinelli, Rosa Maria Bollettieri. 1998a. 'Anna Livia's Italian Sister.' In Lawrence 1998, 193–8.

Bosinelli, Rosa Maria Bollettieri. 1998b. 'Introduction: Anna Livia Plurabelle's Sisters.' In Lawrence 1998, 173–8.

Bosinelli, Rosa Maria Bollettieri. 2000. 'Joyce on the Turrace of Babbel.' In *Classic Joyce: Joyce Studies in Italy 6*, edited by Franca Ruggieri, 417–29. Rome: Bulzoni.

Bosinelli, Rosa Maria Bollettieri. 2001. 'Joyce Slipping across the Borders of English: The Stranger in Language.' *James Joyce Quarterly* 38:395–409.

Buck, Carl Darling. 1988. *A Dictionary of Selected Synonyms in the Principal Indo-European Languages: A Contribution to the History of Ideas.* 1949. Chicago: University of Chicago Press.

Budgen, Frank. 1970. *Myselves When Young.* London: Oxford University Press.

Burgess, Anthony, ed. 1966. *James Joyce: A Shorter Finnegans Wake.* London: Faber and Faber.

Burgess, Anthony. 1975. 'Writing in Rome (pHorbiCEtta).' *Times Literary Supplement*, 31 October, 1296. Includes Italian translation of *FW* 3–14.

Butor, Michel. 1948. 'Petite croisière préliminaire à une reconnaisance de l'archipel Joyce.' *La Vie Intellectuel* 16 (5): 104–35. Reprinted in *Répertoire:*

Études et conférences 1948–1959, by Michel Butor, 195–218. Paris: Les Éditions de Minuit, 1960. Includes translation of *FW* 3.1–3, 196.1–7, 419.5–8.

Butor, Michel. 1957. 'Esquisse d'un seuil pour Finnegan.' *La Nouvelle Revue Française* n.s. 5 (60): 1033–53. Reprinted in *Répertoire: Études et conférences 1948–1959*, by Michel Butor, 219–33. Paris: Les Éditions de Minuit, 1960.

Butor, Michel. 1967. 'La traduction, dimension fondamentale de notre temps.' *James Joyce Quarterly* 4:215–16.

Campbell, Joseph, and Henry Morton Robinson. 1961. *A Skeleton Key to Finnegans Wake*. 1944. New York: Viking Press.

Campos, Augusto de, and Haroldo de Campos, trans. 1957 [*FW*, excerpts: Portuguese]. *Jornal do Brasil* 15 September; 29 December. Seven fragments from *FW* 3, 159, 196, 214–16, 556, 561, 627–8.

Campos, Augusto de, and Haroldo de Campos, trans. 1962. *Panaroma do Finnegans Wake* [*FW*, excerpts: Portuguese]. São Paulo: Comissão de Literatura do Conselho Estadual de Cultura. Eleven fragments from *FW* 3, 143, 159, 189, 196, 214–16, 226, 556, 559, 561, 627–8. Bilingual. The passages from *FW* 214–16 and 627–8 are jointly translated; *FW* 189 is translated by Haroldo de Campos; and the remaining eight are the work of Augusto de Campos.

Campos, Haroldo de. 1978. 'Sanscreed Latinized: The *Wake* in Brazil and Hispanic America.' In *In the Wake of the Wake*, edited by David Hayman and Elliott Anderson, 54–62. Madison: University of Wisconsin Press. Reprinted in *ABEI Journal: The Brazilian Journal of Irish Studies* 3 (2001): 51–60.

Campos, Haroldo de, trans. 1999. 'Dois fragmentos de *Finnegans Wake*, transcriados de Haroldo de Campos.' In *Joyce Revém*, edited by Marcelo Tápia, 30–5. São Paulo: Editora Olavobrás / Associação Brasileira de Estudos Irlandeses. *FW* 292, 449.

Castelain, Daniel, trans. 1964. 'Un itinéraire pour *Finnegans Wake*: Tentative de traduction fragmentaire.' *Two Cities* 9:35–40. Includes French translation of excerpts from *FW* 3, 44, 169–71, 384, 627–8.

Celati, Gianni. 1972. 'Da *Finnegans Wake*: Elaborazioni sul tema visita al museo Wellington: Traduzioni di linguaggi inventati.' *Il Caffè* 19 (3–4): 26–9. Includes Italian translation of *FW* 8.9–10.24.

Chastaing, Maxime, Armand Jacob, and Arthur Watt, trans. 1951. 'Tentatives pour une traduction de *Finnegans Wake*.' *Roman* 3 (June): 270–1. Includes French translation of *FW* 627–8.

Chun, Eunkyung. 2004. 'On the Untranslatability of *Finnegans Wake*: With an Example of a Korean Translation by Kim Chong-keon.' *James Joyce Journal* 10 (2): 173–90.

Conde-Parrilla, María Ángeles. 1997. 'Joyce in Spanish.' *Donaire* 8:20–9.

Corsini, Gianfranco, and Giorgio Melchiori, eds. 1979. *James Joyce: Scritti italiani.* With Louis Berrone, Nino Frank, and Jacqueline Risset. Milan: Mondadori.

Cortanze, Gérard de. 1983. 'Le *Finnegans Wake* de Philippe Lavergne, ou les contorsions de la Sibylle.' *Europe: Revue Littéraire Mensuelle* 649 (May): 179–86.

Costanzo, W.V. 1972. 'The French Version of *Finnegans Wake*: Translation, Adaption, Recreation.' *James Joyce Quarterly* 9:225–36.

Cottle, Basil. 1978. *The Penguin Dictionary of Surnames*. 1967. Harmondsworth, UK: Penguin.

Crispi, Luca, and Sam Slote, eds. 2007. *How Joyce Wrote Finnegans Wake: A Chapter-by-Chapter Genetic Guide*. Madison: University of Wisconsin Press.

Curran, C.P. 1968. *James Joyce Remembered*. London: Oxford University Press.

Debons, Pierre-André. 1983. '*Finnegans Wake* enfin traduit.' *Samedi Littéraire*, 1 January, III.

de Courcy, J.W. 1996. *The Liffey in Dublin*. Dublin: Gill and Macmillan.

del Pozzo, Silvia. 1982. 'Il labirinto violato.' *Panorama*, 31 May, 153–6.

Diacono, Mario. 1961. 'A James Joyce's mamafesta: By the Stream of Zemzem under Zigzag Hill.' *La Tartaruga*. Reprinted in *Joyce Studies in Italy 2*, edited by Carla de Petris, 195–6. Rome: Bolzoni, 1988. Includes translation of *FW* 107.8–108.36.

Diament, Henri. 1996. 'Gallic Joys of Joyce: On Translating Some Names in *Finnegans Wake* into French.' *Names: A Journal of Onomastics* 44 (2): 83–104.

Dinneen, Patrick S. 1927. *Foclóir Gaedhilge agus Béarla/An Irish-English Dictionary*. Irish Texts Society. Dublin: Educational Company of Ireland.

Drews, Jörg. 1993. 'Parforce-Ritt zur Unsterblichkeit, oder In ein teutsches Modell vergossen.' Review of *Finnegans Wehg*, German translation by Dieter Stündel (1993). *Neue Deutsche Literatur* 41:147–55.

Drews, Jörg. 1998. '"Anything Goes" Is My Device? Some Remarks on Dieter H. Stündel's German Version of *Finnegans Wake*.' In Frehner and Zeller 1998, 427–35.

du Bouchet, André, trans. 1950. 'Dans le sillage de Finnegan' [*FW*, excerpts: French]. *L'Âge Nouveau* 45 (January): 24–8. Excerpts from *FW* 619, 624, 625–8. Bilingual.

du Bouchet, André, trans. 1957. 'Les veilles des Finnegans' [*FW*, excerpts: French]. *Nouvelle Revue Française* n.s. 5 (60): 1054–64. Includes an introduction, 'Lire *Finnegans Wake*?' (1054–5), and fragments from *FW* 604–28.

du Bouchet, André, trans. 1962. *Finnegans Wake* [excerpts: French]. Fragments adaptés par André du Bouchet. Introduction de Michel Butor. Suivis de 'Anna Livia Plurabelle.' Paris: Gallimard. Includes *FW* 3–29, 196–201, 215–16, 593–628.

du Bouchet, André, trans. 2003. *Lire Finnegans Wake?* Fontfroide, France: Fata Morgana.

Eco, Umberto. 1978. 'Come si dice in italiano tumptytumtoes?' *L'Espresso* 28 May, 74–83.

Eco, Umberto. 1989. *The Aesthetics of Chaosmos: The Middle Ages of James Joyce.* Translated by Ellen Esrock. Cambridge, MA: Harvard University Press.

Eco, Umberto. 1996. 'Ostrigotta, ora capesco.' In *James Joyce, Anna Livia Plurabelle*, edited by Rosa Maria Bollettieri Bosinelli, v–xxix. Turin: Einaudi.

Eco, Umberto. 2001. *Experiences in Translation*. Translated by Alastair McEwen. Toronto: University of Toronto Press.

Egri, Péter. 1967. 'James Joyce's Works in Hungarian Translation.' *James Joyce Quarterly* 4:234–6.

Elizondo, Salvador. 1992. 'La primera página de *Finnegans Wake*.' In *Teoría del infierno y otros ensayos*, 155–62. Mexico City: El Colegio Nacional, Ediciones del Equilibrista. Includes Spanish translation of *FW* 3.1–24.

Ellmann, Richard. 1982. *James Joyce*. 1959. New York: Oxford University Press.

Enzensberger, Christian, et al., trans. 1985. 'Aus "Glugg's Confession"' [*FW*, excerpt: German]. *Protokolle* 1:103–6. *FW* 241.1–26.

Fanzone, Leandro, trans. 2007. 'Fragmentos de *Finnegans Wake*, de James Joyce' [*FW*, excerpts: Spanish]. *Seikilos*. 8 November 2007. Online. *FW* 159.6–18, 215.31–216.5, 627.34–628.16.

Federici, Fabrizio. 1982. 'Un viaggio al limite del linguaggio.' *Avanti*, 27 July, 8.

Ferrer, Daniel, and Jacques Aubert. 1998. 'Anna Livia's French Bifurcations.' In Lawrence 1998, 179–86.

Flanagan, Deirdre and Laurence. 2002. *Irish Place Names*. Dublin: Gill and Macmillan.

Frehner, Ruth, and Ursula Zeller, eds. 1998. *A Collideorscape of Joyce: Festschrift for Fritz Senn*. Dublin: Lilliput Press.

Fried, Erich, trans. 1985. 'Eine Übersetzung aus *Finnegans Wake*' [*FW*, excerpt: German]. *Protokolle* 1:107–20. *FW* 403.1–404.3.

Frye, Northrop. 1966. *Anatomy of Criticism: Four Essays*. 1957. New York: Atheneum.

Füger, Wilhelm, trans. 1983. '*Finnegans Wake* (German)' [excerpt: German]. *James Joyce Broadsheet*, October. Corresponds to *FW* 4.18–5.5.

Füger, Wilhelm. 2000. *Kritisches Erbe: Dokumente zur Rezeption von James Joyce im deutschen Sprachbereich zu Lebzeiten des Autors*. Amsterdam; Atlanta, GA: Rodopi.

García Tortosa, Francisco, trans. 1992. *Anna Livia Plurabelle* [Spanish]. With Ricardo Navarrete and José Maria Tejedor Cabrera. Edited by Francisco García Tortosa. Madrid: Ediciones Cátedra. *FW* 196.1–216.5. Bilingual.

García Tortosa, Francisco. 1998. 'The Spanish Translation of *Anna Livia Plura-belle.*' In Lawrence 1998, 208–12.

Gardt, Andreas. 1989. *James Joyce auf deutsch: Möglichkeiten der literarischen Übersetzung.* Frankfurt: Lang.

Gibson, George Cinclair. 2005. *'Wake' Rites: The Ancient Irish Rituals of Finnegans Wake.* Gainesville: University Press of Florida.

Gilbert, Stuart. 1955. James Joyce's *Ulysses.* 1930. New York: Vintage Books.

Glasheen, Adaline. 1963. *A Second Census of Finnegans Wake: An Index of the Characters and Their Roles.* Evanston, IL: Northwestern University Press.

Glasheen, Adaline. 1965. 'The Opening Paragraphs.' *A Wake Newslitter* 2:3–8.

Glasheen, Adaline. 1973. Note. *A Wake Newslitter* 10:80.

Glasheen, Adaline. 1976. Note. *A Wake Newslitter* 13:16.

Glasheen, Adaline. 1977. *A Third Census of Finnegans Wake: An Index of the Characters and Their Roles.* Berkeley: University of California Press.

Gordon, John. 1986. *Finnegans Wake: A Plot Summary.* Syracuse, NY: Syracuse University.

Goyert, Georg, trans. 1946. 'Anna Livia Plurabelle' [*ALP*, excerpts: German]. *Die Fähre* 1 (6): 337–40. Also appeared in *das silberboot* 2, no. 8 (1946): 139–41. *FW* 196–8, 213–15, 215–16.

Goyert, Georg, trans. 1970. 'Anna Livia Plurabella' [*ALP*: German]. Reichert and Senn 1970, 141–66. *FW* 196.1–216.5.

Gramigna, Giuliano. 1982. 'Il libro millelingue parla italiano.'*Corriere della Sera*, 27 June.

Graves, Robert. 1960. *The Greek Myths.* 2 vols. Harmondsworth, UK: Penguin.

Green, Miranda J. 1992. *Dictionary of Celtic Myth and Legend.* London: Thames and Hudson.

Grisi, Francesco. 1982. 'Tradurre Joyce: Un'arte difficile.'*Il Borghese*, 26 December.

Groden, Michael. 2007. 'Preface.' In *How Joyce Wrote Finnegans Wake: A Chapter-by-Chapter Genetic Guide*, edited by Luca Crispi and Sam Slote, vii–xi. Madison: University of Wisconsin Press.

Grut, Mario, trans. 2001. *Anna Livia Plurabella* [*ALP*: Swedish]. Lund: Ellerström. *FW* 196.1–216.5.

Hamada, Tatsuo, trans. 2009. *James Joyce: Finnegans Wake (Parts I and IV).* Abiko, Japan: Abiko Literary Press.

Hanks, Patrick, Flavia Hodges, A.D. Mills, and Adrian Room. 2002. *The Oxford Names Companion.* Oxford: Oxford University Press.

Hart, Clive. 1968a. 'The Earwickers of Sidlesham.' In Hart and Senn 1968, 21–2.

Hart, Clive. 1968b. 'The Elephant in the Belly: Exegesis of *Finnegans Wake.*' In Hart and Senn 1968, 3–12.

Hart, Clive, and Fritz Senn, eds. 1968. *A Wake Digest*. Sydney: Sydney University Press.

Hayman, David, ed. 1963. *A First-Draft Version of Finnegans Wake*. Austin: University of Texas Press.

Heath, Stephen, and Philippe Sollers. 1973. 'Joyce in Progress.' *Tel Quel* 54:4–24. Includes translation of excerpts from *FW* 593–628.

Hedberg, Johannes. 1987. 'En bit av *Finnegans Wake* på svenska.' *Lyrikvannen* 4:227–30.

Herms, Uwe, trans. 1985. '"It's Phoenix, dear!"' [*FW*, excerpt: German]. *Protokolle* 1:121–35. *FW* 17.22–5, 55.10–21, 68.28–34.

Higginson, Fred H. 1960. *Anna Livia Plurabelle: The Making of a Chapter*. Minneapolis: University of Minnesota Press.

Hildesheimer, Wolfgang, trans. 1969. 'Übersetzung und Interpretation einer Passage aus *Finnegans Wake* von James Joyce.' In *Interpretationen: James Joyce, Georg Büchner. Zwei Frankfurter Vorlesungen*, 7–29. Frankfurt: Suhrkamp. *FW* 196–7.

Hildesheimer, Wolfgang, trans. 1970. 'Anna Livia Plurabelle.' In Reichert and Senn 1970, 65–97. *FW* 196–216.

Horn, Ingeborg, trans. 1989. In Reichert and Senn 1989, 73–115. *FW* 126.1–168.14.

Ito, Eishiro. 2004. 'Two Japanese Translations of *Finnegans Wake* Compared: Yanase (1991–1993) and Miyata (2004).' *James Joyce Journal* 10:117–52.

Jauffret, Régis. 1982. 'Joyce mode d'emploi.' *Le Monde*, 3 December, 21.

Jauslin, Kurt, trans. 1989. 'I.1 (Der Anfang).' In Reichert and Senn 1989, 36–8. *FW* 3.1–5.29.

Jolas, Maria. 1949. *A James Joyce Yearbook*. Paris: Transition Press.

Jolas, Maria. 1982. 'La musique de James Joyce.' *Libération*, 26 November, 220.

Joyce, James, and Ettore Settanni, trans. 1940. 'Anna Livia Plurabella; I fiumi scorrono' [*ALP*, excerpts: Italian]. *Prospettive* 4 (2): 13–15; 4 (11–12): 14–16. *FW* 196.1–201.21, 215.11–216.5. Reprinted as 'Anna Livia Plurabella,' *Tel Quel* 55 (1973): 59–62.

Joyce, James, and Nino Frank, trans. 1979. 'Anna Livia Plurabella. Passi di *Finnegans Wake* tradotti da James Joyce e Nino Frank, 1938' [*ALP*, excerpts: Italian]. Edited by Jacqueline Risset. In *James Joyce: Scritti italiani*, edited by Gianfranco Corsini and Giorgio Melchiori, 216–33. Milan: Mondadori. Reprinted in Bosinelli 1996, 3–29. *FW* 196.1–201.21, 215.11–216.5.

Joyce, P.W. 1995. *The Origin and History of Irish Names of Places*. 3 vols. Facsimile reprint. Dublin: Edmund Burke Publisher. Originally published London: Longmans; Dublin: Gill, 1869 (vol. 1), 1902 (vol.2), 1913 (vol. 3).

Joyce, Stanislaus. 1971. *The Complete Dublin Diary of Stanislaus Joyce*. Edited by George H. Healey. Ithaca, NY; London: Cornell University Press.

Kim, Chong-keon, trans. 1985. [*Anna Livia Plurabelle*: Korean]. Seoul: Jeong-eumsa.

Kim, Chong-keon, trans. 2002. [*Finnegans Wake*: Korean]. Seoul: Boum-u-sa.

Kim, Chong-keon. 2004. 'On Korean Translation of *Finnegans Wake*.' *James Joyce Journal* 10:153–72.

Knuth, Leo. 1972. 'The *Finnegans Wake* Translation Panel at Trieste.' *James Joyce Quarterly* 9:266–9.

Kot, Jozef, trans. 1965. 'Finnegannovo prebúdzanie' [*FW*, excerpt: Slovak]. *Slovenské pohl'ady* 81 (10): 86–7. *FW* 3.1–5.4.

Królikowski, Adam, trans. 1998. 'Finnegans Wake' [Polish]. *Magazyn Literacki*, 91. *FW* 3.1–24.

Laman, Barbara. 2007. 'ALP Goes to Germany.' In *Joyce and/in Translation*, edited by Rosa Maria Bollettieri Bosinelli and Ira Torresi, 135–41. Rome: Bulzoni Editore.

Laugesen, Peter, trans. 1997. '*Finnegans Wake* (618–28).' Program note for performance of *Alp-Traum*. Copenhagen: Edison Theatre.

Lavergne, Philippe, trans. 1967. 'Shem' [*FW*, excerpt: French]. *Tel Quel* 30 (Summer): 67–89. *FW* 169.1–195.6.

Lavergne, Philippe, trans. 1968. '*Finnegans Wake*' [excerpt: French]. *Change* 1(1). *FW* 3.1–29.36.

Lavergne, Philippe, trans. 1982. *Finnegans Wake* [French]. Paris: Gallimard.

Lawrence, Karen R., ed. 1998. *Transcultural Joyce*. Cambridge: Cambridge University Press.

Le Bihan, Adrien. 2010. *Je naviguerai vers l'autel de Joyce*. Barcelona: Cherche-bruit.

Lernout, Geert. 1990. *The French Joyce*. Ann Arbor: University of Michigan Press.

Lernout, Geert, and Wim Van Mierlo, eds. 2004. *The Reception of James Joyce in Europe*. London, New York: Continuum.

Lewis, Samuel. 1837. *A Topographical Dictionary of Ireland*. 2 vols. Reprint. Port Washington, NY: Kennikat Press, n.d.

Liddell, H.G., and Robert Scott. 1843. *A Greek-English Lexicon*. Oxford: Oxford University Press.

Lobner, Corinna del Greco. 1986. 'Anna Livia Plurabella: La lavandaia antabecedariana di James Joyce.' *Rivista di Studi Italiani* 4 (1): 84–91.

Lobner, Corinna del Greco. 1994. Review of *Anna Livia Plurabelle*, Spanish translation by Francisco García Tortosa (1992). *James Joyce Quarterly* 31:400–3.

Lorenz, Sabine. 1991. 'On the Im?possibility of Translating *Finnegans Wake*.' In *Interculturality and the Historical Study of Literary Translations*, edited by Harald Kittel and Armin Paul Frank, 111–19. Berlin: Schmidt.

Lourenço, Manuel. 1968. '*Finnegans Wake*, I, 3' [*FW*, excerpt: Portuguese]. *O Tempo e o Modo*, n.p. Portuguese translation of *FW* 3.1–24.

MacCana, Proinsias. 1970. *Celtic Mythology*. London: Hamlyn.

MacKillop, James. 1986. *Fionn mac Cumhaill: Celtic Myth in English Literature*. Syracuse, NY: Syracuse University Press.

MacLysaght, Edward. 1980. *The Surnames of Ireland*. 1964. Dublin: Irish Academic Press.

MacManus, M.J. 1927. *So This Is Dublin*. Dublin: Talbot.

MacPiarais. Pádraig [Patrick Pearse]. 1914. *Suantraidhe agus Goltraidhe*. Dublin: The Irish Review.

Magalaner, Marvin, and Richard M. Kain. 1962. *Joyce: The Man, the Work, the Reputation*. 1956. New York: Collier Books.

Malicki, Jacek, trans. 2001. 'Czytanie Joyce'a *Przebudzenie Finnegana*.' 28 September 2001. Online. Includes Polish translation of *FW* 3.1–7.5.

Masoliver, Joan Ramón, ed. 1982. *James Joyce en el seus millors escrits*. Barcelona: Miquel Arimany.

McHugh, Roland. 1980. *Annotations to Finnegans Wake*. Baltimore, London: Johns Hopkins University Press.

McKenzie, John L. 1965. *Dictionary of the Bible*. New York, London: Collier Macmillan.

McLuhan, Eric. 1997. *The Role of Thunder in Finnegans Wake*. Toronto: University of Toronto Press.

Milesi, Laurent. 1985. 'L'idiome Babélien de *Finnegans Wake*.' In *Génèse de Babel: Joyce et la Création*, edited by Claude Jacquet, 155–215. Paris: Éditions du Centre National de la Recherche Scientifique.

Milesi, Laurent. 1996. '*Finnegans Wake*: The Obliquity of Trans-lations.' *Joyce in the Hibernian Metropolis: Essays*. Edited by Morris Beja and David Norris, 279–89. Columbus: Ohio State University Press.

Milesi, Laurent. 1998. 'ALP in Roumanian (with Some Notes on Roumanian in *Finnegans Wake* and in the Notebooks).' In Lawrence 1998, 199–207. Includes Romanian version of *FW* 213.11–216.5.

Milesi, Laurent, ed. 2003. *James Joyce and the Difference of Language*. Cambridge: Cambridge University Press.

Milesi, Laurent. 2004. 'Joyce, Language, and Languages.' In *Palgrave Advances in James Joyce Studies*, edited by Jean-Michel Rabaté, 144–61.London, New York: Palgrave Macmillan.

Mink, Louis O. 1978. *A Finnegans Wake Gazetteer*. Bloomington: Indiana University Press.

Miyata, Kyôko, trans. 2004a. *Finnegans Wake* [Japanese, abridged]. Tokyo: Shueisha.

Miyata, Kyôko. 2004b. 'Translating *Finnegans Wake*.' *James Joyce Journal* 10:257–60.

Mutanen, Miikka, trans. 2006. 'James Joyce: *Finnegans Wake*. 3–10' [*FW* 3.1–10.23: Finnish]. 18 May 2006. Online.

Mutanen, Miikka, trans. 2009. 'James Joyce: *Finnegans Wake*. 10–15' [*FW* 10.24–15.28: Finnish]. 16 April 2009. Online.

Nestrovski, Arthur. 1990. '"Mercius (de seu mesmo)": Notes on a Brazilian Translation.' *James Joyce Quarterly* 27:473–7. Includes Portuguese translation of *FW* 193.31–195.6.

Nishiwaki, Junzaburo, trans. 1933. 'Anna Livia Plurabelle.' In *Joyce shishu* [Joyce's Poems; selections from the poems and from *ALP*: Japanese]. Tokyo: Daiichi-shobo. *FW* 196.1–19, 213.11–216.5.

Norris, Margot. 1976. *The Decentered Universe of Finnegans Wake*. Baltimore, London: Johns Hopkins University Press.

Ó Corráin, Donnchadh, and Fidelma Maguire. 1990. *Irish Names*. Dublin: The Lilliput Press.

Ó Donnchadha, Tadhg. 1933. *Filidheacht Fiannaigheachta*. Baile Átha Cliath: Cómhlucht Oideachais na hÉireann.

Ogden, C.K., trans. 1932. 'Anna Livia Plurabelle' [FW, excerpt: Basic English]. *transition* 21 (March): 259–62. Reprinted in Bosinelli 1996, 141–50. *FW* 213.1–216.5.

O Hehir, Brendan. 1965. 'Anna Livia Plurabelle's Gaelic Ancestry.' *James Joyce Quarterly* 2:158–66.

O Hehir, Brendan. 1967. *A Gaelic Lexicon for* Finnegans Wake. Berkeley: University of California Press.

O'Neill, Patrick. 2000. '*Finnegans Wakes*: Fictions of Translation.' *Canadian Review of Comparative Literature* 27:144–58.

O'Neill, Patrick. 2005. *Polyglot Joyce: Fictions of Translation*. Toronto: University of Toronto Press.

Onions, C.T., ed. 1966. *The Oxford Dictionary of English Etymology*. Oxford: Oxford University Press.

Ono, Kyôko, Koike Shigeru, Junnosuke Sawazaki, Kenzô Suzuki, and Toda Motoi, trans. 1978 [*Finnegans Wake. Giacomo Joyce*]. Edited by Saiichi Maruya. Tokyo: Shueisha. Includes *FW* 169–70, 206–7, 418–19, 593, 627–8. Bilingual.

Osawa, Masayoshi, and Junnosuke Sawasaki, trans. 1968. Selections. *Sekai Bungaku Zenshuu 35* [Selected Works of World Literature, vol. 35]. Tokyo: Shueisha. Includes *FW* 206.29–207.20, 418.10–419.8, 627.34–628.16.

Osawa, Masayoshi, Kyôko Ono, Shigeru Koike, Junnosuke Sawasaki, and Kenzo Suzuki, trans. 1970–2. 'Anna Livia Plurabelle.' *Kikan Paedeia* [Paedeia Quarterly], nos. 7–11, 13, 15. Tokyo: Takeuchi-shoten. *FW* 196.1–208.5, serialized in seven numbers of the journal.

Osawa, Masayoshi, Kyôko Ono, Shigeru Koike, Junnosuke Sawasaki, Kenzo
Suzuki, and Motoi Toda, trans. 1978. Selections. *Sekai no Bungaku* [World
Literature] 1. *FW* 169.1–170.24, 206.29–207.20, 418.10–419.8, 593.1–18,
627.34–628.16.

Osawa, Masayoshi, Kyôko Ono, Shigeru Koike, Junnosuke Sawasaki, Kenzo
Suzuki, and Motoi Toda, trans. 1982. *Anna Livia Plurabelle. Bungei-zasshi Umi*
[Umi Literary Magazine], December, 288–305.

Osawa, Masayoshi, Shigeru Koike, Junnosuke Sawasaki, and Motoi Toda,
trans. 1966. 'Shem the Penman.' *Kikan Sekai-Bungaku* [World Literature
Quarterly] 2:B1–12. *FW* 169.1–170.24.

O'Shea, Michael J. 1986. *James Joyce and Heraldry*. Albany, NY: State University
of New York Press.

O'Sullivan, Carol. 2006. 'Joycean Translations of *Anna Livia Plurabelle*: "It's
translation, Jim, but not as we know it."' In *Italian Culture: Interactions,
Transpositions, Translations*, edited by Cormac Ó Cuilleanáin, Corinna
Salvadori, and John Scattergood, 175–82. Dublin: Four Courts Press.

Pagán, Alberte, trans. 1993. *Contos contados de Finnegan e HCE (Velório de
Finnegans, I.i–ii)* [*FW*, I.i–ii: Galician]. Juncanlinho, Cape Verde: Morabeza.

Pagán, Alberte. 2000. *A voz do trevón: Unha aproximación a* Finnegans Wake.
Santiago de Compostela: Laiovento. Includes most of the Galician translation of *FW* I.i–ii from Pagán 1993.

Parks, Gerald. 1992. 'Blotty Words for Dublin: An Excursus around the
Translation of *Finnegans Wake* by Luigi Schenoni.' In *SSLM Miscellanea*,
197–206. Trieste: Università degli Studi di Trieste, Scuola Superiore di
Lingue Moderne per Interpreti e Traduttori.

Partridge, Eric. 1972. *The Penguin Dictionary of Historical Slang*. Abridged by
Jacqueline Simpson. Harmondsworth, UK: Penguin Books.

Pearse, Patrick [as Pádraig MacPiarais]. 1914. *Suantraidhe agus Goltraidhe*.
Dublin: The Irish Review.

Péron, Alfred, and Samuel Beckett, trans. 1985. 'Anna Lyvia Pluratself.' In *James
Joyce*, edited by Jacques Aubert and Fritz Senn. Paris: Éditions de l'Herne,
1985. Reprinted in Bosinelli 1996, 153–61. Corresponds to *FW* 196.1–201.21.

Pindar, Ian. 2004. *Joyce*. London: Haus Publishing.

Pozanco, Víctor, trans. 1993. *Finnegans Wake* [Spanish]. Barcelona: Editorial
Lumen. Abridged and simplified.

Price, Liam. 1967. *The Place-Names of Co. Wicklow*. Dublin: Dublin Institute for
Advanced Studies.

Quigley, Megan M. 2004. 'Justice for the "Illstarred Punster": Samuel Beckett
and Alfred Péron's Revisions of "Anna Lyvia Pluratself."' *James Joyce
Quarterly* 41:469–87.

Rademacher, Jörg W. 1993. 'Two Approaches to *Finnegans Wake* in German: (Mis)Appropriation or Translation?' *James Joyce Quarterly* 30:482–8.

Rathjen, Friedhelm, trans. 1989. Excerpts. In Reichert and Senn 1989, 44, 45–63, 124–31, 220–37, 256–61, 275. *FW* 3.1–14; 30.1–47.32; 152.15–159.18; 383.1–399.36; 414.16–419.10; 627.24–628.16.

Rathjen, Friedhelm, trans. 1992a. 'Die Alimente der Gehomantie.' *Schreibheft: Zeitschrift für Literatur* 39 (May): 3–8. *FW* 282.1–287.17.

Rathjen, Friedhelm. 1992b. 'Schämes Scheuss wirrdeutscht: Anmerkungen zur Übersetzung von *Finnegans Wake*.' *Merkur* 46 (5): 407–14.

Rathjen, Friedhelm. 1992c. 'Vom Umgang mit Joyce: Ein Rundumblick.' *Schreibheft: Zeitschrift für Literatur* 39 (May): 157–65.

Rathjen, Friedhelm. 1993. '*Finnegans Wake*, plattgemacht.' *Konkret*, September, 52–5.

Rathjen, Friedhelm, trans. 1995a. *Der Mauchs und der Traufen: Eine Fabel aus Finnegans Wake*. Unterreit: Antinous Press. Limited edition (125 copies). Reprinted from Reichert and Senn 1989, 124–31.

Rathjen, Friedhelm. 1995b. 'Quadratur des Kreises: Zur Übersetzung von *Finnegans Wake* ins Deutsche.' *Griffel: Magazin für Literatur und Kritik* 1:65–8.

Rathjen, Friedhelm, trans. 1995c. 'Whas war dhaas?: Bettszene, erste Stellung (*Finnegans Wake* III.iv).' *Griffel: Magazin für Literatur und Kritik* 1:69–76. *FW* 555.1–563.36.

Rathjen, Friedhelm. 1998a. 'Chancelation and Transincidence: How to Deal with Coincidentals in Translating *Finnegans Wake*.' *Papers on Joyce* 4:25–8.

Rathjen, Friedhelm. 1998b. 'On Translating Names, Titles and Quotations: Ten Practitioners' Rules Derived from and Applied to German Renderings of *Ulysses* and *Finnegans Wake*.' In Frehner and Zeller 1998, 407–26.

Rathjen, Friedhelm. 1999. 'Sprakin sea Djoytsch? *Finnegans Wake* into German.' *James Joyce Quarterly* 36: 905–16.

Rathjen, Friedhelm, ed. and trans. 2012a. *Geschichten von Shem und Shaun/Tales Told of Shem and Shaun*. Frankfurt: Suhrkamp. Corresponds to *FW* 152–9, 282–304, 414–19. Bilingual.

Rathjen, Friedhelm, ed. and trans. 2012b. *Winnegans Fake* [*FW*, excerpts: German]. Südwesthörn: Edition ReJoyce. Includes German translation of excerpts from *FW* 3, 6, 11–13, 22–9, 30–47, 58, 92–3, 102–11, 219–24, 229, 250, 257–9, 260–1, 276, 307–8, 316, 336–7, 342, 353, 371–99, 410–12, 420–8, 433–40, 448–73, 483–527, 531–40, 555–90, 627–8. Bilingual.

Reichert, Klaus. 1989. *Vielfacher Schriftsinn: Zu Finnegans Wake*. Frankfurt: Suhrkamp.

Reichert, Klaus, and Fritz Senn, eds. 1970. *Anna Livia Plurabelle*. Introduction by Klaus Reichert. Frankfurt: Suhrkamp. Includes Wolfgang Hildesheimer,

'Anna Livia Plurabelle' (pp. 65–97); Hans Wollschläger, 'Anna Livia Plurabelle, parryotphrosed myth brockendootsch' (pp. 99–133); and Georg Goyert, 'Anna Livia Plurabella' (pp. 141–66). Also includes *FW* 196–216, Beckett and Joyce 1931, and Ogden 1932.

Reichert, Klaus, and Fritz Senn, eds. 1989. *Finnegans Wake Deutsch: Gesammelte Annäherungen* [*FW*, excerpts: German]. With various translators. Frankfurt: Suhrkamp.

Risset, Jacqueline. 1973. 'Joyce traduit par Joyce.' *Tel Quel* 55:47–58.

Risset, Jacqueline, ed. 1979. 'Anna Livia Plurabella: Passi di Finnegans Wake tradotti da James Joyce e Nino Frank, 1938.' In *James Joyce: Scritti italiani,* edited by Gianfranco Corsini and Giorgio Melchiori, 216–33. Milan: Mondadori.

Rodríguez, Leopoldo. 1969. 'Impresións encol do *Finnegans Wake* de James Joyce.' *Grial* 26:475. Includes Galician translation of *FW* 216.

Sailer, Susan Shaw. 1999. 'Universalizing Languages: *Finnegans Wake* Meets Basic English.' *James Joyce Quarterly* 36:853–68.

Sanesi, Roberto. 1982. 'Il risveglio di Finnegan.' *Nuova Rivista Europea* 4 (29–30): 21–4. Includes Italian translation of *FW* 593.

Schenoni, Luigi. 1974. 'Specimen Translation of *Finnegans Wake* 4.18–5.4 into Italian.' *James Joyce Quarterly* 11:405.

Schenoni, Luigi, trans. 1978. [*FW* 3.1–10: Italian]. In 'Come si dice in italiano tumptytumtoes?' by Umberto Eco, *L'Espresso*, 28 May, 79.

Schenoni, Luigi. 1979. 'Il musovoleo willingdone: James Joyce, *Finnegans Wake*, 8.9–10.23: A Translation in Progress.' *Stanford Italian Review* 1 (1): 163–9.

Schenoni, Luigi, trans. 1982. *Finnegans Wake: H.C.E.* [*FW*, excerpts: Italian]. Introduction by Giorgio Melchiori. Bibliography by Rosa Maria Bosinelli. Milan: Mondadori. *FW* I.i–iv. Bilingual.

Schenoni, Luigi. 1986. 'Is There One Who Understands Me?' In *Myriadminded-man: Jottings on Joyce*, edited by Rosa Maria Bosinelli, Paola Pugliatti, and Romana Zacchi, 255–61. Bologna: Università di Bologna. Includes Italian translation of *FW* 627.9–628.16.

Schenoni, Luigi, trans. 1996. 'Anna Livia Plurabelle' [Italian]. In *James Joyce, Anna Livia Plurabelle*, edited by Rosa Maria Bollettieri Bosinelli, 87–139. Turin: Einaudi. *FW* 196.1–216.5. Bilingual.

Schenoni, Luigi, trans. 2001. *Finnegans Wake: Libro Primo V–VIII*. Milan: Mondadori. *FW* I.v–viii. Bilingual.

Schenoni, Luigi, trans. 2004. *Finnegans Wake: Libro Secondo I–II*. Milan: Mondadori. *FW* II.i–ii. Bilingual.

Schenoni, Luigi, trans. 2011. *Finnegans Wake: Libro Secondo III–IV*. Milan: Mondadori. *FW* II.iii–iv. Bilingual.

Schinz, Alfred. 1996. *The Magic Square: Cities in Ancient China*. Stuttgart, London: Axel Menges.

Schmidt, Arno. 1969. 'Der Triton mit dem Sonnenschirm: Überlegungen zu einer Lesbarmachung von *Finnegans Wake*.' In *Der Triton mit dem Sonnen- schirm: Großbritannische Gemütsergetzungen*, 194–253. Karlsruhe: Stahlberg. Includes versions of FW 30.10–31.33; 39.28–36; 63.20–64.21; 142; 166.3–167.4; 175.5–28; 182.28–184.10; 244.1–245.4; 259.1–10; 308.1–36; 403.1–406.21.

Schönmetzler, Klaus J., trans. 1987a. '... *ein sitzam saeculi Phoenis': Sechs deutsche Annäherungen an* Finnegans Wake *von James Joyce* [FW, excerpts: German]. Bad Aibling: privately published. *FW* 3.1–5.29, 152.16–159.18, 169.1–175.28, 383.1–384.32, 414.16–415.22, 605.4–606.12, 626.20–628.16.

Schönmetzler, Klaus J., trans. 1987b. 'Here's another version of ...' [FW, excerpt: German]. *Bargfelder Bote* 113–14:24–5. *FW* 3.1–6.1.

Schrödter, Wolfgang, trans. 1989. 'I.1 (Der Anfang).' In Reichert and Senn 1989, 39–43. *FW* 3.1–4.17.

Schüler, Donaldo, trans. 2003. *Finnicius Revém* [FW, Portuguese]. 5 vols. Pôrto Alegre, Brazil: Ateliê Editorial. Vol. 1 (*FW* I.i), 1999; vol. 2 (*FW* I.ii–iv), 2000; vol. 3 (*FW* I.v–viii), 2001; vol. 4 (*FW* II.i–iv), 2002; vol. 5 (*FW* III.i–iv; IV), 2003. Bilingual.

Schüler, Donaldo. 2004. *Finnício Riovém*. Illustrated by Cristiane Löff. Rio de Janeiro: Lamparina.

Senn, Fritz. 1967a. Note. *A Wake Newslitter* 4 (1967): 108–9.

Senn, Fritz. 1967b. 'The Tellings of the Taling.' *James Joyce Quarterly* 4:229–33.

Senn, Fritz. 1978. '"Entzifferungen und Proben": *Finnegans Wake* in der Brechung von Arno Schmidt.' *Bargfelder Bote* 27 (February): 3–14; Reprinted in Senn 1983, 261–77.

Senn, Fritz. 1983. *Nichts gegen Joyce: Joyce versus Nothing: Aufsätze 1959–1983*. Edited by Franz Cavigelli. Zurich: Haffmans Verlag.

Senn, Fritz. 1984. *Joyce's Dislocutions: Essays on Reading as Translation*. Edited by John Paul Riquelme. Baltimore: Johns Hopkins University Press.

Senn, Fritz. 1993. '"Wehg" zu Finnegan? Dieter Stündel's Übertragung von *Finnegans Wake*.' *Neue Zürcher Zeitung* 10–11 (July): 59–60.

Senn, Fritz. 1995. *Inductive Scrutinies: Focus on Joyce*. Edited by Christine O'Neill. Dublin: Lilliput Press.

Senn, Fritz. 1998. 'ALP Deutsch: "ob überhaupt möglich?"' In Lawrence 1998, 187–92.

Settanni, Ettore. 1955. *James Joyce e la prima versione italiana del Finnegan's* [sic] *Wake*. Venice: Edizioni del Cavallino.

Silva-Santisteban, Ricardo, trans. 1971. 'La última página de *Finnegans Wake*.' *Creación y crítica* 2 (February): 1–4. *FW* 626–8.

Silva-Santisteban, Ricardo, trans. 1982. 'Anna Livia Plurabelle' [excerpts: Spanish]. *Cielo abierto* 7 (April–June): 25–8. *FW* 196.1–197.17, 213.11–216.5.

Silva-Santisteban, Ricardo, trans. 1988. *Anna Livia Plurabelle y otros textos del Finnegans Wake*. Privately published. *FW* 3.1–5.29, 196.1–197.17, 213.11–216.5, 626–8.

Silver, Marc, and Luca Torrealta. 1982. 'La traduzione trovata: Intervista a Luigi Schenoni.' *Quindi*, December, 20–1.

Simpkins, Scott. 1990. 'The Agency of the Title: *Finnegans Wake.' James Joyce Quarterly* 27:735–43.

Škrabánek, Petr. 1973. 'Wassaily Booslaeugh of Riesengeborg.' *A Wake Newslitter* n.s. 10:42.

Skubic, Andrej E., trans. 2000. 'Finneganovo bdenje (izbor)' [*FW*, excerpts: Slovenian]. In *James Joyce: Poezija in kratka proza* [Poetry and Selected Prose], edited by Aleš Pogačnik. Ljubljana: DZS. Includes *FW* 30.1–34.29, 380.6–382.27, 604.28–606.7, 611.4–612.15, 615.12–619.19.

Słomczyński, Maciej, trans. 1972. *Utwory poetyckie* [Poetic Works: Polish]. Kraków: Wydawnictwo Literackie. Includes excerpts from *FW* 44–7, 398–9. Bilingual.

Słomczyński, Maciej, trans. 1985. *Anna Livia Plurabelle* [Polish]. Kraków: Wydawnictwo Literackie.

Sollers, Philippe. 1982. '*Finnegans Wake* de Joyce, version française.' *Libération* 26 (November): 22.

Sonnemann, Ulrich. 1995. 'Das Finneganwunder, oder Die Ausgießung des Heiligen Geistes: Zwei Absätze aus *Finnegans Wake*: Kommentierter Übersetzungsversuch.' In *Müllberge des Vergessens: Elf Einsprüche*, edited by Paul Fiebig, 63–78. Stuttgart: Metzler.

Soupault, Philippe. 1931. 'A propos de la traduction d'*Anna Livia Plurabelle.*' *Nouvelle Revue Française* 19 (212): 633–6.

Soupault, Philippe. 1943. *Souvenirs de James Joyce*. Algiers: Charlot.

Stoltefuß, Helmut, trans. 1989. Excerpt. In Reichert and Senn 1989, 64–72. *FW* 30.1–38.8.

Strzetelski, Jerzy, trans. 1959. 'Noc opłakiwania Finnegana (Urywki)' [*ALP*, excerpts: Polish]. *Twórczość* 12:62–4. Excerpts from *FW* 196–8, 206–7, 215–16.

Stündel, Dieter H., trans. 1993. *Finnegans Wehg: Kainnäh ÜbelSätzZung des Wehrkess fun Schämes Scheuss* [*FW*: German]. Darmstadt: Häusser; Frankfurt: Zweitausendeins. Bilingual.

Suzuki, Yukio, Ryo Nonaka, Koichi Konno, Kayo Fujii, Tazuko Nagasawa, and Naoki Yanase, trans. 1971. *Finnegans Wake* [excerpt]. Tokyo: Tokyodo-shuppan. *FW* 3–74 (I.i–iii).

Szczerbowski, Tadeusz. 2000. *Anna Livia Plurabelle po polsku:* Finnegans Wake *Jamesa Joyce'a ks. I, rozdz. 8*. Kraków: Wydawnictwo Naukowe Akademii Pedagogicznej.

Tindall, William York. 1959. *A Reader's Guide to James Joyce*. New York: Farrar, Straus & Giroux / Noonday Press.

Tindall, William York. 1996. *A Reader's Guide to Finnegans Wake*. 1969. Syracuse, NY: Syracuse University Press.

Titley, Alan. 2008. 'An Seoigheach sa Ghaeilge.' In *Aistriú Éireann*, edited by Charlie Dillon and Ríóna Ní Fhrighil, 108–19. Belfast: Queen's University Press. Includes Irish translation of *FW* 3.1–6.

Topia, André. 1990. '*Finnegans Wake*: La traduction parasitée (Étude de trois traductions des dernières pages de *Finnegans Wake*).' In *Retraduire*, 45–62. Palimpsestes 4. Paris: Publications de la Sorbonne Nouvelle.

Ussher, Arland. 1957. *Three Great Irishmen: Shaw, Yeats, Joyce*. 1952. New York: Mentor.

van der Weide, Jack. 2003. Review of *Finnegans Wake*, Dutch translation by Erik Bindervoet and Robbert-Jan Henkes (2002). *James Joyce Quarterly* 40:625–9.

Van Hulle, Dirk. 2004. 'The Manner of Meaning: Ogden and Beckett Translating Joyce.' *BELL: Belgian Journal of English Language and Literature* 2:75–84.

Van Laere, François. 1968. 'Les traducteurs français devant *Finnegans Wake*.' *Revue des Langues Vivantes* 34:126–33.

Verdin, Simonne. 1979. 'Tradlire Joyce.' *Courrier du Centre International d'Études Poétiques*, 15–25. Includes French translation of excerpts from *FW* 627–8.

Versteegen, Heinrich. 1998. 'Translating *FW*: Translatability and the Translator's Personality.' In *Images of Joyce*, edited by Clive Hart, 2:698–707. Gerrards Cross, UK: Colin Smythe.

Victoria, J.D, trans. 2009. *Estela de Finnegan: Un ensayo de traducción (FW 1.1)* [*FW* I.i: Spanish].Mexico: Lulu.

Volokhonsky, Henri, trans. 2000. *Finneganov Wake* [*FW*, excerpt: Russian]. Tver, Russia: Kolonna Publications. *FW* 3–168.

Vouvé, Solange. 1985. 'Aux limites du langage, aux limites de la traduction: *Finnegans Wake*.' *Texte* 4:209–21.

Wawrzycka, Jolanta W. 1998. 'Transcultural Criticism: "jinglish janglage" Joyce in Polish.' In Frehner and Zeller 1998, 436–43.

Wawrzycka, Jolanta W. 2004. 'Joyce *en slave* / Joyce Enclave: The Joyce of Maciej Słomczyński–A Tribute.' In *Twenty-First Joyce*, edited by Ellen Carol Jones and Morris Beja, 137–56. Gainesville: University Press of Florida.

Weatherall, Maria, Vladimír Procházka, and Adolf Hoffmeister, trans. 1932. *Anna Livia Plurabella: Fragment: Díla v zrodu / Anna Livia Plurabella: Fragment:*

Work in Progress [*ALP*: Czech]. Afterword by Adolf Hoffmeister. Prague: Odeon. Liberec: Dauphin, 1996. *FW* 196–216. Bilingual.

Weninger, Robert. 1984. *The Mookse and the Gripes: Ein Kommentar zu James Joyces Finnegans Wake*. Munich: edition text + kritik. Includes German translation of *FW* 152.15–159.18.

Weninger, Robert. 1985. 'An den Grenzen der Sprache: Bemerkungen zur (Un-)Übersetzbarkeit von *Finnegans Wake*.' *Protokolle* 1:85–102.

Weninger, Robert, trans. 1989. Excerpt. In Reichert and Senn 1989, 116–23. *FW* 152.15–159.18.

Weninger, Robert. 2012. *The German Joyce*. Gainesville: University Press of Florida.

Whatmough, Joshua. 1970. *The Dialects of Ancient Gaul: Prolegomena and Records of the Dialects*. 2 vols. Cambridge, MA: Harvard University Press.

Wilcock, J. Rodolfo, trans. 1961. 'Frammenti scelti da *La veglia di Finnegan*' [*FW*, excerpts: Italian]. In *Tutte le opere di James Joyce*, edited by Giacomo Debenedetti, 3:1125–74. Milan: Mondadori. *FW* 3.1–20, 33.14–34.4, 104.1–109.36, 112.9–27, 169.1–170.9, 179.9–32, 182.30–184.10, 185.14–26, 187.28–188.19, 189.28–191.4, 196.1–24, 206.29–207.14, 219.1–222.17, 249.5–33, 258.19–259.10, 306.7–308.27, 384.6–20, 543.13–545.22, 558.26–559.31, 572.7–575.7, 599.25–606.12, 626.33–628.16.

Winkler, Willi. 1993. 'Ordspindelvaev.' *Die Zeit*, 29 October, 74. Review of *Finnegans Wehg*, German translation by Dieter Stündel (1993).

Wollschläger, Hans, trans. 1970. 'Anna Livia Plurabelle, parryotphrosed myth brockendootsch' [*ALP*: German]. In Reichert and Senn 1970, 99–133. *FW* 196–216.

Yanase, Naoki, trans. 1993. *Finnegans Wake* [Japanese] *I–II* (1991), *III–IV* (1993). Tokyo: Kawade shobo shinsha. Paperback edn. in 3 vols., 2004.

Zanotti, Serenella. 2004. 'L'italiano di Joyce nell'auto-traduzione di Anna Livia Plurabelle.'In *Joyce in Italy/L'italiano in Joyce*, 144–78. Rome: Aracne.

Zanotti, Serenella. 2010. 'The Translator's Visibility: The Italian Translations of Finnegans Wake.' *Mediazioni* (Università di Bologna) 10. 24 June 2010. Online.

Zimmer, Heinrich. 1891. 'Keltische Beiträge.' *Zeitschrift für deutsches Althertum und deutsche Literatur* 35:1–173.

Zoëga, Geir T. 1910. *A Concise Dictionary of Old Icelandic*. Oxford: Clarendon Press.

Index